Institutions, Emotions, and Group Agents

Studies in the Philosophy of Sociality

Volume 2

For further volumes:
http://www.springer.com/series/10961

Anita Konzelmann Ziv • Hans Bernhard Schmid

Editors

Institutions, Emotions, and Group Agents

Contributions to Social Ontology

With the Editorial Assistance of Katharina Bernhard and Ulla Schmid

 Springer

Editors
Anita Konzelmann Ziv
Département de Philosophie
Université de Genève
Genève
Switzerland

Hans Bernhard Schmid
Institut für Philosophie
Universität Wien
Wien
Austria

ISBN 978-94-007-6933-5   ISBN 978-94-007-6934-2 (eBook)
DOI 10.1007/978-94-007-6934-2
Springer Dordrecht Heidelberg New York London

Library of Congress Control Number: 2013949008

Printed on acid-free paper

Springer is part of Springer Science+Business Media (www.springer.com)

Acknowledgements

The project of this volume dates back to the 7th *Conference on Collective Intentionality* held at the *University of Basel* (Switzerland) on August 23–27, 2010 and organized by the research group "Collective Intentionality—Phenomenological Perspectives". The chapters of this volume are a small selection of the papers presented at that conference.

We are grateful to the *Swiss National Science Foundation*, the *Max Geldner Stiftung*, the *Freiwillige Akademische Gesellschaft Basel* and the *University of Basel* for their generous support of the conference and the research leading to this volume.

Also, we wish to thank Ulla Schmid, Katharina Bernhard, and Michaela Bartsch to whom we are indebted for the enormous amount of time and effort they have spent on this project.

Geneva and Vienna   The Editors
December 2012

Contents

Chapter 1
Introduction: Institutions, Emotions, and Group Agents—Contributions to Social Ontology

Anita Konzelmann Ziv and Hans Bernhard Schmid

Social ontology is the philosophical study of the basic constitution and structure of the social world. Social ontology investigates the kinds of entities that make up the social world, its deontological structure, its relations to physical nature and mental attitudes. Social ontology thus engages a wide array of domains in philosophy and neighboring disciplines. Social and political philosophy, ethics, philosophy of mind, and metaphysics contribute to research in social ontology. Also, current social ontology is no pure armchair business. Sociology, legal theory, political science, and economics provide insights into social structures and functions that cannot be ignored by social ontology. Similarly, social psychology, history and linguistics can teach us relevant lessons about the mechanisms of establishing and overthrowing social power.

The contributions gathered in this volume present the state of the art in some selected areas of current social ontology. They are focused on the role of collective intentional states in creating social facts, and on the nature of intentional properties of groups that allow characterizing them as responsible agents, or perhaps even as persons. Many of the chapters are inspired by contemporary action theory, emotion theory, and theories of collective intentionality. Another group of chapters revisits early phenomenological approaches to social ontology, and accounts of sociality that draw on the Hegelian idea of recognition. The variety of philosophical traditions mirrored in this collection provides readers with a rich and multifaceted survey

A. Konzelmann Ziv (✉)
Département de Philosophie, Université de Genève, 2, Rue de Candolle, CH-1211 Genève, Switzerland
e-mail: Anita.Konzelmann@unige.ch

H.B. Schmid
Institut für Philosophie, Universität Wien, Universitätsstraße 7, 1010 Wien, Austria
e-mail: Hans.Bernhard.Schmid@univie.ac.at

A. Konzelmann Ziv and H.B. Schmid (eds.), *Institutions, Emotions, and Group Agents*, Studies in the Philosophy of Sociality 2, DOI 10.1007/978-94-007-6934-2_1, © Springer Science+Business Media Dordrecht 2014

of present research in social ontology. Dependent on the authors' backgrounds, some relevant topics and themes appear and reappear under different angles and in different clothing throughout the volume.

The collection is divided into three parts. The first part contains contributions that discuss themes highlighted in John Searle's work on the ontology of social institutions and facts. John Searle is one of the main protagonists of contemporary philosophical reflections on social reality. His theory (Searle 1995, 2010) provides a conceptual framework for fruitful explorations of a wide variety of finer grained issues. The chapters in this part address, among others, questions concerning the relation between intentions and the deontic powers of institutions, the role of disagreement, and the nature of collective intentionality. While the contributions to Part I roughly pertain to matters of generating and establishing social facts, Part II focuses on joint and collective emotions and mutual recognition. Part III explores the scope and limits of group agency, or group personhood, especially the capacity for responsible agency.

1   Intentionality and Institutions

Searle's basic idea, as developed in his 1995 book, is that institutional facts are typically status functions which involve constitutive rules. An object (X) has a status (Y) if it is collectively accepted that "X counts as Y in context C". Searle's formula for the constitutive rule of the institutional world attempts to bridge the gap between fact and norm by accounting for the relation between the properties of natural objects and minds, on the one hand, and the "deontic powers" deriving as functions from the statuses conferred by collective intentionality on objects, on the other hand. In his 2010 book, Searle has generalized his earlier account in a way that places declarations at the center stage of the creation of institutional reality. A status and the deontic powers deriving from it exists because the status is "declared" to exist; in this theory, the older XYC-formula appears as a special case.

Searle's account has proven to be very successful in current social ontology; however, Searle has met with severe criticism. The opening chapter of the collection, Chap. 2, *Document Acts* by Barry Smith, challenges the consistency of Searle's earlier framework by addressing the problem of how to accommodate an important class of multiply interconnected quasi-abstract entities. Smith points out that the entities targeted in the interlocking manifestations of "document acts", as for instance structured investment vehicles or mortgage securitization, are too abstract in nature to pass for real objects within Searle's professed naturalistic framework. "Document acts" are defined as individual and collective intentional acts that involve all kinds of doings related to documents, as for example issuing a property deed, identifying a person by checking her passport, or electronically paying a bill. Document acts are similar to speech acts in their capacity to state and create facts, and in their having definable conditions of satisfaction. They transcend, however, the capacities of speech acts in creating and maintaining entities of tantalizing complexity. The problem of Searle's theory with entities of this kind as identified by Smith lies in the tension between Searle's alleged strict naturalism, according to which all that exists "consist[s] entirely of physical particles in fields of force", and the claim that the social entity of a status Y comes to exist upon the we-intentional declaration that status Y exist. Whereas this tension is relatively innocuous for a status immediately connected to physical things and states, including the powers and activities of human beings (for example Y: x, z [being married]), it seems fatal in the case of statuses anchored in physical reality in much more intricate ways, such as mortgage securitization. The complex of interrelations manifest in phenomena of this kind is arguably more than a mere pattern of human activities, or a product of "massive fantasy". Smith attempts to show a way out of the dilemma by suggesting that Searle accept in his ontology quasi-abstract entities that, in virtue of their being brought into being by declaration, are "fully a part of the historical world of what happens and is the case", although they lie outside the province of what is described by physics. He considers document act theory as an important device in accounting for the reality of the "historical world" because it explains how relevant portions of the history of institutional quasi-abstract entities are "encapsulated".

The next two chapters in Part I, Chap. 3 (*Searlean Reflections on Sacred Mountains*) and Chap. 4 (*Social Objects without Intentions*), question Searle's intentionalist model of the social world. Their authors, Filip Bueken and Brian Epstein, both challenge the claim that social objects depend on intentions, but they do so in two different ways. Bueken's argument draws on the opacity of social institutions, i.e. on the possibility that institutions appear indistinct from natural facts. He claims that some undoubtedly institutional facts, such as the sacredness of a mountain, might be both unintended and unrecognized as such. In spite of its considerable deontic powers, the "covert" institution of the sacredness of a mountain may be taken as a natural fact, explicable by a "natural etiology", such as the birth of a god on the peak of the mountain. Hence, and in contradiction to what Searle claims, the existence of deontic powers does not seem to require a status Y assigned to X by the members of the relevant community who collectively intend and accept it. Nevertheless, Bueken thinks that Searle's account can accommodate sacredness as a *covert* institutional fact for the creation and maintenance of which shared practices of the members of a collective are responsible, and this in spite of their ignorance about its institutional nature. He argues that uncovering the institutional nature of sacredness need not necessarily disintegrate the powers related to it, even if it leads to a critical re-examination of the relevant practices. A community that shifts towards intentionally recognizing sacredness as an institutional fact thereby accepts its deontic role as deriving from the collectively assigned status. This understanding might, under certain conditions, even increase the force of the deontic powers and make it easier to accept changes or modifications of the institution in question. Emphasizing the possibility of "covert" institutional facts whose deontic role does not derive from institutional status, Bueken seems to suggest a "light" version of a Searlian intentionalist account, which allows deontic powers to result from beliefs about "natural" facts and shared practices emerging from them.

Epstein's approach, in contrast, is more radical. He argues that the role of intentions in accounting for the "anchoring" of social entities is systematically overestimated. By "anchoring", he means the process that makes an object (X) a social object (Y). In Searle's social ontology, he identifies the process of collectively intending or recognizing the constitutive rule "X counts as Y in C" as "anchoring" the "ground" of Y. After a comparison between Searle's constitutive rule and the traditional notion of convention, Epstein discusses a continuum of possible "anchors" for conventions, ranging from the most stringently to the least intentional, i.e. from explicit collective agreement to mere patterns or regularities in practices. He then attempts to show that the complexity of the institution of money, one of Searle's favorite examples of a social fact, does hardly allow for a single intentionalist account of how it is anchored. Expressing similar worries with regard to anchoring other deontic powers in collective acceptance, Epstein casts doubts on the soundness of treating social ontology as a kind of subfield of collective intentionality.

The following chapter (Chap. 5), Jennifer Hudin's The *Logical Form of Totalitarianism*, neatly connects to Bueken's and Epstein's foregoing discussions on the primacy of intentional acceptance or shared practices in establishing social facts. Hudin distinguishes a "vertical" from a "horizontal" account of social structures, the former of which is centered on the capacity of cooperation and summarized in the term "practice", whereas the latter centered on deontic and representative capacities. Hudin then outlines how Searle's formula—(Collective Acceptance) "X counts as Y in context C"—exploits the illocutionary nature of declarations to import "deonticity" into his account of social reality. She restates Bueken's and Epstein's worries by drawing attention to a "split of deonticity" between social authorization, i.e. a linguistic codification of status function, and social expectation, i.e. the non-linguistic perception of social roles. Social expectation, for example of how a wife or a mother is to behave, arguably exhibits deontic power without involving declarative acts of collective acceptance. In order to account for the deontology of social expectation, Hudin suggests focusing on the perception inspired conception of collective recognition rather than on collective acceptance. She underlines the advantages of this conceptual shift by discussing the question of how and why collectives maintain totalitarian regimes. Her account draws on the idea that institutional reality is grounded initially in collective perception, and secondarily in acts of participatory acceptance that maintain their existence without entailing complicity (in the sense of willing cooperation). She proposes, moreover, to distinguish between "happy" and "unhappy" acceptance: the former involves the emotional component of "social bonding" which is absent in the latter. Social bonding is supposed to create a "we" liable to turn social identification into a self-empowering experience by expanding each individual's sense of what one can do and be. With these conceptual tools in place, Hudin shows how to refine Searle's account in a way that meets the challenges of "split deonticity".

The idea that the deontic is a multi-faceted phenomenon the nature of which is not easily explicable by a single model or formula is also central in Rodrigo Sánchez Brigido's chapter on *Groups, Normativity and Disagreement* (Chap. 6).

Addressing the problem of how to explain the genesis of institutional duties, the author argues that a single-type explanation, e.g. in terms of Margaret Gilbert's theory of "joint commitment", is not adequate because normative relations among members of groups seem to appear for a variety of reasons. Accordingly, a variety of explanatory models of "groups with normative unity" (GNU) seems to be required, too. One of the models Sánchez Brigido proposes attempts to account for cases of conforming to membership duties because of considerations pertaining to the value of the joint activity in which individuals engage. Another model that the author suggests draws on classical accounts of agreement. The concept of agreement, according to him, is more flexible and hence more suitable to adapt to the variety of normative unity in groups than the concept of joint commitment. In particular, he intends to show how an agreement-based account can explain why members might disagree on the content of the obligations to which they wish to conform. To this purpose, he discusses the role of intentions and the relevance of a framework of agreement practices in building normative unity.

Seumas Miller's chapter (Chap. 7), *Joint Actions, Social Institutions and Collective Goods: A Teleological Account*, gives an alternative account of the deontic powers of social institutions that draws on the notion of joint action. Miller accounts for the creation and reproduction of social institutions in terms of organizations or systems of organizations that provide collective goods by means of joint activity. His teleological and normative theory of joint action is based on his individualist Collective End Theory (CET) that is relational in the sense of explaining common goal directed activity in terms of individual attitudes and actions and the relations between them. In this chapter, particular emphasis is placed on the question of whether organizations are normative entities, and on the relations between organizations and rights. Miller defines organizations in terms of an embodied formal structure of interlocking roles and a multi-layered structure of joint actions, and distinguishes them by their typical activities and ends. While this definition of an organization does not include any reference to a normative dimension, Miller maintains that most organizations do as a matter of contingent fact possess a normative dimension by virtue of particular (im)moral ends they serve and particular (im)moral activities they undertake. Further normative dimensions ensue from social norms governing the constitutive organizational roles, especially when hierarchical role structures are involved. Miller holds that organizations with such normative dimensions are social institutions and then addresses the issue of the specifically moral dimension of social institutions. In the second part of the chapter, he explains how the moral categories that are deeply implicated in social institutions—human rights and duties, contract-based rights and obligations, rights and duties derived from the production and 'consumption' of collective goods—are to be accounted for in the framework of an individualist theory, e.g. in terms of aggregated rights and joint rights. Miller's joint action based account of institutions challenges the Searlian picture of institutional deonticity that derives from assigned status: it allows the joint moral rights involved in collective goods to be based in aggregated pre-institutional needs-based and non-needs-based human rights.

Part I closes with a methodological study of the central condition highlighted in all recent accounts of social reality and labeled "Collective Intentionality" by John Searle. In Chap. 8, *Three Types of Heterotropic Intentionality: A Taxonomy in Social Ontology*, Francesca De Vecchi suggests analyzing the socially relevant types of intentionality by means of a phenomenologically inspired finer grained taxonomy. Instead of distinguishing between solitary and collective intentionality, she proposes to draw a basic distinction between heterotropic and non-heterotropic intentionality. Heterotropic intentionality is explained as existentially dependent on at least two intentional subjects, and is supposed to manifest in three types: collective intentionality, intersubjective intentionality, and social intentionality. Roughly, the type "collective intentionality" corresponds to what in philosophy is often discussed as "shared" intentional states and attitudes, the type "intersubjective intentionality" is social cognition, and "social intentionality" is what phenomenologists have frequently called "social acts". De Vecchi points out the different conditions of satisfaction these intentionality types have, as well as the relations they bear to each other. Moreover, she attempts to show how collective, intersubjective, and social intentionality contribute to create social entities.

2 Shared Emotions and Recognition

Part II addresses the increasing interest in the nature and role of shared affectivity. Collective emotions, shared feelings, and common moods are an interesting topic by themselves, but they seem to be particularly relevant to social ontology as a background capacity for social action and joint commitments. Shared affectivity is closely related to what has been referred to as "recognition", a notion that links an epistemic ability to affective capacities, such as mutual respect and the desire to be accepted. An important application of accounting for shared affectivity and recognition is the question to what extent groups can be genuine subjects of affective states and attitudes of recognition. This question is not of merely academic interest but pertains to practical issues involving the moral character of groups and group responsibility. An affective capacity that traditionally occupies a central place in discussions of these issues is empathy, that is, the faculty to feel how others feel.

Ronald de Sousa's chapter (Chap. 9), *Emergence and Empathy*, opens the discussion on shared affectivity by examining to what extent empathy corresponds to the image commonly held of it. De Sousa critically examines two claims about empathy: first, that empathy is an emotion, and second, that it is indispensable for moral motivation. He relates these claims to the problem of collective feeling by considering how shared experiences in general might emerge from interactions between individuals. Due to their complex patterns of causation, collective experiences consciously emerge on a level that neither allows determining a single mechanism of causation nor predicting the nature of the resulting experience on the basis of the properties of its constituents. This suggests a component view of collective experiences according to which various types of intentional as well as lower-level sub-personal physiological and psychological states are causally relevant components of what is experienced as, say, a collective emotion. Due to the intersubjective interactions involved, the individual emotions of the participants in a collective emotion depend in part on the collective context in which they appear. This picture of collective emotions as emerging from the concurrence of a variety of individual phenomena has consequences for the role and relevance of empathy. It follows from this conception that claims about specific relations of justification between individual emotions and shared emotion are implausible. Therefore, empathy cannot be ascribed a special role in explaining the *sui generis* collective emotion that emerges. A fortiori, then, it seems impossible to determine whether empathy has a particular function for the moral motivation of groups and in what exactly this function would consist. And since the phenomena constitutive of a collective emotion need not themselves be emotions, empathy, even if considered a relevant ingredient in collective moral emotions, need not be construed in terms of a compassionate emotion. Rather, empathy appears to be an emotionally neutral ability of getting acquainted with the emotional states of others, conceivable in terms of either simple affective contagion or more sophisticated capacities for emotional understanding that might even presuppose the ability to regard someone as "one of us".

The following chapter (Chap. 10), *The Functions of Collective Emotions in Social Groups* by Mikko Salmela, focuses on the functions of collective emotions in the emergence, maintenance, and development of social groups. Salmela evaluates the merits of different theories in accounting for these functions, among them aggregative theories, ritualistic theories, and intergroup emotions theory, as well as Margaret Gilbert's plural subject view and Hans Bernhard Schmid's phenomenological account of collective affectivity. In spite of the many insights provided by these theories, Salmela finds them wanting for a number of reasons, and he suggests a refined approach that is based on the idea of a continuum of collectivity. Emotions seem to be shareable to a lesser or greater degree, resulting in different kinds of collective emotions with different functions in social groups. Salmela suggests that more strongly shared collective emotions serve the emergence, maintenance, and development of social groups more effectively than less strongly shared collective emotions. In order to account for the different kinds and functions of collective emotions, he examines "modes" or degrees of sharing for both emotional content and affective experience. One question considered is how the essential axiological "concern" of an emotion is to be shared, given that affective appraisal of values is usually so fast and modular that collective acceptance of the values in question is impossible. Salmela proposes to account for shared concerns in terms of convergent individual emotions of similar concern, which provides a rational impetus to synchronization of experience. The degree of synchronization achieved bears on the strength of solidarity and commitment among the group members. According to Salmela, moderately collective emotions are experienced as emotions of a group member, but they are still normatively weak because this role is self-appointed and maintained through a private identification or commitment. In strongly collective emotions, however, group membership is immediately felt as shared without implying an act of personal identification. The members of a winning team rejoice in "our winning the championship" or in "our accomplishment". Their feeling responds to prescriptive emotion norms within the group emerging from their collective commitment to their shared concern.

Chap. 11, *Feelings of Being-Together and Caring-With* by Andrés Sánchez Guerrero, takes up the question of how collective affectivity relates to central group concerns. Against the background of Bennett Helm's account of emotions as "felt evaluations" and Heideggerian accounts of ways of being-in-the-world, Sánchez Guerrero investigates the role feelings play with regard to group membership. He suggests explaining the force of the shared evaluative perspective to determine group relevant concerns by the affective attitudes of "caring-with" and "feelings of being-together". Denoting an emotional attitude "about things" that may become the shared concerns relevant for group-belongingness, the term "caring-with" applies to situations in which the involved individuals feel together that the object or occurrence in question matters to their group. Sánchez Guerrero relates this idea to Heidegger's analysis of human intentionality as a shareable orientedness towards an entity, which is embedded in our common care-defined way of being. He contrasts "caring-with" to this shared experiential background of "being-affectively-attuned-to-the-world-in-one-mode-or-another", suggesting that experiences of "caring-with" are marked by a distinct phenomenal character of togetherness describable in terms of a "felt conviction" that the involved individuals jointly care about something. In contrast, "feelings of being-together" are taken to constitute the affective background that prepares the pre-thematic understanding of a concrete situation as one that leads to caring about something as members of a group. Sánchez Guerrero identifies these feelings as a subclass of what Matthew Ratcliffe calls "existential feelings" and whose role is to ground our intentional experiences of being collectively affected. Sánchez Guerrero interprets them as 'sedimented' dynamic structures of experience that prepare us to understand certain circumstances as situations in which we pursue something together in an emotionally motivated way.

A similar picture of the inner structure of we-intentionality is offered in Chap. 12 by Emanuele Caminada, *Joining the Background: Habitual Sentiments Behind We-Intentionality*. The author attempts to acquaint his readers with the early phenomenological account of we-intentionality proposed by Gerda Walther. He shows how Walther conceives of we-intentionality as embedded in a network of intentional habits that shape individual minds. Her claim is that the core of community, or "We", is pre-reflexive and non-thematic and resides in a concrete intentional background founded in a particular structure of affective intentionality. Consisting in a web of conscious and unconscious habitual sentiments of joining, this structure is called "habitual joining" and provides the non-reducible basic "us-background" of community. As such, it is a necessary condition for states and attitudes of "we-intentionality". Accordingly, the latter cannot be understood in terms of the properties of a super-individual subject, and neither in terms of a shared common habit. Rather, it ought to be conceived as a multipolar web of intentional relations involving habits of several kinds. Caminada suggests that the value of

Walther's account for the current debate is to be seen in the fact that habitual joining explains how individual subjects and community reciprocally form each other.

Focusing on recognition, the closing chapters of Part II neatly connect to the foregoing considerations on shared affectivity and its relationship to group ethos and group concerns. In his chapter *Collective Intentionality and Recognition from Others* (Chap. 13), Arto Laitinen examines whether and how a group's status functions, goals and beliefs depend on recognition from outside the relevant group. To this effect, the author outlines different normatively loaded senses in which the term "recognition" is used. His main concern is with uses of "recognition" that refer to "recognitive" attitudes, e.g. having respect for persons because of recognizing them as being persons, feeling esteem for persons because of recognizing them as having merits, feeling concern for beings because of recognizing them as being vulnerable. Other relevant senses of "recognition" pertain to acknowledging the validity of normative entities, and to accepting institutions by those kinds of "taking and treating" which collectively bring institutions into existence and sustain their existence. Drawing on these senses of the term, Laitinen explains that being recognized matters to people because it is constitutive of personhood, it is intertwined with one's self-relation, it affects agentic capacities, and it is required for deontic statuses and powers. The relevance of recognition for analyses of collective intentionality and group behavior is commonly discussed in the context of how intersubjective attitudes contribute to the creation of groups and the constitution of group attitudes. Laitinen takes a different route. Focusing on groups as intentional subjects and the way their self-understanding is determined by "recognitive" attitudes, he suggests that both a group's implicit self-relation— the "attitudinal climate" among group members—and its explicit self-relation—the group's explicit "realm of concern", its "intentional horizon", and its "ethos"— depend in relevant ways on recognition from outside.

In his chapter *The Conditions of Collectivity: Joint Commitment and the Shared Norms of Membership* (Chap. 14), Titus Stahl addresses the theme of recognition from a different angle. Attempting to show that strong collective intentionality depends on the practical acceptance of shared norms and on the establishment of authority relations through mutual recognition, he focuses on those senses of "recognition" that pertain to acknowledging the validity of normative entities and accepting institutions. Stahl challenges the view that collective intentionality is a primitive capacity in the sense of being the absolute prerequisite of sociality. He argues that joint commitment, the core of Margaret Gilbert's account of collective intentionality, can reach beyond individual commitment only on condition of already socially shared "principles of membership". These principles are required to ensure the connection between a shared content and the force of individual commitments. Stahl argues that even if the existence of a set of interpersonal individual commitments between group members is constitutive of the existence and force of a joint commitment of the group, the content of the individual commitments need to be separate from that of the joint commitment supervening on their structure. This content independence implies a relation between the joint commitment of a group and the individual commitments of its members that arguably cannot be given *a priori*.

Drawing on Robert Brandom's theory of language and mind, Stahl points out that the relevant relation needs to be understood as socially created, implying a background of constitutive rules that specify an inferential connection between some normative standards and a collective state or attitude. If a group displays a structure of mutually interlocking commitments to evaluating each other according to such norms, it can count as a plural subject with a strongly collective state or attitude having commitments of its own. Since the individual preconditions of joint commitments are embedded in a structure of pragmatic authority ascription to each other, collective intentionality appears as an achievement of recognitive communities.

3   Collective Reasons and Group Agency

The question of whether and how groups can be proper agents of their own, and perhaps even persons, is a key topic in current social ontology. Christian List and Philip Pettit have recently rekindled this debate, in particular in their Group Agency (2011). Many of the key contributors to the analysis of collective intentionality have developed accounts of group agency, even though their concern is usually not so much with irreducible group agents, but rather with the question of what it means for individuals to act together, as a group. The opening chapter of Part III of this volume, Chap. 15, is Michael Bratman's *Acting over Time, Acting Together*. Bratman compares shared acting to individual acting over time. He starts from the observation that human agency involves the practical capacities both for temporally extended and for shared intentional activity. Both of these capacities require that thought and action be tied together in distinctive ways. In individual temporally extended acting, past, present, and future thought need to be tied to action, whereas in shared activity the thoughts and actions of individual participants need to be tied together in specific ways. Considering conceptual, metaphysical, and normative concerns with regard to the nature of these ties, Bratman's conjecture is that the human capacities for planning agency, a distinctive kind of goal-directed agency, constitute a fundamental common ground for both capacities. His idea draws on the theoretical and practical fecundity of planning structures, stating that the proper exercise of these planning capacities, given relevant contents of the plans, relevant contexts, and relevant interrelations with past, future, and other agents, will yield phenomena of temporally extended or shared intentional activity. The aim of this plan-theoretical account is to understand the metaphysics of "small scale" shared intentional activity as a construct of metaphysical resources already in play in the case of individual planning agency. Bratman thus tries to avoid introducing basic new metaphysical resources, such as Searle's we-intentions or Gilbert's joint commitments. Once individual planning agency is in place, Bratman claims, the step to small scale sociality need not involve a fundamental discontinuity. The basic normative pressures of consistency, coherence, and stability central to individual planning agency already involve the norms of social rationality that are characteristic of shared intentionality. The possibility of intentional and normative resource identity between individual and shared agency, together with the fact that shared intentionality is typically limited in being partial, transitory and cross-cutting, is taken to challenge ontological claims about group subjects. For even given that a shared action is explained by a shared intention, on some notions of agency being the agent of the shared action can come apart from being the subject of the shared intention.

The following chapter (Chap. 16) *How Where We Stand Constrains Where I Stand: Applying Bratman's Account of Self-Governance to Collective Action* takes up and critically assesses some ideas of Bratman's "planning theory of agency". Joseph Kisolo-Ssonko sets out to elucidate the relation between individual autonomy and the constraints that collective intentions allegedly exert on individuals by showing how elements of Bratman's account of the normative force of individual intentions explain the normative interplay between individual and collective intentionality. His particular interest is to carve up the "fuzzy" idea of individual agentive identity by reference to Bratman's point that constraint by one's own intentions does not conflict with autonomy, but is really fundamental to being an autonomous agent. The argument involves a conception of self-governance according to which previous intentions scaffold one's practical life by constraining the valid choices available. By providing a "where I stand" from where one's actions can be governed, these intentions structure future rational deliberation, enabling a subject to consider her actions to be those of a single unified agent. Kisolo-Ssonko holds that an individual's reason for seeing him- or herself as constrained by the intentions of a collective of which he or she is a member is similar to being bound by his or her own intentions. Whereas it is similar in its quality of securing a unitary standpoint with regard to authentic agency, it is different in that securing this standpoint is not an *a priori* necessity for the individual, but becomes a necessity only after the fact of social interaction. This follows from a two-part transcendental argument that starts with people's experience of feeling themselves to be part of collective actions. The argument proceeds by presenting (i) the existence of a collective capable of governing its own actions as necessary for individuals to have this experience, and (ii) the constraint of individuals by collective intentions as conceptually necessary for the existence of the collective as an agent. From this, Kisolo-Ssonko concludes that collective intentions must constrain individuals. In the framework of self-governance, however, this constraint does not in principle endanger personal autonomy, but rather interlocks individual agentive identity with the agentive identity of the collective.

In the following chapter (Chap. 17), *Team Reasoning and Shared Intention*, Abraham Roth addresses the problem of authority and autonomy that emerges from the interplay between participatory intentions in shared activity. In particular, Roth's reflections center on the settling condition that constrains intentions to what one takes to be up to oneself to decide. Applied to collective or shared activity, the settling condition yields a dilemma: having a participatory intention to be A-ing together with other individuals seems to presume having the authority to settle "A-ing-only-in-the-context-where-you-join-in". Yet any such authority exercised by an individual would compromise the autonomy minimally required for the active participation of other individuals. Examining the possibility to resolve this dilemma in the framework of game-theoretical considerations on team reasoning, Roth identifies a profound problem in any such approach. Whereas accounts of team reasoning explain the ranking of outcomes, they cannot explain how this ranking converts to intending one's part. Without one believing that one has the authority to bring about the collective goal, one is not rationally required to intend one's part. Against the background of this problem, Roth argues that if the settling aspect of participatory intention is to be handled within an account of team reasoning, the latter must be fundamentally distinct from individual instrumental reasoning in that it invokes a notion of a rational yet non-evidential warrant for belief. In particular, it requires that a team reasoner's belief or expectation that other participants are also team reasoners is rational, but not acquired in the way that rational belief should be acquired, that is, on the basis of evidence. For acquiring this kind of belief on the basis of conclusive evidence would dispense with the need of team reasoning. Roth thus concludes that the manifest rationality of team reasoning is demonstration enough of a non-evidential yet defeasible entitlement to think that fellow participants are team reasoners.

Juliette Gloor's *Collective Intentionality and Practical Reason* (Chap. 18) takes up the line of Roth's reflections, advancing a similarly skeptical view with regard to the suitability of an instrumentalist conception of rationality for accounts of shared agency. Gloor is less concerned, however, with the puzzle posed by the settling condition of participatory intentions than with the issues of unified action and self-governance addressed in the chapters of Bratman and Kisolo-Ssonko (Chaps. 15 and 16). Her focus is on the question of how the normative power of practical rationality contributes to form unified rational selves, subjects of both individual and shared actions. The main problem the instrumentalist conception of rationality poses to explaining rational selfhood is taken to be its individualistic implication about motivation. This implication becomes manifest in the claim that agents can be motivated solely by their own desires. Accordingly, Gloor's reflections center on the relations between desire and reason in motivating action, and more particularly on the question of how these relations are constitutive of the sort of normativity characteristic of collective intentionality. These issues invoke the debate on practical reason between instrumentalists and Kantians: whereas the latter reproach to the former reason internalism—manifest in their identifying reasons with desires—, the former reproach to the latter reason externalism—manifest in their identifying reasons with desire-independent principles. Roughly, reason internalism is supposed to disable instrumentalism from explaining the normative or binding power of reason, while reason externalism seems to disable Kantianism from explaining the motivating power of reason. In the framework of Christine Korsgaard's Kantian inspired account of agency, Gloor suggests reconciling these positions by adopting the view that a practical reason is a conjunction of an incentive and a value-based principle of choice. This construal of reason-desire-dependency favors a "mattering-relation" over an "instrumentalist-relation" as the primary self-relation of an agent. In contrast to the "instrumentalist-relation" which concerns the question of what means are sufficient to realize an end, the "mattering-relation" concerns the question of what the appropriate means are to realize the end. Agentive self-relation so conceived pertains not only to unified subjects of individual action but likewise to unified subjects of shared action, since shareability of ends seems to presuppose the principled choice of a maxim about the appropriateness of means to an end.

Sara Rachel Chant argues in her paper (Chap. 19) that some responsibility is collective in a "real" sense if it cannot be reduced to the responsibilities of each individual in a group. "Real" collective responsibility presupposes situational features (threats, some degree of coercion) that mitigate the responsibilities of the participating individuals, but fail to mitigate the responsibility of the group as a whole. Chant discusses a series of received attempts to analyze "real" collective responsibility, and she offers an account that uses game theoretic conceptual tools. Real collective responsibility occurs in situations in which there is a morally objectionable Nash-equilibrium that is such that it excuses, to some degree, each participant's respective choice, given his or her reasonable expectations concerning the other participant's choices. In such situations, an element of "coercion" that mitigates each individual's responsibility comes from the group as a whole; thus the group bears moral responsibility for the outcome in a way the individual participants do not. The participants are fully responsible—collectively, but not distributively.

The concluding chapters in the volume challenge the irreducibility of collective properties and group agency, arguing against the need of stipulating an ontological support different from individuals to account for group decisions and responsibility. The first chapter of this group, Chap. 20, *Are Individualist Accounts of Collective Responsibility Morally Deficient?* by András Szigeti, challenges Philip Pettit's claim that attributing responsibility to human individuals only would leave a "deficit in the accounting books". Claims of this kind make individualism about groups appear more than merely methodologically contestable: they make it appear morally deficient. Szigeti counters that the collectivist arguments for claims of this kind are wanting, and consequent worries with regard to the moral insensitivity of individualism can be dispelled. As he claims, collectivist arguments in favor of group responsibility often rely on paradoxes of judgment aggregation that seem to show that a collective can be responsible even when no individual is. Szigeti argues that cases of alleged group responsibility, contrary to what judgment aggregation paradoxes suggest, can be handled by individualist analyses without leaving a responsibility deficit. To this effect, he proposes to examine the relation between moral responsibility and the sources of harm. Harm suffered, so he claims, does either result from culpable wrongdoing or it does not. If harm suffered does not result from culpable wrongdoing, then nobody is morally responsible for it. Individualism does not deny, however, that in these cases, e.g. when harm is the outcome of certain institutional structures, redressing harm might be a moral duty. Therefore, the charge of moral insensitivity against individualist accounts can be rejected. If, on the other hand, the source of harm is culpable wrongdoing, then such harm is due to culpable wrongdoing of individuals. In these cases, harm is to be redressed by holding the culpable individuals responsible. Szigeti expands his defense of individualism in the last part of the paper by showing how collectivist talk about moral responsibility can be used for ethically questionable purposes as well, e.g. for attributing rights to collectives that ought to be prerogatives of individuals only. Therefore, he concludes, collectivists cannot claim the moral high ground over individualists.

Christian List's and Philip Pettit's account of group agency is the target of another critical chapter written by Vuko Andric, Chap. 21, and titled *Can Groups Be Autonomous Rational Agents? A Challenge to the List-Pettit-Theory*. Andric is doubtful whether the List-Pettit theory is able to provide a convincing account of the rationality and autonomy of groups, an account that would justify considering them as agents in their own right. His worry is that the List-Pettit-theory implies an absurd claim, namely that "instrument-user-units", for example the unit formed by a car and its driver, are rational agents over and above those parts of them which are intentional, i.e. the users of the instrument. The *reductio ad absurdum* of the List-Pettit-theory is based on an analogy between groups and the complex entities of instrument-user-units. According to the List-Pettit-theory, the rationality and agential autonomy of a group entity is explicable by the interplay of its members' attitudes and its organizational structure. Andric claims that this *explicans* is analogous to the interplay of the user's attitudes and the constitution of the instrument used in an instrument-user-unit. Therefore, List and Pettit would be committed to say that the networking between the beliefs and desires of Mike driving his Ferrari and the technical properties of the Ferrari give rise to the rationality and agential autonomy of the Mike-and-his-Ferrari-unit, or so Andric claims. The absurdity of this view is, according to Andric, a reason to reject the theory.

In the last chapter of the collection, Chap. 22, *Direct and Indirect Common Belief*, Emiliano Lorini and Andreas Herzig analyze two social phenomena which are supposed to rely on distinct forms of agents' cognitive capabilities. After offering an example that illustrates the envisaged difference between "direct common belief" and "indirect common belief", the authors proceed to give first informal definitions thereof. In the second part of their chapter, they use the framework of public announcement logic (PAL) to provide a more formal analysis. Starting from the example of Giovanni and Maria who commonly believe that they both have Italian citizenship, Lorini and Herzig follow David Lewis in adopting an iterative analysis of common belief: n people have a common belief that p if and only if n people believe that p, n people believe that n people believe that p, and so on *ad infinitum*. The distinction between direct and indirect instances of common belief, then, relates to the way a common belief is generated. According to the authors' definitions, a common belief that p is direct when it is an immediate consequence of an event F that is manifest to all those sharing the prior mutual belief that perceiving F entails the truth of p. Thus, Giovanni and Maria's common belief that they both have Italian citizenship is direct if it is generated by the event of a third person telling them so and their prior mutual belief that hearing a statement to that effect entails their both being Italian citizens. In contrast, a common belief that p is indirect when it is determined by what may be called a "shared inference", i.e. an inference that is "constructive" in the sense that it does not presuppose the prior mutual belief that perceiving F entails the truth of p. Therefore, in order to arrive at the common belief that *p*, the parties have to go through processes of shared inferences accounted for by the definitions the authors offer. Lorini and Herzig suggest that the importance of the distinction between direct and indirect common belief for social ontology lies in the fact that forming indirect common beliefs is cognitively more demanding than forming direct common beliefs. This seems to amount to the suggestion that even complex common capacities are properly explained by the performances of individuals in relation, i.e. need not give rise to postulating ontological collective subjects.

Social ontology has an impressive line of ancestors. As a distinctive area of systematic and cooperative specialization, however, it is a comparatively recent addition to international philosophical research. We hope that this volume will spur further interest in this rapidly evolving field of inquiry. The variety of the styles, methods, and arguments used in the contributions to this volume illustrate vividly the breadth of the current debate. At the same time, they contribute, from their respective perspectives, to deepen our understanding of three interrelated core topics in social ontology, namely, the constitution and structure of institutions, the role of shared evaluative attitudes, and the nature and role of group agents.

References

List, C., and P. Pettit. 2011. *Group agency: The possibility, design, and status of corporate agents.* Oxford/New York: Oxford University Press.

Searle, J. 1995. *The construction of social reality.* London: Allen Lane The Penguin Press.

Searle, J. 2010. *Making the social world: The structure of human civilization.* Oxford/New York: Oxford University Press.

Part I
Intentionality and Institutions

Chapter 2
Document Acts

Barry Smith

Abstract The theory of document acts is an extension of the more traditional theory of speech acts advanced by Austin and Searle. It is designed to do justice to the ways in which documents can be used to bring about a variety of effects in virtue of the fact that, where speech is evanescent, documents are continuant entities. This means that documents can be preserved in such a way that they can be inspected and modified at successive points in time and grouped together into enduring document complexes. We outline some components of a theory of document acts, and show how it can throw light on certain problems in Searle's ontology of social reality.

1 Introduction

The theory of speech acts focuses on the ways in which people use words and sentences in overt speech. They do this, familiarly, not only to convey information but also for a variety of other purposes, from thanking and admonishing to promising and apologizing. In his book *The Mystery of Capital* (2000), the Peruvian economist Hernando de Soto provided an account of the rise of modern civilization in which documents play a central role. In what follows I offer the beginnings of a theory of what I shall call *document acts*—acts in which people use documents, not only to record information, but also to bring about a variety of further ends, thereby extending the scope of what human beings can achieve through the mere performance of speech acts. In the world of commerce, most conspicuously, documents have made possible a vast array of new kinds (and instances) of social institutions, from bank loans and collateral to stock markets and pension funds. But the theory of document acts has implications which extend also to include

B. Smith (✉)
Department of Philosophy, University at Buffalo, Buffalo, NY, USA
e-mail: phismith@buffalo.edu

A. Konzelmann Ziv and H.B. Schmid (eds.), *Institutions, Emotions, and Group Agents,*
Studies in the Philosophy of Sociality 2, DOI 10.1007/978-94-007-6934-2_2,
© Springer Science+Business Media Dordrecht 2014

many types of phenomena outside the commercial realm, from passports to divorce decrees and from university diplomas to wills and testaments (Smith 2008).

I here present a first outline of the theory of document acts and show how it might be used to provide a better understanding of the role played by documents in the coordination of human actions. Where de Soto draws his inspiration from the ways in which documents make possible new kinds of social relations in the domains of law and commerce, our concern here is with document acts in general, where by 'document act' we mean: *what humans (or other agents) do with documents*, ranging from signing or stamping them, or depositing them in registries, to using them to grant or withhold permission, to establish or verify identity, or to set down rules for declaring a state of martial law. Acts of these sorts deal with documents in ways which reflect the status of the latter as documents (rather than as, for example, mere pieces of paper). Thus the coverage domain of the theory of document acts does not include, for example, burning old manuscripts to keep warm.

2 Scope of the Theory

The Oxford English Dictionary defines a document as:

> Something written, inscribed, etc., which furnishes evidence or information upon any subject, as a manuscript, title-deed, tomb-stone, coin, picture, etc.

The documents which interest us here, however, do not merely furnish evidence or information; they also have social and institutional (ethical, legal) powers of a variety of different sorts, summarized by Searle (1995) under the heading 'deontic powers'. They play an essential role in many social interactions, and they can bind people (or organizations, or nations) together in lasting ways which, in the case of wills and testaments or mortgage liens, can create rights and obligations that survive even the death of the authors of the documents involved. Thus (in contrast for example to what is argued in Jansen 2011) documents are like the utterances performed in acts of promising or commanding in that they are not merely of epistemic significance.

The scope of the theory of document acts includes:

1. the different *types of document*, ranging from free-text memos to standardized forms and templates (for example, an uncompleted tax form), and from single documents to entire archives and registries, and incorporating all of the various sorts of riders, codicils, protocols, addenda, amendments, appendices, date stamps, endorsements and other attachments, including maps, photographs, diagrams, signatures, fingerprints, official seals, RFID tags, barcodes, and other marks with which documents can become associated;

2. the different sorts of things *we can do to a document* qua *document* (for example fill it in, sign it, stamp it, inspect it, copy it, file it) and of the different ways in which one document can be transformed into a document of another type (for example when a license is annulled);

3. the different sorts of things we can do (achieve, effect, realize) *with* a document (establish collateral, create an organization, record the deliberations of a committee, initiate a legal action, release funds, confirm flight readiness);
4. the different ways in which, in performing acts involving documents, we may *fail to achieve the corresponding ends* (because of error, forgery, falsification, or invalidity of a document, or because of challenge by an addressee or by some cognizant official);
5. the *institutional systems* to which documents belong in areas such as marriage, law, government, commerce, credentialing, identification, as well as real estate property titling systems, credit reporting systems, credit card payment systems, taxation systems, and so on;
6. the different *positional roles* within such systems which are occupied by those involved in the performance of the corresponding acts, for example as signatory, co-signatory, witness, notary, registrar, and so on;
7. the *provenance* of documents, which means: the different sorts of ways in which documents are *created* as products of document acts of special sorts, as when documents with deontic powers are created through an official act of printing in a parliamentary digest;
8. the ways in which documents are *anchored to extra-documental reality* through the inclusion of photographs, fingerprints, and so forth;
9. the ways in which documents are *authenticated and protected* through security devices such as signatures and passwords.

As Table 2.1 makes clear, there are multiple ways in which we use documents to create new sorts of entities. Note that the listed examples do not involve in every case creation *ab initio*; typically, for example, a title deed is a deed that transfers title to a parcel of real estate from one owner to another. And just as there are document acts which serve to create entities of given sorts, so there are multiple types of document acts which serve to annihilate entities earlier created, as when for instance a divorce decree terminates a marriage, or a notice of dismissal terminates a relation of employment.

Standardly, when documents are used to create new entities or to amend or annihilate existing entities (for example debts or rights), they do this according to certain rules, and the entities created themselves then conform to certain rules in their turn. The two different sets of rules are interconnected, because they have evolved in tandem with the documents which support them. It is in this way that documents have contributed to the formation of the modern system of property rights and to associated systems of commercial obligations involving contracts, titles, collateral, credit, testament, stocks, bills, insurance, bankruptcy, taxes, and so on, as described by de Soto. Other document systems such as marriage, government, universities are governed by, and have co-evolved with, analogous sets of rules, and the same applies for example also to systems of identity documents (of birth and death certificates and public records offices, of visas, passports, consulates and border posts), of legal documents (of codes of law, summonses, police reports, court proceedings), and of employment documents (employment contracts, pay stubs, tax forms, work orders, performance evaluations, ...). Each such system

Table 2.1 Examples of different types of documents and of some of the types of entities which are outputs of the corresponding document acts

Document	Created entity
Contract	Obligation
Statute of incorporation	Corporation
Deed	Privilege
Title deed	Property right
Patent	Exclusive right
Statement of accounts	Audit trail
Marriage license	Bond of matrimony
Stock certificate	Capital
Diploma	Qualification
Registration of baptism	Legal name
Insurance certificate	Insurance coverage
License	Permission
IOU note	Obligation to pay

comprehends, in addition to documents, also other sorts of generic document-related entities such as registries, officials authorized to perform document acts of specific sorts, prescribed channels along which documents can move (for example through a chain of specified officials for inspection and approval), procedures for checking and filling in and storing and registering and validating documents, and also for training in the use of documents of corresponding types. One and the same document may hereby serve multiple successive social acts as it passes through successive recipients. A delivery note fulfils in succession the role of guiding those involved in delivering an object, of allowing the recipient to attest to its receipt, of allowing the deliverer to document successful delivery, and so forth. The signature on your passport plays three roles simultaneously: in initiating the validity of the passport, in certifying that you attest to the truth of the information represented therein, and in providing a sample of your signature for comparison.

Your filling in your tax form fulfills at least the following functions: it supports your performing actions in conformity with a legal protocol; it provides a series of nested questions to which you provide answers (for some of which it provides a protocol—a documentary calculation machine—for their generation); it provides a record of your performance in completing the form; it serves, when signed, to document your attestation to your belief in the validity of the form entries; it serves, when filed, to provide the input to processing by the tax authorities, there by potentially initiating a whole series of further operations (of amendment, verification, calculation of penalties, prosecution, and so forth).

3   The History of Document Acts

The historical dimension of the theory of document acts comes to the fore when we examine the ways in which document systems like those just mentioned have evolved over time in different cultures. Exemplary in this regard are the studies of Michael Clanchy and his associates on how, with the spread of literacy and the evolution of trust in writing in England in the thirteenth century, there occurred a change in the meaning of 'to record' from: *to bear oral witness* to: *to produce a document.* Clanchy shows how a variety of institutions which had hitherto been the preserve of royal or imperial chanceries were in this period progressively disseminated among the laity, so that by 1300 there were hundreds of thousands of peasants' charters giving English smallholders title to their land:

> the use of charters as titles to property made its way down the social hierarchy – from the royal court and monasteries … reaching the laity in general by the reign of Edward I … [when] literate modes were familiar even to serfs, who used charters for conveying property to each other and whose rights and obligations were beginning to be regularly recorded in manorial rolls. … One measure of this change is the possession of a seal or signum, which entitled a person to sign his name. (Clanchy 1993, p. 2; see also p. 35)

Clanchy describes how a range of document-related institutions evolved along the way, including: (1) the safekeeping of master copies of documents in central government archives and bishops' registries; (2) the practice of registering deeds of title in towns; (3) letters testifying to trustworthiness; (4) financial accounts; (5) surveys (from the Domesday book, completed in 1086, onwards); and also the practices of (6) dating and (7) signing documents. Clanchy cites Bracton writing in the mid-thirteenth century and documenting the practice of using documents deliberately to extend the powers of unaided human memory: 'Gifts are sometimes made in writings, that is in charters, for perpetual remembrance, because the life of man is but brief and in order that the gift may be more easily proved' (p. 117).

Through developments such as these, the different parts of English society became bound together in ways mediated by the gradual creation and spread of legal, political, commercial and ecclesiastical document systems at different levels, and accompanied by the acquisition of new document-based skills by ever broader groups in society, whose members thereby acquired the capacity to realize new kinds of collective intentionality, and to occupy new kinds of positional roles within the larger corporate wholes that were gradually evolving.

Analogous accounts of the rise of document systems can of course be provided for other European societies, too (see for example Teuscher 2010), and de Soto and his co-workers have documented the rise of such systems in formerly illiterate cultures of contemporary Africa and elsewhere. As de Soto points out, Tanzanians living in villages far removed from the official legal institutions found in the cities, have in recent times 'created a self-organized system of documented institutions that allows them to govern their actions'. As a result, these village Tanzanians

> live in at least two levels of reality: first, the reality made up of things, both tangible (land, businesses, cattle) and intangible (ideas); and second, the reality of structures of relationships, physically captured in written documents that are the natural habitat of advanced economic and social relationships. (de Soto 2006)

In rural as well as urban areas of mainland Tanzania and Zanzibar, de Soto and his co-workers discovered many thousands of extralegal documents created to enable poor people to make economic decisions, cooperate with each other, structure their collaboration, create property, extract credit and liquidity from physical assets, and structure entrepreneurial associations where they can divide labor internally and trade externally (de Soto 2006).

4   From Occurrents to Continuants

Speech acts are evanescent entities: they are *events* or *occurrents*, which exist only in their executions. Documents, in contrast, are *objects* or *continuants*, which means that they endure self-identically through time and have the capacity to float free from the person or persons who were involved in their creation and thus to live lives of their own. Documents can also have multiple creators, who may make their contributions to the document at different times. Legal and administrative documents may include portions to be filled in at different times, for example when successive decisions have been taken, or successive meetings held, or when the document has been viewed by successive individuals. Documents may also grow through attachment of appendices or through real or virtual incorporation of other documents through document-artifacts such as cross-references (pointing to other parts of a single document) and footnotes and citations (pointing to what lies outside).

Searle, in his *Making the Social World* (2010), has attempted to capture one element of what is involved in the theory of document acts with his idea of 'standing declarations', as for example in the case of the promise from the Chief Cashier of the Bank of England 'to pay the bearer on demand the sum of £5' that is printed on each £5 note. This however is in conflict with Searle's naturalism (discussed in Sect. 7 below). For Searle's idea seems to be that what is printed on the banknote is merely something that stands proxy for an entity which somehow transcends the ontological boundary between event (a declaration) and enduring entity (the declaration somehow *stands*). On the view here proposed, in contrast, some declaration may indeed have taken place at the time of the relevant document act, but the latter gave rise to something which truly did endure, namely a document (or, as in the case of banknotes, a constantly changing collection of documents).

And it is not only the capacity to endure that distinguishes documents from declarations properly so called. No less important are the new enduring dimensions of social reality which arise on this documentary basis. For the capacity of documents to endure brings further the possibility for documents to be stored and registered, and thereby to give rise to a history of changes both in the document itself and in the social reality which falls under its influence. The importance of such changes becomes clear when we consider the list of things we can do *to* documents, including: sign, countersign, fill in, stamp, copy, witness, notarize, transfer, inspect, validate, invalidate, table, ratify, destroy, draft, propose, amend, revise, nullify, veto, deliver, display, register, archive, falsify, redact, and so forth. Only some of these have (in most cases rather rudimentary) counterparts in the domain of speech acts.

Documents differ from speech acts also in virtue of the variety of ways in which pluralities of documents can be chained together (for example to form an audit trail), or combined to form new document-complexes whose structures mirror relations, for example of debtor to creditor, among the persons and institutions involved. As de Soto shows (2000), the practice whereby title deeds become combined and stored with other documents in the granting of mortgages has made an immense contribution to the advance of Western civilization, effectively by allowing the wealth represented by land or buildings to be set free (as capital) for purposes of investment.

5   From Face-to-Face Interactions to the Extended Society

The theory of speech acts provides what seems to be a satisfactory explanation of how entities such as debts or corporations or trusts *begin* to exist: (roughly) people make certain promises. But the question then still arises of what can serve as the physical basis for the *temporally extended* existence of such entities and for their enduring power to serve coordination. In small societies, and in simple social interactions, we might reasonably identify this physical basis with the memories of those involved. In large societies, however, or in what de Soto calls the 'extended market', we are typically dealing with highly complex social interactions, involving principals who may enjoy little or no prior personal acquaintance with each other, and with interactions which may evolve through periods of time which extend beyond the capacity of individual memories.

Our proposal is that, with the growth in size and reach of civilization, the mnemonic powers of individuals have been extended prosthetically through documents in ways which have given rise to a variety of novel artifacts of social reality. Documents of different forms, because they support enduring and re-usable deontic powers, have allowed the evolution of new and more complex forms of social order. Moreover, this process has been iterated, as more complex social orders have themselves given rise to new document forms, and to associated document technologies, which have then given risen in turn to new and more complex social institutions.

As explained in Smith (2012), document acts do not work in isolation from speech acts. Thus acts of creation (of obligations, permissions, rights) of the types referred to above will typically involve not only documents and document-related acts, but also a plethora of speech acts of various sorts ('sign here!', 'your papers, please', ...). The success of a document act will thus depend, too, on the same sorts of felicity conditions as are involved in speech acts of the traditional sort: the person who fills in the document has to have the authority to do so; has to do so with appropriate intentions, in the appropriate sorts of contexts, and so forth.

The fact that documents are involved, however, expands the number and range of different sorts of felicity conditions, because it expands the number of different types of persons and of roles which they can play, either as authors or addressees of documents, or as witnesses or validators (registrars, solicitors, notaries, executors), and so forth. It advances the degree of complexity and also the spatial and temporal reach of what can be achieved. And it thereby also expands the number of ways in which, in the performance of document acts, things can go wrong.

6   Knowledge by Comparison

The speech acts performed in the local contexts of everyday life have an immediate connection to author and addressee, and their deontic consequences are anchored to reality typically through the memories of the persons involved. To bring about deontic consequences that can outlast such memories, a document must be anchored to reality in some lasting way. In the simplest case, an identity document such as a passport is anchored to its bearer through devices such as photographs, signatures, and lists of identifying marks. These encapsulate relevant features of the history of the creation of the document in visible form. They also allow, in the presence of the bearer of the passport, what we might call *knowledge by comparison* whereby, by comparing bearer with photograph, or by comparing one signature with another, we can acquire evidence, for example to the effect that this bearer is who he claims to be, or that the information contained in this passport is veridical.

The photograph allows the gaining of knowledge by comparison only if it is attached in the right way, which means: with the right sorts of signatures, official stamps, seals, watermarks, biometric data, and so forth. Often, the photograph is associated with alphanumeric identifiers, which allow a type of virtual attachment between documents via cross-referencing brought about through the use of the same identifiers in multiple documents, as for example through the use of tracking numbers in parcel shipment, independently accessible not only by sender and recipient, but also by a succession of billing and shipping agents in successive phases of receipt and delivery. The use of the vehicle identification number impressed into the metal of your car in multiple collections of paper and digital documents helps to prevent theft and various kinds of insurance and re-sale fraud, by allowing the creation of a history of the successive physical, commercial, and administrative events in which your car is involved to be compiled automatically over time. The numbers and codes that appear in your passport will appear also in a multiplicity of other documents, for example in records of entry and exit maintained by the immigration authorities. Physically attaching a visa to a passport can in this way have multiple deontic effects: it supports identification of the bearer of the visa; provides evidence that the visa was both legally issued and issued to the person presenting it; and ensures, from both a legal and a practical point of view, that the rules in a given country applying to the carrying of passports are applied automatically to the carrying of visas. It is the registration of your passport number by the immigration official on entry to a foreign country that initiates your state of being legally present in that country, thereby also allowing you to perform legally the act of leaving.

7   Products of Massive Fantasy

At the heart of speech act theory is a thesis to the effect that we can bring about changes in the world through utterances, for example through declarations such as 'I name this ship ...'. In *Making the Social World* Searle (perhaps unwittingly) gives this thesis, which he calls 'the most general logical form of the creation of institutional reality', an explicitly ontological formulation, as:

[A] We make it the case by Declaration that a Y status function exists in a context
     C (Searle 2010, p. 13).

As I attempted to show in Smith (2003, 2012), it is uncertain whether Searle in fact succeeds in formulating a coherent ontology of the social reality that would do justice to this thesis in its full ontological interpretation. This is because on the one hand [A] implies that our declarations are able to bring into existence entities, such as claims and obligations, which fall outside the realm of what is investigated by physics; yet on the other hand Searle himself still embraces a naturalist view according to which:

[B] Everything in the universe 'consist[s] entirely of physical particles in fields of
     force' (Searle 2010, p. 3).

Searle sees himself as contributing in *Making the Social World* to the scientific understanding of society. As he himself puts it:

> I think it is sometimes possible to do good research without worrying about the ontological issues [of social reality], but the whole investigation gets a greater depth if one is acutely conscious of the ontology of the phenomena being investigated. (2010, p. 201)

Unfortunately, however, it appears that Searle himself does not, in the end, succeed in providing a consistent ontology of the most central features of the social world within his naturalistic framework. Already in 1913, Adolf Reinach, a Continental philosopher of genuinely scientific stripe, had pointed the way towards a more rigorous treatment of how social entities are brought into being through Declarations (or through what Reinach calls '*Bestimmungen*'), including a theory of the ways in which such entities may transcend the boundary between what is abstract and what is historical (Reinach 1988; Paulson 1987). In a series of papers on Searle's social ontology (2003, 2008, 2012; see also Smith and Zaibert 2001, and Smith and Searle 2003), I have attempted to show how Searle can quite easily address the problems arising from his naturalism by accepting, with Reinach, that there are quasi-abstract entities—or what I have also called 'free-standing Y terms'—which are both (i) such as to lie outside the province of what is described by physics, yet nonetheless, (ii) because they are brought into being by declaration, are fully a part of the historical world of what happens and is the case.

This departure from naturalism would of course contradict Searle's thesis [B] above. But the departure is at the same time modest, and is indeed consistent with other Searlean statements of his naturalist position, for example to the effect that:

[C] while the basic facts of the world are constituted by the material entities studied by physics and chemistry, *'all the other parts of reality* [emphasis added] are dependent on, and in various ways derive from, the basic facts' (Searle 2010, p. 4),

or that

[D] when status functions are ascribed to freestanding Y terms, then the latter 'always bottom out in actual human beings who have the powers [connected to the status function Y] in question.' (Searle 2010, p. 108)

Even though freestanding Y terms are not made of physical parts, they must nonetheless have some basis in the underlying physical reality—above all in actions of the human beings involved—because every quasi-abstract entity is dependent ontologically on physical entities such as people and documents.

Because Searle holds so firmly to [B], however, he is unable to do justice ontologically to the question of how this basis is secured. Consider, for example, the structured investment vehicles encountered in the realm of commerce (Smith 2012). The needed account of such phenomena would need to refer to quasi-abstract entities at higher levels which are dependent on further quasi-abstract entities on lower levels in a complex hierarchical structure of the sort illustrated for example in Edstrom (2010). Edstrom's chart represents the interrelations between multiple corporations, trusts, government agencies, loan packages, purchase prices, gross proceeds, payments, distributions, assignments, transfers, agreements, filings, deeds, certificates involved in each single act of mortgage securitization.

Edstrom's chart represents a complex set of relations that is part of social reality. Searle, however, withholds commitment to precisely those social entities—such as corporations or trusts or mortgages or securities—between which these relations putatively hold, entities which are referred to in hundreds of relevant legal and financial documents. While for Searle the entirety of these interrelations is a mere pattern of interrelations among the states and activities of human beings (1995, p. 57), in giving an account of what these activities are, he, too, would be called upon to refer to the very entities which he would have fall victim to his naturalistic reduction.

The word 'exists' in [A] is, for Searle, not to be taken literally. Indeed, in *Making the Social World* Searle articulates a view according to which the entities referred to in [A] as being *created by Declaration*, are not really *created* at all. They are, rather, 'products of massive fantasy' (Searle 2010, p. 201). The entire social world is, it turns out, an elaborate confidence trick, in which all participants are involved both as perpetrators and sometimes (as for example in the events triggered by the Lehman bankruptcy) as victims. We are all somehow affected by this massive confidence trick, which extends all the way down to simple social phenomena such as money or marriage. Searle alone is able to see through to the reality beneath—a reality, again, which consists exclusively of physical things such as people, their states, and their activities.

To apply a view of this sort, however, to the task of providing a detailed description of all that is involved in a complex social phenomenon such as mortgage securitization—if it were possible at all—would yield an outcome that is for at least three reasons inadequate. First, it would be orders of magnitude more complicated than the already highly complex accounts provided by the practitioners themselves (see, again, the chart in Edstrom 2010). Second, it would not do ontological justice to the social reality of mortgage securitization, as is seen in the fact that it would make it especially difficult to deal with those modified forms of mortgage securitization in which confidence trickery based on 'massive fantasies' is indeed being deliberately perpetrated on unwitting victims. And third, and most importantly for us here, it would not help our scientific understanding.

8   Creating Quasi-Abstract Entities

Thus while, in accordance with the view expressed by Searle in [C] above, and with the arguments advanced in Johansson (2011), we must accept that the entire edifice of complex social phenomena 'bottoms out' in the actions, powers, and intentional states of the myriad persons who may be involved in such phenomena, this does not mean that these foundational (and, with Searle, naturalistically understandable) components are all that there is. For in the complex cases of the sort discussed in the above, which involve the creation of multiple interconnected quasi-abstract entities existing on multiple levels and enduring across multiple overlapping periods of time, these actions, powers, and states of persons themselves involve myriad identifications and re-identifications of the quasi-abstract entities created. There is thus no way to paraphrase away the latter in terms of statements referring only to the former (Smith 2012), any more than we could paraphrase the language of, say, quantum physics in terms of references to the beliefs and states of mind of physicists.

Note that Searle is not helped, here, by any appeal to the fact that it is not only individual but also collective action that is involved in complex social phenomena such as mortgage securitization. The naturalistic account of collective intentionality presented in (Searle 1995) may indeed be able to suffice for the understanding of, for example, social actions such as dancing a waltz or bearing a coffin; they do not, however, suffice for the understanding of the social actions detailed in Edstrom (2010). For this, we require an analysis of the quasi-abstract entities targeted in multiple interlocking manifestations of individual and collective intentionality. Searle thus owes such entities themselves a home in his social ontology.

9   Coda on Electronic Documents

While I have focused in the above on paper documents, it will be clear that we are all of us currently witnessing the rapid evolution of whole new species of document acts and associated artifacts of social reality as a result of the rise of computerized document systems.

As de Soto has emphasized, the historical growth of the modern system of laws has proved to be the gateway for economic success. It is this system that allowed property documents to be created and standardized and thereby to form a public memory that permits society to engage in an ever-expanding set of economic activities based on the possibility of gaining access to information about individuals, their assets, their legal titles and the associated rights and obligations. In our own day, these possibilities are being expanded still further, allowing suitably authorized persons and institutions to gain access for example to information about your health status (through national electronic health record systems) or the accident status of your car (through vehicle history reporting systems). The international credit card system allows one individual to authorize another individual, who may be on the other side of the world, to gain immediate access to his cash. At the same time, the credit reporting system allows further authorized individuals to gain immediate access to information about each person's credit status, information that is being constantly updated to take account of each new recorded transaction. In this way, individuals in developed societies gain tremendous new opportunities to shape their own lives while at the same time subjecting themselves to new and ever more refined species of accountability.

With the advent of the mobile phone, too, there is occurring a transformation of the traditional telephone into an instrument for the performance not only of speech acts but also of document acts of multiple kinds (Ferraris 2005). At the wave of a hand, your phone sends an order request (a digital document) to a machine standing in front of you with the content: dispense a can of Boss Coffee. Automatically, the transaction is digitally documented in a way that anchors the phone and the person using it to a specific time and place, with multiple further digital documents being created in the computers of your phone company, your credit card agency, and of the company charged to replenish the dispensing machine.

But while digital documents, like the paper documents that preceded them, have certainly given rise to vast new opportunities for mankind, from on-line banking to internet dating, the new possibilities of document aggregation and transmission enabled by the computer have also opened up new opportunities for massive failure, including new opportunities for criminal, terrorist and military attack. One potential benefit of the realistic theory of document acts proposed in the foregoing, therefore, is that it will support the development of the needed scientific understanding of documents and of document artifacts of a sort that might be used in the future in a way which can support a more intelligent appreciation of the changes in social reality that are being effected through the trillions of documents being created daily in the digital realm.

Acknowledgements With thanks to Guglielmo Feis, Ludger Jansen, Ingvar Johansson, Kevin Mulligan and Leo Zaibert for helpful comments.

References

Austin, J.L. 1962. *How to do things with words*. Cambridge, MA: Harvard University Press.

Clanchy, M.T. 1993. *From memory to written record: England 1066–1307*, 2nd ed. Oxford: Blackwell.

de Soto, H. 2000. *The mystery of capital: Why capitalism triumphs in the west and fails everywhere else*. New York: Basic Books.

de Soto, H. 2006. The challenge of connecting informal and formal property systems—Some reflections based on the case of Tanzania. In *Realizing property rights*, Swiss Human Rights book, vol. 1, ed. H. de Soto and F. Cheneval. Zurich: rüffer & rub, http://www.swiss-humanrightsbook.com/SHRB/shrb_01_files/255_02%20de%20Soto.pdf. Last accessed 16 Oct 2012.

Edstrom, D. 2010. *Securities transaction re-engineered*, as cited in: http://goo.gl/IN5nG. Last accessed 12 June 2013.

Ferraris, M. 2005. *Dove Sei? Ontologia del telefonino*. Milano: Bompiani.

Jansen, L. 2011. Konstitution und Dauer sozialer Kontinuanten. In *Persistenz—Indexikalität—Zeiterfahrung*, ed. G. Schönrich and P. Schmechtig, 103–128. Ontos: Frankfurt am Main and Lancaster.

Johansson, I. 2011. John Searle in the year 2010. *Metaphysica* 12(1): 73–85.

Paulson, S. 1987. Demystifying Reinach's legal theory. In *Speech act and Sachverhalt. Reinach and the foundations of realist phenomenology*, ed. K. Mulligan, 133–154. Dordrecht: Martinus Nijhoff.

Reinach, A. 1988. *Sämtliche Werke. Kritische Ausgabe mit Kommentar*. 2 vols. München/Wien: Philosophia.

Searle, J.R. 1969. *Speech acts: An essay in the philosophy of language*. Cambridge: Cambridge University Press.

Searle, J.R. 1995. *The construction of social reality*. New York: Free Press.

Searle, J.R. 2010. *Making the social world: The structure of human civilization*. New York: Oxford University Press.

Smith, B. 2003. John Searle: From speech acts to social reality. In *John Searle*, ed. B. Smith, 1–33. Cambridge: Cambridge University Press.

Smith, B. 2008. Searle and De Soto: The new ontology of the social world. In *The mystery of capital and the construction of social reality*, ed. B. Smith, D. Mark, and I. Ehrlich, 35–51. Chicago: Open Court.

Smith, B. 2012. How to do things with documents. *Rivisti di Estetica* 50: 179–198.

Smith, B., and J.R. Searle. 2003. The construction of social reality: An exchange. *American Journal of Economics and Sociology* 62(2): 285–309.

Smith, B., and L. Zaibert. 2001. The metaphysics of real estate. *Topoi* 20: 161–172.

Teuscher, S. 2010. Document collections, mobilized regulations, and the making of customary law at the end of the middle ages. *Archival Science* 10: 211–229.

Chapter 3
Searlean Reflections on Sacred Mountains

Filip Buekens

Abstract Error theories hold that claims about sacred objects are uniformly false when (and because) their existence is supposed to depend on the occurrence of highly implausible supernatural events involved in their creation or causal history. It is therefore an illusion to believe that the concept of being sacred corresponds to a real property. Social constructionists maintain that sacred entities are constructs of concepts, discourses, or practices, just like gods, angels, witches, and devils. Claims about sacred objects are therefore uniformly true. I present an institutional account of sacred objects as covert institutional entities, and distinguish between true beliefs that help create the institutional facts and false beliefs about their origin.

1 Sacred Objects and Deontic Auras

While religions as such are not institutions, all religions contain "a system of symbols which acts to establish powerful, pervasive, and long-lasting moods and motivations in men" (Geertz 1973, p. 90). In this paper I defend the view that sacred objects can function as covert *institutional objects* in a religious practice. I describe—within Searle's framework—the cognitive effects that accompany a participant's realization that sacred objects are institutional objects.[1] These objects are the ingredients of religious practices, which include institutional reasons,

---

[1] I distinguish unintended social facts and covert institutional facts. An unintended social fact is either a by-product of an institutional practice or a social consequence of individual actions.

F. Buekens (✉)
Department of Philosophy, Tilburg University, Tilburg, Netherlands

Department of Philosophy, University of Leuven, Leuven, Belgium
e-mail: fillip.buekens@hiw.kuleuven.be

A. Konzelmann Ziv and H.B. Schmid (eds.), *Institutions, Emotions, and Group Agents*,
Studies in the Philosophy of Sociality 2, DOI 10.1007/978-94-007-6934-2_3,
© Springer Science+Business Media Dordrecht 2014

narratives about the origin of the world and our ultimate destiny, explanatory schemes, and moral decision procedures, etc. An institutional account of sacred objects allows us to affirm the existence of true beliefs about what is sacred and what isn't. Searle's theory takes the connection between institutional facts and their deontic powers to be fundamental: unlike brute facts, rights and obligations underlie institutional facts. Their deontic powers can to some extent be articulated and codified by participants in the practice (Searle 1995, p. 88; Rust 2010, p. 134). Exposing sacredness as a covert institutional property (that is, covert relative to the community in which a sacred object functions) may modify the deontic powers associated with the institutional object.

The capacity of institutional facts to create deontic powers and desire-independent reasons for action is a central claim in Searle's theory of institutions. The deontic aura of sacred objects in general was brilliantly captured by Clifford Geertz. 'Religion', he writes,

> is never merely metaphysics. For all peoples the forms, vehicles, and objects of worship are suffused with an aura of moral seriousness. The holy bears within it everywhere a sense of intrinsic obligation; it not only encourages devotion, it demands it; it not only induces intellectual assent, it enforces emotional commitment... The powerfully coercive 'ought' is felt to grow out of a comprehensive factual 'is', and in such a way religion grounds the most specific requirements of human action in the most general contexts of human existence. (Geertz 1973, p. 126)

Geertz' description illuminates how rituals, rights and obligations are attached to, and engendered by, symbols and symbolic objects and how they create desire-independent reasons for the participants involved in the practice.[2] Moreover, it seems to be a universal feature of sacred objects that they impose commitments upon those who *accept* and/or *recognize* them (a second Searlean feature of institutional facts). The determination of the hours of worship or the offering of sacrifices presupposes a realm of concrete objects (places, times, etc.) that count as sacred. The objects are surrounded by a deontic aura; at a minimum they elicit reverence and awe in members of the community that is responsible for maintaining their status.[3]

The use of *predicates* like 'sacred' or 'holy' often carries a *colour* that expresses reverence and awe (Frege 1918). One might hold that the predicate, so used, expresses a *thick* concept in the sense that it designates both descriptive and evaluative aspects (Williams 1985). We prefer the Fregean approach, because it acknowledges that meaning and colour can come apart in systematic ways: you, qua outsider, can grant that an object is believed to be sacred (in a community C)

---

[2]Geertz continues: "They are felt to sum up, for those for whom they are resonant, what is known about the way the world is, the quality of the emotional life it supports, and the way one ought to behave while in it" (Geertz 1973, p. 127). Sacred symbols 'thus relate an ontology and a cosmology to an aesthetic and a morality; their particular power comes from their presumed ability to identify fact with value at the most fundamental level, to give to what is merely actual ... a comprehensive normative import.' (ibid.)

[3]My aim in this paper is not to give a full account of the *phenomenon* of the sacred.

without thereby necessarily expressing any (positive or negative) attitude towards it or acknowledging that you yourself (qua outsider relative to C) are the object of the deontic powers associated with it. And even outsiders can respect indirectly sacred objects and places by respecting worshippers. This too is also an appropriate deontic attitude.

It is certainly not *obvious* that sacred objects are Searlean institutional facts. Sacred objects and the practices that surround them have a 'natural' etiology, describable in evolutionary terms. They can continue to function in ceremonial practices that no longer, or only vaguely refer to the original practice. Some hold that if a human anthropological phenomenon f has its origin in evolutionary selection (it has been properly 'selected for' some biological function F), then f's present role can in principle be reductively explained. If you hold such a reductive view, you might join error theorists who hold that beliefs about holy mountains are uniformly false. Social constructionists, on the other hand, hold that sacred objects exist because *all* religious facts are (in some sense) socially constructed (Overing 1990; Beckford 2003 and J.Z. Smith 1987 defend social constructionism applied to sacred places).[4] Both views will be critically assessed and ultimately rejected, and not just because they do not properly acknowledge the deontic dimension of institutional facts. On the other hand, both views offer real challenges to Searle's views. An important issue to examine is the installation of a sensible demarcation between false beliefs about sacred objects and the shared attitudes that create sacred objects. Consider, as an example, shamanism: the role of the shaman and many aspects of shamanic practice are institutional facts, which give them rights and duties. But the core belief of and about the shaman (e.g. 'there exists an Underworld, it is embodied by spirits, the shaman can get in contact with the spirits and direct their powers, these powers are supernatural but can have observable effects which have no natural explanation . . .') are clearly *false*. Of course, such beliefs can be self-fulfilling: predicted events may take place because of psychological looping-mechanisms that make those beliefs true (Hacking 1999); they may encourage supporters to discount contrary evidence; they may have self-fulfilling effects (e.g. placebo effects); or they may encourage supporters to employ immunisation strategies, in order to discount contrary evidence (Jopling 2008).[5] None of these cognitive mechanisms turn their subject matter into institutional facts for they do not create new deontic powers.[6]

---

[4]The constructivist/error theory controversy is discussed by Haslanger (2006), who investigates the concept of *race*.

[5]Langton (2009) distinguishes self-verifying beliefs and self-fulfilling beliefs. Collective acceptance of a certain object's sacredness is self-fulfilling, insofar as it establishes a belief's truth. A belief is self-verifying when it provides *evidence* for itself. These latter beliefs may be false but justified. For example, someone who is ranked as inferior can be made to act as if she is inferior, even when she is not (Langton 2009, p. 11).

[6]There are other senses in which beliefs can be self-validating, as in the case of self-fulfilling prophecies ('There will be thousands of people in the park this evening, and it will be awesome'), but none of these processes and mechanisms create institutional facts in Searle's sense. Thanks to a referee for pointing this out.

2   Searle's Theory of Institutional Facts

In *The Construction of Social Reality* (1995) and *Making the Social World* (2010), Searle develops a theory of institutions, with money, borders, and property as prototypical examples. The distinction between brute facts and institutional facts, originally introduced by John Rawls (1955), is fairly unproblematic. Brute facts such as mountains, rivers, snow or temperature exist independently of human intentionality. Artifacts and institutional objects depend on human intentionality for their existence. Screwdrivers or tennis rackets would not exist unless conscious agents regarded them as such (Searle 1995, p. 41). Searle gives us three essential features of institutional reality: (i) collective intentionality, (ii) the assignment of function, (iii) constitutive rules (1998, p. 124) and (iv) the creation of deontic powers.[7] The key feature of collective intentionality is that the relevant intentions for creating institutional objects must be expressed as 'we-intentions', which reflect the sense in which we do or bring about something together. Collective intentionality is a "biologically primitive phenomenon" that is exhibited in us and in many other species (1995, pp. 24, 38). "The crucial element in collective intentionality is a sense of doing (wanting, believing, etc.) something together, and the individual intentionality that each person has is derived from the collective intentionality that they share" (1995, pp. 24–25).[8]

The second feature involves assigning a status function to some natural object which, if the property obtains, yields an institutional fact, *i.e.* a true proposition about that object. A piece of paper is assigned the status function of money or a contract, and functions that way due to the collective acceptance by relevant members of a collective. The assignment of function is itself based on the third feature, constitutive rules, which create the very possibility of certain types of institutional behaviour. Unlike regulative rules that modify existing behaviour (like speed limits or rules of politeness), constitutive rules create the possibility of new actions. The logical form of constitutive rules is 'X counts as Y in C', where X refers to the object—mostly under a physical description—that is being given an institutional status. 'Y' refers to the status property itself, while C refers to certain conditions under which the status applies. The Y-term itself is sometimes called an 'institutional' term or a 'social concept' (Smith and Searle 2003, p. 299–309). The logical form of the formula has its origins in Searle's work on speech acts (Searle 1969, pp. 52ff; Turner 1999).[9] A final point—not stressed by Searle but important

---

[7]In 2010 Searle stresses the role of deontic powers and desire-independent reasons even more than in earlier works. The whole point of Declaratives is to create deontic powers (2010, p. 101).

[8]Technically, what is at work is an intention to *represent something as something else*: it takes the conditions of satisfaction of a belief-like intentional state and imposes it on a brute object, which is, in this case, a mountain (see Rust 2010, p. 132). Searle (2010, p. 58) seems to acknowledge that there can be institutional facts that do not presuppose collective intentionality.

[9]Searle seems to accept the *uniformity of existence*: everything exists in the same sense of 'exist'. It does not therefore follow that there is a uniform way in which everything came into existence. Institutional properties (status functions, in Searle's terminology) can be imposed on persons, actions, and objects.

for our purposes—is that his account is purely descriptive: when an institutional account of phenomenon X is given or brought into the open, phenomenon X and the practice in which it is embedded need not change just because that account has been given. Searle's aim is *not* (or at least not directly) to question the 'status quo', as Hacking (1999, p. 6) puts it in a critical analysis of social constructionism. Searle often speaks and writes, correctly in our view, as if his theory elucidates deeply embedded cognitive habits; bringing them out into the open need not and does not aim at changing practices and attitudes toward them.[10] Notwithstanding Searle's use of 'acceptance/recognition' for describing attitudes that create and maintain institutional facts, these attitudes do not entail a moral or practical evaluation of the institution or (system of) institutional fact(s) they are directed at.

The fourth claim pertains to how our deontic powers are increased through the creation of institutional facts. Borders, property, money, and marriages create, for those who recognize them, a variety of rights, duties, permissions, and obligations. If you criticize an institution, you often do so because you object to the deontic powers that persons derive from it. I shall assume in this paper that this is indeed the target of criticizing an institution. I shall also assume that the way they come into existence is through implicit or explicit declaratives, a point stressed by Searle (2010). I am not sure this is *always* the case, nor that Searle's functional analysis offers the right order of explanation (see Smit et al. 2011 for an alternative account), but I'll leave that issue aside.

3 Reflections on a Sacred Mountain

Mount Popzatetl is, according to a collective G ('the tribe'), a sacred mountain.[11] Call the proposition members of G believe to be true (the proposition *that Mt. Popzatetl is sacred*) H. Let G designate a collective whose members recognize/accept H, which is essential for Mt. Popzatetl's (designated by the X-term in the constitutive rule)[12] being holy (its agentive function, designated by the Y-term).[13] Because a god born on Mount Popzatetl's summit explains, for members of G, why it is a sacred mountain, members of G will deny that its holiness is an institutional

---

[10]But compare Searle (1995, p. 117), where he complains about 'the steady erosion of acceptance of large institutional structures around the world' and 'the breakdown of national identification in favor of ethnic tribalism'. Institutions come and go, but it is not the purpose of Searle's theory to morally evaluate institutions.

[11]Focussing on a token allows me to bypass some subtle but in this context irrelevant qualifications of the theory involving the type/token distinction.

[12]See Smith (2007) for refinements of Searle's ontology.

[13]Here and in what follows I distinguish a collective from a community. A community may contain apostates and dissenters. The collective is constituted by members who accept/recognize *and* approve of H. Non-members of G may or may not fall under deontic powers of the institutional fact maintained by G (this depends on the tolerance of their religion).

property, even if more theoretically-minded members of G (perhaps those who were graduate students at Berkeley but returned to their community) are willing to accept Searle's theory as a sensible account of *bona fide* institutional facts (e.g., money or borders).[14] Depending on their tolerance for other religious practices (and articulating their view in Searlean terms), they could maintain the sacredness of another mountain (recognized by members of a different community G*) to be merely a covert institutional fact (members of G believe their gods are the only ones that really exist). Members of G could also hold that the beliefs of community G* are *false*. Members of G accept deontic powers that emerge from, or are associated with, the sacred mountain. They know that it is impermissible for children to climb Mt. Popzatetl, and that senior members of the collective must be buried on a day the full moon appears behind its summit.

Even if some members of G accept the general framework of Searle's theory, they would *deny* that it could be applied to Mt. Popzatetl's sacred nature. While they believe that Mt. Popzatetl is sacred, they deny that it is sacred in virtue of the ontological, epistemic and cognitive aspects involving the creation and maintenance of institutions. Below, we conceptualize what members of G would deny in terminology borrowed from Searle's theory (we combine the Searlean account with plausible replies by members of G):

(i) Its holiness is an observer-dependent function that acquires an agentive status function due to collective intentionality (Searle 1995, pp. 21, 26); members of the collective will reply that its sacred character has everything to do with its natural origin (gods were born on its summit, and they believe these gods exist).

(ii) Acceptance and/or recognition of Mt. Popzatetl's holiness is a necessary condition for it to functionally surpass its objective physical features (ibid., p. 39). Its holiness is not a natural (let alone physical) property. The term 'holiness' designates a status function. The reply would be that the mountain's sacred character is not a human-dependent feature, but they might agree that it cannot be derived from its physical features. Holy objects are (again, according to members of G) intrinsically valuable because of a relational property (what happened on top of it, long time ago).[15]

(iii) That Mt. Popzatetl counts as sacred in their religious practice (a concrete instance of the 'X counts as Y in context C' formula) is the logical form of the assignment (Searle 1995, p. 46). For members of G, however, its holiness is neither assigned by them, nor is its validity confined to members of G; members of a wider community, indeed, the whole of mankind ought to accept/recognize that it is true that *H*. Its holiness is not practice-sensitive in the way customs or borders are. There was no 'Status Function Declaration'

---

[14]A building that *counts as* a mosque can be recognized as an intended institutional object, even by a fundamentalist Muslim. I don't hold that all sacred objects are covert institutional facts.

[15]Any object may obtain intrinsic value due to a relational property. Think of relics that have an emotional value for a person because of their origin, their former owner, etc. The value attached to an object on the basis of obtaining these properties does not require acceptance by a collective.

involved in its creation (Searle 2010, p. 85), and if there was, it would have been produced by the deities themselves.

(iv) Deontic powers occasioned by *H*—obligations and permissions, rights and responsibilities—are derived from accepting Mount Popzatetl's status as a sacred object (Searle 1995, p. 100). Members of G would obviously reply that its deontic aura should be explained by some supernatural truth about the mountain. That might explain why, for members of the collective (and as so often observed by anthropologists), those obligations are typically felt to be eternal and unchangeable.[16]

(v) There is real or virtual agency within G which imposed holiness on Mt. Popzatetl and was responsible for maintaining its holiness: in its causal history, a real or virtual Declaration must have contributed to its configuration, intentionally imposing the status of sacredness on the object (Searle 2010, pp. 12–13). It would be plausible to reply that the mountain's sacredness could not have originated in a real or virtual declarative speech acts by a human being. *We* did not create it.

(vi) The deontic powers are symbolic, insofar as the continual collective acceptance (or recognition) of the functional or statutory validity would be exclusively responsible for Mt. Popzatetl's successful performance of its function. However, members of G could reply that the powers are emanating from the object in virtue of its supernatural origin. Its aura has its origin in the acts of a deity, not in collective acceptance.

(vii) Members of G grasp the concept of holiness, but they think it is grounded in a relational property involving supernatural facts. Members of G could accept that, as a matter of fact, *H*'s truth obtains neither in virtue of the material nor physical features of Mt. Popzatetl, and they may admit that holiness is not a perceptual or recognitional property (like being yellow). They would resist the idea that it is a belief-dependent functional property.[17]

In sum, members of G *deny* that what Searle presents as the key function of creating institutional facts applies to deontic powers derived from *H*'s truth: "the whole point of the creation of institutional reality is not to invest objects or people with some special status valuable in itself, but to create and regulate power relationships between people" (Searle 2010, p. 106). For members of G, Mt. Popzatetl's intrinsic religious value is conferred upon it via a relational property:

---

[16]It could be added that if sacred mountains are institutional facts, they may generate 'institutional reasons' for action (Mackie 1977). It is a conspicuous feature of social interaction that we often explain our actions via an appeal to social norms that govern practices ('why are you not willing to climb that mountain?' 'Because it is sacred'). Institutional reasons are usually regarded as the providence of perfectly good explanations but, as Mackie (1977, p. 79) notes, an institutional reason is a reason only for those who accept the underlying institutional practice.

[17]Notice that it is impossible that there could be universal ignorance about an institutional property. 'Mount Popzatetl is sacred, but nobody knows it' is conceptually incoherent. Nothing could be sacred unless someone believed it to be sacred (although some obvious qualifications apply: as an anonymous referee pointed out, if for some community all mountains with the height of exactly 2,412 m are holy, there may be unmeasured mountains no-one has ever heard of that are holy).

a supernatural event that imposed a sacred character on it.[18] Its distinctive deontic powers are due to the holy status of the mountain, which is itself not an agentive fact.[19] They reject the complicity of their ancestors or previous generations (also members of G) in the creation and maintenance of a piece of institutional reality with a view to regulate power relations within G.[20]

It would beg the question to think that members of G could have hereby formulated a cogent argument against the institutional character of their sacred mountain. The conceptual question is how Searle's account can accommodate sacredness as a *covert* institutional fact. Before we give such an account, we discuss two alternative views.

4   Social Constructionist Approaches

If you hold that phenomenon X is a social construction, you are, as Ian Hacking famously put it in his critical analysis of social constructionism, somewhat 'critical of the status quo' (Hacking 1999, p. 7). "Social constructionists about X tend to hold that (1) X need not have existed, or need not be at all as it is. X, or X as it is as present, is not determined by the nature of things, (2) it is not inevitable, and very often they go further and urge that (3) X is quite bad as it is, and (that) we would be better off if X were done away with, or at least radically transformed" (ibid.). Although Searle's institutional theory shares some superficial similarities with social constructionist claims in anthropology, the latter approach is a heterogeneous family of theories, with plausible and modest versions as well as implausible and radical versions.[21]

If social constructionism holds that 'human beings create or construct meanings when they interact with each other' as Beckford (2003, p. 3) puts it in the context of a constructionist account of religion, the theory is almost trivially true, while if social constructionism makes universal claims ('the world is a social construction'),

---

[18]The idea that it should be possible for people to discover that certain facts are based on conventions or institutions was stressed by Burge (1975), who argued that people who act according to a convention (in our case: who believe an institutional fact) may deny that they follow a convention. The status of a convention or institution need not be fully open to participants in order for the convention or institution to exist as such.

[19]Recall Marx' famous claim that religion is the opium of the people.

[20]Members of G may promote belief in *H* to promote, establish, and maintain powers they derive from it. Kings are lucid enough not to take too seriously the idea that they are king by the grace of God.

[21]See Hacking (1999), Haslanger (2003), and Boghossian (2006) for criticism of weak and strong versions of global constructionism, and Turner (1999) for a comparison between Searle's approach and social constructionism.

the position is self-refuting (Boghossian 2006).[22] If sacred mountains are social constructions, why wouldn't the gods born on its summit also be constructions? The factual belief that a god was born on its summit—an empirical statement—cannot be rescued in the same sense in which the existence of a sacred mountain can or should be accounted for, since sacredness is not an empirical property of mountains. Unlike sacred objects, gods are assigned certain physical and psychological powers—the power to rule the weather and to see what you think, for example—that should not be confused with deontic powers that ultimately regulate relations between agents. The alleged physical and psychological powers of gods do not exist, while the deontic powers are a social reality. Moreover, social constructionists tell us that 'ideas' and 'discourses' create objects, but (unlike Searle) they remain vague about how exactly the process of creation takes place. Pronouncements like "the social construction of the meaning of religion is a continuous process of negotiation, reproduction and challenge. The meanings attributed to religion are, in part, a product of social interaction and negotiation at the level of individuals, groups, organisations, and whole societies ... [A] social constructionist approach tries to discover how terms such as 'religion', 'religious', 'sacred', and 'spiritual' are used" (Beckford 2003, pp. 197, 193) are too opaque to be of theoretical value.

Why? Note, for starters, that the key issue between social constructionism and proponents of the austere and descriptive Searlean view is not about the role of terms, discourses or concepts. We (outsiders) share the concept of sacredness with believers whose beliefs are responsible for the existence of sacred mountains. This is consistent with the fact that outsiders' beliefs are *not* involved in 'the production of sacred objects'. (Atheists may deplore that there are holy mountains, and if they are expressivists, they will deny that they exist.[23]) Contrary to Beckford who holds that "the priority (he) assign(s) to 'construction' is not necessarily related to any particular assumption about ontology ('what there is') or epistemology ('what can be known')" (2003, p. 4), we hold that semantic, ontological, and epistemological questions about sacredness require answers in line with other, plausible accounts of what words mean, what determines the extension of the concepts they express, what can be known to exist, and what properties they have. The following key argument is often put forward by social constructivists: "Precisely because conceptions of sacred space are arbitrary and contingent, and not absolute, it does follow that, precisely therefore, they are social constructs" (Thomas 2008, p. 776).[24] There must, of course, be a concept of the sacred in members of a community in which

---

[22] See Appiah (1995) for an error theory about race, and Haslanger (2006) for a social-constructivist approach to race. Haslanger is not a social constructivist in the radical tradition that has its origin in the works of Berger and Luckmann (1966) and Bloor (1976).

[23] The discussion is not about 'institutionalized religions' or the institutional character of religion, but about institutional facts as constituents of religious practices.

[24] In a review of Jonathan Z. Smith's *To Take Place*, widely read as a constructionist approach to sacred space (Smith 1987). That human agency is involved in creation of the sacred is a simple consequence of methodological naturalism and reflects that all artefacts are human-dependent entities. Smith's claim that 'ritual is not an expression of or a response to 'the Sacred'; rather,

sacred objects function, but it does not follow that study of the sacred is reducible to the study of the ways that sacred entities are conceptualized. Moreover, it is not clear how *arbitrariness* (a property of signs, its opposite is being a *motivated or iconic sign*) and *contingency* (a modal property, with *necessity* as its opposite) could entail that sacred objects are social constructs. Many contingently existing entities are not socially constructed; both arbitrary and motivated signs are (in some trivial sense) social constructs. Moreover, the theory should allow for false beliefs about sacred objects, but it is not clear how social constructivism can acknowledge this fact. Finally, it is simply uncontroversial that people have the concepts they do through complex social processes.[25] Just because an individual's (X) possession of a concept *C* has its origin in social facts—a tradition into which X was introduced, for example—does not imply that *C*'s extension must be determined by social acceptance conditions (Haslanger 2003, p. 304). Finally, it should not be a consequence of a viable account of sacred objects that central concepts like 'truth', 'knowledge', and 'reality' should be revised or 'dethroned,' simply because one intends to *debunk* or unmask them as, for example, 'tools of the powerful'. Unlike social constructionists, Searle gives these key concepts a classical realist interpretation; the task is to describe within that framework what sacredness amounts to, what ontological consequences follow from the propositions accepted, and how the ensuing true or false beliefs can be made intelligible.

Searle's general approach draws on distinctions, concepts, and categories, whose full content can be made transparent to whomever possesses them, and which can be seen by them—under rational but accessible conditions—to reflect *manifest* conceptual distinctions.[26,27] Finally, just as a game need not change or be abandoned when its implicit rules are made explicit or when its status as a game is fully exposed, a full awareness of the institutional character of a phenomenon should not necessarily affect its legitimacy.[28] (The question of how and if this can be maintained for sacred objects is important, but will not be further dealt with in this paper.)

---

something or someone is made sacred by ritual' is, when it reflects methodological naturalism, trivially true, not an exciting discovery that vindicates social constructivism.

[25]Haslanger (2006). See Engler (2004) for a critical analysis of social constructionist approaches to religion.

[26]See Rust (2006, p. 162) for further considerations.

[27]Beckford (2003, p. 7) observes that 'social scientific perspectives on religion are sceptical towards common sense definitions of religion'. But note that the distinction between natural facts and institutional facts is a manifest distinction.

[28]But do not confuse this with the elusive ideal of full codifiability: 'A test for the presence of genuine institutional facts is whether or not we could codify the rules explicitly. In the case of many institutional facts, such as property, marriage, and money, these have ... been codified into explicit laws. Others, such as friendships, dates, and cocktail parties, are not so codified.... If the rights and duties of friendship suddenly became a matter of some grave legal or moral question, then we might imagine these informal institutions becoming codified explicitly, though of course explicit codification has its price. It deprives us of the flexibility, spontaneity, and informality that the practice has in its uncodified form.' (Searle 1995, p. 88).

3 Searlean Reflections on Sacred Mountains

5 Error Theories

Error theories assume that talk about mountains being 'sacred' is 'a mere collection of roundabout ways of talking about other things' (Smith 2007, p. 11). The error theorist holds that the extension of the concept expressed by the predicate 'is holy' is empty; talk purportedly referring to sacredness is therefore false or misguided, a bit in the same way that talk about witches is misguided. Searle tentatively defends an error theory about witches in Searle (2006).[29] Two considerations of John Mackie (1977) can be applied in this context: predicates like 'is sacred' (and the concept of sacredness) share with moral predicates both *relativity* and *queerness*. The argument from relativity points to the empirical observation that moral views can vary enormously and that moral disagreements are very often characterized by a high degree of intractability. Mackie concluded that moral judgments merely 'reflect adherence to and participation in different ways of life' (1977, p. 36). There are strong disagreements about what is and what isn't sacred and wars are fought over who 'owns' a sacred place. Such disagreements and disputes are clearly not empirically decidable. Should we not therefore conclude that sacredness fails to designate a property and that propositions involving sacredness are therefore either false or lack truth-value? Or that talk of sacred mountains is purely expressive?

The argument from queerness has a metaphysical and an epistemological reading. The metaphysical reading holds that sacredness, like other moral concepts, would designate 'qualities or relations of a very strange sort, utterly different from anything else in the universe' (Mackie 1977, p. 38). Furthermore, the epistemological reading adds that in order to track such properties we would need some special faculty of moral perception or intuition which, when applied to sacred objects, would amount to an even stranger faculty, one that would allow us to discern instantiations of sacredness. Under an epistemological reading, the queerness argument holds that being sacred is not an objective fact to which some people or cultures (but not all) have superior epistemic access (as Joyce and Kirchin 2009, p. xvii puts it). Sacredness shares non-factuality with other concepts that have no application, like phlogiston or witchcraft.

Zimmerman (2010, pp. 49ff.) points out that the error-theorist must give a debunking explanation, one which *explains* why the beliefs are false. But how could this work? Assimilating the property of being sacred to that of phlogiston begs the question: surely the latter was always intended to be an empirical predicate, but there are many predicates that cannot be reduced to physical predicates, which nonetheless allow for true beliefs. Moreover, the analogous claim that money does not exist is implausible (and sounds naive). Notice that money and borders were (and sometimes still are) supposed to have strange and/or supernatural properties

---

[29]Error theories about race have been defended by Appiah (1995). Musgrave (1999) and Searle (2006b) defend anti-realism about witches (cf. *infra*). A good general argument that supports the inclusion of artefacts in our manifest ontology can be found in Thomasson (2001, 2003).

('a \$ 1 bill has intrinsic value', 'the borders of my country were founded by God').
Still, money and borders are bona fide institutional entities.[30] There is no reason
to assume that certain institutions or institutional entities do not exist just because
people have false beliefs about them.

Moreover, error theories cannot explain how we correct obvious mistakes.
Suppose a member of G observes Mt. Popzatetl from an unusual angle and denies
that *that* mountain is holy.[31] His mistake will be corrected by other members of
G, or even by outsiders: 'No, that mountain (pointing to Mt. Popzatetl) is holy' is
the sensible thing to say here. Error theories deprive not only members of G, but
also outsiders, of knowledge, i.e. true justified beliefs which can be shared with
non-believers and be passed on to future generations.[32]

Still, the error theorist suggests an important objection to the institutional theory.
Suppose you grant that a member of G *knows* that *H*.[33] Knowledge requires that
no false belief enter into the justification for the belief that *H* (if a false belief *q*
enters the justification of one's belief *p*, then the latter belief, even if true, cannot
be counted as knowledge—this is a lesson drawn from the famous 'no false lemma'
requirement on knowledge, see Lehrer 1965). But isn't this the case when the belief
that a god was born on Mt. Popzatetl figures in the justification of the belief that *H*?

The correct answer should be that members of G may be ignorant of, or have
false beliefs about, the social *explanation* of what enabled them to know that *H*:
they lack knowledge (or have false beliefs) about the social etiology of their belief.
Members of G need not know the exact nature of what enabled them to know that
H, in order to know that *H*. The false belief helps to provide justification for the
(false) belief (as it turns out) *that H is a natural fact*, a belief whose content differs
from the unqualified belief that *H*. There is a difference between knowing that *H* (a
justified true belief) and believing (falsely) that the proposition that *H* describes (is
about) a natural fact. The mistake is not in the belief that *H*, but in the belief *that
the mountain's being sacred has its origin in a natural (or supernatural) fact*, which
justifies the further, and false, belief that Mt. Popzatetl's holiness was not the result
of collective acceptance among members of G of (the proposition that) *H*. Outsiders
know that Mt. Popzatetl is sacred because they are told so by a reliable source (a
senior member of G, say), and, if you follow Searle's account of institutional facts,
we outsiders also know in virtue of what the belief is true (it is true in virtue of an
institutional property, created and maintained by a community). Similarly, the belief

---

[30] I owe this suggestion to an anonymous referee.

[31] Compare Frege's example in *On Sense and Reference*.

[32] See Thomasson (2003, p. 590) for a discussion of delicate issues about knowledge and ignorance
involving institutional facts.

[33] Note that members of G may have false beliefs about other communities. If they hold that their
mountain is the only holy mountain in the universe, they are mistaken. What explains their mistake
is, as we shall see, a false belief of what determines the extension of the concept of holiness,
although they correctly grasp the *meaning* of the predicate 'being sacred'.

held by members of G—that Mt. Popzatetl is holy—is justified by their belief *that they were told so—that the scriptures, or the tradition says so*—which, for them, should be (and often is) the end of a justificatory chain.[34] Epistemic externalists or reliabilists hold that at least some privileged members of G (but not necessarily outsiders) will be reliable sources of knowledge about what is and what isn't sacred in their community. If so, reliabilists should therefore have even less problems with the fact that Mt. Popzatetl is known to be holy than their internalist counterparts. And perhaps interpretive charity also plays a role here: while one may deplore the existence of a sacred object—for example because its deontic aura directly or indirectly legitimizes a particularly cruel treatment of women—one shouldn't neglect that making members of G's beliefs and actions intelligible *to us* is crucial. In order to eventually enlighten them about the institutional nature of their sacred mountain, part of what it takes to make them intelligible is to ascribe true and false beliefs to them. The institutional account suggests *which* truths and falsehoods make their actions intelligible.

Insider concepts and descriptions can be understood by outsiders (*pace* cultural relativists), but such understanding does not require joining members of G, to the extent that one thereby becomes co-responsible for maintaining *H*, let alone that they will maintain that *H* is (expresses) a non-institutional fact. This would conflate understanding with conversion. There is a distinction between collectives that are responsible for (unintentionally) maintaining an institutional fact, and an 'enlightened' community that has a full understanding of its institutional etiology. Note again, that in this respect too, the institutional approach cannot be extended to cases like phlogiston.[35] ('Before Lavoisier, phlogiston existed as a covert institutional fact'). Those who believed phlogiston existed were self-consciously involved in empirical research and, at least in principle, open to falsifying evidence. Moreover, they could, independently of a falsification of the theory, accept the distinction between natural and institutional facts, and thus classify phlogiston, even on their own (false) account, correctly as a natural phenomenon ('If it exists, it is a natural phenomenon', they might cautiously formulate). Even for them there would be no deontic powers that could be associated with the existence of phlogiston. All parties involved in the phlogiston-controversy during the eighteenth century agreed that the concept, if it had any extension, designated a natural phenomenon that afforded empirical investigation. And phlogiston's existence did not create deontic powers; there should not be a temptation to hold that now, for us, the existence of phlogiston is an institutional (and not natural) fact. No non-semantic rights and duties are created by designating a non-existent phenomenon as phlogiston.

---

[34]There is a difference between *explaining why* Mt. Popzatetl is holy, and justifying one's belief that it is holy. The latter is justified by evidence, and the only *legitimate* evidence is that 'one is being told so' (it is essentially *knowledge by testimony*). Their own *explanation* of its sacred nature is of course mistaken.

[35]Thanks to Frank Hindriks for pressing me on this issue.

An error theory about sacredness is therefore not *a priori* entailed by the very plausible belief that gods don't exist and can't be born on top of mountains. On this point, atheists and reluctant outsiders are sometimes in a position where they should grudgingly acknowledge the existence of sacred mountains, a bit like the anti-Nazi had to acknowledge that Hitler had a government (Searle 2010, pp. 8, 57).[36] As pointed out earlier, meaning and colour of the predicate 'is sacred' come apart when *outsiders* speak about Mt. Popzatetl's sacredness from their spectatorial point of view.

6 Covert Institutional Facts

Sacred objects can be *covert* institutional facts and in our toy example they do function like that in a community.[37] Members of G do create a sacred object, but they would not acknowledge that 'creating Mt. Popzatetl's sacredness' correctly specifies what they do (they certainly wouldn't acknowledge that they *declared* that Mt. Popzatetl was a sacred mountain). Similarly, they would not believe any presentation of facts about their mountain that explicitly or implicitly presents the target property as an institutional one. Searle explicitly accepts that people may have mistaken beliefs about the nature of specific institutional facts, objects or properties:

> Sometimes (people) believe institutions to be consequences of a Divine Will … Many of them are based on beliefs, such as beliefs in the supernatural, that I think are almost certainly false. (Searle 2010, p. 107)

> Most of these things (the creation of institutional facts, FB) develop quite unconsciously, and indeed people typically are not even aware of the structure of institutional reality. It often works best when they have false beliefs about it. So there are a lot of people in the United States who still believe that a dollar is only really money because it is backed by all that gold in Fort Knox. This is total fantasy, of course. The gold has nothing to do with it. And people hold other false beliefs. *They believe someone is king only because he is divinely inspired, or even believe that marriages have been made by God in heaven, and so on. I am not trying to discourage them because often the institution functions best when people hold false beliefs about it.* (Searle 2001, pp. 37–38; our italics)[38]

---

[36]'Acceptance, as I construe it, goes all the way from enthusiastic endorsement to grudging acknowledgment, even the acknowledgment that one is simply helpless to do anything about, or reject, the institutions in which one finds oneself.' (Searle 2010, p. 8).

[37]My claim is not that they *must* be covert institutional facts. In the Catholic religion, churches are created by a declarative: the consecration of the church in the name of the Catholic Church by a bishop. The Church can therefore acknowledge that a building's counting as a church is a matter of acceptance (by the appropriate authorities).

[38]And see Searle (2010, p. 107), where the point is repeated and generalized: '(People) tend to think of institutions like private property, or human rights or governments as human creations. They tend to think of them as part of the natural order of things, to be taken for granted in the same way they take for granted the weather or forces of gravity… Sometimes, indeed, they believe institutions to be consequences of a Divine Will'.

There are interesting ambiguities in Searle's claims. Is the belief that certain institutions are consequences of a divine will conceptually coherent, given the theory of institutions just developed? Members of G lack beliefs, or have false beliefs about the social enabling conditions of what they believe or know, but those false beliefs need not be part of their justification of their belief that *H*. Recall that even though X (a member of G) has a false belief about what determines the extension of the concept of being sacred, this need not entail that X does not know that Mt. Popzatetl is holy, just as the false belief that Elisabeth II is the Queen because she was divinely elected ("Elisabeth II, by the grace of God" is part of the Queen's official title) does not entail that UK citizens do not know that Elisabeth II is Queen of England or that queens don't exist. The false belief is about the divine origin of her monarchic powers, and there may be further ignorance or even patently false beliefs about the socially enabling conditions of that belief. In this sense, false beliefs can contribute to the maintenance of institutional facts.[39]

A Searlean account of sacred objects as covert institutional entities can therefore accept the error theorist's point made earlier, that institutional properties are in some sense *relative* and *queer*: their assignation is relative to a practice and within a community; they are queer because institutional properties are not natural ones. The institutional account also acknowledges the constructionist point that sacred mountains are part of human institutional reality, but not for reasons that support *global* social constructionism. Although an institutional account is in principle purely descriptive (cf. supra), there is an aspect of the institutional account that allows its proponents to be 'critical of the status quo' (Hacking 1999): since members of a collective are responsible for the creation and maintenance of an institutional fact, but can be ignorant about its institutional nature, uncovering its institutional nature to them may in fact lead to a critical re-examination of the practice.

While it may be true that particular institutional phenomena (sacred objects, kings) work best when people hold false beliefs about them (in the sense Searle suggested in his 1995, pp. 45ff.), coming to appreciate their institutional nature is crucial for assessing and revising ingredients of the deontic aura, i.e. duties and rights institutional facts generate for members of a community. Criticizing— and perhaps even abolishing—deontic powers can be best initiated by explicitly exposing that the object in the X-position has an institutional property Y.[40] Rappaport (1999, pp. 278ff.) pointed out that performative language lies at the root of the sacred (which includes rituals, procedures, the creation of special objects, etc.), and we can see in what deeper sense this might be relevant for revisionary projects: at the heart of institutional reality lies the real or virtual, intended or unintended declarative use of language, which creates a realm of sacred objects,

---

[39]Bruno Celano argues that 'pace Searle, institutional facts being belief dependent is not compatible with people having false beliefs about them' (Celano 1999, p. 249, also quoted—and rejected—in Lagerspetz 2006, p. 302).

[40]Compare the child who pointed out that the emperor has no clothes.

places, books and actions.[41] That is what should be brought into the open, and questioning the beliefs about such objects' origin can make this move. Once you come to believe there are no gods born on top of Mt. Popzatetl, you are open to the suggestion that its sacred character was due to collective acceptance.

Regarding money, Searle himself contends that full awareness of its institutional character may improve the institutional practice. He correctly points out that the relation between the X-property (paper) and the Y-property is arbitrary and was crucial to introduce giral money, checks and credit cards (Searle 1995, pp. 44ff.). Similar remarks hold for borders (compare Searle's genealogy of borders in Searle 1995). But improvement isn't the only option. Once it is fully appreciated by members of G that collective acceptance is responsible for the creation and maintenance of the sacred nature of Mt. Popzatetl, they *eo ipso* discover that the deontic powers attached to it have sublunar origins, and that might be the beginning of a thorough revision of those powers, perhaps eventually leading to their erosion. (Compare the gradual reduction of the monarch's real powers to purely ceremonial ones in constitutional democracies.)

How this process evolves is an empirical question. Perhaps, at a first stage, some individuals in G mentally dissociate themselves from G as a group, and perhaps consciously and explicitly distance themselves from those that steer and monitor the key beliefs. Dissidence means that one no longer wants to be held responsible for maintaining the fact that *H*, which is publicly qualified as an institutional fact. This will have further effects on the assessment of the deontic aura (duties, rights, responsibilities) that comes with (the fact that) *H*. Dissidents may be directly or indirectly questioning the legitimacy of certain practices motivated by and associated with the sacred object. A further possibility unfolds when most, or all members of G come to believe that *H* is an institutional fact maintained by acceptance of *H*. Their problem is how this insight can be reconciled with the belief that a god was born on top of Mt. Popzatetl. How could the existence of a supernatural event be reconciled with the emerging insight that H's truth-maker was an institutional fact, and that it was an institutional fact that engendered the deontic powers? Why should belief in the supernatural event be relevant for the existence of the institution? And consider yet another insight: sacred mountains in other communities will also be seen as institutional objects. Could both insights be consistently combined with a belief about its supernatural origins without irrationality?[42] The crucial consequence is that rights and obligations are now perceived as contingent constructions, for sacred objects in other cultures are now seen as associated with quite different, and perhaps more humane deontic powers.

---

[41]Rappaport's definition of sanctity, as 'the quality of unquestionableness imputed by congregations to postulates in their nature objectively unverifiable and absolutely unfalsifiable' (Rappaport 1999, p. 281) can be straightforwardly translated in Searlean terminology. Also fully in line with Searle's theory is Rappaport's observation that Ultimate Sacred Postulates (his terminology) are beyond empirical verification by scientific methods (see Rappaport 1999).

[42]These perceived inconsistencies, rather than direct attacks based on atheist considerations, have, at least historically, played a key role in secularisation processes.

Be that as it may, various moves and options that come with the insight can be described using Searle's theory of institutional facts: (i) one starts seeing the holiness of Mt. Popzatetl as an observer-dependent fact the status of which is due to collective acceptance. (ii) One thereby comes to see that acceptance/recognition of Mt. Popzatetl's holiness is a necessary condition for its function to surpass the physical features of the object. And one starts to accept that H does not exclude that other mountains can be sacred too (and that this requires different contexts). (iii) Mt. Popzatetl's counting as sacred in a religious practice is recognized as the logical form of the assignment. (iv) The connection between Mt. Popzatetl and the property of being sacred is (now seen to be) arbitrary. No natural fact makes Mt. Popzatetl sacred, and it is recognized that a socially determined enabling condition for the emergence of knowing that Mt. Popzatetl is sacred was key to the emergence of that belief. (v) More importantly, they are in a position to recognize that the deontic powers depend on collective acceptance of H. Powers that emerge from H—obligations and permissions, rights and responsibilities, etc.—have no natural origin. (vi) They will accept that it was human agency that did the imposition of holiness. Once this insight transpires, H can continue to exist or disintegrate, and be studied, perhaps in the context of a Foucauldian 'archaeology' of disintegrated institutional facts and eroded deontic powers. (vii) To avoid expressing reverence and awe, an outsider can assert the complex proposition that *Mount Popzatetl is sacred because they, members of G, collectively accept it as holy*. This avoids the relativism implicit in 'According to them, Mount Popzatetl is holy', which should be avoided (recall that outsiders too know that Mount Popzatetl is holy). (viii) Ex-members of G who come to believe that H is true in virtue of collective acceptance of H continue to grasp the concept of holiness. Contra Celano (1999, p. 248), their *concept* hasn't changed, but what has always (in every possible circumstance or world, if you want) determined its extension is now brought into the open and has become common knowledge.[43]

I end with a semantic proposal that summarizes these views, and which is based on the works of Putnam (1975) and Kripke (1980). A two-dimensional analysis of a concept C represents the content of C as a vector comprising (*a*) stereotypes and/or a reference-fixing factor, and (*b*) an account of what determines its extension (see Schroeter 2010 for a brief introduction). A speaker *fully grasps* a concept C only if she grasps what determines its extension. Members of a collective need not have access to what determines the extension of the concept of being sacred: they can be mistaken about what determines the sacred character of an object although they are usually right about what functions, in their society, as sacred objects and why it is sacred (the beliefs that fix the reference).[44] The approach reflects the fact that 'our

---

[43] An important aspect of enhancing this process is that it requires the allowance to become acquainted with conceptual resources, in order to precisely articulate this insight. If one is deliberately withheld from these concepts, one can be the victim of epistemic injustice (Fricker 2009).

[44] Haslanger (2003, p. 318) applies a two-dimensional framework to biological categories like *woman*.

meanings are not always transparent to us', as Haslanger put it (2006, p. 91). An institutional theory about sacred objects is basically a theory about how beliefs of members of a community, in virtue of shared intentionality, determine the *extension* of the concept in all possible circumstances, not just about what fixes its reference for a particular user or group of users in the actual world.[45] What determines its extension need not be transparent to them. Secularisation is a process by which the institutional character of sacred entities comes into view, often by exposing that beliefs about their supernatural origin are false.[46]

References

Appiah, A. 1995. Race, culture, identity: Misunderstood connections. *The Tanner lectures on human values*, No. 17. Salt Lake City: University of Utah Press, 199: 51–136.

Beckford, J. 2003. *Social theory and religion*. Cambridge: Cambridge University Press.

Berger, P., and T. Luckmann. 1966. *The social construction of reality*. Garden City: Doubleday.

Bloor, D. 1976. *Knowledge and social imagery*. London: Routledge.

Boghossian, P. 2006. *Fear of knowledge*. Oxford: Oxford University Press.

Burge, T. 1975. On knowledge and convention. *Philosophical Review* 84(2): 249–255.

Celano, B. 1999. Collective intentionality, self-referentiality and false beliefs: Some issues concerning institutional facts. *Analyse & Kritik* 21: 237–250.

Engler, S. 2004. Construction versus what? *Religion* 34: 291–313.

Frege, G. 1918. The thought. In *Truth*, ed. S. Blackburn and P. Simmons. Oxford: Oxford University Press.

Fricker, M. 2009. *Epistemic injustice*. Oxford: Oxford University Press.

Geertz, C. 1973. *The interpretation of cultures*. New York: Basic Books.

Hacking, I. 1999. *The social construction of what?* Boston: Harvard University Press.

Haslanger, S. 2003. Social construction: The 'Debunking' project. In *Socializing metaphysics: The nature of social reality*, ed. F.F. Schmitt, 301–325. Lanham: Rowman and Littlefield.

Haslanger, S. 2006. What good are our intuitions? Philosophical analysis and social kinds. *Proceedings of the Aristotelian Society* 80: 89–118.

Jopling, D. 2008. *Talking cures and placebo effects*. Oxford: Oxford University Press.

Joyce, R., and S. Kirchin (eds.). 2009. *A world without values. Essays on John Mackie's error theory*. Dordrecht: Springer.

Kripke, S. 1980. *Naming and necessity*. Oxford: Blackwell.

Lagerspetz, E. 2006. Institutional facts, performativity and false beliefs. *Cognitive Systems Research* 7: 298–306.

Langton, R. 2009. *Sexual solipsism*. Oxford: Oxford University Press.

Lehrer, K. 1965. Knowledge, truth and evidence. *Analysis* 25: 168–175.

Mackie, J. 1977. *Ethics: Inventing right and wrong*. Oxford: Oxford University Press.

Musgrave, A. 1999. Idealism and realism. In *Scientific inquiry: Readings in the philosophy of science*, ed. R. Klee, 344–352. Oxford: Oxford University Press.

Overing, J. 1990. The Shaman as a maker of worlds: Nelson Goodman in the Amazon. *Man* 25: 602–619.

---

[45]This analysis is in line with Thomasson's (2003) analysis of human kinds. A theory that assumes that 'is holy' is ambiguous should be rejected.

[46]I would like to thank Frank Hindriks, Jack Vromen, Paul Post, Anita Konzelmann Ziv, and an anonymous referee for valuable comments and suggestions.

Putnam, H. 1975. *Mind, language and reality. Philosophical papers*, vol. 2. Cambridge: Cambridge University Press.

Rappaport, R. 1999. *Ritual and religion in the making of humanity*. Cambridge: Cambridge University Press.

Rawls, J. 1955. Two concepts of rules. *Philosophical Review* 64: 3–32.

Rust, J. 2006. *John Searle and the construction of social reality*. New York: Continuum.

Rust, J. 2010. *John Searle*. London: Continuum.

Schroeter, L. 2012. Two-dimensional semantics. In *The Stanford encyclopedia of philosophy*, ed. Edward N. Zalta, Winter 2012 ed. Stanford: Stanford University Press. http://plato.stanford.edu/archives/win2012/entries/two-dimensional-semantics/.

Searle, J. 1969. *Speech acts*. Cambridge: Cambridge University Press.

Searle, J. 1995. *The construction of social reality*. London: Penguin.

Searle, J. 1998. *Mind, language and society: Philosophy in the real world*. New York: Basic Books.

Searle, J. 2001. *Rationality in action*. Cambridge, MA/London: The MIT Press.

Searle, J. 2006a. Social ontology. Some basic principles. *Anthropological Theory* 6: 40–44.

Searle, J. 2006b. Reality and relativism. Shweder on a which? hunt. *Anthropological Theory* 6: 112–121.

Searle, J. 2010. *Making the social world: The structure of human civilisation*. Oxford: Oxford University Press.

Smit, J.P., F. Buekens, and S. Du Plessis. 2011. What is money? An alternative to Searle's institutional facts. *Economics and Philosophy* 27(1): 1–22.

Smith, J.Z. 1987. *To take place: Toward theory in ritual*. Chicago/London: University of Chicago Press.

Smith, B. 2007. The foundations of social coordination: John Searle and Hernando de Soto. In *Facets of sociality*, ed. N. Psarros and K. Schulte-Ostermann, 3–22. Frankfurt: Ontos Verlag.

Smith, B., and J. Searle. 2003. The construction of social reality: An exchange. *American Journal of Economics and Sociology* 62: 285–309.

Thomas, C. 2008. Place and memory: Response to Jonathan Z. Smith. *Journal of the American Academy of Religion* 76: 773–881.

Thomasson, A. 2001. Geographical objects and the science of geography. *Topoi* 20: 149–159.

Thomasson, A. 2003. Realism and human kinds. *Philosophy and Phenomeneological Research* 67: 580–608.

Turner, S. 1999. *Brains/practices/relativism*. Chicago: University of Chicago Press.

Williams, B. 1985. *Ethics and the limits of philosophy*. London: Fontana.

Zimmerman, A. 2010. *Moral epistemology*. London: Routledge.

Chapter 4
Social Objects without Intentions

Brian Epstein

Abstract It is often seen as a truism that social objects and facts are the product of human intentions. I argue that the role of intentions in social ontology is commonly overestimated. I introduce a distinction that is implicit in much discussion of social ontology, but is often overlooked: between a social entity's "grounds" and its "anchors." For both, I argue that intentions, either individual or collective, are less essential than many theorists have assumed. Instead, I propose a more worldly—and less intellectualist—approach to social ontology.

1 Introduction

It is often seen as a truism that social objects (such as dollars) and social facts (such as that the Federal Reserve is raising interest rates) are the product of human intentions. As distinct from natural objects and facts, which exist or are the case independently of us, social objects and facts exist in virtue of our having attitudes toward the world, attitudes usually taken with some practical aim in mind.

This postulate is a basic building-block of prevailing theories of social ontology. Lynne Baker, for instance, explains that artifacts "are objects intentionally made to serve a given purpose" (Baker 2004, p. 99). On John Searle's view, institutional facts are created and maintained by collective attitudes:

> Collective intentionality assigns a new status to some phenomenon, where that status has an accompanying function that cannot be performed solely in virtue of the intrinsic physical features of the phenomenon in question. This assignment creates a new fact, an institutional fact, a new fact created by human agreement. (Searle 1995, p. 46)

B. Epstein (✉)
Department of Philosophy, Tufts University, Medford, MA, USA
e-mail: brian.epstein@tufts.edu

A. Konzelmann Ziv and H.B. Schmid (eds.), *Institutions, Emotions, and Group Agents*,
Studies in the Philosophy of Sociality 2, DOI 10.1007/978-94-007-6934-2_4,
© Springer Science+Business Media Dordrecht 2014

My aim in this paper is to argue that focusing on intentions and attitudes distorts our understanding of social ontology. In some sense, it is surely correct that social entities[1] partly depend on people, society, and human intentionality—otherwise, they would not be "social" at all. However, the role of intentions and other attitudes is often overestimated, making prevailing views excessively intellectualist. And it is especially misleading to approach social ontology as if it were a subfield of collective intentionality in particular, an approach that seems to be gaining momentum nowadays.

I begin by introducing a distinction that is implicit in much discussion of social ontology, but is often overlooked: the distinction between what I will call a social entity's "grounds" and its "anchors." Subsequently I discuss the role and limits of intentions in each of the two, respectively. I argue that many social entities have entirely non-intentional *grounds*. I further argue that the role of intentions in *anchoring* is less central than many theorists have assumed. Instead, I propose a more worldly—and less intellectualist—approach to social ontology.

2   Grounds and Anchors: The Intuitive Distinction

The project of social ontology is built on the observation that social facts are not "brute" facts in nature. The fact that Tufts is a university, that the Federal Reserve is raising interest rates, that the word 'Aristotle' refers to Aristotle, and that Mario Batali is a restauranteur, are all the case—at least in part—in virtue of various facts about people. Theories of social ontology identify, implicitly or explicitly, some cohesive set of social facts or objects such as "institutional facts," "semantic facts," "artifacts," etc. For that set, they work to provide an account of the other facts in virtue of which social facts are the case, or in virtue of which social objects exist.

Consider a particular institutional fact. For instance, take the dollar bill I am currently holding. For convenience, we can assign it a name, such as 'B23846598B' (in honor of its serial number). An example of an institutional fact, then, is: *B23846598B is a dollar*. Let us call this fact 'F'. We notice that F is not a fundamental or brute fact in nature, and therefore ask in virtue of which other facts— which more basic facts—is F the case.

In prevailing theories of social ontology, there are two different sorts of answers given to such questions. Consider, for instance, John Searle's account of institutional facts (See Searle 1995, 2010). Searle takes institutional facts such as F to hold in virtue of "constitutive rules" being in place in a context.

In Searle's account, the first answer to the question, *In virtue of what is F the case?* is given *within* the constitutive rule for dollars. Searle says that this constitutive rule is:

---

[1] I will use "entity" to avoid the tedious repetition of "facts or objects," where it is sufficiently unambiguous.

(1) Bills issued by the Bureau of Engraving and Printing count as dollars in the United States. (Searle 1995, p. 28)

The first answer is then that the antecedent clause (what Searle calls the X-term), is satisfied by the object in question. In other words, Searle's view is that the fact that grounds F is simply that B23846598B is a bill issued by the Bureau of Engraving and Printing.[2]

This answer, of course, is incomplete, unless we also explain in virtue of what the constitutive rule itself is in place. Searle's answer to this is a second sort of fact. Constitutive rules are put in place, Searle argues, by our collective acceptance of them. It is in virtue of intentional states of a specific type being realized (i.e., the collective acceptance of a constitutive rule), that the constitutive rule is in place in the context. Thus the second answer given by Searle[3] is that the constitutive rule (1) is in place in the United States in virtue of a fact of the form:

(2) People in the U.S. collectively accept rule (1).

A useful way to look at the difference between (1) and (2) is this: the former has the job of giving the conditions an object must satisfy in order to be a dollar, while the latter has the job of giving the facts that put those satisfaction conditions in place. The facts expressed by (2) are thus not the grounds for F itself, but what I will call F's "anchors." They are what makes it the case that (1) is in place in the context.

This distinction is a crucial one. There are two very different roles for intentions and other factors in various accounts of social ontology. Some theorists take social facts and objects to have intentional grounds, while others take them to have intentional anchors. The considerations for evaluating these two claims are different from one another.

3   Refining the Understanding of Constitutive Rules

Using Searle's own formula for constitutive rules makes it difficult to avoid collapsing grounds and anchors into one another. In this section, I refine the notion of a constitutive rule, so as to clarify the two different questions I will address separately in the remainder of this paper: Must the *grounds* for social entities

---

[2]Searle gives slightly more detailed X-conditions in Searle (1995, pp. 45–56). But this is the explicit constitutive rule he gives, and it is fine for our purposes. In the next sections of this paper, I point out that none of Searle's proposals give plausible X-conditions for dollars, but for the moment I am concerned with clarifying the form of constitutive rules. I use the term 'ground', following Fine (2001), Correia (2005), and others. Grounding is usually understood as holding between sets of facts. But we can also speak of objects, as well as facts, having grounds. A natural way to understand this is to take the grounds of an object, such as the Federal Reserve, to be the grounds of the fact *The Federal Reserve exists*.

[3]This general approach is endorsed by others, including Tuomela (2002) and Hindriks (2008). I discuss Tuomela's more nuanced views below.

involve intentions? Must the *anchors* for constitutive rules for social entities involve intentions? The constitutive rule is best understood as articulating what the grounds are for a social fact like F. Given that it has been anchored—however it has been anchored—the constitutive rule articulates a given set of grounding conditions within the domain where the rule is in place.

Several commentators have pointed out that Searle's constitutive rule formula has problems. Frank Hindriks, for instance, points out that it is unclear what work is done by Searle's "counts as" relation, beyond redundantly marking that the rule is collectively accepted (Hindriks 2008, p. 134). Amie Thomasson observes that there is an unresolved type/token ambiguity in Searle's rule and correspondingly in his treatment of the "self-referentiality" of institutional facts. For instance, it is left unclear whether that account takes us to have collective intentions toward each particular dollar, or toward dollars in general. To remedy this, Thomasson applies Kendall Walton's discussion of "principles of generation" (Walton 1990, pp. 138ff.) to distinguish three kinds of rules, with the following forms (Thomasson 2003, pp. 280ff.):

(3) Singular rules: (Of a) We collectively accept: Ya (where "Y" names a social feature)
(4) General rules: For all z, we collectively accept that (if z meets all conditions in X, then Yz)
(5) Existential rules: We collectively accept that (if all conditions X obtain, then there is some z such that Yz).

While it is useful for Thomasson to notice the inadequacy of Searle's formula in these ways, it is a mistake to separate them into different rules, rather than revising the formula. First, although Thomasson is correct that Searle's formulation involves a type/token ambiguity, her singular rules are superfluous. The reason is that (3) can be treated as a special case of (4), so long as the X-conditions can include object-dependent properties like *being B23846598B*.

Second, by separating the general rules from the existential rules, we lose a basic insight. It is true that the existential rule includes something that the general rule leaves out: that what is done by satisfying the appropriate conditions is that a dollar comes to exist. However, what the existential rule says is only that *some* object is created such that it is a dollar. It misses out the point that *this* bill is a dollar.[4]

But the most critical problem is that Thomasson's rules collapse the intuitive distinction I mentioned above. Even more overtly than Searle's rule does, these formulas include the collective acceptance of the rule as part of the rule. Hence they mix two very different sets of facts: those serving as the grounds for a social fact like F, and those facts in virtue of which the grounds for F are what they are; i.e., the

---

[4]Part of the problem may be that Thomasson wants a general formula to account for the generation of both abstract and concrete objects. Here I only consider concreta.

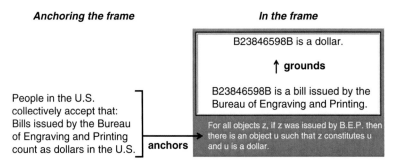

Fig. 4.1 Anchors and grounds for a fact about a dollar bill

facts that serve as the anchors of F. Instead, the constitutive rule is best understood as articulating what the grounds are for a social fact like F. Given that it has been anchored—however it has been anchored—the constitutive rule articulates a given set of grounding conditions within the domain where the rule is in place.

It is useful, if we are to formulate the general fact more precisely, to employ the twin notions of "material constitution" and "coincident objects." The use of "coincidence" may be taken seriously metaphysically, or it may just be regarded as an accounting trick, to keep track of the difference between such things as the paper and the dollar. Altogether, a better formulation of constitutive rules is:

(6) For all objects z, if z is X then there is an object u such that z constitutes u and u is Y,
     where X is the set of sufficient conditions the grounds must satisfy, in order for there to be a coinciding object having property Y.[5]

Applying this to dollars (and using Searle's conditions for being a dollar), we get:

(7) For all objects z, if z is a bill issued by the Bureau of Engraving and Printing, then there is an object u such that z constitutes u and u is a dollar.

Here, the ground is the fact *z is a bill issued by the Bureau of Engraving and Printing*. The relationships among the institutional fact, the constitutive rule (with the "X-conditions" on grounds in bold), and the fact's anchors are depicted in Fig. 4.1.

Searle's formula for constitutive rules obscures this picture. The formula "X counts as Y in C" makes it appear that both the grounds and anchors are facts that have to be in place in a context, in order for an institutional fact to be the case.

---

[5]I have left out the "context" parameter as well. If it is appropriate for some sort of object, a contextual restriction can always be included among the generation conditions. But I see no reason to assume that, for a community, a constitutive rule must only apply to objects in the context of the community in question. I discuss this below (in connection with "cowrie money"). This also differs from Hindriks' formalization (Hindriks 2008, p. 134n143).

But grounds and anchors play different roles. The anchors for a constitutive rule set up the conditions for something to be a dollar, restaurant, or university. With the constitutive rule in place, we can see what satisfies its X-conditions in the actual context. Or we can look around at other contexts—even other possible contexts—to see what things would satisfy the X-conditions in those contexts. I will discuss this further below, in connection with "cowrie-money," which is a monetary instrument whose X-conditions are simply *being a shell of the snail Cypraea moneta.*

Clarifying the constitutive rule allows us to formulate the questions about the role of intention in grounding and anchoring social entities. If we take as a starting point a particular class of social entities S, there are two distinct questions the social ontologist may investigate with respect to S:

(8) What sorts of facts are the grounds for Ss? That is, what properties figure into the X-conditions in the constitutive rules for Ss?

(9) What sorts of facts are the anchors for constitutive rules for Ss?

Questions about the role of intentions are simply sub-questions of (8) and (9):

(10) Must (or can) the grounds for Ss include (only or some) intentional properties?

(11) Must (or can) the anchors for constitutive rules for Ss involve (only or some) intentional facts?

Different theorists implicitly disagree on where to place intentions, in answer to these questions. While Searle and Baker, for instance, agree that intentions are central to social ontology, they disagree on where they figure in. Baker argues that for an object to be a boat, it must be produced intentionally by a maker, to serve some function (Baker 2004, p. 101). Among the necessary conditions for being a boat—i.e., among the grounds—are the functional intentions of its maker. Searle, on the other hand, argues that institutional facts often have brute facts as their "X-terms." That is, they have non-intentional grounds. He, however, holds that anchors are facts of a specific type: facts about the collective acceptance of the constitutive rule itself.

These roles, while easily confused, are distinct. In assessing the claim that social objects and facts are the product of human intentions, (10) and (11) can and should be evaluated separately.

4   Must Grounds for Social Entities Involve Intentions?

In answer to question (10), it is straightforward to see that the grounds for institutional facts do not need to involve intentions at all. I will give a couple of cases.

One institutional fact Searle talks about is *being a murderer* (Searle 1995, p. 50). In our community, along with that status come appropriate punishments. To see that some institutional facts have intentional X-conditions while others have non-intentional X-conditions, compare *being a murderer* to *being an involuntary-manslaughterer.*[6] Murder is the killing of another person with "malice aforethought," i.e., with a particular kind of intention. Thus the X-conditions for *being a murderer* involve intentions: killing another person with malice aforethought. Involuntary manslaughter, on the other hand, is distinguished from murder and voluntary manslaughter by being performed without an intention to kill (or perhaps without any intention at all). The X-conditions for *being an involuntary-manslaughterer* are devoid of intentions.

Turning to the case of dollars, matters are much more complicated than much of the social ontology literature seems to notice. Searle's own quick account, for instance, is contradictory. On the one hand, Searle argues that the "X-term" is a brute fact:

> All sorts of things can be money, but there has to be some physical realization, some brute fact – even if it is only a bit of paper or a blip on a computer disk – on which we can impose the institutional form of status function.[7] (Searle 1995, p. 56)

But Searle's own analysis does not treat the X-term for dollars as brute or non-intentional. Consider, for instance, what it takes for something to be "issued by the Bureau of Engraving and Printing." Plausibly, among the conditions for a bill to be "issued" by an institution requires that a person have had an intention of some sort in doing the issuance. This would make the grounds intentional, not brute.

Indeed, if the grounds for dollars include *being issued by the Bureau of Engraving and Printing*, there are two places where intentions may be implicitly part of these conditions. While not every individual bill is plausibly a product of a specific object-directed intention, there is plausibly a "derivative" or "implicit" intention to print each bill by the person who turns on the press, or by the person authorizing that the bill be printed. Moreover, the Bureau of Engraving and Printing itself has intentional existence conditions. So if this is the correct analysis of the generation conditions for dollars, then dollars are more like murder than manslaughter in this respect.[8]

On the other hand, other monetary instruments have strictly non-intentional grounds. One of the most widely used currencies in history is the cowrie shell. Societies that use cowrie shells as money merely collect them. They do not manufacture them, process them through a mint or central bank, or imprint markings into them. Given whatever anchors it takes to institute cowrie shells as currency in the domain, the conditions for a particular cowrie shell to be a piece of what we might call "C-money" are simply that it is a shell of the snail *Cypraea moneta.*

---

[6] Voluntary manslaughter is either killing with malice aforethought but with mitigating circumstances, or else killing with a different intention—to cause bodily harm but not to kill.

[7] One consideration that puts pressure on this is the question of "freestanding Y-terms." Cf. Smith (2003). Searle responds to this challenge in Searle (2010) by replacing pieces of paper and blips in the "X-term" position with human mental states. I discuss this further below.

[8] One way of addressing the dependence of the Bureau of Engraving and Printing on intention may be, as Searle does, to introduce iterated constitutive rules. But the other cases I've mentioned, such as the intentional requirements for issuance, or for murder, are not treatable in this way.

How can the grounds for *being a piece of C-money* only involve facts about snail shells? Surely a shell would not be a piece of C-money were it not the case that the facts anchoring the constitutive rule were also the case? Here we must be careful about how to evaluate such counterfactuals. The anchors set up the constitutive rule—that is, they set up the *exhaustive* conditions for what it takes to be a piece of C-money. The anchors are not themselves among these conditions, and for the purposes of evaluating ordinary counterfactuals are irrelevant. This can be seen by considering how *being a piece of C-money* would be applied across different circumstances. Given that the person assessing these circumstances has the anchors in place for her, she can identify C-money even outside her own context. For a nineteenth century West African treasure hunter, for instance, it would have been perfectly correct to map out the deposits of C-money lying uncollected at the bottom of the sea. Or to dream of a planet made up only of C-money. The anchors put in place the conditions for something to be a piece of C-money. But the instantiation of the property *being a piece of C-money* only require satisfaction of the grounds. In the treasure hunter's dream, where she stands alone on the planet made entirely of *Cypraea moneta* shells, she is rich. This fact, of course, depends on the treasure hunter assessing that dream from the framework in which the constitutive rule for cowrie-money is anchored as it is. But the facts that anchor that framework should not be confused with the facts that ground the institutional fact.

As for artifacts, the most explicit claims that grounds for social entities must involve intentions arise in discussions of artifacts and artifactual kinds. Thomasson, for instance, says: "an artifactual kind term will pick out entities that are the products of largely successful intentions to create something of that kind (where that intention must involve a substantive, and substantively correct, conception of what features are relevant to being a member of the kind)" (Thomasson 2007, p. 60). For an object to be an artifact of kind K, on this characterization, it must be the product of a largely successful intention to produce something of kind K.

Now, Thomasson does distinguish artifacts from social entities. But the difference between the two is that artifacts are *less* demanding: "Unlike social and institutional objects, the existence of artifacts doesn't seem to presuppose any *collective* intentions of any kind—it makes perfect sense to suppose that a solitary human could create a knife, though not a government or money" (ibid., p. 52). On Thomasson's conception, the grounds for an artifact involve individual intentions, and those for a social entity involve collective intentions. Thus according to Thomasson, institutional facts have more stringent grounding conditions than artifacts. In her view, artifacts are intentionally grounded, while institutional facts are grounded in collective intentions. This suggests that if institutional facts do not need to be intentionally grounded, *a fortiori* artifacts do not either.

There are other reasons as well for suspecting that theorists have gone too far, when they insist that grounds for artifacts must involve intentions. Some artifacts do have intentional grounds. Above I pointed out that institutional entities like dollar bills and murderers have intentional grounds. Likewise, it may be that an artifact like a screwdriver does as well. For instance, it may be that *screwdriver* is a "Proper Function" kind (Cf. Baker 2004; Millikan 1984). On this analysis, for an object to be a screwdriver it must have been designed or manufactured with the intention that it be usable for turning screws. Ruth Millikan and others have convincingly argued that both in biology and the social world, there are certain explanatory kinds that are plausibly "teleonomic" (see Millikan 1999). Historical factors, including the fact of being intentionally produced to perform a function, can be among the grounding conditions for an entity.

In biology, however, it has become clear in recent years that not all biological kinds are teleonomic. As Peter Godfrey-Smith notes, in biology we have to be pluralists about functions; functional kinds such as *camouflage* and *swimming* are far more plausibly interpreted as causal-role functions rather than as teleonomic ones (Godfrey-Smith 1996, p. 23). The Baker-Thomasson view that artifacts must be intentionally grounded implicitly denies that any artifact kinds are causal-role functional kinds. Baker insists that for an object to be a boat, a chair, a cup, and so on, it is insufficient that it satisfy the causal-role conditions we would expect boats, chairs, and cups to have. If Godfrey-Smith is correct, then to be a member of the kind *swimmer* requires only the satisfaction of a causal role. But for something to be a member of the kind *boat* requires that it have been produced intentionally. It is not clear what could justify such a sweeping restriction on the grounds for membership in artifact kinds. And if there were, that would imply a strange asymmetry between the grounds for being an institutional entity, which need not involve intentions, and those for being an artifact.

5   Must Anchors for Constitutive Rules Involve Intentions?

A separate question is whether individual or collective intentions are required for anchoring the constitutive rule for a social or institutional fact. Many theorists will accept that grounds may be either intentional, nonintentional, or hybrid properties, but will claim that where collective intentions are required is in the facts that make the grounds what they are. Here I will not argue as definitively against a role for intention. I will, however, argue that prevailing theories have an overly stringent and intellectualist conception of the attitudes required for anchoring constitutive rules. In particular, I aim to cast doubt on the claim that constitutive rules for social entities are anchored in collective intentions, and indeed, to cast doubt on the claim that there is any single sort of fact that is required for anchoring the social world. Instead, the world of social entities is a diverse one, with a variety of types of facts figuring into determining that constitutive rules are in place for a community.

If we brainstorm on kinds of facts that might serve to anchor a constitutive rule for some social entity Y, it is easy to come up with a long list of candidates. Without attempting to be at all exhaustive, here are a few candidates roughly in order, from the most stringently intentional or intellectualized to the least:

(A1) Explicit collective agreement regarding what it takes to be a Y
(A2) Collective acceptance of the constitutive rule for Y

(A3) Collective acceptance of something other than a constitutive rule for Y

(A4) Widespread common (but not collective) intentions toward Y

(A5) Intentions of one or a few individuals toward Y, with practices spread by intentional reproduction

(A6) Intentions of one or a few individuals toward Y, with practices spread by mere causal transmission

(A7) Patterns or regularities in practices

and so on.

To place Searle on this continuum, he does not insist that facts of type (A1) are required for anchoring a constitutive rule, since explicit agreement is unnecessary. He does, however, require that the facts be at least of type (A2).[9]

There is, of course, a large historical literature that has weighed a range of these candidates for an analogous problem: namely, the analysis of convention. Theories of convention—at least reductive ones, such as Lewis's—mean to give the anchors for a convention to be in place in a community (Lewis 1969).[10] Interestingly, the literature on convention long took it as a given that conventions were products of agreement, explicit or tacit. This seems to have been the default view, perhaps from as early as Plato and Aristotle's discussions of the conventions of law and language at least until early modern treatments of the same topics.[11] Only with Hume's analysis of convention did theorists start considering candidates lower down the list from something like (A2), lowering the explicit and cognitive demands for a convention to be in place (Hume 1978 [1740], pp. 489f).

Lewis's account of convention, for instance, proposes that various beliefs, preferences, knowledge, facts about regularities, and facts about alternatives combine to anchor the presence of a convention. Attitudes are required, but not attitudes towards the convention itself. According to Lewis, a convention is a regularity satisfying certain conditions. If the regularity failed to satisfy those conditions, it would not be a convention. The attitudes of the agents are attitudes toward the regularity (or to the solution of a coordination problem), not attitudes toward the convention. Another interesting feature of Lewis's account is that attitudes are not enough for anchoring a convention. His conditions include not only intentional ones, but also material facts about there being a regularity in practices. Moreover, for there to be a convention, there must also be available alternatives to those practices, which is yet another non-intentional condition. Thus the anchors for a Lewisian convention are a mix of facts of type (A4) and (A7).

---

[9] In Searle (2010), he changes his terminology from "collective acceptance" to "collective recognition." His notion of collective recognition seems to be close to Tuomela's notion of collective acceptance, inasmuch as it does not entail belief. I discuss collective acceptance below.

[10] They do not, of course, use the term 'anchor'.

[11] Plato ascribes this view to Hermogenes in Cratylus 384d, and Aristotle advances a similar view in De Interp. 16b19. Pufendorf (1673), Book I, ch. 10, distinguishes tacit from explicit agreement about conventions.

Other accounts of convention go further, challenging even Lewis's analysis as excessively intellectualist. Burge (1975), for instance, denies both that conventions are solutions to coordination problems, and that participants in a convention must have common knowledge of the convention as a solution. Burge did not provide an alternative analysis, which goes some way to explain why his criticisms have not been taken up by many theorists of convention. However, if the criticisms are correct, and if constitutive rules are conventions, then even facts of type (A5) are unnecessary for grounding constitutive rules.

There is little discussion in the literature on institutional facts on whether the conditions for anchoring constitutive rules must be more stringent than those for anchoring a convention. Searle argues that not all conventions are constitutive rules. He says, for instance, that it is a convention of chess that the pawn is smaller than the king, but this is not a constitutive rule (Searle 1995, p. 28).[12] While this is surely correct, it does not show that constitutive rules have more stringent anchoring requirements (in the sense of (A1)–(A7)) than conventions do.

To cast doubt on the centrality of intentions in anchoring institutional facts, I will suggest that constitutive rules for social entities can be *less* demanding to put in place than conventions are.[13] As I mentioned above, it is always a problem for the theorist of artifacts, institutional facts, and so on, to delineate just which entities ought to be included in these categories. It is all too easy to take 'artifact' or 'institutional fact' to have implicitly stipulated meanings, so that anything that is not intentionally grounded does not count as an artifact, or anything that is not anchored in collective acceptance does not count as an institutional fact. At the end of the day, though, our aim in social ontology is to characterize real phenomena, such as money, universities, screwdrivers, and boats. If some sort of money fails to be anchored in collective acceptance, I am inclined to conclude that collective acceptance is not required for anchoring institutional entities, not that money thereby fails to count as an institutional entity.

Searle, in sentence (1), gives a toy constitutive rule for dollars. It is obvious that it is a toy, since the vast bulk of dollars are not in the form of printed currency. Even if (1) captured one set of sufficient conditions for an entity to be a dollar, there must be many other sets of sufficient conditions as well. My bank does not hold my deposits in paper bills. Instead, it records my deposits, and lends out a multiple of its deposit base to other accountholders, money which they hold and deposit in various ways. Money is created by banks, each of which has different ways of recording assets and liabilities. If we are to follow Searle's model for the constitutive rules for money, where the X-term gives the conditions on the substrate for counting as money, then

---

[12] Searle also discusses this in Smith and Searle (2003, p. 208).

[13] It is always an option for the convention-theorist to weaken the conditions on what counts as a convention. Millikan, for instance, proposes a rather weak set of conditions, where attitudes are not required at all for a convention to be in place. If hers is the correct analysis of convention, and if constitutive rules are conventions in this sense, then intentions are even more unnecessary for grounding constitutive rules than I am arguing here. I have criticized aspects of her theory in Epstein (2006).

we must have an enormous number of constitutive rules, since each bank has its own kind of substrate. They use different kinds of bank notes, ledger books, and so on. There are at least as many substrates as there are banking corporations, probably far more.

Barry Smith has criticized Searle on this point, in response to which Searle has modified his views (Smith 2003; Smith and Searle 2003). Smith argues that electronic money—i.e., records on computer disks—is not actually money, but representations of money. Bowing to this criticism, Searle has eliminated reference to an X-term or substrate altogether for institutional objects like corporations and electronic money. Instead, he asserts that for such entities, we collectively accept that certain agents (e.g., bankers) have certain deontic powers directly, rather than having these powers assigned to a substrate (Searle 2010, pp. 20–22, 101–102). This is meant to obviate the problem of the "X-conditions" for corporations, electronic money, and so on.

It is not clear that this strategy is headed in the right direction. First, it is an error to suppose that these issues arise only for money when it is electronic. Long before the advent of electronic money, the amount of money in circulation was but a small fraction of the money in existence.[14] If Searle must concede Smith's point about electronic money, it is not clear that his constitutive rule (1) is a template for any kind of real money. It is also troubling to remove the substrate entirely from the constitutive rule, since there surely has to be some substrate or record, in virtue of which a bank counts as having a certain number of dollars in its accounts.[15]

My present aim, however, is not to rectify either of Searle's accounts, but only to point out that we are at present far from a satisfactory treatment of the substrates or "X-terms" of constitutive rules for institutional entities like money. It is not clear—even to experts like us—which constitutive rule the community at large is taken to accept.

Moreover, the X-term turns out to be the very least of our problems, if we want to move from a toy constitutive rule for money to an adequate one. As for the function of money, there is no agreement in the economic literature even as to the basics. Any elementary textbook will tell you that the functions of money are to be a standard of value, a medium of exchange, a store of value, and a mechanism for future payments. This statement is useful for helping students think about money quite generically, and may even go a large part of the way toward explaining a social

---

[14]It is not clear which of the various measures economists use for the quantity of money should be identified as the number of dollars outstanding—economists are likely to use "M1", which consists of notes and coins, bank reserves, traveler's checks, demand deposits, and other checkable deposits. Or they may use the "monetary base" or "total currency," which consists only of notes, coins, and bank reserves. For none of these does electronic money have anything to do with it: these measures were in place long before electronic money, and it would be easy to have a dollar-based economy with only checks—no notes, coins, or electronics.

[15]It is also troubling that Searle feels the need to extend this new account to institutional entities like corporations. It seems likely that if this is necessary, then other institutional entities, such as restaurants, universities, churches, nations, and so on, will be subject to the same considerations.

institution that existed among grain-traders in ancient Egypt. But it does little to illuminate the nature of contemporary money.[16] Most economists agree that the key to the nature of contemporary money is tied to the functions of the banking sector, but they disagree on what the primary functions of that sector are. Some economists argue that the key role of banks is as intermediaries for taking on and matching risk, while others argue that their key function is to aggregate the gathering of information about firms in the economy. Corresponding to each of these functions is a different functional understanding of credit instruments, in which money is one role-player.[17]

Petri Ylikoski and Pekka Mäkelä have argued against collective acceptance accounts of institutions with examples that suggest that a wide range of beliefs about money, including non-collective beliefs and false beliefs, can suffice for maintaining the institution and practices of money. They argue, for instance, that the institution can be maintained if all members of a community believe that the monetary value of coins is a natural property of coins (Ylikoski and Mäkelä 2002, pp. 470–73). This is a serious challenge to the collective acceptance theorist, who must show that such systems are not possible, or that there is good reason not to count them as institutions.

Inasmuch as our aim is gain insight into the requirements for anchoring actual institutions, however, it is not clear how instructive it is to debate the possibility and classification of highly stylized and simplified institutions. Above I suggested that the constitutive rules for dollars are enormously more complicated than those that show up in Searle's toy models. Even the toy models are beyond the ken of most users of money—it is easy to explain the role of money as a medium of exchange and a store of value, but not so easy to explain mechanisms of future payments.

In Raimo Tuomela's discussion of the requirements for collective acceptance, he recognizes that not all members of an institution typically have an understanding of the constitutive rules for the institution. He therefore distinguishes "structured" from "egalitarian" collectives. In Tuomela's structured collective, only the "operative" members need to collectively accept the constitutive rules (Tuomela 2000, 2003, p. 125, 2007, p. 198). This may appear to be a route for rescuing collective acceptance theories—i.e., restricting the acceptance requirement only to a privileged subset of community members.

For contemporary money, however, even this weaker demand is not satisfied. In giving an account of the anchoring of contemporary money or some other institution, we are not asking for the anchors of some money-like institution, nor of an ancient or primitive or stylized institution. We are interested in the anchoring of *our* institution. Economists have developed dozens of models of systems that

---

[16]Moreover, plenty of commonplaces about the functions of money are false. For instance, it is widely held that for an instrument to be money, it must be legal tender for future payments. There are many forms of money, however, for which this is not true (e.g. money issued by individual banks in Brazil). And even for dollars, however, there is a spate of exceptions to bills (especially large ones) being legal tender, both in law and in practice.

[17]For instance: Diamond (1984), He et al. (2008), Kahn et al. (2005), Kiyotaki and Moore (2002), Kiyotaki and Wright (1993), and Kocherlakota (1998).

have some money-like characteristics. But there is little sign of agreement among monetary theorists, to say nothing of monetary bureaucrats, on either the X-term or the Y-term of the constitutive rules for our actual institution of money. Tuomela aims to explicate and justify the slogan "what is money is not money unless it is taken to be money," (Tuomela 2007, p. 198) but it is unlikely that even a weak interpretation of the slogan can survive.[18] It is probably correct that the anchors for the constitutive rules for money involve some variety of attitudes towards monetary substrates, and very likely that they involve at least some attitudes. The demand for the collective acceptance of a constitutive rule, however, would insist on a good deal more.

This situation is common. At least since Malinowski in the 1920s, sociologists and anthropologists have investigated social functions that are opaque to all the members of a society. Kinship structures, for instance, have been a staple of anthropological theory for generations. To cite a recent example, using both empirical and agent-based modeling techniques, Bearman et al. (2004) examined sexual selection characteristics among adolescents in a U.S. high school. They found that a set of implicit taboos are in place in sexual partner selection, taboos that are explainable in a number of ways but that required a sophisticated theoretical background on the part of the investigators even to articulate. A fortiori, these taboos were not even conceptualized among the high-schoolers. This example is not unusual; it is a rather pedestrian case among those we might find in the sociology or anthropology literature.

Some theorists seem to have been misled, in theorizing about the anchors for constitutive rules, by the assumption that any constitutive rule involves the *assignment* of a status to material objects. A constitutive rule is simply a "principle of generation" (to use Walton's term) for instances of a property, giving sufficient conditions for the property to be instantiated. As such, we should expect that they can be anchored in heterogeneous ways, whether by the existence of a reproductively established family à la Millikan, or by the existence of a homeostatic property cluster à la Boyd, or by a Lewisian convention, or perhaps even by an accidental regularity à la Hume.

To be sure, a distinction should be made between the properties that count as "social" and those that do not. But it seems likely that those standards are low— all that is needed is a little social salt added to the generative stew. Many people seem also to assume that there must be a bright red line between institutions that carry norms, or that have powers (deontic or otherwise), and those social entities that do not. And that the endowment of these norms or powers requires collective acceptance, which in turn is taken to justify the collective acceptance story for true of "standard" social institutions. This is clearly a larger topic than can be addressed here. But I am suspicious of both parts of this claim—that there is any clean division between institutions that carry norms of some sort and those that

---

[18] If we take it as an ordinary counterfactual, of course, it is a statement about grounds as opposed to anchors, and is straightforwardly false. But if we are to be all charitable, it should be taken to be a counterfactual claim about anchoring.

do not, and that collective acceptance is a special way of endowing such norms. Collective acceptance may be an essential element in certain theories of political legitimacy. But it is hard to imagine that the social institutions that pervade actual societies as they are, societies made up by mortals like us who already have enough on our minds, would have no normative force unless the character of institutions were, as Tuomela says, "all for one and one for all" (Tuomela 2007, p. 64).

All this is not to say that human intentions, individual and collective, are irrelevant to the theory of social facts and objects. However, the claim that constitutive rules for social institutional facts can only be anchored in collective acceptance is highly dubious. And the claim that institutional facts have intentional grounds is flatly mistaken.

References

Baker, L.R. 2004. The ontology of artifacts. *Philosophical Explorations* 7(2): 99–111.

Bearman, P.S., J. Moody, and K. Stovel. 2004. Chains of affection: The structure of adolescent romantic and sexual networks. *The American Journal of Sociology* 110(1): 44–91.

Burge, T. 1975. On knowledge and convention. *Philosophical Review* 84(2): 249–255.

Correia, F. 2005. *Existential dependence and cognate notions*. Munich: Philosophia Verlag.

Diamond, P.A. 1984. Money in search equilibrium. *Econometrica* 52: 1–20.

Epstein, B. 2006. Review of language: A biological model by Ruth Millikan. *Notre Dame Philosophical Reviews*. http://ndpr.nd.edu/news/25029-language-a-biological-model/. Last accessed 10 Jan 2012.

Fine, K. 2001. The question of realism. *Philosopher's Imprint* 1(1): 1–30.

Godfrey-Smith, P. 1996. *Complexity and the function of mind in nature*. Cambridge: Cambridge University Press.

He, P., L. Huang, and R. Wright. 2008. Money, banking, and monetary policy. *Journal of Monetary Economics* 55: 1013–1024.

Hindriks, F. 2008. The status account of corporate agents. In *Concepts of sharedness: Essays on collective intentionality*, ed. H.B. Schmid, K. Schulte-Ostermann, and N. Psarros, 119–144. Frankfurt: Ontos.

Hume, D. 1978 [1740]. *A treatise of human nature*. New York: Oxford University Press.

Kahn, C., J. McAndrews, and W. Roberds. 2005. Money is privacy. *International Economic Review* 46: 377–404.

Kiyotaki, N., and J. Moore. 2002. Evil is the root of all money. *The American Economic Review* 92(2): 62–66.

Kiyotaki, N., and R. Wright. 1993. A search-theoretic approach to monetary economics. *The American Economic Review* 83(1): 63–77.

Kocherlakota, N. 1998. Money is memory. *Journal of Economic Theory* 81: 232–251.

Lewis, D.K. 1969. *Convention: A philosophical study*. Cambridge, MA: Harvard University Press.

Millikan, R.G. 1984. *Language, thought, and other biological categories: New foundations for realism*. Cambridge, MA: MIT Press.

Millikan, R.G. 1999. Historical kinds and the 'special sciences'. *Philosophical Studies* 95: 45–65.

Pufendorf, S. 1991 [1673]. *On the duty of man and citizen according to natural law*, translated by M. Silverthorne, edited by J. Tully. New York: Cambridge University Press.

Searle, J.R. 1995. *The construction of social reality*. New York: Free Press.

Searle, J.R. 2010. *Making the social world: The structure of human civilization*. Oxford: Oxford University Press.

Smith, B. 2003. John Searle: From speech acts to social reality. In *John Searle*, ed. B. Smith, 1–33. Cambridge: Cambridge University Press.

Smith, B., and J.R. Searle. 2003. The construction of social reality: An exchange. *American Journal of Economics and Sociology* 62(1): 285–309.

Thomasson, A. 2003. Foundations for a social ontology. *ProtoSociology* 18–19: 269–290.

Thomasson, A. 2007. Artifacts and human concepts. In *Creations of the mind: Theories of artifacts and their representation*, ed. E. Margolis and S. Laurence, 52–73. Oxford: Oxford University Press.

Tuomela, R. 2000. Belief versus acceptance. *Philosophical Explorations* 2: 122–137.

Tuomela, R. 2002. *The philosophy of social practices: A collective acceptance view*. Cambridge: Cambridge University Press.

Tuomela, R. 2003. Collective acceptance, social institutions, and social reality. *American Journal of Economics and Sociology* 62: 123–165.

Tuomela, R. 2007. *The philosophy of sociality: The shared point of view*. Oxford: Oxford University Press.

Walton, K. 1990. *Mimesis as make-believe: On the foundations of the representational arts*. Cambridge, MA: Harvard University Press.

Ylikoski, P., and P. Mäkelä. 2002. We-attitudes and social institutions. In *Social facts and collective intentionality*, ed. G. Meggle, 459–474. Frankfurt: Dr. Hänsel-Hohenhausen AG.

Chapter 5
The Logical Form of Totalitarianism

Jennifer Hudin

Abstract Theories of social behavior include some notion of cooperation. In light of large social institutions such as government, a paradox ensues in cases where the institution in question is oppressive and not enjoyed by the collective of individuals inhabiting such an institution: How is it possible to cooperate unwillingly yet intentionally? Are such individuals complicity reinforcing the regimes that oppress them? This chapter addresses despotic regimes in general and totalitarian regimes in particular by examining the notion of cooperation within these regimes. An analysis of cooperation is offered in which individual behavior in collectives is logically preceded by perception of the social group as either a set with which the individual identifies or does not. In each case, social identification operates over an individual's social behavior as a reinforcement of the group with which he identifies, or an erosive element of the institution that he finds alien and oppressive.

1 Introduction

A logical account of society considers features that are necessary for societies to exist. Some logical accounts are marked by a particular essential feature, that of cooperation. This essential feature is one which determines how a society will develop through time thereby creating a kind of vertical or horizontal axis through the temporal space of evolutionary social development. Accounts that form a vertical axis are social structures that begin as a matter of simple cooperative behavior among the members of a group and eventually develop into more complex social behaviors. Given a species' capacity for cooperative behavior, there is a simple algorithm for society building according to this type of vertical analysis: if a species

J. Hudin (✉)
Department of Philosophy, University of Berkeley, Berkeley, CA, USA
e-mail: hudin@berkeley.edu

A. Konzelmann Ziv and H.B. Schmid (eds.), *Institutions, Emotions, and Group Agents*,
Studies in the Philosophy of Sociality 2, DOI 10.1007/978-94-007-6934-2_5,
© Springer Science+Business Media Dordrecht 2014

or a group has the feature of cooperation, it is possible for it to have some sort of social structure. If the group or a species lacks the feature of cooperation, it is not possible for it to have social structures. A benefit of an account based solely on observable behavior that appears to be cooperative is that it can be applied in principle to both linguistic and non-linguistic social groups to explain how their social structures evolved.[1]

In contrast to the vertical account, in which society gradually evolves out of cooperative behavior, is a horizontal account in which the basis of society exists the evolutionary moment certain intellectual capacities appear in a species. Although the complexity of social structures do and can evolve on this account, social behavior itself is already a sophisticated activity as soon as the appropriate mechanisms are present. What sort of social cognitive mechanisms are foundational differs according to different cognitive accounts. For example, on some accounts, it is the cognitive capacity for joint perception that bootstraps social behavior. On other accounts, social behavior begins with the intellectual capacity for deontic concepts.[2]

On a deontic account of social behavior, in order to be able to cooperate, members of a group must have the concepts of commitment, obligation, and the ability to represent these concepts with future reference, i.e. they must have the capacity for deonticity and representation. The capacities for deonticity and representation themselves may have evolved gradually in a species, but once present, society exists even in the most basic forms of cooperating, such as pair bonding and family bonding. Humans are a linguistic species and this account is more easily applicable to human society than non-human societies because the linguistic evidence of deonticity is readily apparent.[3]

For brevity's sake, let us call the vertical account the "social practice account", and the horizontal account the "cognitive account". There are many accounts of how human social structures evolved, but in general, all social structures can be characterized in terms of one of the two accounts mentioned above even if they contain elements of both. In this short article, I am going to discuss one account in particular, that of John Searle.

In both *The Construction of Social Reality* (1995) and *Making the Social World: The Structure of Human Civilization* (2010), John Searle's account of the institutional structure of human society is a deontic account. In his earlier book on the subject, *The Construction of Social Reality*, Searle claimed three logical features as the necessary constituents for the creation of social institutions. These are (1) collective intentionality, (2) the imposition of status function and

---

[1] This is a simple picture of a social behavioral account. A more elaborate example of such an account is that given by Haugeland (1982); for a behavioral view of social organization that does not require collectivity or cooperation, e.g. Hayek (1944).

[2] Indeed there are many other types of cognitive accounts, e.g., motor cognition which serves as the foundation of joint attention and cooperative behavior. e.g. Jennerod (2006).

[3] It is not entirely clear that animals do not have comparable capacities. This is an epistemic question that remains unanswered.

(3) codification. It is by means of the imposition of status function and codification both of which require language, that Searle imports deonticity into his account of social reality, as language requires the notion of commitment in Searle's account.

Searle's original logical formula of social construction was simple and elegant: An x as some object, could have a status function imposed on it and become something new, a y, in virtue of this imposition and collective agreement all of which is codifiable in principle given an appropriate context, a c. Along with this imposition of function on the x term, the new y term receives deonticity. Thus the formula:

$$x \text{ counts as } y \text{ in context } c$$

was intended to account for all of institutional reality along with the deontic powers thereof.

An early question about this formula was, How do the institutional statuses, the y's, import collective expectations and individual responsibilities into this equation? How does the formula

$$x \text{ counts as } y \text{ in context } c$$

turn into the fact that the collective accepts that

$$x \text{ counts as } y \text{ in context } c$$

and that the y now has new rights and responsibilities?

As an answer to this question, Searle extended the original formula by adding the logical operator of Collective Acceptance. In this way, he explained in his later book, *Making the Social World*, the formula *x counts as y in context c*, is implicitly or explicitly a declaration, and as a declaration, the speech act states that an x is now a y by means of a double level of illocutionary force: it both states a new state of affairs exists and creates a new state of affairs by making this very statement. Further, because the speaker of this speech act has a double level of commitment, both to the truth of the state of affairs stated and to the sincerity of the underlying desire that this state of affairs be the case, the state of affairs is collectively accepted because the speaker indeed is the collective itself. This is implicit in all declarations regardless of whether they are uttered by single individuals or not. For example, in the case of marriage, the priest marries a couple as a spokesman for the Church. He has no personal power to make such a pronouncement outside of this collectively sanctioned role. In the case of meeting adjournments or anonymous public announcements, the speaker is authorized by the collective to perform the declaration in question. The point in question is that declarations require authorized speakers, and authorized speakers can only act in virtue of collective acceptance.

In other words, they serve as mouthpieces or spokesmen for the collective.[4] In this way, we can say that in the case of the creation of an institutional fact, the collective thus authorizes itself (in the form of an authorized speaker) to create the very state of affairs that the declaration dictates. The formula

$$x \text{ counts as } y \text{ in } c$$

thereby acquires a Collective Acceptance (CA) operator with wide scope when it is used to collectively impose a status function and create an institutional fact:

$$\text{CA [cceptance] } (x \text{ counts as } y \text{ in } c)$$

With this formulation, deonticity is imported into the role of y by means of the collective declaration.

This extended formula raised a new set of objections. For example, concerns were initially expressed over the Collective Acceptance operator reflecting a kind of happy embrace of institutions some people might find objectionable. The institution of slavery is a good example of this objection. Searle was able to avoid this objection by explaining that the operator of Acceptance was not intended as collective approval, but rather something more akin to collective recognition. But another more serious objection to the extended formula was that it could only capture part of the institutional story. It captures institutional facts such as becoming a wife, a president, a licensed driver, a citizen, etc., statuses which have powers *in virtue of* authorization. But the question then arose as to how Searle's extended formula could capture status functions that are unconsciously born by social perception shaped by a given linguistic community—how does Searle's formula capture that part of institutional status which is *social expectation*? (Cf. Anderson 2007; Hudin 2007) For example, how could this formula capture the expectation of how a wife or a mother is to behave, behaviors which are imported by the status functions of wife and mother but not codified? The social expectations of status functions are as powerful as the authorized powers that are codified and imposed by a collective, yet they are difficult to pin down because they are both contextual and timely, always a function of time and place.

A perfect example of the malleability of social expectations is the status function and social expectations of what a mother is. Given the context of the United States and the time, the 1950s, a mother was naturally expected to be married, to be a

---

[4]Because of this impersonal role of being the mouthpiece for the collective, the sincerity conditions are not flouted if the speaker himself personally does not believe nor desire the state of affairs the declaration brings about. For example, it is entirely plausible for a military commander upon following higher orders to announce that the time of attack will be at sunset, yet not desire that the time of attack take place, nor even believe that it will take place at that time.

housewife—itself a status function which implied good housekeeping and cooking.[5] An American mother of the 1950s was not expected to work outside the home.

Now 50 years later, the picture of what a mother is in the United States is quite radically different. As of this date, there is no expectation that an American mother be married. In fact she can have as many children as she wants with no husband whatsoever.[6] The term "housewife" is considered derogatory, replaced by another term for women who do not work outside the home, that of "stay-at-home-mom". "Stay-at-home-mom" is a status function which is not only self-created by those who bear the term, it is a status function that is self-imposed. It refers to a woman who considers taking care of her children as not a function of being a mother but as a career, one which she has chosen to do as one would choose any career, be it a banker or a teacher, etc.[7]

The understanding of what a modern mother is has so changed that my mother or my grandmother would not recognize it. As demonstrated by this one example, social expectations exist and are a function of time and place; these expectations are limitless yet describable, non-linguistic, and non-codified.

In 2007, I suggested emendation to Searle's formula by means of something called *The Deontic Split*. The Deontic Split is characterized by assuming that there are two parts to the imposition of status functions, and indeed, two parts to the acquisition of social power be it positive or negative. The split of deonticity is between social expectation, a non-linguistic perception of social roles, and social authorization, a linguistic codification of status function. I suggested that the deontic split could be easily accommodated by Searle's formula with one small change in his extended formula to allow for non-reflective social expectation. This change is that of allowing the collective acceptance operator (CA) to be a collective recognition operator (CR).

The small change to Searle's formula to incorporate the deontic split would appear in its logical form as:

$$CR [ecognition] (O [bligation] (x \text{ counts as } y \text{ in } c))$$

The power of social expectation is a function of the Collective Recognition operator, which has wide scope over the entire proposition. As I thought at the time, the power of authorization would be a function of the O operator which has a narrower scope and the CR operator which operates over the entire proposition, though, as I will argue later in this chapter, this account is not satisfactory.

---

[5]I used this example in another paper, *Can Status Functions Be Discovered?*

[6]E.g. Nadia Suleyman is an unmarried mother of 14 children in the U.S., eight of whom are octoplets and a product of artificial insemination. The case of Nadia Suleyman has brought her national attention in the United States, but is not the kind of scandal it would have been in the 1950s.

[7]Stay-at-home-moms form their own societies. Self-imposition of the status is collectively recognized once the person who bears it accepts and embraces the status. The deonticity thereby received would be rights such as joining the clubs, exchange of day care, etc.

In his latest book, *Making the Social World*, Searle did not adopt my logical formula but he did adopt the operator, (CR), replacing the (CA) with the (CR) operator. But with this new formula, I now believe that there are new challenges for Searle. Specifically, there are two questions which it raises. These are (1) How can collective perception, a passive cognitive event, create and maintain unpopular regimes? and (2) How is the power of the unpopular regime maintained by mere collective perception? In this chapter, I will suggest a logical formula which can account for both the creation of objectionable institutions, along with the perpetuation of despotic power.

2 How Collectives Support and Maintain Oppressive Regimes

Scholars from various disciplines have given us a picture as to why despots have gained power throughout history. The phenomenon of despotism is not a mystery. But what is mysterious is the continued maintenance of the oppressive regimes over which despots reign. A simple question which is often asked about oppressive regimes is, How could they let it happen? "They" are the collectives whose cooperative activities make social structures possible.

In this chapter, I am going to focus on one type of oppressive regime in particular, that of totalitarianism. Totalitarian regimes are a particular kind of oppressive regime in that every aspect of individual behavior is governed by the ruling state party, or the ruler of the state. This total control over individual behavior provides an interesting case for either a behavioral or a cognitive logical account for the very reason that both accounts require cooperation, and cooperation implies some form of complicity in the sense that people are motivated by their desires whatever they might be. Without further examination, this feature of cooperation leaves the logical analysis with a strange result: totalitarian regimes are both sanctioned, and accepted and maintained by the collective. To put it bluntly, they are what the people wanted.

In *Making the Social World* (2010), Searle attempts to answer this very dilemma. In order to do this, Searle departs in several respects from his earlier position in *Collective Intentions and Action* (1990) and *The Construction of Social Reality* (1995) to the logical features of institutional reality. There are at least two note-worthy departures, one with respect to the primacy of collective intentionality and another, with respect to the essential feature constitutive of institutional reality, that of codification. In first *Collective Intentions and Action* and then *The Construction of Social Reality*, Searle claimed that collective intentionality cannot be reduced to individual intentionality and mutual belief. His example of the Harvard Business School graduates illustrates two paradigms of collectivity, one in which there is a collective goal that is irreducible to individual intentions and mutual belief, and another in which the goal of the members of the group is identical in content, but is not collective. In the first case, the graduates agree on the collective goal of enriching the state of the economy by means of their individual wealth; in the second case, the graduates agree on becoming individually rich, the incidental feature of which is a general rise in the economy. In the group effort that is made as a pact, defection of any member spoils the collective goal regardless of whether the general economy rises or not, i.e., the original intention of the collective state is not satisfied. In the second case in which there is no pact, defection of a member ruins nothing at all as there is no collective goal but rather a general effect which may or may not be affected by individual defection, i.e., the original content of each individual intention is satisfied. The important point is that the psychological content of the members of the group is different in both cases depending on whether the goal can only be achieved by the collective or by individuals.

In *Making the Social World*, Searle considers the problem of unpopular regimes in relation to the constitutive and essential feature of cooperation in the structure of institutions. In order to allow for the maintenance of oppression regimes and also explain unwilling individual participation in those regimes, Searle states that contrary to what our theories originally claimed, cooperation is *not* essential to the structure of institutions. Rather, what institutions require at the very minimum is *collective recognition* and this type of collective intentionality—collective recognition—can indeed be reduced to I-intentionality and mutual belief. Thus, he maintains, in this way it is not hard to see how an individual can participate in a regime which he finds disagreeable. The situation is no different from the institution of money. An individual may loathe money, but nonetheless recognizes the institution of money, believes others recognize its value also, and uses it in virtue of this recognition (see Searle 2010, pp. 56–58).

To extend this example then to totalitarianism, an individual might find himself under the control of a totalitarian state. He may not like the regime but he recognizes it exists in virtue of the fact that others recognize it exists, and he shares mutual belief about its existence with others in the community. Because of this fact, he acts within the institution because it is his institutional reality. The proof that this must be the case is that the individual is powerless to change what he does not like. Even if a single individual decides neither to accept nor recognize the institution of money nor the political regime under which he lives, this rejection does not affect the reality of these institutions at all if the collective still recognizes their validity. Institutional reality thus is grounded initially in collective perception, and then secondarily in the acts that maintain its existence. Again, there is a proof of the sequencing of these acts: Once lack of participation in the institutional reality reaches critical mass, the institution no longer is recognizable nor recognized as functional.

As appealing as this explanation is, there is a chicken-egg problem for a logical analysis. This problem is tightly connected with Searle's second essential institutional feature, that of the imposition of status functions as power-endowing. In Searle's original formula, power is conferred on a y in virtue of collective acceptance which lent itself to be interpreted as implemented in either non-reflective or reflective behavior. In Searle's new formula, power is conferred on a y in virtue of collective perception-recognition, a passive state of the collective which at best can be interpreted as recognizing a y has a status function, and not interfering in this state of affairs. The real question then is, What is the nature of collective-recognition conferral of power? Perceiving that some proposition holds is not sufficient to make it the case. At its weakest interpretation, collective recognition is a negative state of affairs in which the collective does not interfere in the power of the y, i.e., simply put, the conferral of collective recognition must be a negative conferral in that an individual or a group of individuals are allowed to act without interference. And negative conferral of power does occur in cases of coups and revolutions where power is usurped. But not all totalitarian regimes are cases of coups and revolutions. Some totalitarian regimes are authorized, voted in, and legitimated by the collective. In a word, they are positive cases of conferral in which the collective takes active steps towards conferring power on some y.

But even in the cases of coups and revolutions, once the totalitarian regime has been established, it is the collective that maintains the power of the despot or the state by means of their daily acts within the institutions of these states. This is not merely a case of passive perception-recognition, but also a matter of acceptance. *Acceptance is participation in an institution*, no matter how oppressive the institution might be. And, as it has been argued in this chapter, acceptance is behavioral. Acceptance defined as participation, even unwilling participation in an unpopular government or institutional state of affairs, is still a matter of cooperation. This fact forces us to the conclusion that every single individual capable of active participation within totalitarian state, young or old, is in equal regard responsible for the oppressive state he might find himself in. This result is not only intolerable, but false.

Thus, at this point, we are left with two dilemmas: (1) How to incorporate the chicken-egg problem into a logical analysis; i.e., how to reflect the fact that both collective recognition and collective acceptance (as participation) simultaneously construct and maintain totalitarian regimes, and (2) How to account for the possibility that acceptance (as participation) does not necessarily entail complicity (in the sense of willing cooperation) in the construction and maintenance of totalitarian states.

In order to resolve these dilemmas, we first need to return to the primitive notion of social analysis, that of cooperation. Human institutions are constructed and maintained by human cooperation. This includes the construction of marriages, parties, conferences, as well as wars and governments. All of these phenomena require human cooperative actions, what Searle originally called *Collective Acceptance*. But collective acceptance is not at all at odds with the notion that individuals can accept and loathe at the same time the institutions which they maintain since by our definition of collective acceptance as mere behavior, cooperation does not entail complicity. How then can this fact be built into the notion of cooperation as acceptance?

In the same way that power can be divided into both an active and passive conferral (the Deontic Split), acceptance can also have two forms depending on the attitude of the participants in the collective. One form I will call "happy" and the other, "unhappy." Happy acceptance arises from a strong form of collective recognition, one in which the perceiver identifies with the regime or the despot in some manner, and bonds with this state or person who represents the state, i.e., the despot. This form of identification does not need to be a deliberative process nor rise to the level of thought. In fact, it quite likely can be the case that an individual cannot pinpoint the exact cause of attraction to another, be it an individual or a set of individuals. Rather, this state is a perceptual capacity that allows individuals to perceive in an other an attractive familiarity. To put the experience perhaps more abstractly, it is the ability to see oneself in others, or to see others as a larger form of oneself. Social identification is a necessary step towards forming social relations and it occurs at all levels, from one-on-one pair bonding or friendships, to the more abstract level of joining a set of individuals.

Social bonding is the emotional component of social identification. It is logically separate from social identification in that one can understand oneself to be part of a larger set unified by some property, be it familial or representational (underscored by a principle), yet feel no emotional bond with the group whatsoever. But in situations which interest us, individuals who socially identify with a cause, more perspicuously, a set of individuals who represent a cause, feel a bond to act with the set in question. It is social bonding that is the emotional component of collective identity and motivates the individual to act in the interest of the group. It is this crucial element in human psychology that is required for all collectives to be able to act, to have effect and be a unified force. This crucial element of emotional bonding in oppressive societies is purchased through frequent use of propaganda, including music, art, parades, symbols such as flags. In the case of totalitarian regimes, the parades, flags, symbols, music, art, etc. are means to moving the collective's conferral of power on the despot in particular, the state at large.

So what exactly is the experience of social bonding? Social bonding with individual(s) is an experience in which power is given to the set, be it a set of two or two million. The kind of power given over to another is not of the type, "power over" in which the individual is subjugated to another, but rather, the kind of power that enables the set to become enabled to act as a single unit. For example, in the case of pair bonding, individuals bond with each other, thereby creating a new thing, a "we" which acts together. This new enablement allows pairs to have children, or to make a home, to create an estate, etc. In the case of larger groups, an individual's bonding with a group empowers the group to act more forcefully towards whatever aim the group might have. Thus, the phenomenology of social bonding is one in which the individual gives power to the group and in doing so feels empowered by expanding his or her own sense of what one can do and be. This is true not only of individual relationships but of political, social, religious groups also.

In political regimes of any kind, happy acceptance arises when an individual identifies and bonds with the political group and thus commits him-herself to the collective. In this commitment, the individual gives power to the group and thereby experiences an expanded sense of his-her own power through group membership. Happy acceptance thus motivates individuals to actively strengthen the collective by engaging in activities of legitimation through such acts as voting, engaging in various civic duties such as becoming a party member, becoming the chairman of a cooperative, volunteering for citizen night patrols, etc. The individual who happily accepts the collective in question feels larger than himself or herself, empowered by the collective power of the group. In some groups, the power is returned in fact, as in the cases of benign institutions as marriages, universities and so on. In the case of totalitarian regimes, the power derived from the state by the individual is only phenomenological as individuals under totalitarian regimes are institutionally powerless.

Unhappy acceptance, on the other hand, is a case in which there is perception-recognition that y has a given status function, but social identification and therefore social bonding is lacking. Unhappy acceptance, at its best, thus leads to begrudging participation in the state, at its worst, erosive activities against the state. Ultimately, without any active effort on the parts of the collective members, unhappy acceptance is a dangerous state of affairs for a totalitarian state because members have little motivation to expend energy on its institutions. And, naturally, members who do not have social identification with the state at large will form identifications with other groups, even with each other, a cause for totalitarian states to have increased police policies, including terrorizing its citizenry.[8]

In light of this twofold distinction, and the fact that collective recognition operates in tandem with collective acceptance, how would we reflect this in logical form?

First of all, unlike in non-institutional reality, in institutional reality perception is logically prior to action. There are two arguments to support this claim. First, deferential behavior alone towards some agent does not add up to conferring power on that agent. For example, alpha males in wolf packs command a certain kind of deferential behavior from their pack in virtue of brute power, but the deferential behavior does not confer the kind of power that is required for institutional status functions. In order for institutional deontic powers to be conferred, the collective must have the capacity to grasp the deontic properties of the y in the absence of y and this requires representational abilities which are perceptual. As an example of this, in a tribe of humans with minimal linguistic abilities that include symbolization and tense, an alpha male or female can also have the status function of "chief" if the collective is capable of perceiving his or her deontic powers even in his or her absence. Thus, the capacity for recognizing social hierarchy with deonticity is logically prior to behaving towards social hierarchy with deonticity.

Second: As argued above, it is in virtue of social identification, a perceptual property, that collective acceptance is made possible. Without the capacity to see some property in others as one's own, one cannot be social at all.

Thus, as in the logical form saw earlier, the **CR** operator operates before the **CA** operator. We are now in a position to reformulate our formula in the following way, allowing the **CA** operator wide scope over the entire proposition.

---

[8]C. Milosz (1990 [1951]) expands the notion of what I call "unhappy" and unwilling cooperation in a totalitarian regime by dividing up such participation into various types. As he points out, the participants in such regimes are for the most part not willing cooperators, but engaging in the upkeep of the institution for a variety of reasons.

$$\mathsf{CA}\,[\text{cceptance}]\ (\mathsf{CR}\,[\text{ecognition}]\ (x \text{ counts as } y \text{ in } c))$$

And as before, this captures the tacit power of social expectation as a function of the Collective Recognition operator which has primacy over the legitimizing power of collective acceptance which has wide scope over the entire proposition. The power of authorization is a function of the CA operator. The power of social expectation is a function of the CR operator.

To make a complete logical description, we need to add the tags of happy and unhappy to the CA[cceptance] operator. In order to do this, we will note them with + for "happy" and − for "unhappy", and put them as subscripts to the Collective Acceptance operators:

$$\mathsf{CA}\,[\text{cceptance}]_{(\pm)}\ (\mathsf{CR}\,[\text{ecognition}]\ (x \text{ counts as } y \text{ in } c))$$

A final question remains as to whether an unpopular regime can exist with a critical mass of members who join the collective but unhappily. The answer is not straightforward. The continued existence of oppressive regimes depends on how successful they are at convincing individuals of their own powerlessness outside the collective in question. If an unpopular regime is successful enough at frightening its members so that they only feel empowered by being part of the collective, then the regime can exist for a certain amount of time based solely on ensuring individuals' fear of loss of personal power by leaving the collective. The security of such regimes is always at stake though, and the fragility is apparent in the size of its internal policing and propaganda directed at enemies of the collective. At this point in the analysis, it is safe to make the claim that the oldest and most secure collectives are those that are the most successful at ensuring the experience of personal power through the collective and expanding the actual power of the individual because of membership in the collective.

References

Anderson, A. 2007. *Power and social ontology*. Malmo: Bokbox Publications.
Haugeland, J. 1982. Heidegger on being a person. *Nous* 16(1): 15–16.
Hayek, F. 1944. *The road to serfdom*. Chicago: University of Chicago Press.
Hudin, J. 2007. Can social statuses be discovered? *The Journal for the Theory of Social Behavior* (submitted).
Jennerod, M. 2006. *Motor cognition*. Oxford: Oxford University Press.
Milosz, C. 1990 [1951]. *The captive mind*. New York: Vintage Books.
Searle, J.R. 1990. Collective intentions and actions. In *Intentions in communication*, ed. P. Cohen, J. Morgan, and M. Pollack. Cambridge, MA: MIT Press.
Searle, J.R. 1995. *The construction of social reality*. New York: The Free Press.
Searle, J.R. 2010. *Making the social world*. Oxford: Oxford University Press.

Chapter 6
Groups, Normativity and Disagreement

Rodrigo E. Sánchez Brigido

Abstract We are members of many groups to which we ascribe the performance of intentional actions, and belonging to these groups seems to give rise, in many cases, to special normative relations. For instance, as a member of the university I have certain duties, as a member of the football team I have others, and yet I have other duties *qua* member of my law firm. But what is special about some groups that claims of the form "I am under a duty *qua* member of the group" seem adequate? This paper claims that the standard answer to this question faces two main difficulties. Firstly, most accounts appeal to one special normative notion (e.g. the idea of a joint commitment, or an agreement) to explain such relations, a notion such that, if instantiated, it gives rise to duties that are independent of the value of the joint action. But there are cases where participants think that they are under a duty *qua* members because the joint activity is valuable, and only because it is valuable. Secondly, most accounts seem unable to explain disagreements among participants about the content of their duties. The paper proposes a model of group action and of normative relations among participants that attempts to overcome both difficulties.

1 Introduction

We are members of many groups to which we ascribe the performance of intentional actions, and some of these groups have a particular characteristic: belonging to them seems to give rise to special normative relations, for members believe that they have certain duties *qua* members. Thus, my university is involved, primarily, in the

R.E. Sánchez Brigido (✉)
Filosofía del Derecho, Universidad Nacional de Córdoba, Córdoba, Argentina

Department of Philosophy, Universidad Blas Pascal, Córdoba, Argentina
e-mail: rodrigosanchezb@uolsinectis.com.ar

A. Konzelmann Ziv and H.B. Schmid (eds.), *Institutions, Emotions, and Group Agents*, 81
Studies in the Philosophy of Sociality 2, DOI 10.1007/978-94-007-6934-2_6,
© Springer Science+Business Media Dordrecht 2014

activity of teaching. And my university would be a completely different entity if its professors thought that they are at liberty to perform activities such as teaching, that they had no duty *qua* members to teach their subjects. I shall label this sort of groups "groups which act with a normative unity" (GNU). Schools, armies, religious orders, banks and, in general, most institutions are GNUs. Despite our familiarity with GNUs, they seem to resist explanation.

First, consider the general strategy to explain members' beliefs in duties *qua* members. Most accounts appeal to one special normative notion such that, if instantiated, it gives rise to duties that are independent of the value of the joint action. Thus, Gilbert (1996, p. 8, 2002a, pp. 73–74) claims that participants are "jointly committed" to doing something. Given that the notion of a joint commitment is a normative, irreducible notion, that would explain beliefs in duties *qua* members. Tuomela (1995, chapter 3) claims that the relevant notion is that of an agreement to do one's part of a joint action. Bratman (1999, p. 126) and Kutz (2000, p. 85) make similar suggestions. The general strategy is, nevertheless, subject to counterexamples. For, however one conceives of joint commitments or agreements, they create duties (if they do) that are partially independent of the value of the action which participants are jointly committed to pursuing, or have agreed to pursue. And one can easily think of cases where this is not so. Consider two individuals working together to rescue an individual from drowning. As participants in the joint activity of saving somebody's life, they may well think of themselves as members of this small, sporadic group. And they may well think that they are under a duty *qua* members of such a group because the joint activity (saving somebody's life) is valuable, and only because it is valuable. This same belief may occur in larger institutional groups, from charities devoted to fighting global poverty to pro bono consulting agencies.

Secondly, the general strategy seems unable to explain why participants disagree about the content of their duties. Suppose that a group of pro bono lawyers has provided legal advice to individuals for many years, and that now a non-governmental organization requests legal advice. Half of the lawyers argue that they should disregard this request, for their only duty *qua* members is to provide advice to individuals. But half of them claim that their duty *qua* members is, and has always been, to provide advice to organizations too; it so happens that, so far, there has been no opportunity to do so. And each side grounds its views by claiming that this is what their collective practice, properly understood, really requires. This sort of situation appears to be fairly common. And it poses a challenge for the general strategy. For, if participants had in effect become jointly committed to doing something together (or reached an agreement to do something together), it seems that they should have had the same idea of the content of their joint commitment (or the agreement) and hence of their duties. But participants disagree about this.

In this chapter I propose an account of GNUs that attempts to overcome both difficulties. I begin by suggesting a general model of collective intentional action where no normative relations among members exist. This is a starting point to provide an analysis of GNUs (Sect. 1). I then focus on Gilbert's account and criticize its faults. If my contentions are correct, it follows that any account appealing to only one normative notion (such as the idea of a joint commitment, or an agreement) is unsatisfactory (Sect. 2). I then propose a model of GNUs. According to this model, GNUs may take on different normative structures (Sect. 3). When the group is normatively structured by an agreement, as happens frequently but not necessarily, disagreement can be explained if one considers how the content of voluntary undertakings is determined (Sect. 4).

2 Collective Intentional Action without Normative Unity

Many groups which act are not groups whose members believe that they have duties *qua* members. Two or more individuals may be seriously coerced to work together on (what they believe is) a morally repugnant joint activity, or pursue the achievement of a joint goal that is (considered) morally indifferent and act together out of pure personal interest. Members may act motivated by convenience, ambition, fear, or for other reasons, without believing that they have (or indeed without having) any duties *qua* members. I shall label this sort of groups "groups which act *without* normative unity". A good way to provide an account of GNUs is, I believe, to focus on groups which act without normative unity in the first place. For they seem to be more simple than GNUs.

One way of explaining groups which act without normative unity is to examine the relevant intentions. For, as with individual actions, it seems that there is no collective action if the action is not jointly intended.

An account that focuses on the relevant intentions of collective action is Christopher Kutz's, and I use it as a starting point.[1] Kutz (2000, pp. 89, 94, 103–104) claims that there is a collective or joint intentional activity if, and only if, there is a set of individuals who are acting with participatory intentions, a participatory intention being an intention to do one's part of a collective or joint act.

Notice that, despite its attractive simplicity, the key notion of a participatory intention seems to make the model uninformatively circular. For it employs the same idea (the notion of a collective act) that the analysis claims to elucidate. Naturally, whether there is a circularity problem is debatable. But to remove any doubts on the matter, Kutz's model can be easily modified to avoid the appearance of circularity. Consider the following argument.

Suppose I conceive of a particular state of affairs to be brought about: that a house be painted. I conceive of certain actions as standing in a sort of instrumental relation to this state of affairs. Say, getting the brushes and the paint, painting the front first, the back next, and so on, such that, if these actions are performed, the state of affairs will likely be brought about. Of course, the state of affairs might be brought about otherwise, by performing other actions. But this is how I conceive of the matter now.

---

[1] I think Kutz's proposal is promising for several reasons. See Rodrigo Sánchez Brigido (2010).

In other words, I conceive of a state of affairs the bringing about of which involves performing these actions. Suppose I decide to perform these actions myself. I plan in advance what to do: the first day I will paint the front, the second day the back, etc. I am essentially dividing labour among my inner-selves. Something similar might happen if I decide to hire two painters to paint the house. I divide the labour among them, and assign tasks to each such that, if my plan is followed, the state of affairs (that the house be painted) will likely be brought about. And a similar situation may occur if the agents are you and me. Just as I can divide labour among my inner-selves, and between the two painters, you and I can divide labour among ourselves. If we do this, each of us will see his own actions, and the actions of the other, as standing in a sort of instrumental relation to the state of affairs. So we can say that some collective ends are just states of affairs, the bringing about of which is conceived of as involving the actions of two or more individuals. These actions can be conceived of as the parts each individual is to perform in order to bring about the state of affairs.

This definition of some collective ends does not employ any notion of collectivity. True, there is some kind of coordination among the relevant individuals. But this sort of coordination does not involve collectivity in any sense. The definition only relies on the simple idea of an activity that can be divided in parts. Or, to be more precise, it simply relies on the idea of states of affairs, the bringing about of which is conceived of as involving the performance of certain acts by several individuals, an idea with which we are very familiar. And with this idea of collective ends we can characterize at least some participatory intentions. Some of them can be characterized as intentions to perform certain acts that the agent conceives as, together with the actions of other agents, bringing about a state of affairs, the realization of which involves his doing certain things and their doing certain things. I find no uninformative circularity involved here.

Not all participatory intentions can be characterized thus, however. Some collective ends are states of affairs which are *constituted* by the performance of certain acts by different individuals. Suppose an assembly wants to honour a guest by offering a toast. Assume that there is a common conception of what counts as 'an assembly offering a toast'. Say, it consists of each member of the assembly, when prompted by one of the members, facing the guest and raising his or her glass of wine for a couple of seconds as a way of showing respect. This counts as the assembly offering a toast. So it is a state of affairs, the bringing about of which is seen as constituted by the actions (and attitudes) of different individuals. Notice the difference between the first type of collective act and this one. Here the actions do not stand, in any plausible sense, in an instrumental relation to the state of affairs. Besides, the state of affairs is not achievable in ways other than the individuals performing the relevant actions and displaying the relevant attitudes. So their intentions to do their part of their giving a toast (a collective action) are just intentions to perform certain actions (coupled with certain attitudes) that, together with the actions (and attitudes) of the others, are seen as constitutive of the bringing about of a particular state of affairs. Again, I find no uninformative circularity involved here.

These two characterizations of participatory intentions seem to cover all cases. We can use this argument to propose a model of collective intentional action that, purportedly, does not face the problem of uninformative circularity. My provisional suggestion is this:

There is a **collective intentional activity with no normative unity** if, and only if, there is a set of individuals (defined extensionally or intensionally) such that:

(a) Each conceives of a state of affairs, the bringing about of which involves, or is constituted by, the performance of certain actions (and the display of certain attitudes) by all members of the set,
(b) their conceptions of this state of affairs overlap,
(c) each intends to perform these actions (and displays the relevant attitudes), and each conceives of these actions (and attitudes) as related in the way described to the state of affairs,
(d) and each executes his or her intention, such that the state of affairs mentioned in (b) is brought about.[2]

Some comments and clarifications are in place. Firstly, the idea of overlap should be understood as requiring that there must be a non-empty intersection of the states of affairs that each participant has in mind. This notion is necessary in order to capture the fact that, for there to be a collective intentional action, it must be the same joint enterprise in which agents intentionally participate. So, for instance, I may intend that we go together to a friend's house for a quiet dinner, while you intend that we go there for a surprise party. While our going to the surprise party is not jointly intentional, our going to our friend's house is.[3]

Secondly, the model is minimalistic.[4] By this I mean that it should be interpreted as proposing necessary conditions for there to be any instance of joint intentional action with no normative unity, and also as providing sufficient conditions for there to be the simplest type of instance. However, this does not deny that the model has to be supplemented by adding further conditions if it is to capture cases which are, in an intuitive sense, more complex. For instance, it is difficult to explain what takes place in many groups unless one supposes that each participant knows what the other intends, and that all this is common knowledge. But, again, this situation seems not necessary, as the example of the two painters above shows. And, besides, it can be captured by adding the relevant clause (one that requires the relevant beliefs) to the model. This is possible due to its minimalistic character.

---

[2]Clause (d) implies, as an anonymous referee has rightly pointed out, that the group would be unsuccessful if the relevant intentions are not executed. This does not mean, however, that one could not attribute to the group an intentional action in another sense. The same happens with individual action. I may intend to do A knowing that, in my attempt to do A, B (an unwanted consequence) will occur. Even if I end up being unsuccessful in doing A, I may have done B intentionally. The same applies, I think, to group action.

[3]The idea of overlap, and the example, are taken from Kutz (2000, p. 94).

[4]Kutz (2000, pp. 74–75, 89–90) introduces the idea of a minimalistic model, although I am not sure of whether he would interpret it in the way I do in the text.

Many other clarifications could be made, but the foregoing considerations should suffice. My only aim was to provide a plausible model of collective intentional action with no normative unity that could remove any doubt about the circularity problem and the model appears to fulfill such purpose. Let us focus now on GNUs.

3   Normative Relations among Members of Groups

As previously mentioned, on many occasions participants regard themselves as under a duty, *qua* members of the group, to perform the actions conducive to the joint end. This need not be the case, as the examples above show. But this might be, and perhaps normally is, the case. Given that the model I have just proposed is minimalistic, it could be further developed to capture these cases. Before doing so, however, I shall consider Gilbert's account. It is one of the most elaborated models in this respect, and examining it will provide guidance in suggesting an alternative.

3.1   Gilbert's Account

Gilbert's account can be stated thus: two or more people are involved in the collective action of J-ing if, and only if, they are jointly committed to accepting the goal of J-ing as a body and each one is acting in a way appropriate to the achievement of that goal in the light of the fact that each is subject to the joint commitment (1996, p. 8, 2002a, p. 68, 2002b, pp. 73–74).

Consider the general notion of being *jointly committed* to accepting the goal of J-ing. The basic idea is that agents join forces toward the achievement of a goal by committing themselves to each other in a particular way, i.e. by becoming *jointly committed*. The main properties of a joint commitment are these: (a) the parties become individually committed through the joint commitment simultaneously, and these individual commitments are interdependent; thus, if Jack and Sue are on a walk together, it is because they have become individually and interdependently committed to doing what is necessary for them to walk together; (b) relevant entitlements and obligations will be in place; so, if Jack inadvertently draws ahead, he would accept Sue's criticism for violating the joint commitment; (c) normally, the joint commitment is not rescindable unilaterally—thus, if Jack wishes not to walk together anymore, he will seek for Sue's approval (Gilbert 2002a, pp. 77–79, 90–91). Notice that feature (b) would explain normative relations among members of groups.

3.2   Criticism of Gilbert's Account. An Alternative Solution

Gilbert's model entails, *inter alia*, that all groups which act are groups whose members think of themselves as being under a duty *qua* members. For, in her view, there is a group only if members are jointly committed and, by definition of being "jointly committed", this entails that they are under a duty to act accordingly (as members of the group). Her definition, insofar as it attempts to be an analysis of our ordinary concept of group intentional action, is, it seems to me, incorrect. There are clear cases where it seems undeniable that there is a group acting intentionally and where members do not conceive of themselves as under a duty *qua* members, such as the case of the painters above.

We may consider then whether Gilbert's account is an adequate analysis of GNUs only, and focus on joint commitments, the key notion of her analysis. If individuals are jointly committed, the following takes place by definition (see properties (a–c) of joint commitments above): several agents are each individually committed in a particular way; each commitment is interlocked with the others (the individual commitments are interdependent, are arrived at simultaneously, and cannot be rescinded without the concurrence of all); this gives rise to duties to act in accordance with the commitments, and these duties are independent of the value of the actions which participants are individually committed to doing, and in fact they are independent of the value of the joint action itself.

This does not seem to capture all cases. Recall the case of the painters, but suppose now that the two individuals want the house to be painted because it is going to be a rest-home for elderly people. They do consider themselves under a duty *qua* members now, for the joint activity is seen by them as something valuable in relation to individuals other than themselves.[5] Does Gilbert's account capture this sort of case?

The individuals intend to perform the relevant actions, and hence they are committed to doing them. The commitments are interdependent in some sense, for they all concern actions which, taken together, are related in a special way to a state of affairs (that the house should be painted). But these commitments need not have been arrived at simultaneously. In other words, joining in to this set of interdependent commitments might have taken place in other ways. For instance, one of the painters might intend to perform the relevant actions first, in the hope that the other will join him. These commitments need not be non-rescindable without the concurrence of the other painter either. For example, the joint action might be taking place and one of the painters might simply change his mind as to the valuable character of the activity and opt out. He does not need the concurrence of all to do this in any sense. The conditions put forward by Gilbert seem, then, too demanding. More importantly, Gilbert requires that participants think that they are under a duty regardless of the value of the collective action and, as we saw, this is not the case. Participants think of themselves as under a duty precisely because the joint action is

---

[5]I am assuming that values are normally seen as being grounds of duties. If you think that the assumption is too controversial, think of any case where participants would consider themselves under a duty based on other moral grounds which make reference to the intrinsic or instrumental desirability of the relevant action. It is still the case, as I argue in the next paragraph, that Gilbert's account would not capture it. Unless you think, of course, that the only ground of duties is a joint commitment.

valuable in relation to others. Moreover, Gilbert thinks that participants *are* actually obligated. But it is easy to think of collective actions where individuals believe that the activity is valuable and are completely wrong in so believing.

In short, there are groups whose members think of themselves as under a duty *qua* members because they think of the joint activity as particularly valuable in relation to other individuals. In those groups, which I shall label "GNUs of type (I)", Gilbert's main conditions are not met. So the idea of joint commitment is not necessary to understand these groups.

It seems, in fact, that one can propose an account of GNUs of type (I) by expanding the model I suggested in the previous section. Consider this proposal:

There is an intentional activity of a **GNU of type (I)** if, and only if, there is a set of individuals (defined intensionally or extensionally) such that:

(a) each of them conceives of a state of affairs the bringing about of which involves, or is constituted by, the performance of certain actions and the display of certain attitudes by all members of the set;
(b) their conceptions of this state of affairs overlap;
(c) each intends to perform the relevant actions (and displays the relevant attitudes), and conceives of these actions (and attitudes) as related in the way described to the state of affairs;
(d) each executes his intentions and, as a result, the state of affairs mentioned in (b) is being achieved;
(e) each believes that the previous conditions are satisfied, and that the state of affairs being brought about is valuable in relation to individuals other than themselves;
(f) each thinks that applying to them is a normative consideration according to which everyone who is in a position of, together with others, bringing about a state of affairs that is valuable for individuals other than themselves, should do his part.[6]

This model is just an expanded version of the model deployed in the previous section. It only contains some additions, which are highlighted, namely clauses (e) and (f).[7] They are introduced to explain why participants believe that they are under a duty *qua* members. And the expanded model simply claims that they so believe because they think that a normative consideration demands that they do their parts because of the valuable character of the activity. This normative consideration appears to be quite abstract. But it is a plausible normative consideration. And it explains why members might think of themselves as under a duty *qua* members, i.e. as individuals who belong to the group (as individuals described in terms of clauses

---

[6]I am assuming that this normative consideration is normally thought of as grounding duties. It may be argued that the normative consideration need not make reference to individuals other than participants in order to be thought of as imposing duties. If that is so the model should be modified.

[7]Notice that adding more conditions to the initial model does not imply that GNUs are a special case of groups with no normative unity. For both models contain necessary and sufficient conditions, and the conditions are not identical. It does imply, however, that if there is a GNU, there is also a group with no normative unity with some additional conditions.

(a) to (d)) and to whom the normative consideration is applicable. The model is, as far as I can see, adequate to capture cases of GNUs of type (I).

We still need, nevertheless, an account of groups where participants conceive of themselves as under a duty *qua* members even if they do not think of the activity as particularly valuable in relation to other individuals. I label them "GNUs of type (II)".

Gilbert's account seems to be an inadequate analysis of these groups as well. The main difficulty is that we do not know exactly what a joint commitment is.[8] Gilbert refuses to break down the notion, and this makes it unclear. This concern may be defused—as Gilbert herself suggests—by arguing that a joint commitment is just a particular set of individual commitments. Thus, if I intend to do A, I am individually committed to doing A. A joint commitment would be, then, a set of individual commitments but with the particular properties mentioned above: they are interdependent, arrived at simultaneously, non-rescindable unilaterally, and give rise to duties. But these notions are still mysterious. For even if individual commitments could become interlocked in the way described, one might sensibly ask why duties arise out of that mesh. Just as individual commitments do not create duties (for instance, if I intend to do A, it does not follow that I have a duty to do A), a meshing set of individual commitments does not create duties either. Gilbert's explanation of why duties arise out of joint commitments is that this is so analytically. That is, because it is part of the concept of being jointly committed.

This idea appears inadequate. Notice, first, that certain restrictions should apply. If one is seriously coerced, no obligation should appear. But Gilbert claims explicitly that, even if somebody is forcing another to become jointly committed by putting a gun to his head, he becomes obligated (1996, pp. 351–52). This sounds extremely odd, to say the least. Explanations of duties must involve a normative argument, an argument that brings in normative considerations, of what is good, valuable, worthwhile, etc. Gilbert's account is problematic because it is not of the relevant form. According to her, duties arise of necessity.

Suppose, nevertheless, that we accept that joint commitments create duties by definition. The idea would still be problematic. For a theory is not supposed to introduce new theoretical constructs unnecessarily. And all the main features of the phenomenon that the concept of a joint commitment is supposed to capture can be captured in other terms. That is, by employing the idea of an agreement to do one's part of a joint act. Consider the following proposal:

There is a **GNU of type (II)** if, and only if, there is a set of individuals, defined intensionally or extensionally, such that:

(a) each conceives of a state of affairs the bringing about of which involves, or is constituted by, the performance of certain actions (and the display of certain attitudes) by all the members of the set; *the relevant actions are the actions which each has agreed (explicitly or implicitly) to perform*;

---

[8]The remarks that follow provide an additional reason for thinking that Gilbert's account is inadequate as an account of GNUs of type (I).

(b) each has an overlapping conception of the state of affairs;
(c) each intends to perform the relevant actions (and displays the relevant attitudes), and conceives of these actions (and attitudes) as related in the way described to the state of affairs;
(d) each executes his intentions and, as a result, the state of affairs mentioned in (ii) is brought about; and
(e) each thinks that the previous conditions are satisfied.

This model needs to be completed and elaborated. But the point is that all of the main features of the phenomenon that Gilbert attempts to capture seem to be captured by employing the idea of agreements, a notion with which we are familiar, and dispensing with the idea of joint commitments, which is a new theoretical construct.

In effect, agreements, under any plausible construal, are ways of voluntarily undertaking obligations. In this sense the relevant obligations are created by the parties. Accordingly, participants can conceive of themselves as under an obligation *qua* members of the group, i.e. *qua* individuals who have agreed. When agreements are reached, the parties think that they have become obligated regardless of whether the thing one has agreed to is particularly valuable. The obligations are also thought of as arrived at simultaneously (when one agrees, no party becomes obligated first), and normally the agreement is not rescindable unilaterally. And since participants intend to fulfill the agreement, they are committed to performing the relevant actions. Agreements, finally, create duties because there is a normative principle according to which agreements should be kept and, arguably, this principle is valid for certain normative reasons.[9] It is not my intention to discuss those reasons, although my view is that the principle is valid insofar as it gives assurance that one's part will be performed, regardless of whether one thinks that the relevant action is convenient for oneself or not. And assurance is a valuable thing.[10] Nevertheless, whatever your view about the reasons why agreements might bind, the point is that the idea of agreements, and of their normativity, is familiar to us. The notion of joint commitments is not.

Gilbert is aware of the parallel between agreements and joint commitments. But she rejects the idea that joint commitments can be replaced by the idea of agreements because, in her view, agreements themselves are instances of joint commitments. They are instances of being "jointly committed to upholding a decision as a body" (1996, pp. 292–96). Her rejection, nevertheless, brings us back to all the problems I have mentioned.

In short, Gilbert's account is problematic. There are GNUs of type (I) where her conditions are not met. I have, in fact, proposed a model to capture these cases. Moreover, there are GNUs of type (II) where her conditions are not met either, and where the idea of a joint commitment could be replaced easily by the idea of an agreement.

---

[9]Notice that it is not the case that agreements are considered binding without any type of restrictions, e.g. when serious coercion takes place.

[10]I have taken a stab at the normativity of agreements in Sánchez Brigido (2010).

3.3 Refining the Provisional Model

The provisional model of GNUs of type (II) I have proposed should, nevertheless, be revised. Agreements are voluntary undertakings. But they are not the only kind of voluntary undertaking. Vows, for instance, are voluntary undertakings that exhibit certain important differences with agreements. *Inter alia*, vows need not involve several parties (and hence obligations need not be arrived at simultaneously), and they need not be rescindable with the concurrence of others. Some GNUs of type (II)—think of gangs, and certain religious orders—are groups where members have made a vow, instead of having agreed to perform their parts. Moreover, agreements and vows are but examples of voluntary undertakings. There are others, such as making oaths, consenting, or promising.

To capture all these possibilities we could create a model of GNUs that incorporates the idea of voluntary undertakings. But the model would still be unsatisfactory. The normative consideration according to which voluntary undertakings should be honoured is "content-independent". That is, there is no direct connection between the action which, according to the normative consideration, one ought to perform, and the particular value of the action considered alone.[11] And groups may be structured by content-independent normative considerations other than the voluntary-undertakings principle. For instance, participants might be doing something together because a legitimate authority has issued an order to that effect. And the normative principle according to which one must obey, within certain limits, legitimate authorities is, arguably, a content-independent normative consideration too.

I shall not propose any particular account of these moral principles. My only point is that they are plausible, and that, when applicable, they may give different normative structures to GNUs of type (II). Moreover, there might be other content-independent normative considerations, and one should leave this possibility open. Perhaps the best way to proceed, then, is to propose a very general and abstract characterization of the activities of GNUs of type (II). My suggestion is that there is such a group if, and only if, the following conditions are met:

There is a **GNU of type (II)** if, and only if there is a set of individuals (defined extensionally or intensionally) such that:

(a) each conceives of a state of affairs the bringing about of which involves, or is constituted by, the performance of certain actions (and the display of certain attitudes) by all members of the set; the relevant actions are the actions which, together with certain facts (e.g. the fact that they are the actions which they have voluntarily undertaken the obligation to perform, or have been ordered to perform by a particular authority), appear in the antecedent of a content-independent normative consideration;
(b) their conceptions of this state of affairs overlap;

---

[11]Cf. Raz (1972, p. 95) and (1986, pp. 35–36).

(c) each intends to perform the relevant actions (and displays the relevant attitudes), and conceives of these actions (and attitudes) as related in the way described to the state of affairs;
(d) each executes his intentions and, as a result, the state of affairs mentioned in (b) obtains;
(e) each thinks that the previous conditions obtain, and that the content-independent normative consideration mentioned in (a) is in effect applicable to them.

I think that this model has sufficient descriptive coverage. Many aspects of it should be discussed. But I would rather leave them open. My only point in suggesting the model was to propose an account of the normative relations among members of groups and, as far as I can see, the models of GNUs of type (I) and type (II) capture all the possibilities. GNUs may take on different normative structures and, accordingly, appealing to only one normative notion, such as the notion of a joint commitment, is unsatisfactory.

I have not considered other accounts of GNUs. Tuomela, for instance, proposes a very sophisticated model based on the idea of an agreement,[12] and other theorists make similar suggestions. But if my contentions above are correct, any model which appeals to the notion of an agreement to explain *all* possible normative relations among members of groups is unsatisfactory as well.

4   Disagreement about Duties

The reason why theorists focus on the idea of an agreement, or on normative notions which are very close to it (such as the idea of a joint commitment), is because many GNUs are groups structured by agreements. One difficulty with that strategy, nevertheless, is that members often disagree about the content of their duties, as in the example of the pro bono lawyers mentioned above. It seems that a model based on the idea of an agreement could not explain this kind of dispute. For, it could be claimed, the parties should have the same ideas as to what they are committing themselves to in order to reach an agreement.

In this section I try to show that this objection is only apparent. It is based, I argue, on an incorrect assumption of how the content of agreements is determined.

4.1   The Content of Agreements

There are several views about the nature of agreements.[13] Despite this variety, the issue of how the content of agreements is determined can be examined, I believe,

---

[12]Tuomela's notion of "proper social norms" may help to deflect the criticism but, for reasons of space, I cannot consider that issue here.

[13]For a brief examination, see Rodrigo Sánchez Brigido (2010, ch. 8).

without presupposing any particular view of what an agreement is and why it binds. This is the case if one concedes (as most theories of agreements in fact do) that there are agreeing practices. That is, if one concedes that, as a matter of fact, there are social rules according to which performing certain actions counts as agreeing to perform a particular action (say, A). One can concede, moreover, that there are special relationships (among friends, relatives, colleagues, etc.) constituted by rules according to which performing certain actions counts as agreeing to do A. In what follows, then, I assume that, whatever the nature of agreements, there are practices of agreeing and special relationships of the sort described, and I focus only on the question of how the content of agreements is established.

There are three general views in that respect: the subjective view, the objective view, and the mixed view.

According to the subjective view, for there to be an agreement to do A, the intentions of the parties must coincide.[14] The difficulties of this view seem obvious, for there are plenty of counterexamples. Consider cases where one party makes an ambiguous offer. The individual intended to bind himself to do A, but becomes aware that the recipient will reasonably think that he intended to bind himself to do B because the context clearly supports that view. So he acknowledges that he agreed to do B, despite not having the intention to obligate himself to do B. The same applies to many other cases like blunders, mistakes as to the identity of the other party, errors about the nature of the action proposed, and so on. In many cases of this sort, an agreement has been reached and, contrary to the subjective view, the intentions do not coincide.

According to the objective view, whether one has agreed to do something depends on whether the parties have performed some actions that count as agreeing as defined by a practice of agreeing, regardless of whether the intentional states are present.[15] This view is "objective" only in the sense that it is not subjective. And the approach is unsatisfactory for a simple reason: agreeing practices may require some intentions to be present.

According to the mixed view, some mental states are relevant while others are not. Endicott's views are a good example of this approach. He claims that whether the parties have agreed to do A is determined by the meaning of the conduct by which the parties agreed as interpreted by a reasonable person. The only "subjective" aspect of agreement is that the parties must do intentionally what counts as entering into an agreement to do A. For instance, in Endicott's view, if X reasonably thinks that she is signing an autograph (not a form of contract), then she has not agreed to anything, even if Y, a reasonable person, would interpret her conduct otherwise, e.g. because Z arranged things so that everything looked to Y as if X was signing a contract (2000, pp. 152–53, 157, 162–63).

---

[14] Cf. Treitel (2003, p. 1) and Atiyah (1979, pp. 407–8, 731–33).

[15] Along these lines, see Goddard (1987) and Langille and Ripstein (1997).

This view is also subject to counterexamples. In some cases the "subjective" aspect that it requires may not be met. For instance, there might be (justified) agreeing practices which, while providing a remedy against Z for misleading X, stipulate that X has acquired an obligation by merely signing a form of contract, even if X reasonably thinks that she is signing an autograph, in order to enable third parties like Y to perform transactions rapidly and without bothering about X's mental states. In other cases no "objective" aspect is required. For instance, Peter acts in a way that leads his intimate friend, John, to think that he has agreed to do A, where Peter's doing A is something that both of them consider relatively unimportant. John thinks that Peter has agreed to do A because that is what a reasonable person would make of Peter's conduct. John begins to act accordingly, and when Peter notices this, he promptly claims that he had no intention to bind himself. So John apologizes, and claims that he was wrong in thinking that Peter has agreed to do A. It seems clear that Peter has not agreed to anything, so the objective aspect that the view considers indispensable is absent.

One could attempt to provide more sophisticated arguments in favour of each of these views, but the result will always be unsatisfactory. It is clear that sometimes we adopt the "objective" view, sometimes the subjective view, and sometimes the mixed view.

This remains true because agreements normally take place within the framework of on-going relationships or agreeing practices that are thought to promote certain values. These relationships and practices may require that certain acts count as agreeing to do A. They may demand that the subjective view be adopted. That is the case of the friends, where agreeing requires the presence of all the relevant mental states because the relationship as such requires that one takes into special consideration what a friend intends. The relevant practices may require that the "objective" view be adopted, as in the case of the contract signed by mistake where a remedy exists for the misled person, such that one has agreed regardless of whether all the mental states are present. In other cases, the mixed view is appropriate, as in Endicott's example.

Perhaps the best way of establishing when one has agreed to do A, where agreeing takes place within the framework of special relationships or agreeing practices, is in these terms: two individuals have agreed to do A, when agreeing takes place within the framework of special relationships or agreeing practices, when, and only when, the relevant practices, or the relevant relationships, require that their actions count as agreeing to do A. Whether they have agreed to do A in these contexts is, then, an objective question in the following sense: it depends on what the practices or relationships require, and what the practices or relationships require is something that is independent of what the parties to the alleged arrangement think in this respect. In fact, we can claim that, in these scenarios, the agreement to do A creates obligations to do A when, and only when, the relevant relationships or the agreeing practices are in effect valuable. That is, when a value is in effect promoted by the relevant relationship or practice requiring what they require.

This explains all cases, and shows that neither the "objective" view nor the subjective view nor the mixed view is correct.

4.2   Disagreement Reconsidered

Acknowledging the existence of these agreeing practices or special relationships helps explain the kind of disagreement which interests us. Notice that some of these practices have this form: two individuals have agreed to do A when their actions can reasonably be interpreted as if they intended to bind themselves to do A, regardless of whether this was their intention. A "reasonable interpretation" is an interpretation that assumes that the persons are reasonable in the context of the interaction. The contexts may vary but, typically, the interaction is nested within the framework of second-order practices which are taken to promote certain values, or within the framework of shared understandings, to the effect that certain values ought to be promoted. And these values are, normally, seen as objective, in the sense that what they amount to does not depend on what the parties think about that matter.

Consider agreements among tradesmen. There are agreeing-practices stipulating that two tradesmen have agreed to do A when they have performed certain actions that can reasonably be interpreted as if they intended to bind themselves to do A. A reasonable interpretation is one that assumes that the individuals are reasonable in the context of the interaction. And the context is normally nested within the framework of a second-order, broader commercial practice which is taken to promote values such as rapidity, security and fairness in profitable transactions. These values are normally seen as objective values. A reasonable tradesman is, then, a person who is acquainted with this second-order practice and, accordingly, he is a person who has a good grasp of how the relevant values bear on the matter. So what the agreeing practice demands is that the relevant actions be interpreted, assuming that the individuals who performed them are reasonable tradesmen, that is, individuals who have a good grasp of how the applicable values bear on the matter. To adapt the example mentioned before, if a tradesman signs a document that he had every reason to believe was a form of contract but negligently failed to acknowledge as such, everyone would understand that the first individual has bound himself to do what the document provides for, even if he did not intend to do so. Tradesmen would argue in favour of such a view by claiming that this is what the agreeing practice requires, that this is so because his actions can reasonably be interpreted as if he intended to bind himself to do what the document provides for. Other times, tradesmen disagree as to whether an agreement has been reached. Cases of mistakes, blunders, and ambiguities as to the thing agreed to are but examples. And when they disagree, they appeal to what they deem is the reasonable interpretation of the relevant actions, a disagreement that runs deep and is genuine because this depends on how the values in play (rapidity, security, and fairness), which are seen as objective and sometimes are in conflict, bear on the matter.

In short, when this sort of agreeing practices appear, participants may have agreed and still have a genuine disagreement about their duties.

Let us come back to the case of the pro bono lawyers. Assume that their providing legal advice (their collective action) is structured by an agreement, and that this agreement has been reached within the framework of an agreeing-practice of the sort considered, i.e. a practice according to which two or more individuals have agreed to do A when their actions can reasonably be interpreted as if they intended to bind themselves to do A. A reasonable interpretation is one that assumes that they are reasonable persons in the context. And the context of the interaction is, let us assume, a second-order shared understanding: free legal advice is necessary to promote fairness and equality in their local community.

It seems clear that there could be a genuine disagreement about whether they have agreed to provide advice to individuals only or to individuals and organizations. Which actions they have agreed to perform depends on what the agreeing-practice requires. Some of them think that it requires that the relevant actions count as having agreed to provide advice to individuals only. In their view, the relevant actions can reasonably be interpreted as if they intended to bind themselves to that. Put otherwise, they claim that the relevant actions can be seen, assuming that they were acting as reasonable individuals at the time the interaction took place (i.e. assuming that they had a good grasp of how the applicable values bore in the context), as if they intended to bind themselves to provide advice to individuals only. For, as they see it, fairness and equality require that free legal advice be provided only to persons without economic resources, as happens with individuals in their local community. And some of them might think that the practice requires that the relevant actions count as having agreed to provide advice to organizations too. For, in their view, fairness and equality require that free legal advice be provided to anyone who faces a legal problem regardless of its economic capacity. And they can significantly disagree about this matter, as it is an objective matter in the sense described.

The foregoing remarks are sufficient to show, I hope, that some normative relations among members of GNUs can be explained by the idea of an agreement to do one's part of a joint act, and that this is compatible with the presence of disagreement about duties.

5   Conclusion

Normative relations among members of groups appear for a variety of reasons. However, there is a tendency in the literature to ignore this variety. That is, there is a tendency to appeal to only one particular normative notion that (allegedly) gives rise to duties that are independent of the value of the joint action. This ignores that members, in some cases, think that they are under a duty precisely because of the value of the joint action. It also ignores that, in other cases, they think that they are under a duty because content-independent normative considerations (principles not related to the value of the joint action, such as the principle that agreements should be kept, or that authorities should be obeyed) are deemed applicable. It is plausible to claim, nevertheless, that most groups are structured by agreements. And the fact that participants often disagree about the content of their duties should not be considered an objection. Normally, agreements take place within the framework of agreeing practices, and some of these practices leave room for this possibility: one might have agreed to do something even if not fully aware of what obligation one has acquired, as this is an objective issue over which participants may disagree.

References

Atiyah, P. 1979. *The Rise and Fall of Freedom of Contract*. Oxford: Clarendon Press.

Bratman, M. 1999. *Faces of intention*. Cambridge: Cambridge University Press.

Endicott, T. 2000. Objectivity, subjectivity and incomplete agreements. In *Oxford essays in jurisprudence* (152), ed. J. Horder, 151–171. Oxford: Oxford University Press.

Gilbert, M. 1996. *Living together: Rationality, sociality and obligation*. Lanham: Rowman and Littlefield.

Gilbert, M. 2002a. Considerations on joint commitment: Responses to various comments. In *Social facts and collective intentionality*, vol. 73, ed. G. Meggle, 73–101. Frankfurt: Dr. Hansel-Hohenhausen AG.

Gilbert, M. 2002b. Acting together. In *Social facts and collective intentionality*, vol. 73, ed. G. Meggle, 53–71. Frankfurt: Dr. Hansel-Hohenhausen AG.

Goddard, D. 1987. The myth of subjectivity. *Legal Studies* 7(3): 263–278.

Kutz, C. 2000. *Complicity*. Cambridge: Cambridge University Press.

Langille, B., and A. Ripstein. 1997. Strictly speaking—It went without saying. *Legal Theory* 2(1): 63–81.

Raz, J. 1972. Voluntary obligations and normative powers. *Proceedings of the Aristotelian Society* 46: 59–102.

Raz, J. 1986. *The morality of freedom*. Oxford: Clarendon.

Sánchez Brigido, R. 2010. *Groups, rules and legal practice*. Dordrecht/Heidelberg/London/New York: Springer.

Treitel, G. 2003. *The Law of Contract* (11th ed.). Londo: Sweet & Maxwell.

Tuomela, R. 1995. *The importance of us*. Stanford: Stanford University Press.

Chapter 7
Joint Actions, Social Institutions and Collective Goods: A Teleological Account

Seumas Miller

Abstract Social institutions are complex social forms that reproduce themselves such as governments, police organizations, universities, hospitals, business corporations, markets, legal systems. Moreover, social institutions are among the most important of collective human phenomena; they enable us to feed ourselves (markets and agribusinesses), to protect ourselves (police and military services), to educate ourselves (schools and universities), and to govern ourselves (governments and legal systems).

Sometimes the term institution is used to refer to complex social forms that are arguably not organizations such as human languages or kinship systems. However, my concern is only with institutions that are also organizations and/or systems of organizations.

In this chapter I will offer a teleological normative theory of social institutions which is based on an individualist theory of joint action (Much of the content in this chapter is a highly condensed version of parts of Miller (The moral foundations of social institutions: a philosophical study. New York: Cambridge University Press, 2010)). Put simply, on this account social institutions are organizations or systems of organizations that provide collective goods by means of joint activity. The collective goods in question include the fulfilment of aggregated moral rights, such as needs based rights for security (police organizations), material well-being (businesses operating in markets), education (universities), governance (governments) and so on.

S. Miller (✉)
Centre for Applied Philosophy and Public Ethics, Charles Sturt University,
Canberra, Australia

3TU Centre for Ethics and Technology, Delft University of Technology,
The Hague, The Netherlands
e-mail: semiller@csu.edu.au

A. Konzelmann Ziv and H.B. Schmid (eds.), *Institutions, Emotions, and Group Agents*,   99
Studies in the Philosophy of Sociality 2, DOI 10.1007/978-94-007-6934-2_7,
© Springer Science+Business Media Dordrecht 2014

1 Joint Actions

The central concept in the teleological account of social institutions is that of *joint action*. Joint actions are actions involving a number of agents performing interdependent actions in order to realize some common goal. Examples of joint action are: two people dancing together, a number of tradesmen building a house, and a group of robbers burgling a house. Joint action is to be distinguished from individual action on the one hand, and from the 'actions' of corporate bodies on the other. Thus an individual walking down the road or shooting at a target are instances of individual action. A nation declaring war or a government taking legal action against a public company are instances of *corporate* action. In so far as such corporate 'actions' are genuine actions involving mental states such as intentions and beliefs then they are, in my view, reducible to the individual and joint actions of human beings.

Over the last decade or two a number of analyses of joint action have emerged. These analyses can be located on a spectrum at one end of which there is so-called (by Frederick Schmitt (2003)) strict individualism, and at the other end of which there is so-called (again by Schmitt (2003)) supra-individualism.

A number of these theorists have developed and applied their favored basic accounts of joint action in order to account for a range of social phenomena, including conventions, social norms and social institutions. One such theory is my Collective End Theory (CET) elaborated elsewhere (Miller 2001, ch. 2, 2010, ch. 1). CET is a form of individualism. I will use it throughout this chapter, although other closely related individualist theories of joint action might also suffice for my purposes here.

Individualism, as I see it, is committed to an analysis of joint action such that ultimately a joint action consists of: (1) a number of singular actions; (2) relations between these singular actions. Moreover, the constitutive attitudes involved in joint actions are individual attitudes; there are no *sui generis* we-intentions and other like we-attitudes. Here it is important to stress that individualism can be, and in the case of CET certainly is, a form of relationalism. It is relational in two senses. First, as mentioned above, singular actions often stand in relations to one another, e.g., two partners dancing, and the joint action in part consisting of the singular actions, also in part consists of the relations between the singular actions. Second, the agents who perform joint actions can have inter-subjective attitudes to one another, e.g., they mutually recognize who one another is; and some (but not all) of these attitudes are *sui generis*. Specifically, some *cognitive* (but not conative) inter-subjective attitudes may well be *sui generis*, e.g. mutual consciousness of one another's consciousness (Eitan et al. 2005, ch. 14). In virtue of such inter-subjective attitudes they will also typically have interpersonal relations to one another. Inter-subjectivity and interpersonal relations in this sense are not necessarily, or at least are not by definition, social or institutional. To suggest otherwise would be to beg the question against individualism (specifically, relational individualism) in any interesting sense of the term.

By contrast, according to supra-individualists when a plurality of individual agents perform a joint action the agents necessarily have the relevant propositional attitudes (beliefs, intentions, etc.) in an irreducible "we-form" which is *sui generis*, and as such not analyzable in terms of individual or I-attitudes. Moreover, the individual agents constitute a new entity, a supra-individual entity not reducible to the individual agents and the relations between them.

Basically CET is the theory that joint actions are actions directed to the realization of a collective end. However this notion of a collective end is a construction out of the prior notion of an individual end. A collective end is an individual end more than one agent has, and which is such that, if it is realized, it is realized by all, or most, of the actions of the agents involved; the individual action of any given agent is only part of the means by which the end is realized, and each individual action is interdependent with the others in the service of the collective end. Thus when one person dials the phone number of another person, and the second person picks up the receiver then each has performed an action in the service of a collective end: a collective end that each has, namely, that they communicate with each other.

On the basis of this individualist notion of a joint action, a number of social notions can be constructed including the notion of a convention. A convention can be understood as being in essence a set of joint actions each of which is performed in a recurring situation (Miller 2001, ch. 3). Thus driving on the right hand side of the road is a convention that each of us adheres to in order to realize a collective end, namely, to avoid collisions. Another social action notion which can be derived from our notion of a joint action and which is crucial to our understanding of social institutions is that of organizational action.

2 Organizational Action

Organizations consist of an (embodied) formal *structure* of interlocking roles (Miller 2001, ch. 5, 2010, ch. 1). An organizational role can be defined in terms of the agent (whoever it is) who performs certain tasks, the tasks themselves, procedures (in the above sense) and conventions. Moreover, unlike social groups, organizations are individuated by the kind of activity that they undertake, and also by their characteristic *ends*. So we have governments, universities, business corporations, armies, and so on. Perhaps governments have as an end or goal the ordering and leading of societies, universities the end of discovering and disseminating knowledge, and so on. Here it is important to emphasize that these ends are, firstly, collective ends and, secondly, often the latent and/or implicit (collective) ends of individual institutional actors.

A further defining feature of organizations is that organizational action typically consists in, what can be termed, a *multi-layered structure of joint actions* (Miller 2001, pp. 173f., 2010, p. 48). One illustration of the notion of a layered structure of joint actions is an armed force fighting a battle. Suppose at an organizational level a number of joint actions ('actions') are severally necessary and jointly sufficient to achieve some collective end. Thus the 'action' of the mortar squad destroying enemy gun emplacements, the 'action' of the flight of military planes providing air cover, and the 'action' of the infantry platoon taking and holding the ground might be severally necessary and jointly sufficient to achieve the collective end of defeating the enemy; as such, these 'actions' taken together constitute a joint action. Call each of these 'actions' level two 'actions', and the joint action that they constitute a level two joint action. From the perspective of the collective end of defeating the enemy, each of these level two 'actions' is an individual action that is a component of a (level two) joint action: the joint action directed to the collective end of defeating the enemy.

However, each of these level two 'actions' is already in itself a joint action with component individual actions; and these component individual actions are severally necessary (let us assume this for purposes of simplification, albeit it is unlikely that every single action would in fact be necessary) and jointly sufficient for the performance of some collective end. Thus the individual members of the mortar squad jointly operate the mortar in order to realize the collective end of destroying enemy gun emplacements. Each pilot, jointly with the other pilots, strafes enemy soldiers in order to realize the collective end of providing air cover for their advancing foot soldiers. Further, the set of foot soldiers jointly advance in order to take and hold the ground vacated by the members of the retreating enemy force.

At level one there are individual actions directed to three distinct collective ends: the collective ends of (respectively) destroying gun emplacements, providing air cover, and talking and holding ground. So at level one there are three joint actions, namely, the members of the mortar squad destroying gun emplacements, the members of the flight of planes providing air cover, and the members of the infantry taking and holding ground. However, taken together these three joint actions constitute a single level two joint action. The collective end of this level two joint action is to defeat the enemy; and from the perspective of this level two joint action, and its collective end, these constitutive actions are (level two) individual actions.

It is important to note that on this (stipulative) definition of organizations they are, *qua organizations*, non-normative entities (other than in the minimal sense in which an end is normative because successful or unsuccessful, or a belief is normative because true or false). In this respect they are analogous to conventions, as we have defined conventions above. So being an organization is not of itself something that is ethically good or bad, any more than being a convention is in itself ethically good or bad. This can be consistently held while maintaining that organizations, as well as conventions, are a pervasive and necessary feature of human life, being indispensable instruments for realizing collective ends. Collective ends are a species of individual end; but merely being an end is in itself neither morally good nor morally bad, any more than being an intention or a belief are in themselves morally good or morally bad.

While this definition of an organization does not include any reference to a normative dimension, most organizations do as a matter of contingent fact possess a normative dimension. As was the case with conventions, this normative dimension will be possessed (especially, though not exclusively) by virtue of the particular moral/immoral ends (goods) that an organization serves, as well as by virtue of the particular moral (or immoral) activities that it undertakes.

Further, most organizations possess a normative dimension by virtue (in part) of the *social norms* governing the constitutive organizational roles (Miller 2001, ch. 4). More specifically, most organizations consist of a hierarchical role structure in which the tasks and procedures that define the individual roles are governed by norms; and in hierarchical organizations some of these norms govern the relations of authority and power within the organization. It is not simply that an employee in fact undertakes a particular set of tasks, or tends to comply with the directives of his employer. Rather the employee undertakes those tasks, and obeys the directives of his employer, by virtue of the social and other norms governing the employee's (and employer's) roles, and the relations of authority and power that exist between these roles.

Organizations with the above detailed normative dimension are *social institutions* (Giddens 1984; Parsons 1982). So—and as already noted—institutions are often organizations, and many systems of organizations are also institutions.

3 Joint Mechanisms

A feature of many social institutions, whether they be of the organizational or non-organizational variety, is their use of what I will refer to as *joint mechanisms* (Miller 2001, pp. 174 f., 2010, pp. 50f.). Examples of joint mechanisms are the device of tossing a coin to resolve a dispute, voting to elect a candidate to political office, use of money as a medium of exchange and, more generally, exchange systems such as markets for goods and services. Importantly, from my theoretical perspective, action in accordance with joint mechanisms—like organizational action—can be understood as derivable from the prior notion of a joint action.

Joint mechanisms consist of: (a) a complex of differentiated but interlocking actions (the input to the mechanism); (b) the result of the performance of those actions (the output of the mechanism); and (c) the mechanism itself. Thus a given agent might vote for a candidate. He will do so only if others also vote. But further to this, there is the action of the candidates, namely, that they present themselves as candidates. That they present themselves as candidates is (in part) constitutive of the input to the voting mechanism. Voters vote *for candidates*. So there is interlocking and differentiated action (the input). Further there is some result (as opposed to consequence) of the joint action; the joint action consisting of the actions of putting oneself forward as a candidate and of the actions of voting. The result is that some candidate, say, Barack Obama, is voted in (the output). That there is a result is (in part) constitutive of the mechanism. That to receive the most number of votes is to be voted in, is (in part) constitutive of the voting mechanism. Moreover, that Obama is voted in is not a collective end of all the voters. (Although it is a collective end of those who voted for Obama.) However, that the one who gets the most votes—whoever that happens to be—is voted in is a collective end of all the voters, including those who voted for some candidate other than Obama.

Money, markets and other systems of exchange are also a species of joint mechanism. Such exchange systems coordinate numerous participants seeking to exchange one thing for another thing, and to do so on a recurring basis with multiple other participants. For participants A, B, C, D etc. and exchangeable token things w, x, y, z etc. (possessed by A, B, C, D etc., respectively), the individual end of each participant, say A, on any single instance of a recurring exchange enabling situation, e.g. a marketplace, is to exchange w for something (x or y or z etc.) possessed by B or C or D etc.; similarly for B, C, D etc. Moreover, on any such occasion at, or near, the point of exchange two participants, say A and B, will have a collective end; thus A and B each has the collective end that A and B exchange w and x on this occasion. Here the realization of the collective end constitutes a joint action; however, it is a joint action—and its constitutive collective end—in the service of the individual end of each participant.

The set of realized collective ends of these (coordinated) single joint actions of exchange constitutes the output of the joint mechanism, i.e. that A exchanges w for x with B, C exchanges y for z with D, and so on. Naturally, the *particular* configuration of joint actions (individual exchanges) that results on some occasion of the recurring situation is not aimed at by anyone, e.g. it is not a collective end of A or B that C and D exchange y and z. However, that there be *some* coordinated set of exchanges is the point or collective end of the system; certainly the regulators and designers of the system have or had this as a collective end, and even the participants all have this as a collective end, even if unconsciously. The latter point is evidenced by attempts on the part of participants to remedy defects or problems with the system, for example, by communicating to all participants any change in the location of the points of exchange.

Since the occasions for exchange are instances of a recurring situation, each participant has a *standing* individual end with respect to a single open-ended set of future recurring such occasions for exchange, i.e. that on each of these occasions s/he, (say, A), will make such an exchange of some relevant thing with B or C etc. Likewise, each of the participants has a *standing* collective end with respect to a single open-ended set of associated future joint actions of exchange of some relevant thing with B or C etc. Finally, each of the participants has a standing collective end with respect to a single open-ended *set of sets of coordinated multiple* future joint actions of exchange, i.e. each has a collective end with respect to the results of the future workings joint mechanism, namely, that there be on each future occasion of the recurring situation some coordinated configuration of joint actions of exchange.

Note that an exchange system is institutionalized when it is 'regulated' by social norms—and typically by enforceable formal regulations and laws—as a consequence of its constitutive joint actions and/or collective ends having moral significance. This might be as a result of competition between participants for scarce items that provide benefits to their possessors, e.g. social norms of fair competition, promises to hand over the scarce item at the jointly decided exchange rate.

4   Acting *qua* Member of a Group/*qua* Occupant of an Institutional Role

Some theorists, such as John Searle (1995) and Margaret Gilbert (1989) have suggested that actions performed by individuals *qua* members of a group and (relatedly) *qua* occupants of an institutional role constitute a problem for individualist accounts. In any case the notion of acting qua member of an institutional role is central to understanding institutional action (Miller 2001, pp. 204f., 2010, pp. 52f.).

The notion of acting qua member of a group is often quite straightforward since the group can be defined in part in terms of the collective end or ends which the group of individuals is pursuing. Here I am assuming that the members of the group are engaged in interdependent action in the service of this collective end, as described above. Individual agents or numerically different collections of agents who each aim at some common outcome do not necessarily have a collective end in my sense; specifically, there is not necessarily interdependence of action in relation to the aimed-at outcome.

Consider a group of individuals building a house. Person A is building a wall, person B the roof, person C the foundations, and so on. To say of person A that he is acting *qua* member of this group is in large part to say that his action of building the wall is an action directed toward the collective end that he and the other members of the group are seeking to realize, namely a built house.

Notice that the same set of individuals could be engaged in different collective projects. Suppose persons A, B, C, etc. in our above example are not only engaged in building a house but also—during their holidays—in building a sailing boat. Assume that A is building the masts, B the cabin, C the bow, and so on. To say of A that he is acting *qua* member of this group is just to say that his action of building the masts is an action directed toward the collective end that he and the other members of the group are seeking to realize, namely a built boat. Accordingly, one and the same person, A, is acting both as a member of the "house building group" (G1) and as a member of the "boat building group" (G2). Indeed, since A, B, C, etc. are all and only the members of each of these two groups, the membership of G1 is identical with the membership of G2.

Moreover, when A is building the wall he is acting *qua* member of G1, and when he is building the mast he is acting *qua* member of G2. But this phenomenon of one agent acting as a member of different groups in no way undermines individualism. Indeed, CET is able to illuminate this phenomenon as follows. For A to be acting *qua* member of G1 is for A to be pursuing—jointly with B, C, etc.—the collective end of building the house; for A to be acting *qua* member of G2 is for A to be pursuing—jointly with B, C, etc.—the collective end of building the boat.

Further, let us suppose that G1 and G2 each have to create and comply with a budget; G1 has a budget for the house and G2 has a budget for the boat. The members of G1 and G2 know that they must buy materials for the house and the boat (respectively) and do so within the respective budgets. Assume that A, B, C, etc. allocate $50,000 to pay for bricks for the house. This is a joint action. Moreover, this joint action is one that A, B, C, etc. have performed *qua* members of G1. G1 is individuated by recourse to the collective end of building the house, and the proximate (collective) end of buying bricks is tied to that group, G1, and to its ultimate end of building a house. Accordingly, A, B, C, etc. are not in buying the bricks acting *qua* members of G2. For G2 is individuated by the collective end of building a boat, and A, B, C, etc. do not *qua* members of G2 have any plans to build their boat from bricks!

Thus far we have focused on the notion of acting *qua* member of a group in the sense of a mere set of individuals engaged in joint activity. However, there are other related but more structured collectives whose members act qua members of the collective in question. Specifically, there are social groups and institutions.

The notion of a social group is somewhat opaque but it is certainly more than a mere collection of agents who have a collective end. For example, social groups typically conform to a shared set of conventions and social norms (Miller 2001, ch. 6). Accordingly, the notion of acting qua member of a social group consists in more than simply acting in accordance with a collective end; it also consists in compliance with conventions and social norms. However, acting in accordance with a collective end (or collective ends) is a necessary condition for acting qua member of a social group; indeed, it is the central necessary condition.

Given this distinction between mere groups and social groups, it is evident that some members of a group might be members of a given social group, while others might not be. Accordingly, two members of a group might have the same collective end but not be acting qua members of a social group (e.g. two voters who vote for Obama but come from different social groups). And the same point can be made in relation to other collectivities, such as institutions, e.g. two friends contributing to the building of a house who are not doing so as members of any organization or institution.

Here the notion of acting *qua* occupant of an institutional role is simply that of performing the tasks definitive of the institutional role (including the joint tasks), conforming to the conventions and regulations that constrain the tasks to be undertaken, and pursuing the purposes or ends of the role (including the collective ends).

Note the relevance here of the above-introduced notion of a *layered structure of joint actions*. As described above, a layered structure of joint actions is a set of joint actions each of which is directed to a further collective end; so it is a macro-joint action comprised of a set of constituent micro joint actions. This account of a layered structure of joint actions can be supplemented by recourse to concepts of conventions, social norms and the like, and especially by recourse to the explicitly normative notions of rights, obligations and duties that are attached to, and in part definitive of, many organizational roles. It is not simply that organizational role occupants *regularly* jointly act in certain ways in preference to others, or in preference to acting entirely individualistically; rather they have institutional duties to so act and—in the case of hierarchical organizations—institutional rights to instruct others to act in certain ways.

At any rate, the point to be made here is that my account of the notion of acting *qua* member of a group in terms of acting in accordance with collective ends can be, and should be, complicated and supplemented by the normative notions of rights and duties in order to accommodate various different kinds of acting *qua* member of an organized group, including acting in hierarchical roles such as that of President of the U.S., for example. So role occupants such as Barack Obama take on the tasks definitive of the role. More specifically, they take on the institutional rights and duties definitive of the role, and some of these institutional rights and duties are also moral rights and obligations. Accordingly, it makes sense to say of Obama that he has this and that moral obligation *qua* President but not necessarily *qua* husband or father.

5   The Varieties of Social Institution

Self-evidently, social institutions have a multifaceted ethico-normative dimension, including a moral dimension. Moral categories that are deeply implicated in social institutions include: human rights and duties, contract-based rights and obligations and, importantly I suggest, rights and duties derived from the production and 'consumption' of collective goods.

Collective goods of the kind I have in mind have three properties: (1) they are produced, maintained or renewed by means of the *joint activity* of members of organizations or systems of organizations, i.e. by institutional actors; (2) they are *available to the whole community* (at least in principle), and; (3) they *ought* to be produced (or maintained or renewed) and made available to the whole community since they are desirable goods and ones to which the members of the community have an (institutional) *joint moral right*.

Such goods are ones that are desirable in the sense that they ought to be desired (objectively speaking), as opposed to simply being desired; moreover, they are either intrinsic goods (good in themselves), or the means to intrinsic goods. They include, but are not restricted to, goods in respect of which there is an institutionally prior moral right, e.g. security.

Note that the scope of a community is relativized to a social institution (or set of interdependent social institutions). Roughly, a community consists in the members of an organization; those who jointly produced a collective good and/or who have a joint right to that good. In the case of the meta institution, government, the community will consist in all those who are members of any of the social institutions that are coordinated and otherwise directed by the relevant government. So the citizens of a nation-state will count as a community on this account.

Roughly speaking, on my account, aggregated needs-based rights, aggregated non-needs-based human rights and other desirable goods generate collective moral responsibilities which provide the ethico-normative basis for institutions, e.g. business organizations in competitive markets, welfare institutions, police organizations, universities etc., which fulfill those rights.

For example, the aggregate need for food generates a collective moral responsibility to establish and maintain social institutions, such as agribusinesses, the members of which jointly produce foodstuffs; once the relevant institutions are established, then the needy have a joint moral right, and ought to have a joint institutional right, to the food products in question. Accordingly, the needy have a right to buy the food products (they cannot be excluded from purchasing them) or, if they are unable to do so, then the products ought to be provided to the needy free of charge.

I note that in modern economies there is a derived moral right to paid work, i.e. a right to a job (some job or other), since (other things being equal) without a job one cannot provide for one's basic needs (and one's family's needs) and one cannot contribute to the production, maintenance and renewal of collective goods, e.g. via taxes. Naturally, if no paid job can be made available to some person or group then they have no moral right to one, but if so then (other things being equal) they will have a moral right to welfare.

I also note that some quite fundamental moral rights, values and principles are logically prior to social institutions; or, to be more precise, logically prior to social institutions that are also organizations, or systems of organizations. Basic human rights, such as the right to life, the right not to be tortured, and the right not to be incarcerated are logically prior to social institutions. A further important set of right that are in some cases, at least, logically prior to social institutions are needs-based rights to water, food and shelter. There are, of course, other needs-based rights that are not logically prior to social institutions, e.g. the need of a business actor for an accountant or of an alleged offender for a lawyer.

Many of these basic human rights provide the *raison d'être* (by our lights, collective end) for a number of social institutions. Consider, for example, police institutions. The police role consists in large part in protecting persons from being deprived of their human rights to life, bodily security, liberty and so on; they do so by the use, or threatened use, of coercive force.

Now consider business organizations operating in competitive markets. Many business organizations do not have the protection of human rights or the fulfillment of needs-based rights as a primary purpose; nor should they. On the other hand, human rights are an important *side constraint* on business activity.

5.1   Institutional Moral Rights

Notwithstanding that human rights and some other moral phenomena are logically prior to social institutions, many moral rights, duties, values, principles and so on are *not* logically prior to social institutions. Consider in this connection the moral right to vote, the moral right to a fair trial, the right to buy and sell land, and the moral right to a paid job; the first right presupposes institutions of government of a certain kind (democratic government), the second criminal justice institutions of a certain kind (e.g. courts of law that adjudicate alleged crimes), and third and fourth economic institutions of a certain kind. Let us refer to such institution-dependent moral rights as "institutional moral rights" (as opposed to natural moral rights).

Evidently, institutional moral rights depend in part on rights-generating properties possessed by human beings *qua* human beings, but also in part on membership of a community or of a morally legitimate institution, or occupancy of a morally legitimate institutional role.

Such institutional moral rights and duties include ones that are: (a) derived at least in part from collective goods and; (b) constitutive of specific institutional roles, e.g. the rights and duties of a fire officer. They also include moral rights and duties that attach to all members of a community because they are dependent on institutions in which all members of the community participate, e.g. the duty to obey the law of the land, the duty to contribute to one's country's national defense in time of war, the right to vote, the right of access to paid employment in some economy, the right to own land in some territory, the right to freely buy and sell goods in some economy. These moral rights and duties are institutionally relative in the following sense.

Even if they are in part based on an institutionally prior human right, (e.g. a basic human need, the right to freedom), their precise content, strength, context of application (e.g. jurisdiction) and so on can only be determined by reference to the institutional arrangements in which they exist and, specifically, in the light of their contribution to the collective good(s) provided by those institutional arrangements. So, for example, a property regime, if it is to be morally acceptable, must not only reward the producers of goods, e.g. by protecting the ownership rights of the producers of goods to the goods that they produce (e.g. would-be consumers cannot steal their goods), it must also ensure that consumers are benefited and not harmed (e.g. producers are required to meet health and safety standards). More particularly, a property regime, if it is to be morally acceptable, must satisfy the requirements of institutionally prior human rights; specifically, it must ensure that the needs-based rights of consumers are fulfilled (e.g. producers are required to compete under conditions of fair competition, or are otherwise constrained, to ensure that their products are available at prices the needy can afford).

We need to make a further distinction between: (a) institutional moral rights; and (b) institutional rights that are not moral rights. The right to vote and the right to stand for office embody the human right to autonomy in the institutional setting of the state; hence to make a law to exclude certain people from having a vote or standing for office, as happened in apartheid South Africa, is to violate a moral right. But the right to make the next move in a game of chess, or to move a pawn one space forward, but not (say) three spaces sideways, is entirely dependent on the rules of chess. In other words, these rights that chess players have are *mere* institutional rights; they depend entirely on the rules of the 'institution' of the game of chess (Searle 1995). Likewise, (legally enshrined) parking rights, such as reserved spaces and 1 h parking spaces in universities are *mere* institutional rights, as opposed to institutional *moral* rights.

I will now consider in more detail the moral rights and collective goods that underpin social institutions.

6 Joint Rights

As outlined above, social institutions involve the production of collective goods by means of the joint activity of members of organizations. In the case of any given institution there is a collective moral responsibility to produce the collective good in question and there is a joint moral right of access to that good once it is produced. In many instances the collective moral responsibility to produce the collective good is based on an aggregate of individual moral rights, including basic needs-based rights. However, it is only when a certain threshold of aggregate of actual or potential aggregated rights violations (or otherwise unrealized rights) exists that the establishment of an institution takes place; agribusinesses or welfare institutions, for example, are not established because a single person's need for food has not been realized. Only when such a threshold aggregate of unrealized rights exists does the collective moral responsibility arise to engage in joint activity in order to realize the rights in question.

As discussed, a key notion in my account of social institutions is that of a joint moral right (Miller 2001, ch. 7). It will turn out that not only are there joint rights to collective goods once they are produced, but also, at least in some cases, joint rights which provide the grounds for the 'production' of those goods in the first instance.

Let me now consider one way in which certain human rights, notably the individual human right to autonomy (Griffin 2008), can underpin social institutions and constitute collective goods. In the kind of case I have in mind human rights underpin social institutions via joint moral rights, and do so in a particular way. Let me explain.

Consider the right to political secession. Arguably, the Kurds in Iraq have a right to secede. But, if this is a right, it is not a right that some Kurdish person has as an individual. After all, an individual person cannot secede. The right of the Kurds to secede—if it exists—is a right which attaches to the individual members of the Kurdish social group, but does so jointly. Similarly, the related right of the Kurds to exclude others from their territory, if it exists, is a joint right; some Kurdish person acting as an individual does not have a right to exclude, for example, would-be immigrants.

Now consider the right to political participation. Each Canadian citizen has a moral right to participate in political institutions in Canada; non-Canadians do not have a right to such political participation in Canada. Moreover, the right to political participation of each Canadian is dependent on the possession of the right to political participation in Canada of all the other Canadians; Canadians have a joint moral right.

Such joint rights need to be distinguished from universal individual human rights. Take the right to life as an example of a universal individual human right. Each human being has an individual human right to life. However, since one's possession of the right to life is wholly dependent on properties one possesses as an individual, it is not the case that one's possession of the right to life is dependent on someone else's possession of that right.

Notice that joint rights can be based in part on properties individuals possess as individuals. The right to participate in political institutions is based in part on membership of a political and legal community, and in part on possession of the individual human right of autonomy.

Consider the right to vote. This is an individual, institutional moral right. Nevertheless, it is based in part on the prior individual human right to autonomy. In a social or political setting requiring collective or joint decision-making this individual human right is transformed into an individual institutional moral right to vote via a joint right: the joint right to political participation. Indeed, properly speaking, the individual institutional moral right to vote is itself a joint right; each only has a right to vote if each of one's fellow *bona fide* members of the political community in question likewise has a right to vote.

Here there are four related points to be made. First, the institution, (say) representative government, is not directly based on an aggregate of individual human rights, but rather directly on a joint moral right; a joint moral right that is in turn in part based on the individual human right of autonomy. (Note that while many joint moral rights are institutional rights, many are not, e.g. the natural joint right of non-institutionally based producers to their product.) Second, the exercise of the joint right of political participation is an end in itself; it is not simply a means to some further end (although in fact it is also a means to other ends). Third, the exercise of the joint right to political participation is a collective end; it is an end that is realized by the actions of many, and not by one person acting alone. Finally, it is a collective end that morally ought to be realized (by virtue of being the fulfillment of moral rights), and that is enjoyed in being realized; so it is a collective good.

In fact the institution of representative government is grounded in a number of collective goods. Representative government not only has as a collective end to embody, or give expression to, the joint right to political participation, but also to provide various other collective goods, e.g. the coordination and regulation of other social institutions (the education system, the health system, the criminal justice system, the financial system etc.) to ensure that they realize their (respective) collective ends.

In short, political participation is joint activity that morally ought to be performed. Moreover, it is joint activity that is constitutive, both of the collective end-in-itself that it serves, and of the collective good that it is; the producers are the consumers, so to speak. In this respect political institutions differ from, say, welfare institutions. The latter institutions are instruments in the service of prior needs-based rights, rather than an expression or embodiment of those rights. Accordingly, the producers are not necessarily the consumers.

7   Aggregated Moral Rights, Joint Rights, and Collective Goods

Let me now explain how it is that the realization of aggregated needs-based rights, and of other aggregated moral rights, are collective goods in my sense, i.e. jointly produced (or maintained or renewed) goods that ought to be produced (or maintained or renewed), and that are, and ought to be, made available to the whole community since they are desirable goods and ones to which the members of the community have a joint moral right (Miller 2010, ch. 2).

As one might expect of something claimed to be a collective good, the fulfillment of aggregated rights is not something that is available to only one person. Of course, the fact that it is *aggregated* rights that are in question makes this trivially true. Moreover, since it is moral rights that are in question then each and every rights-bearer ought to have available to them the good to which he or she has a right; hence the good ought to be made available to the whole community.

However, the enjoyment of rights is typically thought to be an individual affair; and indeed in many respects it is. If, for example, my right to individual freedom is fulfilled then I enjoy the exercise of *my* right and no-one else enjoys the exercise of *my* right (even if they enjoy the exercise of their own). It is also true that the exercise of my right to freedom (at least in part—see below) is logically consistent with the inability of others to exercise their respective rights to freedom, e.g. if I am Robinson Crusoe and everyone else lives in an authoritarian state.

It is, of course, a commonplace of political philosophy, that the establishment of government and the rule of law is instrumentally necessary for the preservation of the freedom of each of us, albeit under the restriction not unduly to interfere with others; the alternative, as Hobbes famously said, is the state of nature in which life is nasty, brutish and short. However, I want to make a somewhat different point; there is another reason that most of us rely on the fulfillment of the rights to freedom of others in order to enjoy adequately our own freedom.

Specifically, I cannot engage in freely performed *joint* activity with others if they cannot exercise their rights to freedom. Here, the property of being free qualifies the joint activity per se, and not simply the individual action of each considered independently of its contribution to the collective end which is constitutive of that joint activity. Accordingly, a joint action is a freely performed joint action if and only if each freely performed their contributory action qua contributory action.

For example, I cannot freely participate in an election, unless others can also freely do so. Of course, I could freely cast a vote in an election in which all the other votes were cast in accordance with (say) the instructions of the dictator of my country. However, such an arrangement is a pseudo-election. It defeats the point of an election which is to provide a mechanism for participants to jointly arrive at a result which is acceptable to all—even if not voted for by all—because each participant has had his/her say but none on his/her own can guarantee any particular result. Accordingly, if there are to be elections, as opposed to pseudo-elections, then they will be free (and fair) elections. Moreover, whether or not I can vote, and do so freely, is dependent not only on whether others can vote—elections are a form of joint activity—but on whether others can do so freely. So one person's freedom to vote is dependent on the freedom to vote of others.

Again, I cannot freely engage in a market, unless others can do likewise. Of course I could freely offer goods for exchange under a regimented arrangement in which all other participants are required by law to exchange their goods with one another according to some pre-determined configuration, but in which I alone can exchange my goods for whatever goods I unilaterally determine. However, such an arrangement is a pseudo-market. It defeats the point of a market which is to provide an efficient and effective means to coordinate numerous participants seeking to make freely chosen exchanges. Under such an arrangement there are no freely chosen exchanges. Even the exchanges which I make are not freely performed *exchanges*. They are not freely performed exchanges since one party in the exchange is not acting freely. Here an exchange is to be understood as a joint action in which the participants A and B have as a collective end that x be exchanged for y. Accordingly, if there are to be markets, as opposed to pseudo-markets, then they will be free markets. Moreover, whether or not I can exchange my goods, and do so freely, is dependent not only on whether others can exchange their goods—markets are a form of joint activity—but on whether others can do so freely. So one person's freedom to exchange goods is dependent on the freedom to exchange goods of other persons.

So much for aggregated moral rights to freedom. What of aggregated needs-based rights—the right to basic foodstuffs and shelter, for example? In modern economies these aggregated needs are fulfilled by means of joint activity, e.g. by business organizations in competitive markets. So these morally required goods, i.e. fulfilled (aggregated) needs-based rights, are *jointly produced*; so they meet this defining condition for being collective good. What of their enjoyment? In what further respects, if any, does the enjoyment of aggregated needs-based rights meet the defining conditions for being a collective good?

As we saw in the case with aggregated rights to freedom, the fact that the fulfilled needs-based rights in question are *aggregated* makes it trivially true that the members of the community in general enjoy these rights. Likewise, since it is moral rights that are in question then each and every rights-bearer ought to have available to them the good to which he or she has a right. Again, if my right to basic foodstuffs is fulfilled then I enjoy the exercise of *my* right and only I enjoy the exercise of *my* right (even if others also enjoy the exercise of theirs). It is also true that the exercise of my needs-based rights to basic foodstuffs, shelter and so on is logically consistent with the inability of others to exercise their respective rights to these goods, e.g. if I am a successful subsistence farmer, but one living in a failed state in which many are starving. Moreover, others can exercise their needs-based rights without me doing so, e.g. if the needed goods are only available in a market and I cannot afford to pay for them while others can.

Nevertheless, each of us, albeit indirectly, relies on the fulfillment of the needs-based rights of others in order to enjoy adequately our own needs-based rights. The reason for this is twofold.

First, in modern societies most individuals rely on social institutions, e.g. agribusinesses, manufacturers of building materials etc., operating in competitive markets, to produce the foodstuffs and other necessities to fulfill their needs-based rights. Indeed, even if they were disposed to do so, few modern individuals are even capable of producing sufficient food, clean water, adequate shelter, medicine etc. for themselves; few of us living in modern societies are, or could easily become, subsistence farmers.

Second, most individuals rely on business organizations operating in competitive markets to provide paid jobs that: (a) enable them to pay for the basic necessities of life, and; (b) generate taxes to fund a variety of other collective goods necessary for the production and distribution of these basic necessities, e.g. transport, communications, research and training, and other infrastructure.

So there is a complex structure of direct, and indirect, interdependence (as opposed to one-way dependence) and overlap between the needy and those who fulfill their needs. For example, there is direct interdependence between agribusinesses and the paying consumers of basic foodstuffs; and there is indirect interdependence between the former and all the other organizations which pay their employees and, thereby, enable them to become paying consumers of basic foodstuffs.

For our purposes here, an important feature of this complex structure of economic interdependence and overlap is the indirect interdependence between the bearers of needs-based rights themselves, i.e. the consumers of basic necessities; they rely on one another economically to maintain the agribusinesses etc. which provide their basic necessities. Accordingly, in modern economies, speaking generally, if one person's needs-based right to food or shelter etc. is fulfilled then so are the relevant needs-based rights of many other persons.

This *de facto* indirect web of economic interdependence between the bearers of needs-based rights does not, of course, necessarily encompass *all* the members of a community, e.g. there might not be any dependence of the employed on the unemployed. Nevertheless, under conditions of full employment (or near full employment in conjunction with welfare payments to the unemployed) and sufficient production of basic necessities to meet the needs of all, then this *de facto* indirect web of economic interdependence will encompass all members of the community; the web of economic interdependence will be complete.

This web of economic interdependence is, of course, not of such a kind that the meeting of the needs of a single person is a necessary or sufficient condition for the meeting of the needs of any other single person, let alone of all other persons taken in aggregate. Rather the interdependence between individuals, between small subsets of the whole community, and between individuals and small subsets is partial and incremental. Roughly speaking, the larger the subset, the greater the dependence on it of its members (taken individually) and of individuals and subsets outside it; and the less dependent it is on any particular subset outside it (or on any small subset of itself).

Each and every member of the community has a needs-based right to the basic necessities of life. Accordingly, if the *de facto* web of economic interdependence is complete—and there are adequate production levels—then the needs-based rights of all will be fulfilled. Moreover, such a completed web of economic interdependence will parallel a deontic structure of interdependent (aggregated) needs-based rights. The (aggregated) needs-based rights in question are interdependent by virtue of being joint rights. Let me explain.

As mentioned above, a needs-based right is not *per se* a jointly held right; it follows that an aggregate of needs-based rights is not necessarily a set of jointly held rights. However, a needs-based right and, likewise, an aggregate of needs-based rights, are such only in the context of the possibility of their fulfillment (either by the rights bearers themselves, or by others); one cannot have a right to something, if it is impossible (logically or practically) for it to be provided.

The context in question, i.e. a well-functioning modern economy, is one in which aggregated needs-based rights are fulfilled (and realistically can only be fulfilled) by economic institutions characterized by a completed web of economic interdependence among the consumers of basic necessities, i.e. the bearers of the needs-based rights in question. But in that case—given that rights exist only if it is possible for them to be fulfilled—then the needs-based rights in question are *joint* rights. One member of the community in question only has a right to basic necessities if others do, and vice-versa. The institutional arrangements in question are not such that they could provide for one person, or even a small group of persons; they are designed to provide for aggregate needs, i.e. for large groups of consumers. Since it is not possible to provide for one person (or even a small group) that person cannot have a right to the basic necessities independent of others having this right. That is, the right of any one person to the basic necessities is a jointly held right; the needs-based rights in question are joint rights.

I have defined collective goods as jointly produced goods that ought to be produced and made available to the whole community, since they are desirable goods and ones to which the members of the community have joint moral rights. The fulfillment of aggregated needs-based rights is a collective good in this sense.

References

Eitan, N., C. Hoerel, T. McCormack, and J. Roessler. 2005. *Joint attention: Communication and other minds*. Oxford: Oxford University Press.

Giddens, A. 1984. *The constitution of society: Outline of the theory of structuration*. Cambridge: Polity Press.

Gilbert, M. 1989. *On social facts*. Princeton: Princeton University Press.

Griffin, J. 2008. *On human rights*. Oxford: Oxford University Press.

Miller, S. 2001. *Social action: A teleological account*. New York: Cambridge University Press.

Miller, S. 2010. *The moral foundations of social institutions: A philosophical study*. New York: Cambridge University Press.

Parsons, T. 1982. *On institutions and social evolution*. Chicago: Chicago University Press.

Schmitt, F. 2003. Joint action: From individualism to supra-individualism. In *Social metaphysics: The nature of social reality*, ed. F. Schmitt, 129–66. Lanham: Rowman and Littlefield.

Searle, J. 1995. *The construction of social reality*. New York: Free Press.

Chapter 8
Three Types of Heterotropic Intentionality.
A Taxonomy in Social Ontology

Francesca De Vecchi

Abstract I will focus on the phenomenon of heterotropic intentionality, on its role in the creation of social reality and on its relation to social ontology. I will argue *five theses* on heterotropic intentionality: (i) the heterotropism thesis identifies a great divide within the vast domain of intentional phenomena: solitary ones (which need just one individual in order to exist) *vs.* heterotropic ones (which need at least two individuals in order to exist); (ii) the three-types-of-heterotropic-intentionality thesis maintains that there are at least three types of heterotropic intentionality: collective, intersubjective and social intentionality; (iii) the three-modes-of-intersubjective-and-collective-intentionality thesis claims that, like solitary or individual intentionality, collective and social intentionality also involve different modes of intentionality: practical, affective and cognitive; (iv) the sub-personal-and-personal-level thesis maintains that collective and intersubjective intentionality are both sub-personal and personal intentionality, while social intentionality is always a personal intentionality; (v) the ontological-efficacy thesis claims that all three types of heterotropic intentionality create social entities, and that social entities are ontologically dependent on heterotropic intentionality, and not on solitary or individual intentionality. Moreover, I will integrate my theses by putting forward a taxonomy which points out the family resemblances and the strong diversities of these types of heterotropic intentionality.

F. De Vecchi (✉)
Faculty of Philosophy, Università Vita-Salute San Raffaele, Milan, Italy
e-mail: francesca.devecchi@unisr.it

A. Konzelmann Ziv and H.B. Schmid (eds.), *Institutions, Emotions, and Group Agents*, 117
Studies in the Philosophy of Sociality 2, DOI 10.1007/978-94-007-6934-2_8,
© Springer Science+Business Media Dordrecht 2014

1   Introduction

1.1   On the Expression "Heterotropic Intentionality"

"Heterotropic" is a neologism composed of two ancient Greek words: the more familiar "*héteros*" which means "*other/another* [*autrui, fremd, altro*]" and the less familiar "*trépō* which means *turn towards* [*se tourner vers, sich wenden an, rivolgersi a*]".[1]

"Heterotropic intentionality" refers to intentional states, acts and actions, which are in some way turned towards other subjects and which also need other subjects to exist. Examples for this are collective intentions, acts of empathy, social/speech acts like promising or commanding. They are all turned towards other subjects in order to be performed. Thus, in a larger sense, by "heterotropic intentionality" I mean each type of intentionality which involves at least two subjects.

1.2   On the Idea, Theses and Taxonomy of This Paper

The basic idea grounding my chapter is that the intentionality types which inhabit our social and institutional world and play a constitutive role in it include more than—the most famous—type of collective intentionality. I claim that collective, intersubjective and social intentionality are all intentionality types we experience and perform in our social and institutional everyday lives.

A lot of work has been done in analyzing collective intentionality and explaining its role in the creation of social reality and its relation to social ontology.[2] In contrast, much less effort has been spent on the analysis and explanation of intersubjective

---

[1] I would like to be precise that the adjective "heterotropic" and the noun "heterotropism" are neologisms born in the philosophy of law and social ontology group of the Universities of Pavia and Milan (members of the group are: Amedeo Giovanni Conte, Giampaolo Azzoni, Paolo Di Lucia, Giuseppe Lorini, Lorenzo Passerini Glazel, Stefano Colloca, Francesca De Vecchi and others). "Heterotropic" and "heterotropism" are "variations on the theme" of "nomotropic" and "nomotropism", which are neologisms by A.G. Conte and P. Di Lucia, and which are, in their turn, "variations on the theme" of "heliotropic" and "heliotropism". "Heliotropic" and "heliotropism" are constituted by the ancient Greek words "*hēlios*" [*sun*] and "*trépō*" [*turn towards*] (think of heliotropic plants such as sunflowers). "Nomotropic" and "nomotropism" are composed by the ancient Greek words "*nomos*" [*rule*] and "*trépō*" [*turn towards*]. "Nomotropism" means an acting which is in some way turned towards rules and implies ontological dependence on rules (nomotropism is not conformity to rules; the cardsharper is an example of nomotropic acting), see Conte (2000) and Di Lucia (2002). Similarly, "heterotropism" means turning towards other subjects and implies ontological dependence on other subjects (see also De Vecchi and Passerini 2012).

[2] See the works of Searle (1990, 1995, 2010), Tuomela and Miller (1988), Tuomela (2007), Bratman (1992), and Gilbert (2002), among others.

and social intentionality. A main reason for this might be the tendency in the social ontology debate to subsume the phenomena and the meanings of "intersubjective intentionality" and "social intentionality" under the phenomenon and the meaning of "collective intentionality".

Moreover, in the domains of philosophy of mind, cognitive sciences and neurosciences we frequently find the expression "social cognition" referring to both, phenomena of intersubjective and of collective intentionality. In other terms, there is some confusion regarding these different intentional phenomena.

Starting from this philosophical picture and its *lacunae*, I intend to focus in this chapter on the distinction of collective, intersubjective and social intentionality as three types of heterotropic intentionality, and to shed light on the nature, the "family resemblances" and the strong diversities of these three types, as well as on their role in the construction of social reality.

From this perspective, I will argue five theses on heterotropic intentionality and also present a taxonomy of heterotropic intentionality. I will defend my theses both through phenomenological and conceptual arguments. The five theses are the following:

(i)   The heterotropism thesis.
(ii)   The three-types-of-heterotropic-intentionality thesis.
(iii) The three-kinds-of-collective-and-intersubjective-intentionality thesis.
(iv)   The sub-personal-and-personal-level thesis.
(v)   The ontological-efficacy thesis.

The heterotropism thesis identifies a great divide within the vast domain of intentional phenomena: solitary ones *vs.* heterotropic ones; in contrast to solitary intentional phenomena, heterotropic intentional phenomena relate to and ontologically depend on at least two individuals.

The three-types-of-heterotropic-intentionality thesis maintains that there are at least three types of heterotropic intentionality—collective, intersubjective and social intentionality—, i.e. three intentionality types which depend on and relate to at least two individuals.

The three-kinds-of-intersubjective-and-collective-intentionality thesis claims that, like solitary intentionality, collective and social intentionality also involve different kinds of intentionality: practical, affective and cognitive.

The sub-personal-and-personal-level thesis argues that collective and intersubjective intentionality can be both on a sub-personal and a personal level, whereas social intentionality is always on a personal level.

The ontological-efficacy thesis claims that all three types of heterotropic intentionality create social entities, even if each of them creates social entities of different kinds. Social entities ontologically depend on heterotropic intentionality; contrary to what many philosophers in social ontology traditionally assume, they do not depend on solitary intentionality.[3]

---

[3]See, among others, Searle (1995, 2010), Thomasson (2003), and Ferraris (2009). More precisely, Searle maintains that social and institutional facts depend on collective intentionality, but according

My taxonomy will bring into focus 12 distinctions, based on phenomenological data and on phenomenological contributions to collective, intersubjective and social intentionality and to social ontology.[4] The 12 distinctions are the following:

(i) Solitary intentionality *vs.* heterotropic intentionality.
(ii) Collective intentionality *vs.* intersubjective intentionality.
(iii) Collective intentionality *vs.* social intentionality.
(iv) Intersubjective intentionality *vs.* social intentionality.
(v) Social acts *vs.* heteroscopic states, acts and actions.
(vi) Cognitive *vs.* practical *vs.* affective collective intentionality.
(vii) Cognitive *vs.* affective *vs.* practical intersubjective intentionality.
(viii) Affective collective intentionality *vs.* affective intersubjective intentionality.
(ix) Practical collective intentionality *vs.* practical intersubjective intentionality.
(x) Sub-personal cognitive collective intentionality *vs.* personal cognitive collective intentionality.
(xi) Sub-personal intersubjective intentionality *vs.* personal intersubjective intentionality.
(xii) Social entities created by social intentionality *vs.* social entities created by collective intentionality *vs.* social entities created by intersubjective intentionality.[5]

2 The Heterotropism Thesis: Heterotropic Intentionality *vs.* Solitary Intentionality

The fundamental idea which grounds the concept of "heterotropic intentionality" is that we may divide the *vast domain of all intentional mental states, all intentional acts and actions* into two classes:

(i) The *solitary intentionality* class.
(ii) The *heterotropic intentionality* class.

---

to Searle collective intentionality can also be the intentionality of a very solitary brain in a vat. About Searle's individualism, see infra, footnotes 6, 8 and 27.

[4]See: Husserl (1905–1935: XIII, 1912–1928), Reinach (1911a, 1913), Stein (1917, 1922, 1925), Scheler (1923), Hildebrand (1930), and Walther (1923); about the early phenomenological accounts, see Mulligan (1987), Smith (1990), and De Vecchi (2010, 2012, 2013). My claims also refer to some of the recent accounts of collective intentionality and social cognition. See: Searle (1990, 1995, 2010), Bratman (1992), Tuomela and Miller (1988), Gilbert (1989, 2002), Ferraris (2009), Gallagher and Zahavi (2008), Gallese (2005), and Goldman (2005).

[5]This taxonomy is not to be considered exhaustive. It rather attempts to give a sample of the varieties of heterotropic intentionality within the framework of its three main types.

Solitary intentional states, acts and actions are characterised by the fact that they may be performed and experienced by one single individual without referring to and depending on other individuals.

There is a great deal of solitary states, acts and actions. For instance: cognitive experiences like perceiving or imagining or remembering the sea in front of me, or believing that the seawater in front of me is warm; conative or practical acts like having the intention to go to the sea, and deciding to do it; actions like swimming in the sea; affective experiences like feeling good and happy when I swim in the sea, *etc.* These are manifestly all intentional states, acts and actions that can be performed and experienced by myself alone, without any reference to or interaction with other subjects. Thus, they are all cases of *solitary intentionality*. Only single individuals can be the subjects of solitary states, acts and actions.

In contrast, heterotropic intentional mental states, intentional acts and actions cannot be performed and experienced by a single individual: heterotropic states, acts and actions necessarily refer to and depend on other individuals, i.e. they involve at least two individuals.

There is also a great variety of heterotropic intentional states, acts and actions. For instance: practical acts, like intending to go to the movies together; actions, such as going to the movie together; social or speech acts, such as my promising to go to the movies with you; affective experiences, like my feeling that you are enthusiastic about the film we have seen, *etc.* These are all cases of *heterotropic intentionality*: a solitary subject cannot perform any of them; they need to be performed and experienced by at least two subjects, although the role of the subjects involved may change in each of them.

These considerations bring into focus the first phenomenological distinction of my taxonomy:

Taxonomy

(i) Solitary intentionality *vs.* heterotropic intentionality.
   Ex.: I swim in the sea *vs.* I see you are enjoying swimming in the sea.

3   The Three-Types-of-Heterotropic-Intentionality Thesis

I claim that there are at least three types of heterotropic intentionality: collective, intersubjective and social intentionality. As types of heterotropic intentionality, they all necessarily involve and depend on at least two individuals, even if each of them is heterotropic in its own specific way.

I will point out that here I am not taking position for externalism in the internalism *versus* externalism debate on collective intentionality.[6] By distinguishing between solitary intentionality and heterotropic intentionality, on the one hand,

---

[6]As it is well known, Searle maintains an internalist collective intentionality account (Searle 1990, 1995, 2002, 2010), while other philosophers argue for an externalist collective intentionality account (Meijers 2003; Pacherie 2007; Schmid 2003, among others). For a very clear presentation

and identifying collective, intersubjective and social intentionality as three types of heterotropic intentionality, on the other hand, I intend to catch, according to phenomenology, an essential character shared by these three types of intentionality. Phenomenology is neither externalist nor internalist, indeed; phenomenology merely attempts to catch the essential, a priori structure of phenomena. Now, it is phenomenologically manifest that collective, intersubjective and social intentionality involve more than one individual, whereas solitary intentionality need not involve more than one individual.

More precisely, *collective intentionality* is constituted by states, acts and actions shared by two or more persons, for instance: collective feelings, beliefs, intentions, and collectively intended bodily movements (e.g. playing tennis or a piano/violin duet together). *Intersubjective intentionality* is constituted by states and acts of one or more persons directed towards an understanding of the experiences of other subjects, for instance my understanding of your feeling joyful or sad. *Social intentionality* is constituted by social acts performed by one or more persons in the very acts of speaking, turned towards one or more persons and grasped by them. Among the acts of social intentionality are promising, commanding, informing, demanding, promulgating, *etc.* Social acts are *speech acts*[7]—most of them are declarations, and in particular *status functions declarations* (Searle 2010). John R. Searle would not agree with the distinction between collective and social intentionality I make. According to Searle, social and speech acts have to be subsumed under collective intentionality.[8] But phenomenologically, the essential character of social acts is their need to be communicated to and grasped by their addressees, who play a counterpart role in the performance of the act, and this is not an essential character of collective intentionality (and of intersubjective intentionality), too. Hence, on the basis of this essential difference, I state that social acts are not reducible to collective states or acts.

These considerations bring into focus three further phenomenological distinctions of my taxonomy:

Taxonomy

(ii) Collective intentionality *vs.* intersubjective intentionality.
   Ex: *We* intend to go to the movies together *vs. I* see that *you* intend to go to the movies.

---

of the salient issues of the internalism versus externalism collective intentionality debate and also a defence of Searle's internalism see Gallotti (2010, ch. 3).

[7] Social acts were discovered and defined by Adolf Reinach, a phenomenologist and philosopher of law who was a pupil of Edmund Husserl at the beginning of the twentieth century (Reinach 1911a, 1913). Before Reinach, Thomas Reid had already spoken of "social operations" (Reid 1788). Reinach's social acts anticipate by some 50 years the discovery of Austin's speech acts (Austin 1962). About the history and theories of social and speech acts, see Smith (1990), Mulligan (1987), Schuhmann and Smith (1990), Searle (1969, 1995, 2010), and De Vecchi (2010).

[8] This is a very significant point characterising Searle's individualism and internalism, see Searle (1990, 1995, 2010), Meijers (1994), Bratman (1999), and Schmid (2009).

(iii) Collective intentionality *vs.* social intentionality.
   Ex: *We* intend to go to the movies together *vs. I* promise *you* to go to the movies with you.
(iv) Intersubjective intentionality *vs.* social intentionality.
   Ex: *I* see that *you* intend to go to the movies *vs. I* promise *you* to go to the movies with you.

Moreover, it is worth highlighting that we could also identify another type of heterotropic intentionality which is similar to (but nonetheless different from!) social intentionality: I will call it "heteroscopic" intentionality. Examples of heteroscopic states, acts and actions are: I envy you; I forgive you (see Reinach 1913: § 3); I focus my webcam on you. I call them "heteroscopic" (according to the ancient Greek "skopós" which means "target") because in this case the addressee is also the target of the act. Like social acts, heteroscopic states, acts and actions have an addressee, but unlike social acts, they do not need to be communicated to the addressee and grasped by her/him in order to be performed, i.e. they do not need the addressee to play a counterpart role. In order to be performed, heteroscopic states, acts and actions only need to be addressed to someone else. In other terms, simply in addressing to someone else they reach their target. So, we can focus on a fifth phenomenological distinction of the taxonomy:

Taxonomy

(v) Social acts *vs.* heteroscopic acts (states and actions).
   Ex: I ask you to do P *vs.* I forgive you for P (I envy you for P; I take a picture of you).[9]

3.1   On the Phenomenological Account of States, Acts, and Actions

I will now point out a very relevant phenomenological issue: the distinction among *intentional states*, *acts* and *actions* and the correlated account of *persons as subjects of acts*. This issue is crucial to understand because in contrast to many philosophers I do not speak only of intentional collective and intersubjective mental states and actions, but also of intentional collective, intersubjective and social *acts* (see *supra* § 2, where I spoke of collective, intersubjective and social acts).

In philosophy, and also in common language, the meaning of "act" is ambiguous. Many analytic philosophers tend to call mental acts "mental states", and to identify acts with actions. On the contrary, phenomenologists distinguish among states,

---

[9] Although heteroscopic acts, states and actions are also a heterotropic intentionality type, I will not pore on them in my chapter because of constraints on the chapter's length. I will focus just on collective, intersubjective and social intentionality which are the main types of heterotropic intentionality. About heteroscopic states, acts and actions, see De Vecchi and Passerini (2012).

acts and actions, and hold this distinction to be very important. The basic idea grounding this distinction is that a person's mental life is not to be conceived as a flow of mental states; persons are subjects of states, like other animals, but they are specifically subjects of acts of different "positionality" levels. Persons have an emerging and hierarchically ordered structure constituted by states, by acts of first level positionality, and by acts of second level positionality. So, very schematically, the idea is that by acts of first level positionality (e.g. beliefs), persons take a position (yes-no) on their states (e.g. perceptions and emotions), which happen to them and are not in their power to avoid (states are understood as causal effects). By acts of second level positionality (e.g. intentions), persons take positions on their acts of first level positionality.

For instance, by believing that this movie is a good one, we endorse a certain perceptual and/or emotional state about the movie (about the existence of the movie and about some positive value of the movie): so, this is a first level position taking act. By forming the intention to go to see this movie, we take a position on our belief that this movie is a good one: so, this is a second level position taking act. By performing this second level position act, we take the belief—first level position act—as a ground for our decision to go to the movie, or also as a ground for informing (speech/social act) other friends that this movie is a good one, *etc*. Second order position taking acts are *free*, *spontaneous* acts, and they are characterised by *authorship* or *agency*.[10]

Finally, *actions* are bodily movements that satisfy intentions. So, actions are goal-directed intentional movements: they are intended bodily movements, which aim to satisfy the content of the intention.[11]

3.2   Two Criteria for the Distinction among Collective, Intersubjective and Social Intentionality

I shall now point out two phenomenological criteria for the distinction among collective, intersubjective and social intentionality I have been claiming.

3.2.1   The Different Roles of the Subjects Involved

The first criterion I put forward concerns the fact that the subjects involved in heterotropic intentionality have different roles depending on the type of heterotropic intentionality they are involved in. I shall now outline these different roles.

---

[10]About the phenomenological account of acts and persons as subjects of acts, see Reinach (1911a, b, 1913: § 3), Husserl (1912–1928: § 61), Stein (1922) and De Monticelli (2007a, b).

[11]About this account of action, see Searle (1983, 1990, 2010), Gallagher and Zahavi (2008), and Reinach (1913).

(i) *Collective states, acts and actions*

The subjects to whom collective states, acts and actions refer and on whom they depend are all *agent-partners*. Thus, in the case of collective intentions or actions, or collective perceptions and beliefs, or collective feelings, *etc.*, the subjects involved in them are all joint agents. Accordingly, the subjects referred to by "we" in sentences of the form "we intend to do P", "we believe P", "we feel P" are all joint agents who intend or believe or feel together P. Needless to say, I am just identifying the essential conditions about the subjects' roles for collective intentionality to exist, i.e. for collective intentionality to exist the subjects who intend, believe or feel together have to play the role of partners. Thus, I am only giving a minimal picture, which of course may be enriched and extended by introducing further roles and subjects. For example: we have the intention to prevent you to do P with respect to her/him. In this case, the subjects referred to by "we" are the agent-partners of the collective intention, while the subjects referred to by "you" and "she/he" are not the agent-partners of the collective intention at all.

(ii) *Social acts*

The subjects to whom social acts refer and on whom they depend are the *addressees* of the act. The addressee is the *counterpart* of the agent of the act. Also in this case, I just want to outline the essential structure of social acts and the minimal roles required by the subjects in this structure. For social acts to exist, the subjects to whom social acts refer and on whom they depend play necessarily the role of the *addressees* of the act. Like in the case of collective intentionality, this essential structure may be modified and enriched by introducing more subjects and roles. Take, for instance, a promise performed in the name of someone else and concerning further subjects: on behalf of you, I promise your sister to take care of her child (see Reinach 1913: § 3). Here, "your sister" plays the essential role of the addressee of my promise (without an addressee grasping my promise, my promise would not exist), while the other subjects involved in this case (you and the child of your sister) do not play the role of addressee.

(iii) *Intersubjective states and acts*

The subjects to whom intersubjective states and acts refer and on whom they depend are neither partners nor addressees. Intersubjective intentionality is directed towards other persons, and specifically it is directed towards the understanding of experiences of other persons, but these other persons do not in any way—neither as partner-agents nor as addressees—perform intersubjective states and acts. For instance, my understanding of your feeling depends on you and on your feeling, because your feelings are the *object* of my intersubjective intentionality; without them, my intersubjective intentionality cannot be performed. But my act of understanding your feeling does not require that you play either the agent-partner role or the addressee role. For the most part, you totally ignore my understanding of your feeling.

3.2.2   The Different Directions of Each Type of Heterotropic Intentionality

The second criterion I put forward for distinguishing among collective, social and intersubjective intentionality is that they have different directions.

(i) *Collective intentionality is a mono-directed intentionality towards a shared object*
Collective intentionality is directed towards a shared object that is external to the individuals' minds (*lato sensu*) and that is an object of the public, social and institutional world. For example: if we intend to walk together on the hills, and if we both believe that the Appennines are a good place for our walking together on the hills, then it is manifest that walking together in the Appennines is an intentional content which concerns the external world.

(ii) *Intersubjective intentionality is a mono-directed intentionality towards experiences of other subjects*
Intersubjective intentionality, like collective intentionality, is mono-directed intentionality but, differently from collective intentionality, it is directed towards other subjects' experiences. Hence, intersubjective intentionality is basically mind-to-mind intentionality, and not mind-to-world intentionality in the sense that collective intentionality and social intentionality are.

Intersubjective intentionality remains on the I-you level and does not reach a third objective level beyond the intersubjective level. In the case of intersubjective intentionality, my mental states or acts are always directed towards your mental states or acts, and hence towards a mind-internal object. In other terms, it is an intentionality which is fundamentally performed *intra* subjects: if I feel your joy or if I see what you are thinking about, then my intentional object is always a *mental object*, even if it is a mental object belonging to *mente tua* and not to *mente mea*. In conclusion, intersubjective intentionality is basically a face-to-face encounter.[12]

(iii) *Social intentionality is a double-directed intentionality towards both other subjects and a common targeted object*
Social intentionality is addressed to other subjects for a common object. The intentionality of the agent's act is directed both towards another subject, the addressee of the act, and towards the object of the act. The intentionality directed towards the addressee is a *medium* of the intentionality directed

---

[12] As Dan Zahavi claimed, there are, both in analytical philosophy of mind and in phenomenology, quite diverse accounts of intersubjectivity which transcend the face-to-face encounter between individuals and which posit the world as a common field of experiences among individuals (Zahavi 2001). I am by no means denying this. I am convinced that the encounter between individuals is the encounter between individuals that are subjects in a common world, i.e. in a common field of experiences and bodily interlacements of selfhood and otherness. But I think that this perspective is fully compatible with the attempt to outline a distinction among intersubjective, collective and social intentionality by the criteria of the directionality of intentionality: in the case of intersubjective intentionality, the direction of intentionality is always an I-you direction, even if between I and you there is, of course, the world.

towards the object: I command *you* to do x; you are the *medium* through whom x is done, and x is the *aim* of the act. Through the other subject—you, the addressee of the act—, social intentionality aims at the commanded (requested, promised, *etc.*) thing.[13]

As in the case of collective intentionality (but not in the case of intersubjective intentionality), the object of social intentionality is an object of the external, social and institutional world.

4 The Three-Modes-of-Intersubjective-and-Collective-Intentionality Thesis: Practical, Cognitive, Affective

I maintain that, like individual intentionality, also collective and intersubjective intentionality involve different modes of intentionality: practical, affective and cognitive.

4.1 Practical, Cognitive and Affective Collective Intentionality

Collective intentionality may be *practical*, *cognitive* or *affective*: hence, it becomes manifest in *intentions* (*prior intentions*, *intentions-in-actions*[14], *volitions* or *desires*), *beliefs* (or *perceptions*), or *feelings* (including a variety of feelings: moods, emotions, passions *etc.*) respectively. Thus, I focus on a sixth phenomenological distinction of my taxonomy:

Taxonomy

(vi) Cognitive *vs.* practical *vs.* affective collective intentionality.[15]
      Ex: We believe that *The Apartment* by Billy Wilder is a beautiful movie *vs.* we intend to go to see *The Apartment*, or we are going to see *The Apartment vs.*

---

[13] See Reinach (1911a, 1913), and Mulligan (1987).

[14] About the notion of *prior intentions* and *intentions-in-actions*, see Searle (2001, 2010): "prior intentions begin prior to the onset of an action and intentions-in-action are the intentional components of actions" (Searle 2010, p. 51).

[15] The distinction between *practical collective intentionality* and *cognitive collective intentionality* is now more or less accepted (Gilbert 1989, 2002; Bratman 1999; Searle 2010; Zaibert 2003; Tollefsen 2005; Schmid 2009). The individuation of affective collective intentionality as a third kind of intentionality, internal to the type of collective intentionality, on the other hand, is much more recent (see Schmid 2009), and not widely adopted. Michael Tomasello seems still to give a priority to cognitive states: he talks about "cognitive representations" for both collective intentions and collective beliefs, without paying particular attention to affective states (Tomasello et al. 2005; Tomasello 2009).

we both are amused by *The Apartment* and we share the same enthusiasm for this movie.[16]

I would like to point out that these examples of cognitive, practical and affective collective intentionality are also cases of collective states, acts, and actions. Our *collective feeling* of being amused and enthusiastic for *The Apartment* is a mental state. Our *collective belief* that *The Apartment* is a beautiful movie is a collective mental act of first level positionality; our *collective intention* to go to see *The Apartment* together is a collective *spontaneous, free act*, i.e. an act of a second level positionality. Finally, our going to see *The Apartment* together is a collective action.

4.2 Practical, Affective and Cognitive Intersubjective Intentionality

Intersubjective intentionality may be *affective* or *cognitive*. Affective and cognitive intersubjective intentionality are respectively directed at the *understanding of affective and cognitive experiences of other persons*. Moreover, we may also identify a third kind of intersubjective intentionality: *practical intersubjective intentionality*.

The distinction among affective, cognitive and practical intersubjective intentionality has not yet been really adopted in philosophy: philosophers, but also and especially psychologists, cognitive scientists and neuroscientists tend to speak generically of "*social cognition*" which may indistinctly concern the understanding of cognitive, affective and practical experiences of other subjects. In other terms, "social cognition" means intersubjectivity, without distinguishing among cognitive, practical and affective intersubjectivity. Consistent with the phenomenological tradition, I distinguish, rather, among cognitive, affective and practical intersubjective intentionality: they are three different phenomena indeed.

Thus, I focus on a seventh phenomenological distinction of my taxonomy:

Taxonomy

(vii) Cognitive *vs.* affective *vs.* practical intersubjective intentionality.
       Ex: I see that you are thinking about *The Apartment vs.* I see that you are still amused and enthusiastic about *The Apartment vs.* I see that you intend to go to see *The Apartment* again.

---

[16]Among these different kinds of collective intentionality, the more problematic phenomenon to grasp and to define is affective collective intentionality: what exactly does it mean that we share the same feeling, that we feel it together or collectively? In which specific sense are we both amused and enthusiastic for *The Apartment*? Or, in which sense are we both deeply sad and moved by a tragic existential event? In this regard, I will mention Scheler's famous case of *feeling-together* (*Mit-einanderfühlen*): a father and mother feel the same pain standing by the dead body of their beloved child (Scheler 1923). In this case, we properly have an example of "emotional sharing", indeed. About this issue, see Schmid (2009: § 15 "Phenomenological Fusion"), Krebs (2010), Zahavi (2008), and De Vecchi (2011), where I outlined an account of collective affective (but also cognitive and practical) intentionality in terms of shared intentionality.

4.3 Intersubjective Intentionality vs. Collective Intentionality

Affective intersubjective intentionality is not to be confused with affective collective intentionality, and practical intersubjective intentionality is not to be confused with practical collective intentionality.

I focus on an eighth and ninth phenomenological distinction of my taxonomy:

Taxonomy

(viii) Affective collective intentionality *vs.* affective intersubjective intentionality.
Ex: We are both moved by *The Apartment* and we share the same enthusiasm for this movie *vs.* I see (I feel) your amusement and enthusiasm for *The Apartment*.

(ix) Practical collective intentionality *vs.* practical intersubjective intentionality.
Ex: We intend to go to see *The Apartment* together *vs.* I see (I intend) your intention to go to see *The Apartment*.

The possibility of confusing affective and practical collective with affective and practical intersubjective intentionality is directly connected with the *criteria that characterise* the mode of intersubjective intentionality.

Firstly, we may characterise the mode of intersubjective intentionality through the *content* of mental states or acts and say: If I see your *intention*, this is a case of practical intersubjective intentionality; if I see your belief, this is a case of cognitive intersubjective intentionality; and if I see your *feeling*, this is a case of affective intersubjective intentionality.

Secondly, we may characterise the mode of intersubjective intentionality in a stronger way, involving not only the content but also the *quality* of the mental states or acts.[17] According to this second criterion of characterisation, I may see your intention, your belief, your feeling—the content of your experience—only if I personally have the same intentional mode you have: only if I intend your intention, I believe your belief, I feel your feeling.[18]

These different criteria of characterisation depend clearly on the account of intersubjective intentionality (social cognition) we adopt.[19] Our choice of such

---

[17]The distinction between content and quality of intentional experiences is a classic phenomenological distinction: we find it already in the early Husserl (1901). It is also a classic analytical distinction: Searle, for example, distinguishes between "intentional content" and "intentional mode" (Searle 1983).

[18]I think that particularly in the case of intersubjective affective intentionality it makes sense to adopt the stronger criterion: it really could be difficult to see that you are feeling joy or pain without feeling it, i.e. without having the same intentional mode you have. This is also the position of phenomenologists like Scheler and Stein: according to them, empathy (called *Nachfühlung* by Scheler and, more traditionally, *Einfühlung* by Stein), the act by which I see the feeling of the other, is characterised by an affective nuance of knowing. Scheler speaks properly of "*verstehend fühlen*" (see Scheler 1923 and Stein 1917).

[19]There are different accounts which try to describe or explain the phenomenon of intersubjective intentionality or social cognition. The crucial problem is: *how* do I understand the experiences of

an account carries over to the distinction between intersubjective and collective intentionality. Why? Well, if we adopt the second and stronger criterion that characterises intersubjective intentionality, then it is manifestly more difficult to distinguish between different types and modes of intersubjective and collective intentionality. Nonetheless, I claim that even if we adopt the stronger criteria, we are able to distinguish between these different types and kinds of intentionality. The reason for this is that they still essentially differ with regard to the intentionality direction and to the *role of the subjects* involved in them (see *supra* § 2.2.1 and 2.2.2).[20]

5   The Sub-personal-and-Personal-Level Thesis

I maintain that collective and intersubjective intentionality can appear on a sub-personal or a personal level with regard to the mental states, acts and actions of the subjects. On the sub-personal level, subjects will not have a reflexive, conscious awareness of their states and their taking a position of the first level, whereas on the personal level they always take a position of second level.

Differently from collective and intersubjective intentionality, social intentionality is always personal intentionality in the pregnant sense that it implies authorship and agency, because social acts, as we have seen, are always position-takings of second level.

I will now discuss two cases of personal *vs.* sub-personal collective intentionality and intersubjective intentionality.

5.1   Sub-personal Cognitive Collective Intentionality vs. Personal Cognitive Collective Intentionality

I focus on a tenth phenomenological distinction of the taxonomy:

---

others? Do I understand them by *inferences* (the inference which I can make from the expressions or bodily appearance of the other and from my own experience)? Do I understand them by *simulating* them? Do I understand them by feeling them, if they are feeling, by intending them, if they are intentions, *etc.*? Can I understand the experiences of the others without engaging myself in such experiences? Neurosciences maintain that mirror neurons are the heroes of social cognition. But the neurobiological data are interpreted in many ways according to the different accounts (Simulation theory, Theory of Mind, called also Theory-theory, *etc.*). About this debate, see: Gallese (2005), Goldman (2005), Rizzolati and Sinigaglia (2006), Gallagher and Zahavi (2008). See also Lipps (1913): Lipps represents the proto theorist of the present "Simulation Theory".

[20]They are also intrinsically different because collective intentionality is essentially shared intentionality, while intersubjective intentionality is not. About this argument, see De Vecchi (2011).

Taxonomy

(x) Sub-personal cognitive collective intentionality *vs.* personal cognitive collective intentionality.
Ex: We are buying some books in the bookshop and we pay with a 50 euro bill: this implies that *we recognise* that this piece of paper in my hand *counts as* a 50 euro bill *vs.* we are at the notary's to sign a property contract: before signing it, we ask the notary about the rules by virtue of which the piece of paper on the notary's table *counts* as a property contract.

These examples are built on Searle's account of collective recognition or belief: according to Searle, collective recognition has an essential role in imposing "status functions" (one piece of paper counts as a 50 euro bill and the other counts as a property contract). Collective recognition always belongs to a *Network* of conscious or unconscious intentional states and is grounded in a *Background* of pre-intentional, pre-reflexive and sub-personal abilities, attitudes, know-how, *etc.*, which is the basis of our intentional (individual and collective) mental states and actions (see Searle 1995, 2010).

The point I will focus on is that, normally, when we pay something with a 50 euro bill, we implicitly, pre-reflexively and sub-personally recognise the piece of paper as a 50 euro note: we do that without being aware of it, without having reflected on the nature of the bill or on the constitutive rules of money, and without having taken the second level position of awareness.

On the contrary, if we reflect on the nature of the property contract we are going to sign, and ask the notary about the rules which regulate and constitute the property contract, we will then be fully aware that this piece of paper on the notary's table counts as a property contract because we and all the other people in our country recognise or accept it as such. Thus, we will be aware of having taken a position on it, i.e. we will be aware that we have recognised that this piece of paper counts as a contract. In other words, we will have recognised at the personal level—i.e. have taken a position on—the constitutive rules of the institution of the property.

This example shows that sub-personal cognitive collective intentionality, when it creates social and institutional entities by imposing *status* functions, plays a very important role in the construction of social reality.

5.2   Sub-personal Intersubjective Intentionality vs. Personal Intersubjective Intentionality

I focus on an eleventh phenomenological distinction of my taxonomy.

Taxonomy

(xi) Sub-personal intersubjective intentionality *vs.* personal intersubjective intentionality.
Ex: I am swayed by your sadness *vs.* I see (I feel) that you are sad.

Here, following Max Scheler's masterpiece on *Wesen und Formen der Sympathie* (1923), where he presents an extremely rich phenomenological taxonomy of affective intentionality, and Edith Stein's dissertation *Zum Problem der Einfühlung* (1917), I distinguish between *emotional contagion (Gefühlsansteckung)* and *empathy (Einfühlung, Nachfühlen)*.

In the case of *emotional contagion*, I feel the same feeling you feel without being aware of it and without having taken a position about it. In the case of *empathy*, I see the feeling of another, I know it, and I can avoid or endorse this feeling. *Emotional contagion* is a state, whereas *empathy* is an act, which implies positionality.

According to Scheler, we find at least two more kinds of affective intersubjective intentionality: *emotional fusion* and *sympathy*. Whereas emotional fusion belongs to what I call "sub-personal affective intersubjective intentionality", sympathy belongs to the opposite pole of what I call "personal affective intersubjective intentionality". *Emotional fusion (Einsfühlung)* is a borderline case of emotional contagion in which one self absorbs another. It belongs to sub-personal affective intersubjective intentionality because one feels another's feeling without taking a position on it. Awareness of the feeling of the other, which characterises empathy, may then become the basis for further position-taking: the compassion or fellow-feeling wherein I rejoice in your joy and I commiserate with your sorrow (*Mit-fühlen mit jemandem*), which we may roughly call *sympathy*.

We have said that intersubjective intentionality is basically a face-to-face encounter between individuals. We may now specify this claim: the encounter between individuals may take place in a personal or a sub-personal way. Thus, we may also distinguish between weak intersubjective intentionality and strong intersubjective intentionality, which I suggest calling *inter-personal intentionality*.[21]

The social relevance of the sub-personal affective intersubjective intentionality is impressive. Let us only think of all the mass-phenomena of medium and macro scale and their presence in our everyday life: we go to a party and are swayed by the gaiety of the party; we go to the football match and are affected by the rage of our fellow supporters. Or think about the famous case of the fall of the *Third Reich* in Berlin during Second World War: a soldier gives up and lays down his weapons, another soldier sees it and does the same. What has happened here? A case of *emotional contagion* has just happened: a diffused mood of fear and desperation has affected the soldiers, and thus, when one laid down his weapons, the others imitated him.[22]

---

[21] Gallagher and Zahavi also distinguish between *primary inter-subjectivity and secondary inter-subjectivity* (see Gallagher 2005 and Gallagher and Zahavi 2008). By "intersubjectivity" Costa means just inter-personality (Costa 2010).

[22] Ferraris quotes this historical case and its representation in the movie *Der Untergang* (2004) as a counter-example against collective intentionality (Ferraris 2009). Instead, I think that this case is not a case of collective intentionality, but a case of emotional contagion. Thus it is not a valid example against the collective intentionality claim.

6 The Social-Efficacy Thesis

I claim that all types of *heterotropic intentionality are socially and/or institutionally effective*. Each of the three types of heterotropic intentionality—collective, intersubjective and social—contribute to the creation of social reality. An important corollary of this claim is that *social entities are ontologically dependent on heterotropic intentionality*, i.e. they do not depend on solitary intentionality but on intentionality which involves, in the different ways we have seen, at least two subjects. In other terms, in order to create social and institutional entities of any type (rights, obligations, football matches, money, corporations, marriages, parties, families, friendships *etc.*), one subject is not enough. What is required are at least two subjects who deal with one another, be it by performing social/speech acts, by sharing collective intentions, beliefs and feeling, by understanding the other in an act of empathy or sympathy, *etc.*[23]

Moreover, I also state that collective, intersubjective and social intentionality are both *praxis* and *poiesis*. Let us consider some cases:

(i) *The efficacy of collective intentionality*

Collective intentionality has a normative efficacy: it produces a *joint commitment* with respect to, for instance, a joint action (walking together) as well as to a joint creative activity (baking a cake together).[24]

It is worth noticing that collective intentionality may be both a *poiesis* and a *praxis* (baking a cake together is a *poiesis*, whereas walking together is a *praxis*). In the case of *collective beliefs* (recognitions) which impose "*status functions*", cognitive collective intentionality is generally a *poiesis*. This piece of paper in my hand is a five euro bill because we believe or accept that it is so (see Searle 1995, 2010). This case is very meaningful because it shows that also theoretical acts, such as beliefs—and not only practical acts like intentions or actions—may be poietic.

(ii) *The efficacy of social acts*

Social acts are both poiesis and praxis: asking, informing, or asserting are practical social acts, they are simply actions; promising, commanding, promulgating a law, *etc.* produce normative entities (for instance, rights and obligations), so they are poietic acts. I will highlight that poietic social intentionality is immediately effective on the normative level, while it is not immediately effective on the practical level. This becomes evident in the difference between performing a social act and satisfying this act by performing the action that realizes its content. For instance, if a government

---

[23] Another way to formulate this thesis is that social entities presuppose always a society in order to exist, i.e. at least two individuals which constitute a society in miniature. This is the thesis of Czesław Znamierowski (1921).

[24] On the normative significance of "walking together", see the famous account of Margaret Gilbert (2002).

promulgates a law, then some obligations and rights are immediately produced by the promulgated law; in contrast, the actions of the citizens that satisfy these obligations and rights are not an effect of the promulgated law.[25]

(iii) *The efficacy of intersubjective intentionality*
Intersubjective intentionality is *ontologically effective*, too, specifically in the case of *mutual* intersubjective experiences. Mutual intersubjective intentionality has been identified by Husserl as characteristic of interpersonal relations of knowing each other, which imply *understanding* each other, i.e. mutually understanding what the other intends, believes and feels. On the basis of this mutual understanding (be it affective, cognitive or practical) proper to interpersonal relations, we can ground the creation of the social world and the performing of collective acts and actions, as well as of social/speech acts.[26] Consider the case of mutual feelings (such as mutual love, respect and trust) or the cases of mutual beliefs and intentions: in virtue of the mutual (affective, cognitive and practical) understanding, they create interpersonal relations which are the necessary conditions—as Husserl maintains—for the creation of social world (think of social entities like friendships, families, communities, philosophical societies, political parties, *etc.*) and for the performing of collective acts and actions and social acts. In other words, in order to share intentions and cooperate, or in order to promise, inform, command, *etc.*, we need to have a mutual understanding of each other.[27]

We can now sum up this analysis of different kinds of efficacy, i.e. of the different roles played by different types of heterotropic intentionality in the creation of social reality, by focusing on this last distinction of the taxonomy:

Taxonomy

(xii) Social entities created by social intentionality *vs.* social entities created by collective intentionality *vs.* social entities created by intersubjective intentionality.

Ex: Promising creates normative entities like obligations and claims *vs.* collective recognition creates status functions of institutional entities (money,

---

[25] See Reinach (1913), Conte (2002), Mulligan (1987), and De Vecchi (2013), where I worked on the relation between normative and practical level in social intentionality and social ontology.

[26] On the contrary, some philosophers, e.g. Searle, hold that collective intentions could also be intentions of an extremely solitary brain in a vat. Most philosophers and cognitive scientists—with rare exceptions—pay very little attention to the inter-personal relation, and do not claim that it is a necessary condition of collective experience. See Searle (1990). For arguments against Searlian individualism in collective intentionality and in support of an account of collective intentionality based on relational intentionality, see Meijers (1994, p. 7), Bratman (1999), and Schmid (2009, p. 37).

[27] See Husserl (1905–1935, XIII, 98, 102–104), "Die für Sozialität konstitutiven Akte, die 'kommunikativen'" and "Soziale Ontologie und deskriptive Soziologie", and Husserl (1912–1928: § 51), "Die Personen in der Kollektivität der Personen". See also Hildebrand (1930), Walther (1923), Scheler (1923), and Stein (1922).

prime minister, universities, corporations) *vs.* intersubjective feelings create interpersonal relations which ground the creation of the social world (friends, families, communities, political parties).

References

Austin, J.L. 1980 [1962]. *How to do things with words.* Oxford: Oxford University Press.

Bratman, M. 1992. Shared cooperative activity. *Philosophical Review* 101: 327–341.

Bratman, M. 1999. *Faces of intention: Selected essays on intention and agency.* Cambridge: Cambridge University Press.

Conte, A.G. 2000. Nomotropismo: Agire in funzione di regole. *Sociologia del Diritto* 27: 1–27.

Conte, A.G. 2002. Atto performativo: il concetto di performatività nella filosofia dell'atto giuridico. In *Atto giuridico*, ed. G. Lorin and G. Lorini, 29–108. Bari: Adriatica Editrice.

Costa, V. 2010. *Fenomenologia dell'intersoggettività.* Bologna: Carocci.

De Monticelli, R. 2007a. L'attualità degli atti. Spunti per una teoria unificata. *Rivista di Estetica* 36(3): 81–96.

De Monticelli, R. 2007b. The phenomenological revolution and the emergence of persons. *Encyclopaideia* 22: 9–30.

De Vecchi, F. 2010. Per una preistoria degli atti sociali: gli atti di significare di Edmund Husserl. *Rivista internazionale di filosofia del diritto* 3: 365–396.

De Vecchi, F. 2011. Collective intentionality vs. intersubjective and social intentionality. An account of collective intentionality as shared intentionality. *Phenomenology and Mind* 1: 72–87.

De Vecchi, F. 2012. Platonismo sociale? In difesa del realismo fenomenologico in ontologia sociale. *Rivista di Estetica* 52(50): 75–90.

De Vecchi, F. 2013. Ontological dependence and essential laws of social reality. The case of promising. In *The background of social reality*, Studies in the philosophy of sociality, ed. B. Kobow, H.B. Schmid, and M. Schmitz. Dordrecht: Springer.

De Vecchi, F., and L. Passerini Glazel. 2012. Gli atti sociali nella tipologia degli Erlebnisse e degli atti spontanei in Adolf Reinach (1913). In *Eidetica del diritto e ontologia sociale. Il realismo di Adolf Reinach*, ed. F. De Vecchi, 261–280. Milano: Mimesis.

Di Lucia, P. 2002. Efficacia senza adempimento. *Sociologia del diritto* 29: 73–103.

Ferraris, M. 2009. *Documentalità. Perché è necessario lasciar tracce.* Bari: Laterza.

Gallagher, S. 2005. Phenomenological contributions to a theory of social cognition. *Husserl Studies* 21: 95–110.

Gallagher, S., and D. Zahavi. 2008. *The phenomenological mind. An introduction to philosophy of mind and cognitive science.* London: Routledge.

Gallese, V. 2005. Being like me: Self-other identity, mirror neurons and empathy. In *Perspectives on imitation I*, ed. S. Hurley and N. Chater, 101–118. Cambridge, MA: MIT Press.

Gallotti, M. 2010. *Naturally we. A philosophical study of collective intentionality.* Doctoral dissertation, University of Exeter.

Gilbert, M. 1989. *On social facts.* New York: Routledge.

Gilbert, M. 2002. Acting together. In *Social facts and collective intentionality*, ed. G. Meggle, 53–71. Frankfurt: Hänsel-Hohenhausen.

Goldman, A. 2005. Imitation, mind reading and simulation. In *Perspectives on imitation II*, ed. S. Hurley and N. Chater, 79–94. Cambridge, MA: MIT Press.

Husserl, E. 1952 [1912–1928]. Ideen zu einer reinen Phänomenologie und phänomenologischen Philosophie, Zweites Buch, Phänomenologische Untersuchungen zur Konstitution. In *Husserliana, IV*, ed. M. Biemel. Den Haag: Nijhoff.

Husserl, E. 1973 [1905–1935]. Zur Phänomenologie der Intersubjektivität. In *Husserliana, XIII–XV*, ed. I. Kern. Den Haag: Nijhoff.

Husserl, E. 1975/1984 [1901]. Logische Untersuchungen. In *Husserliana XIX/1, XIX/2*, ed. U. Panzer. Den Haag: Nijhoff. English translation: 1976. *Logical investigations*. London: Routledge.

Krebs, A. 2010. Vater und Mutter stehen an der Leiche eines geliebten Kindes. Max Scheler über das Miteinanderfühlen. *Allgemeine Zeitschrift für Philosophie*. 35(1): 9–43.

Lipps, T. 1913. Zur Einfühlung. In *Psychologische Untersuchungen*. Leipzig: Engelmann.

Meijers, A.W.M. 1994. *Speech acts, communication and collective intentionality: Beyond Searle's individualism*. Doctoral dissertation, Utrecht University.

Meijers, A.W.M. 2003. Beyond Searle's individualism. *The American Journal of Economics and Sociology* 62: 167–183.

Mulligan, K. 1987. Promisings and other social acts: Their constituents and structure. In *Speech act and Sachverhalt. Reinach and the foundation of realist phenomenology*, ed. K. Mulligan, 29–90. Dordrecht: Kluwer.

Pacherie, E. 2007. Collective intentionality really primitive? In *Mental processes: Representing and inferring*, 3rd ed, ed. M. Beaney, C. Penco, and M. Vignolo, 135–175. Cambridge: Cambridge Scholars Press.

Reid, T. 1969 [1788]. On the nature of a contract. In *Essays on the active powers of the human mind*. Cambridge, MA/London: MIT Press.

Reinach, A. 1989 [1911a]. Nichtsoziale und soziale Akte. In A. Reinach, *Sämtliche Werke*, ed. K. Schuhmann and B. Smith, 355–360. München: Philosophia Verlag.

Reinach, A. 1989 [1911b]. Zur Theorie des negative Urteils. In A. Reinach, *Sämtliche Werke*, ed. K. Schuhmann and B. Smith, 95–140. München: Philosophia Verlag.

Reinach, A. 1989 [1913]. Die apriorischen Grundlagen des bürgerlichen Rechts. In A. Reinach, *Sämtliche Werke*, ed. K. Schuhmann and B. Smith, 141–278. München: Philosophia Verlag. English translation: 1983. The Apriori foundations of the civil law (trans: Crosby, J.) *Aletheia*, III: 1–142.

Rizzolati, G., and C. Sinigaglia. 2006. *So quel che fai. Il cervello che agisce e i neuroni specchio*. Milano: Raffaello Cortina Editore.

Scheler, M. 1973 [1923]. Wesen und Formen der Sympathie. In M. Scheler, *Gesammelte Werke, VII*, 3rd ed, ed. M. Frings. München: Francke Verlag. English Translation: 1954. *The nature of sympathy*. London: Routledge.

Schmid, H.B. 2003. Can brains in vats think as a team? *Philosophical Explorations* 6: 201–218.

Schmid, H.B. 2009. *Plural action: Essays in philosophy and social science. Contributions to phenomenology*. Dordrecht: Springer.

Schuhmann, K., and B. Smith. 1990. Elements of speech act theory in the work of Thomas Reid. *History of Philosophy Quarterly* 7: 47–66.

Searle, J.R. 1969. *Speech acts. An essay in philosophy of language*. Cambridge: Cambridge University Press.

Searle, J.R. 1983. *Intentionality*. Cambridge: Cambridge University Press.

Searle, J.R. 1990. Collective intentions and actions. In *Intentions in communication*, ed. P. Cohen, J. Morgan, and M. Pollack, 401–415. Cambridge, MA: MIT Press.

Searle, J.R. 1995. *The construction of social reality*. London: Allen Lane.

Searle, J.R. 2001. *Rationality in action*. Cambridge, MA: MIT Press.

Searle, J.R. 2002. *Consciousness and language*. Cambridge: Cambridge University Press.

Searle, J.R. 2010. *Making the social world. The structure of human civilization*. Oxford: Oxford University Press.

Smith, B. 1990. Towards a history of speech acts. In *Speech acts, meanings and intentions. Critical approaches to the philosophy of John R. Searle*, ed. A. Burkhardt, 29–61. Berlin/New York: de Gruyter.

Stein, E. 2006 [1925]. *Eine Untersuchung über den Staat*. Collected Works Vol 7, Freiburg: Herder.

Stein, E. 2010 [1922]. Individuum und Gemeinschaft. In *Beiträge zur philosophischen Begründung der Psychologie und der Geisteswissenschaften*, In Gesamtausgabe, vol. 6, Freiburg: Herder.

Stein, E. 2012 [1917]. *Zum Problem der Einfühlung.* (Halle University.) In Gesamtausgabe, vol. 5, ed. E. Stein. Freiburg: Herder.

Thomasson, A. 2003. Foundations for a social ontology. *ProtoSociology: An International Journal of Interdisciplinary Research* 18/19: 269–290.

Tollefsen, D. 2005. Collective Intentionality. *Internet Encyclopedia of Philosophy.*

Tomasello, M., M. Carpenter, J. Call, T. Behne, and H. Moll. 2005. Understanding and sharing intentions: The origins of cultural cognition. *Behavioural and Brain Sciences* 28: 675–735.

Tomasello, M. 2009. *Why we cooperate.* Cambridge, MA/London: MIT Press.

Tuomela, R. 2007. *The philosophy of sociality: The shared point of view.* Oxford: Oxford University Press.

Tuomela, R., and K. Miller. 1988. We-intentions. *Philosophical Studies* 53: 367–389.

von Hildebrand, D. 1955 [1930]. *Metaphysik der Gemeinschaft. Untersuchungen über Wesen und Wert der Gemeinschaft.* Regensburg: Habbel.

Walther, G. 1923. Zur Ontologie der sozialen Gemeinschaften. *Jahrbuch für Philosophie und phänomenologische Forschung* 6: 1–158.

Zahavi, D. 2001. Beyond empathy. *Journal of Consciousness Studies* 8(5–7): 151–167.

Zahavi, D. 2008. Simulation, projection and empathy. *Consciousness and Cognition* 17: 514–522.

Zaibert, L. 2003. Collective intentions and collective intentionality. *American Journal of Sociology and Economics* 60: 209–232.

Znamierowski, C. 1921. Social objects and social facts [O przedmiocie i fakcie społecznym]. *Przegląd Filozoficzny* 25: 1–33.

Part II
Shared Emotions and Recognition

Chapter 9
Emergence and Empathy

Ronald de Sousa

> *'I weep for you', the Walrus said:*
> *'I deeply sympathize.'*
> *With sobs and tears he sorted out*
> *Those of the largest size,*
> *Holding his pocket-handkerchief*
> *Before his streaming eyes.*
> Lewis Carroll

1 Emergence and Externalism

If there are collective emotions in some interesting sense, they must consist of more than the mere conjunction of a number of individual emotions. But what could be meant by this "something more"? In a collective or compound phenomenon, what counts as being "more than the sum" or "merely the sum of its components" is notoriously difficult to define. These phrases stir the passions of defenders and opponents of "reductionism"—another contentious term—and touch on live questions about "externalism" and "emergence" in the philosophy of mind. Externalists place the locus of certain mental states outside the individual brains where common sense tends to place them. And if externalism accounts for some features of individual minds and bodies, perhaps it can do the same for individual consciousness. Perhaps the very nature of some emotions might best be understood in terms of facts outside the mind of the person said to be experiencing them. Even an individual emotion, then, might be what it is as a consequence of certain collective facts.

R. de Sousa (✉)
Philosophy Department, University of Toronto, Toronto, Canada
e-mail: sousa@chass.utoronto.ca

A. Konzelmann Ziv and H.B. Schmid (eds.), *Institutions, Emotions, and Group Agents*, 141
Studies in the Philosophy of Sociality 2, DOI 10.1007/978-94-007-6934-2_9,
© Springer Science+Business Media Dordrecht 2014

For an example of a claim about the emergence of a social phenomenon, consider this passage from a recent interview in *Wired* of Nicholas Christakis, who has become something of a celebrity for his study of "social emotional contagion". Christakis notes that the average Facebook user has about 105 friends, and claims that those 105 "friends" do not influence your opinions and taste, whereas your (five or six) actual friends do. He speaks of such social effects as "emergent". In his explanation of that term, however, it is not entirely clear whether we are being given an analogy, another example of the very same phenomenon, or a distinct species of a generic concept of emergence:

> The example I give ... is graphite and diamond. ... The properties of graphite are completely different than the properties of diamond, and those properties do not reside in the carbon. They arise as a result of the patterns of interconnections between the carbon atoms. Therefore a group of carbon atoms can have different properties that have nothing to do with the carbon per se and have everything to do with the ties between the carbon [sic]. And that's what we're seeing about social networks. The same people assembled in different ways can give rise to different properties. (Zetter 2010)

Talk of "emergence" is a standard strategy for blocking the perceived threat of reductionism. But what is that threat, and why does it bother anyone? If having a certain atomic structure, say, H_2O, is necessary and sufficient for a phenomenal property such as liquidity to arise, does it mean that there is *nothing but* that structure in the world, and that the property in question is merely epiphenomenal? To worry about that question is to feel what I've called the threat of reductionism.

The objection to reductionism is temperamental rather than rational. Broadly interpreted, reductionism is no more and no less than the fundamental project of science. It rests on the methodological presupposition that explanations of complex phenomena are to be sought in terms of the nature, arrangement and interactions of their parts. But while it is often assumed that emergence and reduction are mutually exclusive, a clarification of those terms can show that assumption to be false: rightly understood, reduction is compatible with emergence. To show this, it is helpful to distinguish several grades of emergence, depending on the conditions, if any, under which facts about the base level *suffice to predict* those on the emergent level.

At level zero, the properties of a whole can be seen to follow immediately from those of its components. If I arrange four coins in a square, the pattern's property of squareness is immediately seen to follow from that arrangement of its components. Putting it this way merges two ideas: the psychological obviousness of the pattern, which is a contingent fact about our ability to detect a given "Gestalt"; and the logical fact that the spatial relations among the coins *constitute* necessary and sufficient conditions to form a square. The psychological fact is commonly taken to attest to the logical fact, but neither entails the other. Some analytic truths are not obvious. I might have to work hard to deduce the behaviour of the whole from the behaviour of the parts, even if it can be done using only the laws of logic. The same might be said of mathematical theorems. In these cases, although one would not normally speak of emergence, I might have trouble figuring out the deducible consequence. Theorems are said to be "contained" in their premises, but they are generally opaque to mere common-sense even when those premises are known. I therefore suggest that we think of this as a case of "epistemic emergence", where the inference is hampered by logical complexity. Call this, then, *Epistemic Emergence of level 1*. Obviously there is nothing troublesome about it.

Epistemic Emergence of level 2 is the most common case. Here mere logic and mathematics no longer suffice. Instead there are law-like connections between the phenomena at one level and those at the other. Typically, for example, there are bridge laws linking individual and global (or micro and macro) phenomena. These must be discovered empirically. Once discovered, they can serve to yield information about the behaviour of the whole on the basis of information about the parts. Thus I am told by those who know such things that many (if not all) properties of a never-before-seen protein can be deduced on the basis of three lower-level facts: what amino-acids compose it, the "secondary" structure determined by the sequence of those components, and the "tertiary" or folding properties of the whole structure. That can be done only on the basis of laws or regularities that must be discovered empirically. If that were not so, it would imply, if it could be generalised, that all science could ultimately be done a priori. Assuming an irreducible need for empirical input in such scientific matters, then, this represents a genuine level of emergence in relation to purely logical deducibility.

Epistemic Emergence of level 3 relates to level 2 in a way analogous to the way level 1 relates to level zero: in both cases, epistemic justification does not ensure psychological accessibility. Level 3 typically applies to deterministic chaotic systems. Prediction is a logical possibility; but in a chaotic system small differences in the values of some parameters can generate, after a sufficiently long time, arbitrarily large differences in outcome. In practice, these outcomes are therefore effectively unpredictable. Their surprising nature justifies calling them emergent, but again there is nothing there that seems mysterious or metaphysically incompatible with the spirit of scientific reductionism.

It is at the next step that we get the kind of emergence about which disputes arise and ideology makes claims for ontology. We get *Epistemic Emergence of level 4* when there is no logical possibility of prediction, because the correlation between facts at the lower level and those at the emergent level can be established *only* on the basis of ad hoc empirical correlations. No independently established general laws and principles exist from which the specific relation between micro and macro levels can be inferred. This is what bothers people about the emergent character of consciousness in relation to its neural underpinnings: it's that we *can't imagine* how the latter can give rise to the former. Perhaps, at a more advanced stage of science, we will come to understand why consciousness *has* to exist when certain sets of neural connections are made in a certain sort of wetware. But is that not, after all, just like the relation between the atomic structure of carbon and the divergent properties of graphite and diamonds alluded to by Christakis? On that criterion, the fact that just this divergence of properties arises from just that difference in arrangements is equally mysterious. And yet, for reasons that remain unclear, most people worried about the supposed irreducibility of consciousness would remain unperturbed by Christakis's example.

Armed with this taxonomy of grades of emergence, bothersome or not, we can reformulate the question of the reducibility of a shared or collective emotion to the component events that constitute it. There are two ways to think of the grounding level. One alternative is to think of a collective emotion as arising out of the emotions of the individual members of the collectivity. A more intriguing possibility is that the collective emotion arises not from individual emotions, but out of sub-emotional and sub-personal characteristics of the individuals involved. The analogy then would be with the way that, on some "component theories" of emotion, an individual emotion is ascribed on the basis of a number of components—behavioral, experiential, physiological, situational, and cognitive—which taken separately do not suffice to warrant the name of emotion. One might be led to that hypothesis by the notoriously bewildering characteristics of crowd behaviour, which seem to amount to more than the sum of the individual emotions of group members. Under certain conditions, it seems that a "psychological law of the mental unity of crowds" comes into play. Gustave Le Bon anticipated by a century the situationist point of view of John Doris (2002) when he noted:

> It is only in novels that individuals are found to traverse their whole life with an unvarying character. It is only the uniformity of the environment that creates the apparent uniformity of characters ... All mental constitutions contain possibilities of character which may be manifested in consequence of a sudden change of environment. (Le Bon 1896, p. 7)

That suggests that the individual emotions involved at the time a collective emotion is being manifested are not merely the constituents of that collective emotion, but are partly caused by the fact that each individual is a member of that particular group. That leaves indeterminate the mechanism responsible for producing the collective emotion as well as the individual emotions that are implied by it, allowing for the possibility that the types of basic interactions responsible are not in themselves (yet) emotions, but some sort of attunement of lower-level states. This might be comparable to the mechanism, whatever it may be, that commonly results in the synchronization of menstrual periods among members of a single household. In this last case, there may well be a kind of emotional harmonization that also takes place, but that emotional attunement is the result of a prior physiological attunement, rather than an emergent effect of the existence of individual emotions.

Recall that level 4 emergence is defined by the impossibility of deducing, from the examination, however thorough, of a single particle, what properties will be generated when that particle is associated with other particles in a configuration that has never yet been tested. This is precisely the point made by Le Bon in connection with the minds of individuals in a crowd. No amount of investigation of a particular individual's dispositions to behave in this or that way in isolation, including the dispositions such an individual might avow when asked about counterfactual situations, can yield a reliable prediction of what that same particle or individual will contribute to a group phenomenon.

This presents an intriguing analogy with the "problem of externalism" figuring elsewhere, in several versions, in the philosophy of mind and language. Hilary Putnam's claim that "meanings ain't in the head" was based on the fact that the reference of a term was not adequately fixed by any individual speaker's knowledge of its sense. I can accurately refer to an elm without having any idea what one looks like or how it differs from an oak. My reference is fixed, not by my mental state setting up adequate conditions of recognition, but by the fact that elms and oaks are reliably identified by others who speak my language and on whose expertise my reference tacitly depends (Putnam 1973). This is a straightforward externalist thesis about meaning.

Sue Campbell (1998) has put forward a more contentious thesis applicable specifically to the identity of our emotions. She focuses on the predicament of Roxane, in *Cyrano de Bergerac*, who thinks she loves Christian, not just because he is handsome and brave, but because, as she falsely believes, he is the author of the fine poetic words actually spoken or composed by Cyrano. After Christian is killed, Cyrano's sense of honour stops him from revealing himself when Roxane insists she would love Christian even if he were ugly. (But then how does she know …? That love is rare indeed that does not "alter when it alteration finds". Our insight into counterfactuals is shaky at best, and particularly so where the counterfactual concerns emotions.) In the play's final scene, Cyrano asks to see Christian's last letter. He gives himself away by "reading" it aloud when it has become too dark for him to see it. Whom then does Roxane love? Campbell insists that it is too late now to say that Cyrano is Roxane's true love. This is not because he is also now conveniently dying, but because the question has at least in part been decided against Cyrano, by Roxane's past actions over a long period of time: kissing Christian, marrying Christian, speaking of her love for Christian, mourning him for years.

Campbell's analysis is "externalist" in two ways. First, there is a genuine indeterminacy about the object of Roxane's love. Her feelings may have been caused or *prompted* by Cyrano's fine words, but it was *directed*, together with her letters, her kisses, and her thoughts, at Christian. The second point is both bolder and more subtle. It is the claim that to individuate a changing emotion requires an act of "collaborative individuation". We can see this as an extended form of Putnam's externalism about meaning: just as we don't have privileged access into the meanings of our own words, so also we fail to be the sole authority over the nature and object of our emotions. This thought might encourage an anxious awareness of the perils entailed by the power of others to define us, as well as a resolve to master whatever additional power we might claim over our own emotions by controlling the way we express ourselves. "To change emotionally," Campbell writes, "we appear to need situations to work through, and some history of success" (p. 102). The point can be conservatively glossed in terms of classical learning theory: a habit is extinguished not in the absence of the stimulus. Extinction requires the presence of the stimulus coupled with the absence of the response. It's the response, therefore, that holds the key to change, and while by definition (some definitions, anyway) emotional expression is *involuntary*, that term is sufficiently elastic to allow for some more or less indirect control of at least some of our responses.[1]

Insofar as the identification of an emotion is a social rather than exclusively an individual fact, we have a specifically emotional version of externalism. This identifies two respects in which the collective phenomenon is not "merely the sum" of its individual components: one is that it is emergent, at what I've characterized as level 4, in relation to the individual emotions; the second is that the individual emotions themselves are in part defined by the collective context in which they appear. The individual emotion undergone by participants in a collective emotion depends in part for its very identity on what is happening outside of each individual.

2   Modes of Sharing

How then, in practice, might a collective or shared emotion be built out of multiple individual states? I begin by briefly surveying some standard ways in which two or more people can share an emotion. In speaking of "standard ways", I mean that for the moment I will confine myself to cases that presuppose no special group phenomena such as those alluded to by Le Bon, that is, no emergence beyond Level 3; but we shall soon see that Level 4 may become implicated as well. The basic cases I have in mind exemplify only three familiar patterns of causation: common, mutual, or reciprocal. Without any claim to be exhaustive, I distinguish joint attention, one-way influence, mutual influence, and purely epistemic influence.

(i) *Joint attention*

The capacity for joint attention emerges in the first 6 months of life (Butterworth and Cochran 1980). In the simplest case, joint attention might be merely coincidental. When two people are looking at the same thing then, if they approach the common point of focus equipped with similar background assumptions, very likely their responses to it will be somewhat similar. Such similarity could be due to an entirely general mechanism involving common knowledge, attitudes, assumptions, and perceptual capacities. Or it could be due to some specific prior agreement which leads the subjects to interpret the situation in similar ways, when that would otherwise be difficult or unlikely. (A convention establishing the meaning of symbols might be required, for example.)

---

[1]To draw the starkest contrast with Campbell's thesis, one can turn to the purest form of existentialism, illustrated by Sartre's play *Les Mains Sales*. The central character, Hugo, a Communist Party member, had been ordered to kill a deviationist Party leader. He did indeed kill him, but out of sexual jealousy. The party having now adopted the dead leader's line, Hugo could save his life by admitting that he killed out of jealousy, not political conviction. But in the climactic scene of the play he chooses to be "non-recuperable" by the Party, by retroactively construing his motive as political. In this existentialist view, the psychological and collective facts don't matter. The individual can just choose by fiat the nature of his past act (Sartre 1948).

In simple cases of this kind, the common feeling that results need involve no interaction between subjects. Interpreted in this way, the case of joint attention can be conceived as a species of a general type, where a single cause acts on several subjects. The common cause might not necessarily be that on which attention is focused. On the contrary, it might affect two or more people's moods and feeling without generating any awareness of its nature. A smell, for example, or worse an odorless chemical affecting the nervous system, might go undetected as such by those whom it affects, and yet result in shared moods of depression, anxiety, or panic. Or it might force itself into the consciousness of the subjects, but without being the object of intentional focus, as when, for example, several people are subjected to some unpleasant condition. Think of lining up for a show in the sun on a hot muggy day.

In practice, few cases will fall within this simple pattern of mere common causation. Unless neither is aware of the other, each will be influenced by the other. There is evidence that attention itself is not a purely cognitive phenomenon but involves emotional engagement. In the psychological literature about "joint attention", the term is reserved for cases where two or more people don't just happen to focus on the same object, but the common focus itself derives from a prior emotionally tinged engagement with one another. Thus Peter Hobson regards the capacity of an infant to engage in joint attention as the culmination of a three phase process:

> 1. The infant engages with someone else. 2. The infant engages with someone else's engagement with the world—and is 'moved'. 3. The infant achieves a new level of awareness that she is engaging with someone else's engagement with the world (in part through the process of being engaged with the other's engagement with herself) (Hobson 2005, p. 188).

In this kind of case, then, the mutual engagement is prior to the common focus, and jointness is a result rather than a simple cause of mutual engagement. If a certain emotional attunement is a precondition rather than a result of shared attention, we might have to concede that there is really no simple case of joint attention (unless we mean to speak merely of cases where two unconnected observers just happen to be looking in the same direction). Genuine cases of joint attention are really more akin to the complex type (iii) described below.

First, however, let us look at an intermediate case.

(ii) *One-way influence*
One-way influence could take several forms resulting in the two parties experiencing similar, different or even opposite emotions (as in escalating antipathy). The case of empathy, of which more in a moment, is often of this sort, for the object of empathic feeling might not even be aware of the existence of the empathizing individual. In the most interesting cases, however, which are also those most likely to generate unexpected consequences giving rise to ascriptions of emergence, the causation is not one way.

When all goes well, a one-way influence can result in a harmony between two people, manifested in similar emotional attitudes and attested by similarity of patterns of brain activity. So much is indicated by an experiment in which fMRI observations were made of the patterns of brain activity in a storyteller and that of a listener (Stephens et al. 2010). The authors found a remarkable correlation between the extent to which the listener understood the speaker's story as the latter meant it and the extent of overlap in brain activity. Another experiment showed that meaningful physical gestures of the sort involved in playing charades also gave rise to overlapping regions of activity in the various participants, linked to mutual understanding (Schippers et al. 2010). In all these cases, the agreement between participants is not necessarily emotional: all that the brain evidence shows is that something is shared at a sub-personal level linked to cognition. But if cognition, when shared, involves similar brain activity, there is no reason to expect that the same would not also apply to emotions.

Conversely, the absence of common presuppositions can be a serious obstacle. In a particularly demoralising piece of research, Brendon Nyhan and Jason Reifler have shown that when people have misconceptions, confronting them with evidence of their mistake can be counterproductive, serving only to entrench their erroneous conviction (Nyhan and Reifler 2010). As Aristotle remarked in another connection, "when you choke on water, what will you wash it down with?"

(iii) *Mutual influence*
The most complex case, at least when just two people are involved, involves causation that goes in both directions. If the resulting experiences are similar in both individuals, we might get the slow dance-like emulation involved when two people are communicating in a harmonious way, whether in therapy (Charny 1966) or in ordinary conversation (Kimura and Daibo 2006). In such cases the outcome of the emotional coupling might be shared emotions; but it could also be, on the contrary, a growing estrangement that might still count as a collective feeling insofar as it is generated by the emotionally affecting interaction between the two participants. Once again, however, it must be noted that the original component individual states may not be of precisely the same emotional species as the collective fact we describe as "mutual estrangement".

The dynamics of mutuality are highly diverse. Some of the diversity results from the fact that the feedback given and received by the participants might be positive or negative, and that it can involve sympathetic entrainment or antithetical entrainment. An illustration of the former is provided by Tom Nagel's Sartrean analysis of mutual seduction (Nagel 1979). On this model, each lover's desire is enhanced by perceiving the other's desire, which is simultaneously enhanced by perception of his own. The structure of desire, then, is analogous to that of reflections in a pair of facing mirrors. But there is a disanalogy, which is that the images in the mirrors get fainter, whereas on Nagel's model the desire is intensified by each reflection. This is a case of positive feedback, and since all cases of positive feedback are inherently unstable, no general prediction can be made about where it will end.

Where the feedback is negative, we can expect a stable equilibrium. An example of such an oppositional model is provided by the emotional phenomenon that Alain de Botton has called "Marxism", in homage not to Karl but to Groucho, who disdained to join any club so vulgar as to admit him as a member. Here the natural dialectic tends to foster contempt for anyone so undiscriminating as to fall in love with such an unworthy object as me: the less you love me, then, the more I can love you; but if both are subject to the same dialectic, the two will find an equilibrium (de Botton 1993, pp. 53–64). In actual love affairs, even when there isn't the premise required by the Marxist dialectic idea, similar dialectics take place that sometimes enable a relationship to find equilibrium.

If mutual love is enhanced by positive feedback, on the other hand, the lovers can end up swallowing one another in a kind of dance that can end only in death, as in the legendary stories of Tristan and Isolde, or of Nagisa Oshima's *Realm of the Senses*. Scaling back, under the influence of negative feedback, means restraint, and constraints, and brings back Romantic love into the Classical fold of proportion and moderation.

(iv) *Purely epistemic influence*
By way of comparison with more general ways in which the mental states of various individuals can be brought into harmony, we should also, if only by way of contrast, note cases where a collective belief is generated by rational considerations of evidence. These needn't involve emotions. This is ideally what happens in the scientific community when someone publishes a convincing paper that establishes a fresh piece of knowledge, perhaps requiring most people to change their minds— showing, for example, that stomach ulcers are caused by a bacterium when orthodox medical opinion assumed they were due to stress. It is noteworthy that such rational conversions are in fact rare, precisely because people's previous convictions tend to be emotionally invested.

In (i)–(iv), we have seen four patterns of causation resulting in a collective phenomenon. It is time now to ask what forms of sharing might be most likely to apply to emotional states. Here emotion theorists generally agree that we should make a three-fold distinction.

(a) *Contagion* appears to take place without the intervention of any subtle cognition, or perhaps any cognition at all, in small babies as well as other animals. Contagion is reflexive, not reflective: it involves no effort of imagination or thought.

(b) *Empathy* appears to be something like a primitive perceptual state, differing from contagion in that it does not necessarily result in similar states in observer and observed.

(c) *Sympathy*, in which there is a more detached form of resonance between observed and someone observed to be in a given emotional state. As Jesse Prinz has put it, "Sympathy is a third person emotional response, whereas empathy involves putting oneself in another person's shoes" (Prinz 2011, p. 212). This point can be slightly confusing for, as Prinz points out, the British moralists "used 'sympathy' in a way that is similar to the way I want to use 'empathy'." Sympathy is more clearly a cognitive phenomenon. It seems to be based on understanding the situation, or building a model of someone else's mind.

Before discussing how empathy might work, and how it might serve morality and politics, let me note in passing that some forms of emotional influence discovered by recent research seem downright bizarre. There is evidence that we are susceptible to being influenced by our friends but "we are also beholden to the moods of friends of friends, and of friends of friends of friends—people three degrees of separation away from us who we have never met, but whose disposition can pass through our social network like a virus." (Bond 2008, p. 24). This applies not only to moods but to obesity. According to Nicholas Christakis, whom I quoted above, the range of states that are subject to such transmission is surprisingly broad. It reportedly applies to "happiness and depression, obesity, drinking and smoking habits, ill-health, the inclination to turn out and vote in elections, a taste for certain music or food, a preference for online privacy, even the tendency to attempt or think about suicide" (Ibid.).

Many thinkers, including the early modern sentimentalists such as Hutcheson and Hume—and Mencius long before them—have regarded our capacity for empathy as fundamental to our capacity for morality. The capacity to share feelings that results from the basic faculty of empathy is undoubtedly important. But empathy is not directed equally to all. This becomes apparent, if we look at the patterns of influence that distinguish closer friends from more distant acquaintances. So much, at least, is claimed by Christakis in the previously quoted interview with *Wired* magazine:

> Our friends' friends' friends affect us—meaning that there's a kind of social domino effect or a social contagion. Things ripple through the network and we can come to be affected, not just by what the people around us are doing, but by what people further away, that we don't even know, are doing. The best example of this is a children's game of telephone. You're the fifth in line, and the person whispers something in your ear that is erroneous. But it doesn't just include the errors that that person introduced. It includes all the accumulated errors of everyone else. So that's how we come to be affected by people downstream. (Zetter 2010)

Actually that seems a little strange, because in the kind of case they are talking about the influence is predictable, whereas the telephone game admits of random branchings—limited, to be sure, since one can't misunderstand just anything as just anything else—but it is never a case of there being a definite probability of X turning into Y on the basis of the influence of Z.

Still, the analogy is interesting for that very reason. Given the diversity of temperaments among participants, the phenomenon of uniform causal influence— happiness increases happiness, depression deepens depression, etc.—demands an explanation. Even if a single person's mood has *some* effect on that of another, there was no a priori reason to expect the influence in question to be the same for all those affected. People can resist as well as endorse what other folks are thinking. In the case of emotion, however, it seems plausible that the influence should simply be based on imitation. What are we imitating? Well, there's evidence that posture is naturally imitated, as is facial expression, and on a broadly Jamesian view of emotion we would expect some feedback-type influence of that behavioral process on the participants' emotional state. But while imitation is a powerful strategy, it turns out to be most successful if not everyone else is doing it too (Boyd and Richerson 2005). This makes good intuitive sense: savvy investors know that contrarian strategies often work best. But that leads us to expect that not everyone is pre-wired for imitation. And this fact, in turn, should prepare us for the possibility that mechanisms akin to imitation and empathy are unlikely to be central to the human capacity for moral response. Yet several authors have recently made just such a claim for empathy. I turn, then, to look a bit more closely at the possible uses of empathy.

3   Sceptical Thoughts on Empathy

It is consoling to imagine that even if we can't trust in God, Nature does everything for the best. Empathy, the etymology of which suggests that it implies "feeling as if you were on the inside" of another's experience, looks like one of Nature's best inventions: a shortcut to the motivation of altruistic actions. Mencius noted, 2,300 years ago, that when you see a baby about to fall into a well, you don't need to think about it before leaping to save it. That involves a kind of reflex-like response often mentioned in this connection; but it isn't actually obvious that it requires empathy. At that moment, the baby in question might not be feeling anything at all. Whatever we call it, the feeling that drives the response was not yet, for Mencius, a virtue: rather it was the emotional "root" of what, with proper education, becomes the virtue of benevolence ("ren"). Recently Jeremy Rifkin (2009), an author of blockbuster books on issues of public significance, and Frans de Waal (2009), a leading primatologist, have taken up the theme in a big way. The converse idea, that evil is the result of a lack of empathy, underlies a book by Baron-Cohen (2011).

Rifkin and de Waal argue that humans are blessed with a capacity to respond empathically to one another's emotions. Both suggest that empathy has evolved for the benefit of humanity, along with our smarts, our language, and our love of kin. If we would only *realize* this, in both senses of the word, we could have what Rifkin refers to as an "empathic civilization": a whole new golden age.

There are a couple of reasons for the current interest in empathy, as global social glue or panacea for cultural conflict. One is that when globalisation brings mutually antipathetic value systems into direct confrontation, empathy promises a shortcut to mutual understanding. Empathising with another's pain, we earnestly hope, will automatically motivate us to alleviate it. Another is the scientific discovery of "mirror neurons" (Gallese and Goldman 1998), which seem to provide a mechanism, triggering the speculation that we have a neurologically guaranteed access to others' emotions and especially their pain.

Both these ideas are questionable. Not every brain scientist is convinced of the existence of mirror neurons in humans; but if they do exist, it isn't clear that they relate directly to empathy. Mirror neurons light up when the motor system is activated, and they owe their name to the fact that they also light up at the sight of someone else doing the same thing. One can imagine different ways in which we might interpret this observation. The most obvious is that mirror neurons have evolved to facilitate imitation by simple observation. But the fact that a bunch of neurons are observed to light up under these two different sets of circumstances doesn't suffice to establish that hypothesis. In addition, only humans imitate from birth, and in humans mirror neurons remained conjectural until very recently. They were first clearly observed only in monkeys. But, as Alison Gopnik pointed out, monkeys "don't actually imitate what other monkeys do: so the ubiquitous and powerful imitation we see in human babies can't just be there because they have mirror neurons" (Gopnik 2009, p. 207). Her observation about the difference between humans and monkeys remains valid, despite recent evidence that mirror neurons do indeed exist in human brains as well (Mukamel et al. 2010). One form of such imitation arises at an amazingly early age: newborns are liable to pull out their tongue in response to seeing someone pulling theirs. As Gopnik interprets this, "this means that for babies imitation is both a symptom of innate empathy and a tool to expand and elaborate that empathy" (Gopnik 2009, p. 205). In itself, it's not clear why we have to assume that this necessarily implicates emotions or feelings, except in the simple sense of "the feeling of pulling my tongue out"; but insofar as we go along with the Jamesian view that physical behaviour itself, as well as visceral responses, are reflected in subjective emotional feeling, it seems likely that the capacity for imitation will be linked to emotional experience:

> Psychologists have shown that people unconsciously copy the facial expressions, manner of speech, posture, body language and other behaviours of those around them, often with remarkable speed and accuracy. This then causes them, through a kind of neural feedback, to actually experience the emotions associated with the particular behaviour they are mimicking. (Bond 2008, p.25)

So what can we expect of empathy as a source of positive shared emotions?

Jesse Prinz (2011) has given several reasons for thinking that the answer is: Not much. First, he points out that we cannot assume—as do Rifkin and most of the commentators that have gushed about Rifkin's book on the web—that empathy necessarily includes concern. That obviously begs the question in the context of a debate about the role of empathy as a necessary, sufficient, or even essentially relevant factor in the motivation of moral responses. Prinz also points out that "empathy in its simplest form is just emotional contagion: catching the emotion that another person feels" (p. 213). As I observed above, contagion resembles a reflex more than an emotion. This means that if contagion counts as empathy, then a sophisticated act of imagination is not required for empathy; yet it is undoubtedly required for morality.

Prinz notes that our moral judgment does not generally track our empathetic responses: "for example one might charge that it is bad to kill an innocent person even if his vital organs could be used to save five others ... Arguably, we feel cumulatively more empathy for the five people in need than for the one healthy person" (Prinz 2011, p. 214). Actually, that might not be true, if we take account of Paul Slovic's finding that people are more likely to respond emotionally to the picture of a single needy person without further discursive information than they are to the same picture accompanied by a caption pointing out that many other children are suffering the same plight (Slovic 2007). Prinz's point, however, stands. Prinz also points out that other emotions can be involved in generating moral judgments. In itself, that need not point away from empathy, because it seems to imply that empathy is itself an emotion: in fact, however, empathy is a capacity to resonate with somebody else's emotion, not an emotion in itself. It is not so much *an* emotion as a *window* onto another's emotion: the resulting experience can be of almost any emotion.

Prinz makes another remark worthy of a small detour. "There are crimes against nature: such as necrophilia, incest, or bestiality. In these cases, the dominant emotional response is disgust, when the action is performed by another, and shame if we perform or even consider performing such an action ourselves" (Prinz 2011, p. 215). Needless to say, that depends on who "we" are. Some of us regard the very concept of a "crime against nature" as an offense against rational thought. To anyone who shares this view, Prinz's argument will seem feeble. But it raises a couple of interesting points. I myself am unable to empathize directly with the desire to perform any of the three sorts of actions Prinz alludes to; the idea of the first and third, at any rate, provokes a modicum of disgust (though the second leaves me indifferent). But I am equally unable to sympathize with the view that any of these behaviours are in themselves *immoral*. And in this case I find myself empathizing with precisely the people who commit such acts. I do so not in the sense of sharing their desire, but in the sense of feeling their hurt for the condemnation that their inclinations are liable to call down on them. This suggests that some forms of empathy, far from being simply contagion, result from a sophisticated selection that imagination is able to make between different aspects and levels of appraisal. As we'll see in a moment, there is actually some evidence for this from brain science.

There is an asymmetry between moral approbation and disapproval. Prinz suggests that "the sentiment of disapprobation" towards a kind of action is what a negative moral judgement amounts to. The asymmetry arises from the fact that, while approbation can indeed be directed at acts that one finds particularly admirable, most actions that are not immoral elicit no sentiment of either kind. A further problem with this proposal is that whatever empathy might contribute to moral judgment, there are many kinds of disapprobation and many grounds for it. If I disapprove of the aesthetics expressed in your choice of hats, that does not show that I find you immoral on that ground. It is notoriously difficult to say just what is specific about moral disapproval as opposed to other kinds of disapproval. Prinz seems to me to be on firmer ground when he mentions the important emotions of guilt and anger, which Alan Gibbard has singled out as crucial to moral judgements (Gibbard 1990). The kind of disapprobation that involves anger or guilt is unlikely to pertain to matters aesthetic. So I endorse his conclusion that a sentimentalist theory can be based on such emotions as anger and guilt, while empathy is of only minor importance.

As for the moral incompetence of psychopaths, it is not, contrary to the central thesis defended in (Baron-Cohen 2011), due to a lack of empathy; rather it seems related to a more general deficit in their capacity to experience genuine negative emotions in response to present pain in others and even to the prospect of future pain for themselves (Blair et al. 2005). In fact, as we shall see below, there is no evidence that the psychopath lacks empathy. On the contrary, it is plausible to suppose that some of our power to hurt is due to the accuracy of their perception of other people's moods, emotions, and vulnerable points.

The fact that empathy is not in itself an emotion also provides good reason for Prinz's rejection of empathy as motivation. Motivation is entailed by actual specific emotions, rather than by empathy as such. In some cases, however—and these are the cases that have led people to think that empathy is developmentally important in small children—the appropriate emotions will be elicited in a child capable of empathy, while they may remain opaque to a child who is defective in that regard.

I will conclude by adding a few considerations that might strengthen Prinz's reservations about empathy, drawing on the main threads of the foregoing discussion. To begin with, empathy appears to be above all an epistemic tool: an avenue into the minds of others. It isn't evil psychopaths who lack empathy, but harmless autistic individuals. If empathy very likely evolved to yield insight into others' minds, that affords no particular reason to think its function is to make us nicer to one another. As Mark Rowlands (among others) has suggested, our primate intelligence shows signs of having been designed above all to manipulate and outwit the competition (Rowlands 2009). Knowledge of others' states of mind is highly important in the pursuit of those "Macchiavellian" aims. The mechanical capacity for empathy seems to be just one tool, together with calculation, mirror neurons and perhaps direct mood contagion, in the arsenal of Macchiavellian intelligence. Like those other tools, it is just as likely to serve selfish ends as altruistic ones. Knowing how others think and feel is imperative for hypersocial beings such as we are, but it is no guarantee that we'll *care* about the people we're thus equipped to know about.

That empathy evolved not to make us nicer, but to make us better able to deceive, control, and manipulate, doesn't mean it isn't a good thing. Lots of good things, in evolution, have arisen as "exaptations", mere side-effects of adaptations that originally had quite different functions (Gould and Lewontin 1979). (The delicate bones in our inner ear that enable us to parse music and speech started out as jawbones with which our crocodilian ancestors crushed their prey). But exaptations, by definition, weren't primarily shaped to fill that novel role.

In the case of empathy, one indication that empathy didn't primarily evolve for the sake of mutual aid is that there is surprisingly little correlation between feeling another's pain and being inclined to help. If you happen to dislike the person suffering, you can respond with glee, not sympathy. Brain studies confirm the distinction made above on purely conceptual grounds, namely that empathy is not emotional contagion (though the two are sometimes confused). On the contrary, unlike contagion, it is strongly modulated by attitudes. Painful experience endured by another person is viewed with remarkable indifference if that person is thought to "deserve" it. Vignemont and Singer (2006) have provided evidence that the triggering of empathic responses is modulated by prejudices and opinions and depends on our appraisal of the situation. And we don't need brain scanners to tell us that people can be entirely placid, or even enjoyably entertained, when witnessing the torments of some person or animal that isn't judged to be part of their crowd.

In fact, although empathy and compassion are commonly said to promote greater inclusiveness in our attitude to others, the truth may be precisely the reverse: in order to feel empathy, we must first regard someone as "one of us". All too often, empathizing humans are like Lewis Carroll's walrus weeping for the oysters he is gobbling. Without a prior commitment to doing good, feeling another's pain is just as likely to move you to give them a wide berth as to close in to help. If you're in pain, it's unpleasant to feel what you feel. If I allow myself to feel it, rather than just turn away or turn it off, it could be either because I already care about you, or because it is worth it for me to know what you're feeling, just so that I can be forewarned about what you might do.

Neither is it obvious that empathy is an indispensable condition of behaving morally. Kant was wrong in insisting that emotion should have no part in moral motivation. But even if motivation does require emotion, there are many powerful emotions that can move us to respond to the needs of others without empathy. You may want to help someone you pity; but pity isn't the same as empathy. You may want to help someone in need out of a commitment to equality, or fairness, without feeling the slightest empathetic resonance. In defence of noble ideals of freedom, you might fight for the rights of someone for whom you feel nothing but repugnance. You may be moved to fight against an injustice, not out of empathy for the victim, but out of indignation against the perpetrator. Or, to turn things upside down altogether, your righteous indignation might even be bolstered by empathy with the perpetrator rather than the victim: guilt at your kinship with the bad guys, together with shame at your very lack of empathy for the oppressed, has been known to out a check book more effectively than the next person's tearful compassion.

Jeremy Rifkin reminds us that "two and a half billion people in more than 190 countries watched the worldwide satellite transmission of [Lady Diana's] funeral ... broadcast in forty-four languages ... the most watched event in all of history." (Rifkin 2009, p. 425). But what good did that do for anybody? None whatever. It may have been empathetic, but it was a fine illustration of sentimentality at its worst: what Oscar Wilde defined as wanting to have a feeling without paying for it. Paul Slovic has shown that while a picture of a single suffering child might prompt people to give \$20, they are likely to give only \$18 if they have to read any text with the picture, especially information about the many other children who share this one's plight. Their empathy works well enough, but a capacity for sober arithmetic might do a lot more good.

Boosting the possibility of moral progress are the indubitable advantages of collaboration, division of labour, the "win-win" strategies of trade, and other cooperative undertakings. This prompts Rifkin to suggests that perhaps "human beings are not inherently evil or intrinsically self-interested ... and that ... drives that we have considered to be primary—aggression, violence, selfish behavior, acquisitiveness—are in fact secondary drives that flow from repression or denial of our most basic instinct" for empathic cooperation (Rifkin 2009, p. 18).

But it makes no evolutionary sense to suppose *anything* deserves the title of "most basic instinct". We are a patchwork of "modules" set up by natural selection to solve countless types of problems of living faced by our ancestors at all stages of evolution. These sometimes act independently and not seldom antagonistically, leading to the experiences of inner conflict noted by philosophers and psychologists ever since Plato decreed the soul to consist in three potentially warring parts. So we are all those things, good and bad, and many others besides. When Rifkin proclaims, in the face of the many instances of social collaboration afforded by complex modern societies, that "cooperation bests competition" (Rifkin 2009, p. 17), he is oblivious to the self-refuting character of that slogan. "*Bests*" is a meaningless term outside a framework of competition. And the logic of natural selection is ineluctable: cooperation will indeed win out, if and only if it succeeds, at some appropriate level of selection, in *besting* competing strategies.

It's good to care about other people's pain and to be motivated to promote their welfare. We can all agree to that, but it won't usher in a new age. And while the capacity for empathy is one of the mental dispositions that sometimes might move us to promote social good, it is neither necessary in any particular case, nor ever sufficient in general. My money's still on the values of the Enlightenment: a little less stupidity, a little more passionate reason.

4 Conclusion

I began with a methodological plea for regarding different grades of "emergence" as reflecting differences in predictability from one level of analysis to another. None, I suggested, should be regarded as especially mysterious. When applied to collective emotions, this perspective leads us to expect that such emotions can arise as the sum of individual ones, but that they might also be causally grounded in sub-emotional, sub-personal physiological events, intensified and transformed by mutual causation. Among the forms of causation involved, it is often assumed that empathy plays a pre-eminent role, and functions as a crucial mechanism underlying our capacity for moral responses. I questioned both whether there is just one single mechanism underlying empathy and whether empathy should in turn be relied on to provide us with necessary emotional tools of moral response. In the course of making this argument, I distinguished three modes of causation pertinent to the states of two or more persons: simple common causation, one-way influence, and more complex forms of mutual causation in which reverberations can become indefinitely complex. In the more interesting cases of collective or joint emotion, involving all three of these levels of causation, the resulting collective emotion can be emergent at level 4. This means that it will not be possible to predict the nature of such a collective emotion on the basis of the properties of its constituents. The force of the externalist thesis I endorsed, when applied to the identification of shared emotions, is that the components of the collective emotions may not themselves be emotions. This provides a further reason why empathy—consisting either in simple contagion or in more sophisticated capacities for emotional understanding—will have no special role in explaining the *sui generis* collective emotion that emerges from the concurrence of individual phenomena. When a collective phenomenon results from complex interactions, not of merely additive individual emotions, but of sub-personal physiological and psychological states, implementing unpredictable and unstable causal processes, there will be no plausibility to the claim that the shared emotion is either justifying of or justified by the individual emotions. The bearing of such emergent phenomena on moral consciousness or the disposition to moral behaviour seems bound to remain equally unpredictable, and we have very little reason to think it must be invariably benign.[2]

References

Baron-Cohen, S. 2011. *The science of evil: Empathy and the origins of cruelty*. New York: Basic Books.

Blair, J., D. Mitchell, and K. Blair. 2005. *The psychopath: Emotion and the brain*. Oxford: Blackwell.

Bond, M. 2008. How your friends' friends can affect your mood. *New Scientist* 2689, December 30, 24–27.

Boyd, R., and P.J. Richerson. 2005. *The origin and evolution of cultures*. Oxford/New York: Oxford University Press.

Butterworth, G., and E. Cochran. 1980. Towards a mechanism of joint visual attention in human infancy. In *Thought without language*, ed. L. Weiskrantz, 5–25. Oxford: Oxford University Press.

Campbell, S. 1998. *Interpreting the personal: Expression and the formation of feeling*. Ithaca: Cornell University.

Charny, E.J. 1966. Psychosomatic manifestations of rapport in psychotherapy. *Psychosomatic Medicine* 28: 305–315.

de Botton, A. 1993. *On love*. New York: Grove Press.

de Waal, F. 2009. *The age of empathy: Nature's lessons for a kinder society*. New York: Three Rivers Press.

Doris, J.M. 2002. *Lack of character: Personality and moral behavior*. Cambridge/New York: Cambridge University Press.

Gallese, V., and A. Goldman. 1998. Mirror neurons and the simulation theory of mind-reading. *Trends in Cognitive Sciences* 2(12): 493–501.

Gibbard, A. 1990. *Wise choices, apt feelings: A theory of normative judgment*. Cambridge, MA: Harvard University Press.

Gopnik, A. 2009. *The philosophical baby: What children's minds tell us about truth, love, and the meaning of life*. New York: Farrar, Straus and Giroux.

Gould, S.J., and R.L. Lewontin. 1979. The spandrels of San Marco and the Panglossion paradigm: A critique of the adaptationist programme. *Proceedings of the Royal Society of London B* 205: 581–598.

Hobson, G. 2005. What puts the jointness into joint attention? In *Joint attention: Communication and other minds. Issues in philosophy and psychology*, ed. N. Elian, 198–220. Oxford: Oxford University Press.

Kimura, M., and I. Daibo. 2006. Interactional synchrony in conversations about emotional episodes: "A measurement by 'the between-participants pseudosynchrony experimental paradigm'". *Journal of Nonverbal Behavior* 30: 115–126.

Le Bon, G. 1896. *The crowd: A study of the popular mind*. New York: Macmillan.

Mukamel, R., A. Ekstrom, J. Kaplan, M. Iacoboni, and I. Fried. 2010. Single-neuron responses in humans during execution and observation of actions. *Current Biology* 20(8): 750–756.

---

[2]I wish to thank conference participants for discussion at the 2010 Basel Conference at which these ideas were first presented, and I am particularly grateful to an anonymous reviewer for extremely helpful criticisms of an earlier draft of this chapter.

Nagel, T. 1979. Sexual perversion. In *Mortal questions*, 39–52. Cambridge: Cambridge University Press.

Nyhan, B., and J. Reifler. 2010. When corrections fail: The persistence of political misperceptions. *Political Behavior* 30: 303–330.

Prinz, J. 2011. Is empathy necessary for morality? In *Empathy: Philosophical and psychological perspectives*, ed. P. Goldie and A. Coplan, 211–229. Oxford: Oxford University Press.

Putnam, H. 1973. Meaning and reference. *Journal of Philosophy* 73(19): 699–711.

Rifkin, J. 2009. *The empathic civilization: The race to global consciousness in a world in crisis*. New York: Jeremy P. Tarcher/Penguin.

Rowlands, M. 2009. *The philosopher and the wolf: Lessons from the wild on life, death and happiness*. London: Granta.

Sartre, J.-P. 1948. *Les mains sales: Pièce en sept tableaux*. Paris: Gallimard.

Schippers, M.B., A. Roebroeck, R. Renkena, L. Nanetti, and C. Keysers. 2010. Mapping the information flow from one brain to another during gestural communication. *Proceedings of the National Academy of Sciences USA* 107(20): 9388–9393.

Slovic, P. 2007. When compassion fails. *New Scientist*, April 7, 18.

Stephens, G.J.S., J. Lauren, and U. Hasson. 2010. Speaker-listener neural coupling underlies successful communication. In *Proceedings of the National Association for Science* 107(32): 14425–14430.

Vignemont, F., and T. Singer. 2006. The empathic brain: How, when and why? *Trends in Cognitive Science* 10(10): 435–444.

Zetter, K. 2010. TED 2010: "Nicholas Christakis: Does this social network make me look fat?" *Wired*. http://www.wired.com/epicenter/2010/02/ted-2010-nicholas-christakis-does-this-social-network-make-me-look-fat/. Last accessed 14 Jan 2011.

Chapter 10
The Functions of Collective Emotions in Social Groups

Mikko Salmela

Abstract In this article, I evaluate the merits of existing empirical and philosophical theories of collective emotions in accounting for certain established functions of these emotions in the emergence, maintenance, and development of social groups. The empirical theories in focus are aggregative theories, ritualistic theories, and intergroup emotions theory, whereas the philosophical theories are Margaret Gilbert's plural subject view and Hans Bernhard Schmid's phenomenological account. All of these approaches offer important insights into the functions of collective emotions in social dynamics. However, I argue that none of the existing theories offers a satisfying explanation for all established functions of collective emotions in social groups. Therefore, I offer a new typology that distinguishes between collective emotions of different kinds in terms of their divergent degrees of collectivity. In particular, I argue that collective emotions of different kinds have dissimilar functions in social groups, and that more collective emotions serve the emergence, maintenance, and development of social groups more effectively than less collective emotions.

1 Established Functions of Collective Emotions in Social Groups

Collective emotions have several functions in the dynamics of social groups, as suggested by both empirical and philosophical researchers.[1] Collective emotions are important both for the *emergence* of social groups as well as for their *maintenance*

---

[1] In this article, I use the notion of "collective emotions" in a wide sense to refer to shared, group, and collective emotions that are understood as referring to the same phenomena. I prefer

M. Salmela (✉)
Helsinki Collegium for Advanced Studies, University of Helsinki, Helsinki, Finland
e-mail: mikko.salmela@helsinki.fi

A. Konzelmann Ziv and H.B. Schmid (eds.), *Institutions, Emotions, and Group Agents,* 159
Studies in the Philosophy of Sociality 2, DOI 10.1007/978-94-007-6934-2_10,
© Springer Science+Business Media Dordrecht 2014

and *development*. Beginning from the first aspect, collective emotions contribute to the formation of social groups. Religious, political, ideological, and other identity groups often arise when the emotions of several individuals converge on an important topic, urging them to act in accordance with their emotions. For instance, shared anger at oppression or shared guilt about collective wrongdoing to a third party plays an important role in the emergence of social and political movements. In this process, collective emotions contribute to the formation of goals, values, and evaluative beliefs—a certain *ethos* (Tuomela 2007)—that are partially constitutive of those groups. Anger at oppression associates with the goal of removing the relevant injustice that aroused this shared emotion, whereas shared guilt gives rise to groups whose members believe that they should apologize and possibly also compensate for the wrong that either they or some other members of their ingroup have inflicted (e.g. Goodwin et al. 2001; Branscombe and Doosje 2004; Flam and King 2005; Scholtz 2008). Finally, collective emotions motivate collective behavior, both expressive and purposive, that contributes to the satisfaction or maintenance of the group ethos. Thus, shared anger motivates protests, both spontaneous and organized, and shared guilt motivates apologetic and reparative actions towards the wronged outgroup (Jasper 1998; Branscombe and Doosje 2004).

Secondly, collective emotions contribute to the maintenance of social groups. Here too we can distinguish several mechanisms. First of all, collective emotions have informative value as they are capable of providing important information about the significance of external events for the group members. Thus, group members feel angry when their group goals are unjustly thwarted or threatened, sad when the group loses something that is important to its goals, proud when the group's goals are achieved as a result of the group members' own efforts, shame when respect for the group is diminished as a result of group members' actions, and so on; (Spoor and Kelly 2004; Parkinson et al. 2005). In addition to their informative value, collective emotions provide group members affective experiences of "being in the same boat" with each other. Experiences of this kind are intrinsically rewarding as they involve feelings of closeness and solidarity, which in turn foster affective bonds, cooperative ties, and group loyalty, especially if the shared emotions are hedonically positive rather than negative (e.g. Smith 2002; Collins 2004; Spoor

the concept of "collective emotions" to "shared emotions", which I have employed elsewhere (Salmela 2012), because the latter concept is ambiguous. On the one hand, the notion "sharing of emotion" refers to a phenomenon in which one person's expressed emotion is perceived by another person (see e.g. Michael 2011; Rimé 2007). On the other hand, it may refer to several individuals experiencing an emotion of the same type and content, such as joy about the success of their favorite team, with mutual awareness of their respective emotional state. My analysis of collective emotions invokes the notion of sharing in the latter sense as I suggest that emotions become collective by virtue of being shared—to lesser or greater degree—with other individuals. Accordingly, I occasionally use the notions of "collective" and "shared" emotion interchangeably for stylistic reasons.

and Kelly 2004; Rimé 2007; Smith et al. 2007; Knottnerus 2010).[2] Central to the emergence of affective solidarity is behavioral synchrony and entrainment among group members: coordination of bodily movements, which underlies emotional contagion and levels emotions in groups (Barsade and Gibson 1998; Collins 2004; Spoor and Kelly 2004). Collective emotions coordinate group activity both through their informative and affiliative functions, which are closely related and mutually reinforcing, as Spoor and Kelly (2004) point out.

Finally, in addition to maintenance, collective emotions are capable of contributing to qualitative changes in the normative structure of social groups. The phenomenon I have in mind is the group members' relation to the constitutive ethos of their group. Tuomela (2007) suggests that the weakest type of commitment to group ethos is private, meaning that the commitment is up to each group member to embrace, revise, or renounce on private reasons alone. Accordingly, Tuomela characterizes social groups whose members have committed themselves to their group ethos in this way as *I-mode* groups. Their opposites are *we-mode* groups, whose members have collectively committed themselves, either explicitly or implicitly, to the group ethos. I argue that collective emotions are capable of contributing to the transformation of social groups from I-mode to we-mode, thus providing an important vehicle for the development of social groups.

In this article, I focus on existing theoretical accounts of collective emotions, asking to what extent they are capable of accommodating these functions of collective emotions in social groups. My approach is then hermeneutic as I begin from certain established (with the exception of the last one) functions of collective emotions and proceed backwards to the features that these emotions must possess in order to serve those functions. Obviously, existing empirical studies have been conducted with some heuristic understanding of the nature of these emotions. In many cases however this understanding is not very explicit, or even if it is, the particular account does not offer a satisfying explanation for all the functions that empirical studies *together* ascribe to collective emotions. Moreover, philosophical accounts of collective emotion have not always been developed with much interest in empirical research. However, philosophical concepts should be at least compatible with existing empirical evidence on the functions of collective emotions, whatever other features they ascribe to these emotions.

I begin my survey from those concepts that have underlain empirical research on the functions of collective emotions. Here I discuss three approaches: aggregative views, intergroup emotion theory, and ritualistic views. Then I move on to philosophical concepts of collective emotions, where I focus on Margaret Gilbert's plural subject view and Hans Bernhard Schmid's phenomenological view. While all existing approaches, both empirical and philosophical, offer several important

---

[2]There is evidence that negative collective emotions such as sadness, disappointment, guilt, and shame, with the exception of anger toward outgroup, decrease commitment to the group, unless these emotions are occasional and controllable (Smith et al. 2007; Kessler and Hollbach 2005; Stryker 2004).

insights into those aspects of collective emotions that explain their functions in social dynamics, I suggest that all of them need to be supplemented with important details. Therefore, I end with a sketch of my own typology that distinguishes between collective emotions of different kinds in terms of their divergent degree of collectivity. In short, I suggest that collective emotions of different kinds have importantly dissimilar functions in social groups, and that more collective emotions generally serve the emergence, maintenance, and development of social groups more effectively than less collective emotions.

2 Empirical Concepts of Collective Emotions

2.1 Aggregative Accounts

Several empirical researchers understand collective emotion on an aggregative basis; as a "group affective tone" (George 1996), "affective group composition" (Barsade and Gibson 1998), or "emotional climate" (de Rivera 1992). Aggregative views model collective emotion as the sum of individual group members' emotional experiences and dispositions. Thus, for instance, the concept of affective group composition "examines how the emotions of individual group members combine to create a group-level emotion, and how group emotion may be seen as the sum of its parts" (Barsade and Gibson 1998, p. 88). The combinatorial process starts from sharing of individual feelings, emotions, and moods in an actual group context, such as at workplace. In this process, we can distinguish between implicit and explicit sharing processes. Implicit, often unconscious processes involve emotional contagion, behavioral entrainment, and vicarious experience of affect through modeling, whereas explicit, conscious processes of sharing include people's active attempts to influence the affects of other group members through 'affective impression management' and other means. Together, "these processes combine individual-level affective experiences of group members to form the affective composition of the group" (Kelly and Barsade 2001, p. 112).

The basic problem with aggregative accounts is that they do not distinguish between very dissimilar collective emotions, some of which should not qualify as collective because the individuals do not have the same emotion in the first place. In some cases, the various sharing processes give rise to intuitively strongly collective emotions. Team members' joy about winning a national championship is an example of this kind of emotion. Yet in other cases, the combinatorial processes produce only weakly collective emotions or rather moods. This is the case for instance when "some aggregate of individuals is feeling something that is sufficiently alike to be identified as the common emotion of the group" (Kemper 2002, p. 61). This characterization allows us to ascribe a collective emotion to a bunch of suburbanites who are waiting for an early morning bus to downtown at the same bus stop, each grumpy for some private reason. While this may be an example of a very weakly collective emotion, the individuals' affective states are at least homogeneous with each other. Nevertheless, affective homogeneity is not necessary for group or collective emotion, as defined by Barsade and Gibson (1998), Barsade (2002), or Sanchez-Burks and Huy (2009). Yet without affective homogeneity, there is no robust sharing of emotions within the group. Therefore, I conclude that insofar as we understand collective emotions on an aggregative basis, their capacity to account for the emergence, maintenance, and transformation of social groups is contingent at best.

2.2   Ritualistic Accounts

In contrast to aggregative theories, ritualistic theories that emerge from the seminal work of Émile Durkheim (1984 [1893]) take the collectivity of collective emotions seriously. Durkheim emphasized the role of collective effervescence in the emergence and maintenance of social groups, but he was not very explicit on the nature of this phenomenon *as an emotion* of certain kind. In a like manner, later researchers in the ritualistic tradition have focused on the causal role of collective emotions in social dynamics rather than on their specific nature as emotions. Nevertheless, Randall Collins' elaborate account of the emergence of collective effervescence in interaction rituals offers a glimpse into the anatomy of this phenomenon as well.

Collins characterizes collective effervescence as heightened intersubjectivity. "The key process is participants' mutual entrainment of emotion and attention, producing a shared emotional/cognitive experience" (Collins 2004, p. 48). The ingredients of an interaction ritual include first of all a group of people who are physically assembled in the same place and separated by some barrier from others who are excluded. The group members focus their attention on some common object or activity, and by communicating this focus to each other become mutually aware of their shared focus of attention.

Finally, the group members share a common mood or emotion.[3] These initiating affects spread and intensify in the group's interaction rituals, such as chants, songs, dances, or games, through emotional contagion and rhythmic synchronization of the group members' bodily responses as well as through their mutual awareness of the shared experience. The result is collective effervescence, "high degree of absorption in emotional entrainment, whatever the emotion may be" (ibid., p. 108). A successful interaction ritual produces emotional energy—confidence, enthusiasm, and good self-feelings—for the participants; collective symbols—emblems, signs,

---

[3]Collins uses the notions of emotion, feeling and mood interchangeably. Here is a striking example: "Members share a common *mood*. It is unessential what *emotion* is present at the outset. The *feelings* may be anger, friendliness, enthusiasm, fear, sorrow, or many others" (Collins 2004, pp. 107–8; my italics). This kind of conceptual vagueness is very unhappy as moods and feelings, unlike emotions, are widely agreed to lack particular intentional objects.

slogans, buzzwords, ideas, or other representations—also infused with emotional energy; feelings of solidarity; and standards of morality: respect for the group and its symbols and anger at violations against either two.

The main problem with Collins' account of collective emotions is their lack of intentionality. Collins follows William James in rendering emotions first and foremost as feelings of bodily arousal, whatever cognitions are contingently involved. Collins speaks about focusing of attention on the same object as a precondition of collective effervescence, but he does not clarify whether or not this object is the object of collective emotion. Instead, shared emotional mood and mutual focus of attention are independent variables that *accompany* and *causally reinforce* each other as ritual ingredients, without becoming *constitutive* aspects of collective effervescence. Indeed, Collins never claims that collective effervescence *as an emotion* possesses an intentional object. Instead, he describes this phenomenon in terms of rhythmic entrainment in conversational turn-taking, speech patterns and rhythms, bodily movements, and feelings. Together these aspects of rhythmic entrainment build up high levels of emotional energy. This energy is attributed to symbols that become means of preserving and reviving the energy in individual minds between interaction rituals in which the participants' emotional energy is "recharged". Unfortunately, these hydraulic metaphors betray an outdated noncognitive view of emotions. Collins' model includes neither collective nor individually convergent appraisal of the object of mutual focus of attention, as a *component* or *function* of *any* emotion.[4] This problem undermines the capacity of his ritualistic theory to explain several functions of collective emotions in social groups.

Collins aptly analyzes the rhythmic synchronization of individual emotional responses that contributes to the experience of collective effervescence. This kind of synchronized sharing is important for the experience of affective solidarity among individuals, which in turn contributes to the emergence of social groups with affectively laden symbols. The affective congruence of group members also fuels expressive collective behavior, such as spontaneous aggression or panicked flight. Nevertheless, these effects remain ephemeral insofar as Collins' collective emotions do not possess an intentional and evaluative content. For instance, the power of symbols to unite the group seems weak if symbols are arbitrary emblems, signs, buzzwords, slogans, chants or ideas that catch the participants' shared attention during an interaction ritual. Collins maintains that symbols reinforce commitment to the group between rituals, but this commitment has no independent *normative* force apart from its *psychological* force that is associated with the amount of emotional energy created in the group's previous interaction rituals. Moreover, it is difficult

---

[4]There is wide agreement among emotion researchers, both empirical and philosophical, that the function of emotions is to evaluate perceived changes in our environment for their significance to our concerns. Cognitive theories (e.g. Frijda 1986; Lazarus 2001; Scherer 2001; Nussbaum 2001; Solomon 2007) maintain that emotions serve this function by virtue of involving evaluations of their particular objects, whereas non-cognitive theories (e.g. Damasio 2003; Prinz 2004; Robinson 2005) argue—in various ways—that emotions can serve this evaluative function even without involving appraisals in their content.

to see how collective effervescence could give rise to purposive and cooperative group action in the service of long-term goals, such as the elimination of some social injustice. Cooperative behaviors may contingently emerge from feelings of solidarity, but these feelings and behaviors are precarious since they tend to fade as time from interaction rituals goes by. The only type of social behavior that Collins' theory of collective emotions non-contingently explains and predicts is then ritualistic behavior in which people engage recurrently in order to recharge their emotional energy. All other behavior is motivated instrumentally by the need to gain resources for emotionally energizing interaction rituals, as Collins admits.

2.3   Intergroup Emotions Theory

The intergroup emotions theory (IET) was developed in order to understand the nature of emotions that arise from group identification or membership. The basic premise of IET is that "when an individual identifies with a group, that ingroup becomes part of the self, thus acquiring social and emotional significance" (Smith et al. 2007, p. 431). Thus, the theory predicts that if my favorite football team is losing an important game, I am desperate about the situation, whereas if it wins, I rejoice. Individuals identify with some groups more closely than with others. Accordingly, more important groups possess more emotional significance than less important ones.

IET makes four specific claims about group-level emotions. First, group-level emotions are distinct from the same person's individual-level emotions. This can be seen from the fact that people may experience group emotions in response to events that affect other ingroup members without affecting the perceivers themselves. Second, group-level emotions depend on the person's level of group identification. In general, the theory predicts that people who identify more strongly with a group should experience and express group emotions—with the exception of guilt—to a greater extent than weak identifiers. Third, group-level emotions are socially shared. By this, Smith et al. (2007) mean that the emotions of group members converge towards a prototypical profile in the group. And fourth, group-level emotions motivate and regulate intragroup and intergroup attitudes and behavior. Thus, Mackie et al. (2008, pp. 1874–75) argue that "knowing whether a group regards another with anger, fear, disgust, guilt, or even admiration and respect tells you whether to expect confrontation, avoidance, exclusion, a desire to repair past wrongs or actions of affiliation and support."

The intergroup emotions theory has many virtues in explaining the functions of collective emotions in social groups. In contrast to ritualistic theories, the IET emphasizes the evaluative function and content of group-level emotions that allows these emotions to focus on specific events and objects that are relevant from the group perspective. This intentional aboutness of collective emotions is vital for their informative function as well as for their role in motivating specific goal-directed group behaviors. The theory also regards group identification or membership as a precondition of group-level emotions and not only as their consequence even if those emotions, with the exception of guilt, reinforce this identification as well.

However, the theory is unclear about the subjective basis and quality of group identification, which reduces its capacity to explain the role of collective emotions in the emergence of groups. Not all similarities between individuals constitute salient grounds for group identification, yet we cannot take the existence of groups and their boundaries for granted. Moreover, the IET does not address the embodied dimension of collective emotions. The main reason is methodological: group-level emotions are typically studied by asking individuals how they feel when they think of themselves in terms of some identity, either in general or in some hypothesized group-relevant situation. The first approach yields reports on the prevalence of distinct emotion-types within certain groups, such as Republicans or students of Indiana University. In contrast, the second approach yields reports on real emotions about hypothesized group-relevant events. These emotions are argued to have similar consequences for arousal, perception, information processing, judgment, and decision-making as emotions about actual events. Even so, the theory only predicts collective emotions proper insofar as these require some kind of co-presence, either physical or virtual, of the participants. This is a serious deficit of IET, because shared affectivity, which is possible only among co-present individuals, is vital for the emergence and reinforcement of affective solidarity between the group members. Without an account of shared embodiment, IET is incapable of explaining all functions of collective emotions in social groups.

3   Philosophical Concepts of Collective Emotions

Philosophical analyses focus on the collective intentionality of shared emotions. In this article, I discuss the capacity of three philosophical accounts—Margaret Gilbert's, Hans Bernhard Schmid's and my own—to accommodate the functions of collective emotions in social groups.

3.1   Gilbert's Plural Subject Account

Gilbert presents her account on collectively intentional emotions, and guilt in particular, in her article "Collective Guilt and Collective Guilt Feelings" (2002). She distinguishes collectively intentional guilt feelings from two kinds of aggregate feelings: feelings of personal guilt and feelings of membership guilt. According to Gilbert, guilt over some personal wrongdoing or over some acts that directly contributed to one's groups' collectively performed wrongdoing does not qualify as an instance of "proper" collective guilt, as it does not constitute guilt over a wrongful collective action. Membership guilt fares somewhat better in this respect, since it is supposed to be guilt over some action that the members of one's group have collectively performed on the basis of a joint commitment. However, individual group members' guilt over the group's actions is not the same thing as the group's guilt over its own actions. Therefore, we need a plural subject account of collective guilt feelings.

Gilbert formulates her plural subject account of collective guilt in two ways:

(i) For us *collectively to feel guilt over our action A* is for us to be jointly committed to feeling guilt as a body over our action A.
(ii) For us *collectively to feel guilt over our action A* is for us to constitute a plural subject of a feeling of guilt over our action A.

A significant difference between this and other accounts of collective guilt is the involvement of joint commitment to feeling guilt as a body. Gilbert presents anecdotal evidence in favor of the idea that subjects can jointly commit themselves to feeling emotions. Further still, she claims that a properly installed authority can commit an entire group to feeling in a certain way and that the members of the group are bound by such commitment even if they are unaware of it. While it is unrealistic to assume that an authority could commit all or even most members of his or her group to actually experiencing emotions, a joint commitment can be expressed by acting and talking in ways that are consistent with the relevant emotion. Gilbert claims that the feelings of collective guilt exist in and through the individual group members' pangs and twinges. But since pangs and twinges of collective guilt do not possess specific phenomenology as distinct from pangs of other sorts—"a pang is a pang is a pang" as Gilbert (2002, p. 141) points out—she claims that feelings of collective guilt can be distinguished from other, phenomenally similar feelings only by their responsiveness to the plural subject's collective guilt. Thus, a collectively intentional pang should not go away unless the group members jointly decide that the action they collectively performed was not wrongful after all.

Gilbert aptly highlights the role of shared judgments, desires, and intentions in collective emotions. These intentional and evaluative elements of emotion are crucial for understanding how emotions are capable of giving rise to social groups whose aims and values resonate with the intentional content of the eliciting emotions. Nevertheless, Gilbert has been criticized for relegating feelings into a contingent role in collective emotions (Wilkins 2002; Konzelmann Ziv 2007; Schmid 2009). What has not been emphasized is that this problem seriously undermines the power of Gilbert's account to explain several functions of collective emotions in social groups. The first problem is that individual members of a plural subject are said to participate in collective guilt *feelings* even if they have *no* phenomenal experiences of guilt as long as they behave in accordance with this emotion. However, it is not obvious in what sense we are entitled to speak about *feelings* here. Second, without feelings, group members are incapable of experiencing affective solidarity with each other. Both of these experiences depend on sharing full-fledged emotions rather than mere propositional attitudes with others. The role of bodily and behavioral synchronization and entrainment is also important here: mere phenomenal similarity of individual feelings may not amount to a robust shared experience that reinforces group commitment. Indeed, if behavioral compliance provides sufficient evidence for participation in a plural subject, then it becomes difficult to distinguish genuinely committed, emotionally involved group members from individuals who comply in behavior for merely private and instrumental reasons.

3.2   Schmid's Phenomenological Account

Hans Bernhard Schmid (2009) avoids the problems of Gilbert's view by starting from a more plausible notion of emotion. He follows Peter Goldie (2000) and Bennett Helm (2001) in rendering emotions as affective perceptions with *target*, *focus*, *mode*, and underlying *concern*. For instance, if I am afraid of a dangerous dog, the mode of my emotion is fear, the target is the dog, I am in focus, whereas the underlying concern is my well-being. While target and focus are important, only shared concerns are necessary for shared emotions. Schmid suggests that if individuals share concerns, they are capable of experiencing a phenomenal fusion of their feelings into a shared feeling, interpreted as "our" feeling. Schmid's argument for the phenomenological collective subject is founded on the idea that "all conscious states are—pre-reflectively and un-thematically—*conceived* and *interpreted* by the subjects who have them" (Schmid 2009, p. 77). Thus, it may be possible for an individual A to interpret his or her feeling as the feeling of another individual B, as when Bill Clinton famously claimed that he feels the pain of the AIDS-activist Bob Rafsky. Schmid is not naïve about the sincerity of this claim, but he asks us not to dismiss the possibility that individual subjects can take part in each others' feelings by virtue of interpreting their feelings as part of *your* or *our* feeling. When this "phenomenological fusion of feelings" happens, the *phenomenal subject* of feeling differs from the *ontological subject*.

Schmid's example of an emotion with a phenomenally collective subject, adopted from Max Scheler, is the shared grief of parents over the dead body of their beloved child. Scheler (1973) suggests that the bereaved parents feel this emotion together (*Mit-einanderfühlen*) rather than separately. Schmid argues that differences in the *intensity* and *quality* of feeling between the participants of a collective emotion do not threaten the emergence of a phenomenological "we" if the participants' feelings "match" with those of the others "according to the different roles the participants play in the joint activity" (ibid., p. 79). Thus, he suggests that joy at the successful first performance of a symphony may possess a phenomenally collective subject even if the composer, the stage manager, the man at the triangle, and a member of the audience each feel the joy about the performance in a somewhat different manner: the composer as exuberant exaltation, the man at the triangle as silent contentment, a member of the audience as delight, and so on. I believe that it is an empirical question whether or not different roles, or rather, how different roles, in a joint activity allow the experience of a phenomenally collective subject, so I won't discuss this question further. A more general problem with phenomenally collective subject is that it may not *alone* indicate very strong sharing if it is possible for individuals to experience a phenomenal fusion of feelings in the context of otherwise dissimilar emotions. Schmid's two examples of shared emotions provide evidence for this worry.

The parents' shared grief manifests their deeply shared concern for the deceased child, and it affectively glues the parents to each other in their mourning. Nothing similar is present in the latter example. The aims of the musicians and the audience, including the composer, are compatible as the latter hope to hear an excellent performance, while the former intend to provide one. Yet only the musicians can commit themselves to this goal, because the audience cannot influence the quality of the performance but only hope that the orchestra plays well. Satisfaction of this convergent goal gives rise to shared joy among everyone present, but the emotion manifests and reinforces only the musicians' commitment to offer excellent performances, because the audience did not participate in this act and commitment in the first place. Likewise, affective solidarity among the attendants is ephemeral and confined to the event, except for the members of the orchestra. These examples indicate that Schmid's model is not sensitive enough to importantly dissimilar collective emotions, even if it is capable of accommodating all functions of collective emotions in social groups more or less adequately. However, I believe that we can improve this account by paying more attention to the preconditions of a phenomenological fusion of feelings on the one hand, and to shared concerns of different kind on the other hand.

4   Collectivity as a Continuum

I suggest that we should understand the collectivity of emotions as a continuum rather than as an on/off question. If collectivity is a matter of sharing emotions with others, then it seems possible to share emotions to a lesser or greater degree. Both main dimensions of collective emotions, their intentional content and their affective experience, allow for a continuum in terms of their sharing. I first highlight different ways in which individuals can share the intentional content of emotion, and then discuss the sharing of affective experiences. However, I believe that the former dimension of collectivity is more important for the overall collectivity of emotions, because strongly shared affective experiences may occur in the context of otherwise weakly collective emotions.

There is a wide interdisciplinary agreement among emotion researchers that emotions could not exist without underlying concerns. When a group of people experiences a collective emotion, it is plausible to assume that they have some shared desires or goals or norms or values—representations with the world-to-mind direction of fit, which I henceforth call "concerns" for brevity's sake. Nevertheless, emotional appraisals are often so fast and modular that it is impossible to make, let alone accept, them collectively. Sharing an emotional appraisal can therefore be only a matter of converging on such appraisal with other individuals. But how can we understand the collectivity of emotional appraisals if not in terms of their collective generation or acceptance? My proposal focuses on shared concerns of different kinds.

In the weakest form of collectivity, people share a concern if they have *overlapping* private concerns. Insofar as people pursue their own survival, security, health, happiness, and attachment these are private concerns. So are altruistic goals insofar as we have them for purely private reasons. Tuomela (2007) calls concerns of this kind *plain I-mode* concerns. Individuals can establish groups whose members cooperate in promoting their convergent private concerns. Groups of this kind may include economic sharing groups and self-help groups, such as dieting groups, alcoholics anonymous, and so on. The fact that private concerns or goals are general or even universal among all humans does not amount to their collectivity but merely to their *commonality*, which is a different thing.

Concerns can be shared in a somewhat stronger sense when individuals are privately committed to some concern [in part because of] believing that the others in the group have the same concern, and also believing this is mutually believed in the group. Thus, for instance, when I as a Liverpool fan am concerned about the future of this prestigious football club, not only do I believe that the other Liverpool fans have the same concern, but also that the other fans believe the same about my and other fans' having the concern in question. The bracketed clause refers to the fact that many of our shared concerns (as well as beliefs) are *socially grounded*. That is, we come to have concerns, because we believe that other members of our group have them, where this belief is either *a reason* or *a cause* or both for my adopting the same concern. The commitment is still private, but the concern is shared with others, unlike in the first case where these too are private. Tuomela has characterized this type of collectivity as *pro-group I-mode* or, more recently, *weak we-mode* collectivity. In my terminology, concerns of this kind are *moderately collective*. The main point is that the commitment is still up to the individual to revise and renounce for private reasons alone. Groups based on concerns of this kind may include loose associations, such as unorganized fan groups or social and religious movements.

The strongest mode of collectivity in sharing concerns is founded on the group members' collective commitment, either explicit or implicit. In addition, there is a mutual belief among the group members that they share the same concern to which they have collectively committed themselves. Through their collective commitment, the group members adopt the concern as *theirs* in a *strong we-mode* sense. Collective commitment provides the group members authoritative group reasons to think, want, feel, and act in ways that are in accordance with their shared concern. Moreover, the group members are allowed to revise their commitment to the shared concern only by reasons that are acceptable from the group's point of view. The collective commitment implies that the group members necessarily "stand or fall together" when acting as group members. Formulated for group goals, this Collectivity Condition states that a group goal is satisfied for one group member if and only if it is satisfied for all group members. For instance, individual players of a team win a match if and only if their team wins the match. Other examples of groups with shared concerns in the strongest sense may include religious groups, workgroups, theater ensembles, bands, orchestras, and families.

Collective commitment to a concern emerges from a collective acceptance that individuals give as group members; typically in the form of an explicit agreement. This kind of voluntaristic commitment suits well with Tuomela's typical examples of we-mode groups that carry pianos, paint houses, or clean parks. However, it suits ill with those cases that intuitively involve shared concerns of the strongest kind, such as Scheler's example of mourning parents. Those parents may not have given an explicit collective acceptance of their shared concern for the child's well-being during the child's life. Instead, they may have grown into this kind of understanding of their relationship to the child and each other. The parents' emotions, attitudes, and actions testify to such concern if they share a single evaluative and practical perspective whose focus is the child and its well-being (Helm 2010). Indeed, Tuomela allows that the "thinnest" form of collective acceptance of a content "is based on some kind of shared implicit understanding of the situation and the other participants' relevant mental attitudes" (Tuomela 2007, p. 92). Nevertheless, this kind of commitment is psychologically strong, because the parents' strongly shared concern for the child's well-being is supported by their convergent private concerns with the same aim.

While shared concerns are the most important background condition for shared emotional appraisals, they are embedded within a more comprehensive set of attitudes that subjects of these emotions share. People who share emotions often have a history of common experiences in the context of shared social practices as well as representations thereof, as Parkinson et al. (2005), Schmid (2009), Konzelmann Ziv (2009), and—most comprehensively—von Scheve ("Towards a Theory of Collective Emotion Elicitation", unpublished conference presentation) point out. Therefore, in addition to concerns, group members typically also share other cognitive, conative, and evaluative attitudes in a more or less collective sense, analogously to sharing concerns. Together such shared attitudes constitute the *intentional background* from which collective emotions can emerge in situations that impinge on some shared concern or concerns of individuals. Convergent emotional appraisals depend then on sharing at least *some* other attitudes besides concerns, of which the latter are still the most important because without them, collective emotions would not emerge in the first place.

As the typology of shared concerns purports to account for the shared intentional content of collective emotions, it does not suffice to explain the kind of non-reflective absorption in shared affective experience that sometimes takes the form of a phenomenological fusion of feelings. Shared concerns provide both a psychological cause and a rational reason for the emergence of emotional responses in individuals whose shared concerns are affected favorably or adversely. However, the emotional responses of individuals are hardly capable of giving rise to shared emotional experiences unless the various dimensions of individual emotional responses—physiological changes, facial expressions, action tendencies, and subjective feelings—are synchronized in the manner proposed by ritualistic theories.

Causal mechanisms that contribute to the synchronization of individual emotional responses in interaction situations include attentional deployment (Collins 2004), emotional contagion (Hatfield et al. 1994), facial mimicry (Bourgois and Hess 2008), motor mimicry and imitation (Chartrand and Bargh 1999), and neural mirroring (Decety and Mayer 2008). Shared concerns provide a *rational* impetus to causal processes of synchronization, and the degree of synchronization is the criterion of collectivity for shared affective experiences. Together, shared intentional content and shared affective experience constitute the two dimensions—intentionality and embodiment—of collective emotions that explain their function in maintaining and reinforcing interpersonal solidarity among individual group members as well as their commitment to the group. However, since it seems possible to experience highly synchronized affective experiences in the context of all kinds of collective emotions, the intentional dimension of collectivity is nevertheless more important than the embodied dimension for the overall collectivity of these emotions.

5   Types of Collective Emotions and Their Social Functions

Beginning from the weakest type of collective emotion, I suggest that these emotions emerge when a group of individuals appraise the emotion-eliciting event convergently in relation to their overlapping private concerns, and such mechanisms as attentional deployment, emotional contagion, facial and motor mimicry, and behavioral entrainment synchronize the individuals' emotional responses, producing a shared affective experience among the co-present individuals who are mutually aware that others are feeling the same. Collective emotions of this type can sometimes contribute to the emergence and maintenance of social groups. For instance, shared private anger about downsizing can help individual workers to realize that they have shared concerns as workers, which may foster their mutual solidarity and lead them to establish a trade union to promote those shared interests to which they commit themselves as a group. In this way, collective emotions of the weakest type are capable of contributing to the transformation of groups from I-mode to we-mode. However, the beneficiality of weakly collective emotions is ephemeral and contingent. Panicked shareholders who rush to sell their stocks exacerbate the financial crisis, thus adding to the losses of everyone. Curiously, enthusiasm has the same effect in the stock market: everyone has to pay more for stocks that become more expensive. These examples indicate that collective emotions of the weakest type may, at worst, give rise to collective behavior that is harmful to the overlapping private concerns of the affected individuals.

I suggest that moderately collective emotions emerge when individuals evaluate the emotion-eliciting event convergently in relation to their moderately shared concern that is constitutive of a social identity or group in terms of which the individuals identify themselves, and such mechanisms as attentional deployment, emotional contagion, facial and motor mimicry, and behavioral entrainment synchronize the individuals' emotional responses, producing a shared affective experience among the co-present individuals who are mutually aware that other group members are feeling the same. Shared group membership reinforces the synchronization process, adding to the intensity of the shared affective experience. Moderately collective emotions are functionally and phenomenologically experienced in the role of a group member, but the group membership is still normatively weak because it is self-appointed and maintained through a private identification or commitment. I believe that the functional differences between moderately and strongly collective emotions are subtle, and they can be highlighted only after a brief account of the latter.

I propose that strongly collective emotions emerge when members of the group appraise the emotion-eliciting event convergently in relation to their strongly shared concern, and such mechanisms as attentional deployment, emotional contagion, facial and motor mimicry, and behavioral entrainment synchronize the members' emotional responses producing a shared affective experience among the co-present group members who are mutually aware that other group members are feeling the same. The strong collectivity of an emotion is reflected both in the degree of synchronization of individual emotional responses and in the evaluative content of the group members' emotions. The members of a winning team do not rejoice merely in winning the championship but instead in "*our* winning the championship" or in "*our* accomplishment". Also, the emotion is felt as a group member in a strong sense. In this way, collective *content* in the sense of indexicality and *mode* are built into collective emotions of the strongest kind.[5]

I believe that moderately and strongly collective emotions are capable of maintaining and reinforcing more robust and resilient solidarity and group identification than weakly collective emotions. They can also motivate behavior that is more probably conducive to the concerns that individuals share as a group. This is possible because collective emotions of stronger types inform individuals about how their shared concerns are faring in the world, quite the same way as private emotions inform individuals about the destinies of their private concerns. Collective emotions of stronger types also motivate group members to adaptively respond to the eliciting situations of those emotions, either separately or together as a group. I surmise that strongly collective emotions are capable of motivating even more persistent and reliable group-conducive behavior than moderately collective emotions. I realize that this hypothesis requires empirical support, which I am not able to provide here. However, I offer an argument for the plausibility of this hypothesis.

---

[5]My account of strongly collective emotions resembles Gilbert's membership account in which there is a joint commitment to the goal or intention or action that underlies the group members' convergent emotional evaluations. I supplement this account with the dimension of affective synchronization which is absent from Gilbert. Moreover, I distinguish between two dissimilar membership accounts, weaker and stronger, whereas Gilbert only has one.

Group membership has normative implications to the group members' emotions. The most general implication is the norm to feel and display appropriate emotions when the group members' shared concerns are affected favorably or adversely. However, there is an important difference in the nature of this norm between privately and collectively committed groups. In the former case, the emotion norm is *descriptive* and anonymous, and it is adopted in conjunction with one's identification with the group. Accordingly, one is bound to the norm by standards of individual rationality on the one hand, and by anonymous social pressure emerging from other group members' compliance on the other hand. In the latter case, by contrast, the norm to respond with appropriate emotions to changes in the status of the group members' shared concern emerges from the members' collective commitment to the concern, which implicitly gives rise to *prescriptive* emotion norms within the group.[6] I suggest that this group-internal normativity renders strongly collective emotions more resilient in serving the functions of collective emotions in social groups than shared emotions of weaker types. Thus, I surmise that the group-eroding effects of collective guilt and shame, which empirical research has established, are stronger in those groups whose members share concerns in a weak or moderate sense rather than in a strong sense.[7] However, an empirical validation of this hypothesis is a topic for another, interdisciplinary rather than merely philosophical study.[8]

References

Barsade, S.G. 2002. The ripple effect: Emotional contagion in groups. *Administrative Science Quarterly* 47: 644–675.
Barsade, S.G., and D.E. Gibson. 1998. Group emotion: A view from top and bottom. In *Research on managing on groups and teams*, ed. D. Gruenfeld, B. Mannix, and M. Neale, 81–102. Stamford: JAI Press.
Bourgois, P., and U. Hess. 2008. The impact of social context on mimicry. *Biological Psychology* 77: 343–352.
Branscombe, N.R., and B. Doosje (eds.). 2004. *Collective guilt. An international perspective.* Cambridge: Cambridge University Press.
Chartrand, T.L., and J.A. Bargh. 1999. The chameleon effect: The perception-behavior link and social interaction. *Journal of Personality and Social Psychology* 76: 893–910.
Collins, R. 2004. *Interaction ritual chains*. Princeton/Oxford: Princeton University Press.
Damasio, A.R. 2003. *Looking for Spinoza. Joy, sorrow and the feeling brain*. Orlando: Harcourt.
de Rivera, J. 1992. Emotional climate: Social structure and emotional dynamics. In *International review of studies on emotion*, vol. 2, ed. K.T. Strongman, 197–218. Chichester: Wiley.

[6]On the difference between descriptive and prescriptive emotions norms, see von Scheve ("What Kind of Norms are Emotion Norms?" Unpublished conference presentation).

[7]On the group-eroding effect of negative emotions, see footnote 2 above.

[8]I would like to extend my thanks to the anonymous referees of my chapter as well as to the editors of this volume. Their perceptive comments helped me to improve the article in many respects. Any remaining shortcomings are solely my responsibility.

Decety, J., and M. Meyer. 2008. From emotion resonance to empathic understanding: A social developmental neuroscience account. *Development and Psychopathology* 20: 1053–1080.

Durkheim, É. 1984 [1893]. *The division of labor in society.* Trans. W.D. Halls with an Introd. L. Coser. New York: The Free Press.

Flam, H., and D. King (eds.). 2005. *Emotions and social movements.* London: Routledge.

Frijda, N. 1986. *The emotions.* Cambridge: Cambridge University Press.

George, J.M. 1996. Group affective tone. In *Handbook of work group psychology*, ed. M.A. West, 77–93. Chichester: Wiley.

Gilbert, M. 2002. Collective guilt and collective guilt feelings. *Journal of Ethics* 6: 115–143.

Goldie, P. 2000. *The emotions.* Oxford: Oxford University Press.

Goodwin, J., J.J. Jasper, and F. Polleta (eds.). 2001. *Passionate politics. Emotions and social movements.* Chicago/London: The University of Chicago Press.

Jasper, J.M. 1998. The emotions of protest: Affective and reactive emotions in and around social movements. *Sociological Forum* 13: 397–424.

Hatfield, E., J. Cacioppo, and R. Rapson. 1994. *Emotional contagion.* Cambridge: Cambridge University Press.

Helm, B. 2001. *Emotional reason.* Cambridge: Cambridge University Press.

Helm, B. 2010. *Love, friendship, and the self.* Oxford: Oxford University Press.

Kelly, J.R., and S. Barsade. 2001. Mood and emotions in small groups and work teams. *Organizational Behavior and Human Decision Processes* 86: 99–130.

Kemper, T. 2002. Predicting emotions in groups: Some lessons from September 11. In *Emotions and sociology*, ed. J. Barbalet, 53–68. Oxford: Blackwell Publishing.

Kessler, T., and S. Hollbach. 2005. Group-based emotions as determinants of ingroup identification. *Journal of Experimental Social Psychology* 41: 677–685.

Knottnerus, J.D. 2010. Collective events, rituals, and emotions. In *Advances in group processes*, vol. 27, ed. R. Thye, J. Lawle, and J. Lawler, 39–62. Bingley: Emerald Publishing.

Konzelmann Ziv, A. 2007. Collective guilt revisited. *Dialectica* 61: 467–493.

Konzelmann Ziv, A. 2009. The semantics of shared emotion. *Universitas Philosophica* 52: 81–106.

Lazarus, R. 2001. *Emotion and adaptation.* New York: Oxford University Press.

Mackie, D.M., E.R. Smith, and D. Ray. 2008. Intergroup emotions and intergroup relations. *Social and Personality Psychology Compass* 2(5): 1866–1880.

Michael, J. 2011. Shared emotions and joint action. *Review of Philosophy and Psychology* 2: 355–373.

Nussbaum, M.C. 2001. *Upheavals of thought.* Cambridge: Cambridge University Press.

Parkinson, B., A. Fischer, and A. Manstead. 2005. *Emotion in social relations.* New York: The Psychology Press.

Prinz, J.J. 2004. *Gut reactions. A perceptual theory of emotion.* New York: Oxford University Press.

Rimé, B. 2007. Interpersonal emotion regulation. In *Handbook of emotion regulation*, ed. J.J. Gross, 466–485. New York: The Guilford Press.

Robinson, J. 2005. *Deeper than reason.* Oxford: Clarendon Press.

Salmela, M. 2012. Shared emotions. *Philosophical Explorations* 66(1): 33–46.

Sanchez-Burks, J., and Q.N. Huy. 2009. Emotional aperture and strategic change: The accurate recognition of collective emotions. *Organization Science* 20: 22–34.

Scheler, M. 1973 [1912–1916]. *Formalism in ethics and non-formal ethics of values: A new attempt toward the foundation of an ethical personalism.* Trans. M.S. Frings and R.L. Funk. Evanston: Northwestern University Press.

Scherer, K.R. 2001. Appraisal considered as a process of multilevel sequential checking. In *Appraisal processes in emotion. Theory, methods, research*, ed. K.R. Scherer, A. Schorr, and T. Johnstone, 92–120. Oxford: Oxford University Press.

Schmid, H.B. 2009. Plural action. Essays in philosophy and social science. In *Contributions to phenomenology*, vol. 58. Berlin: Springer.

Scholtz, S. 2008. *Political solidarity.* University Park: Pennsylvania University Press.

Smith, A. 2002 [1759]. *The theory of moral sentiments.* Cambridge: Cambridge University Press.

Smith, E.R., C.R. Seger, and D.M. Mackie. 2007. Can emotions be truly group level? Evidence regarding four conceptual criteria. *Journal of Personality and Social Psychology* 93: 431–446.

Solomon, R.C. 2007. *True to our feelings*. New York: Oxford University Press.

Spoor, J.R., and J.R. Kelly. 2004. The evolutionary significance of affect in groups: Communication and group bonding. *Group Processes and Intergroup Relations* 7: 398–412.

Stryker, S. 2004. Integrating emotions into identity theory. In *Theory and research on human emotions*, Advances in group processes, vol. 21, ed. J. Turner, 1–23. Englewood: JAI Press.

Tuomela, R. 2007. *The philosophy of sociality*. New York: Oxford University Press.

Wilkins, B. 2002. Joint commitments. *Journal of Ethics* 6: 145–155.

Chapter 11
Feelings of Being-Together and Caring-With

H. Andrés Sánchez Guerrero

Abstract In this chapter I address two important roles feelings play in collective affective intentional episodes. I do so by elaborating on the suggestion that our emotions may disclose the significance something has for us as members of a group we care about. Seeking to anchor the notion of collective affective intentionality in the Heideggerian theme of a human care-defined way of being, I first develop the idea of an affectively enabled and essentially shareable 'world-belongingness'. I propose the term 'caring-with' to refer to a mode of caring about things that may be said to rely on the fact that the involved individuals have come to share a number of concerns. Arguing that the role affective states play in cases of collective affective intentionality is not exhausted by the capacity our emotions have to disclose the mentioned structure of shared concerns, I further introduce the notion of 'feelings of being-together' and suggest that certain pre-intentional feelings might serve as 'sedimented', dynamic structures of experience that prepare us to understand certain circumstances as situations in which we are pursuing something together in an emotionally motivated way.

1 Introduction

In an attempt to elaborate on the suggestion that the intentionality of an emotion is inextricably intertwined with its phenomenology (cf. Goldie 2000, ch. 3), Hans Bernhard Schmid (2008, 2009) has recently claimed that in order to provide a *phenomenologically adequate account of collective affective intentionality* we are required to solve a concrete problem. This problem, which we might call 'the problem of shared feelings', concerns the conflict between two apparently

H.A. Sánchez Guerrero (✉)
Institute of Cognitive Science, University of Osnabrück, Osnabrück, Germany
e-mail: hsanchez@uni-osnabrueck.de

A. Konzelmann Ziv and H.B. Schmid (eds.), *Institutions, Emotions, and Group Agents*,
Studies in the Philosophy of Sociality 2, DOI 10.1007/978-94-007-6934-2_11,
© Springer Science+Business Media Dordrecht 2014

incompatible intuitions: the intuition that emotions can be shared and the intuition that only individuals (and not groups) can have feelings—and, what is more, that they can only have their own feelings. By urging us to elucidate the sense in which the feelings involved in a case of collective affective intentionality may *straightforwardly* be said to be shared, i.e. to be identical *numerically* (2009, pp. 69ff.), Schmid has made a substantive philosophical problem of this conflict.

In this chapter I shall try to show that in order to make room for the idea that feelings are at the heart of collective affective intentionality, we are not required to solve Schmid's problem of shared feelings. I shall do so by discussing two distinct roles feelings (of different sorts) may be said to play in those situations in which we take ourselves to be *affectively connected to certain others in relation to something*. Following a suggestion made by Schmid himself, I will try to redefine the task to be accomplished in order to make visible the central role feelings play in collective affective intentionality (Sect. 2). Subsequently, I shall prepare my proposal by discussing the relation between our emotions and the significance something has for us (Sect. 3). Seeking to ground the notion of collective affective intentionality in the Heideggerian theme of a care-defined way of being, in a third step I will attempt to show that human intentionality in general might be understood in terms of an affectively enabled and essentially shareable 'world-belongingness' (Sects. 4 and 5). Finally, I shall try to clarify what is distinct about collective affective intentionality (Sects. 6 and 7). In the course of this discussion, I will introduce two notions: the notion of *caring-with* and the notion of *feelings of being-together*.

2   Feeling Together That It Matters: An Attempt to Recast Our Philosophical Task

As soon as we distinguish between two possible senses of the expression 'subject of a feeling', Schmid argues, the philosophical problem of shared feelings becomes tractable. These two meanings concern, on the one hand, the *ontic* subject *of* a feeling, i.e. the actual individual who has this feeling, and on the other, its *phenomenal* subject, i.e. the self-concept implicit in this affective experience (2009, p. 65).

Schmid suggests that even having endorsed the assumption that only individuals can have feelings (and only their own feelings), by means of this distinction, we make room for the idea that, under certain conditions, the involved individuals may be correct in *pre-thematically understanding themselves* as individuals that constitute a sort of community of affective experience. The idea being that we could safely assume that in at least some of those cases in which the (phenomenal) subject appears as a 'we-subject' *in* the affective experiences of a number of individuals— as a *subject-we*, as Schmid, drawing on Sartre, prefers to call it (pp. 173ff.)—the conditions could be met under which these individuals would not be mistaken in taking their feelings to be had by the other members of the relevant group. Schmid proposes to consider those cases in which these conditions (whatever they turn out to be) are met as cases in which, by virtue of what he calls a 'phenomenological fusion of feelings', the individuals' feelings come to constitute *a unique shared feeling* (pp. 77ff.).

A particularly interesting point of Schmid's proposal concerns the idea that such a fusion of feelings could obtain even in situations in which qualitative differences may be assumed to exist between the feelings of the involved individuals. Schmid illustrates this point by considering the shared feeling of joy at the success of the first performance of a symphony. He writes:

> If the man at the triangle, the composer, some member of the audience and the stage manager take themselves to share a single feeling of joy, this is because, in their perception of the situation, their individual feelings 'match' with that of the others rather than being qualitatively or even numerically identical. (Schmid 2009, p. 79)

Presumably because of the intuitive appeal of this image of 'matching feelings', in his initial proposal, Schmid (2008) makes no effort whatsoever to offer a criterion by reference to which we could determine in a concrete situation whether or not qualitatively different emotional feelings may be said to 'match one another'. In a later version of this account, however, Schmid makes a remark that one could consider particularly illuminating in this respect. In the relevant passage, he submits that if a feeling connects two individuals in a given situation, it is ultimately 'by means of the shared *concern* behind the target-focus relation' (2009, p. 68) of their individual emotions.[1]

One certainly might be tempted to read Schmid's remark as an attempt to provide the lacking criterion. It is important, however, to realize that Schmid does probably not feel any urge to look for such a criterion. For he never questions a prima facie plausible assumption that makes the search for it appear redundant. According to this assumption, we would be entitled to speak of a collective affective intentional episode just in case the involved individuals' feelings could be understood as instances of the *same sort* of emotion.

This is, however, an assumption we could easily cast doubt on by just considering a situation in which the non-type-identical emotions of two or more individuals may be taken to 'match one another' in such a way as to connect the participating individuals to each other in the context of the relevant situation.

Suppose that someone is playing with a ball in the vicinity of a fragile object that Adrian and Beatrice particularly value. Both Adrian and Beatrice respond emotionally to the threat posed to the valued object by the flying ball, but they do so in completely different ways. Adrian turns in anger towards the person who is carelessly playing with the ball and shouts at her loudly, while Beatrice turns back in fear and closes her eyes.[2]

---

[1] I shall discuss Bennett Helm's notion of an *emotion's focus* as well as his idea of a target-focus relation below (in Sect. 3).

[2] I am here extending an example offered by Helm (2001, p. 69).

Not only would we, in such a situation, probably assume some substantial qualitative differences between Adrian's and Beatrice's feelings. What is more, it would be utterly inaccurate to speak of a shared emotion here. But the significant fact is that both of them are responding emotionally and at least simultaneously to the threat posed to the integrity of the relevant object. Their individual emotional responses, one could say, make visible that this object has value for both of them. And for this reason, I think, we could understand such a situation, provided a particular condition (to be discussed below) is met, as a case of collective affective intentionality; as a situation in which the involved individuals are *feeling together that the object or occurrence in question matters to them.*[3]

Against the background of this basic finding, according to which a number of individuals might be said to be feeling together even in situations in which their individual emotions would clearly belong to different kinds, in the remainder I shall try to elaborate on the idea that what we find at the centre of interesting cases of collective affective intentionality is a shared concern (or set of concerns). In doing so, I shall attempt to make plausible a claim concerning the task to be solved in order to offer a phenomenologically adequate account of the phenomenon at issue: We can elucidate the sense in which feelings can be claimed to be at the heart of collective affective intentional episodes by developing the idea that collective affective intentionality may be understood, using Bennett Helm's (2008) terminology, as a phenomenon grounded in a *shared evaluative perspective.*

3   Being Affected and Caring about Something

I shall begin this account by discussing a proposal on which I will elaborate in a number of ways in the rest of this chapter. The proposal concerns the idea that our emotions *disclose* and *constitute* our *unified evaluative perspective* (Helm 2001). This is a suggestion Helm defends by explaining two different ways in which our emotions may be said to involve evaluative content, namely as responsive to and as constitutive of the particular worthiness something has.

Conceiving of this worthiness as something that is 'imparted by a subject's concern for something' (2001, p. 49), Helm makes an elaborate effort to show that this *import*, as he calls it, also has an objective character, in the sense of not being merely projected by the relevant emotion onto the world. He does so by showing that the significance something has for us can be understood as something we might either discover, erroneously think to discover, or fail to discover. In this sense, Helm argues, import serves as a 'standard of warrant' for our assent to the particular view of the world an emotion presents.

---

[3]Let me emphasize that an additional condition is met in those situations in which the involved individuals can be taken to *really* be feeling together. For *independently* valuing the object in question, Adrian and Beatrice could show the simultaneous affective response just described.

Helm develops this point by writing that 'an emotion is *warranted* just in case the target of the emotion has, or intelligibly seems to have, the import defined by the emotion's formal object' (p. 64).[4] An emotion, he explains further, would be warranted in a concrete situation just in case this 'emotional assent', as he calls it, could be said to *reflect* the significance the relevant object has for the subject in question. So the objective character of the significance something has for a given person becomes visible when considering the role an appeal to this import can play while trying to make sense of some of her behaviors as genuine emotional responses or 'actions out of emotion' (Goldie 2000, pp. 37ff.).

Based on the idea that a particular emotional response 'exerts *rational pressure* on one' (p. 71) to continue to have certain other emotions in the relevant circumstances, Helm contends that the way emotional feelings constitute the import they respond to is by constituting *patterns of evaluative attitudes tied together by rational connections*. If you are, for instance, hoping to get a grant for a project you are very interested in, you *ought to* feel disappointed if you are informed that you are not going to receive the expected financial support. Otherwise it would be questionable that this project was really significant to you. In this sense, Helm argues, a concrete emotion (hope, in this example) could be said to *commit* you to having certain other emotions (e.g. disappointment), given some relevant circumstances.

Against the background of this idea of a series of *emotional commitments*, as he calls these rational connections, Helm coins the notion of an *emotion's focus* in order to refer to the background object of import that 'makes intelligible the evaluation implicit in the emotion' (p. 69); the idea being that this focus defines the range of emotions to which a particular emotion commits one. In this context, Helm contends that having the capacity to respond emotionally in a given situation presupposes something more than the discussed internal consistency of the relevant pattern of emotions. For if we are to make sense of the idea that an emotion can be seen as a response to the significance its focus has, the relevant pattern of emotions also has to cohere *for the most part* with certain patterns of evaluative attitudes of different kinds (e.g. desires or evaluative judgments) that have the same focus. In other words, we have to understand our general capacity to respond emotionally as a capacity grounded in our being disposed both actually and counterfactually to evaluate certain situations in certain ways 'when rationally required and not when rationally prohibited' (p. 70). And we have to understand this disposition as a disposition to attend to the focus of the evaluations in question and to 'act appropriately on behalf of that focus' (p. 78). In this way, Helm argues, we eventually come to understand our emotions as '*conceptually indivisible* states of felt evaluations that both evaluate and motivate' (p. 80; my emphasis).

---

[4]The *target* of an emotion is the particular object or event towards which this (token) emotion is directed. The *formal object* of an emotion can be understood, in turn, as an evaluative property implicitly ascribed by the relevant emotion to its target; a property that defines this token emotion as an instance of a given type of emotion. Someone's fear, for instance, may be said to present the dog this person is afraid of as something that is dangerous for her or worth avoiding.

But the idea that our emotions disclose and constitute a *singular* evaluative perspective only becomes clear when considering our capacity to prefer one thing to another. Helm argues that we can understand the strength of our motivation to pursue something in terms of the *relative* import different things can have by presupposing that some rational connections also hold 'between patterns *with different foci*' (p. 112; my emphasis). Concretely, he suggests that the intensity of an emotion, which would be warranted in a particular situation, may be 'properly dampened because of the way in which preferences are involved in defining the circumstances' (p. 112). We should, thus, understand our emotions not only as commitments to have (in the relevant circumstances) certain other emotions that have the same focus, but also as commitments 'to dampen felt evaluations, the import of whose foci is of lesser degree' (p. 113).

Helm concludes this reflection by observing that we cannot understand our general receptivity to the significance certain things and occurrences have in terms of a series of independent concerns. 'Rather, given the sensitivity to *relative* import required by the dampening effect, we must understand these distinct cares and values to be *unified into a single evaluative perspective*—as both a commitment and receptivity to import in general' (p. 115; my emphasis).

Against the background of this line of reasoning—according to which, in order to be able to understand an emotion as a state that reveals the significance something has, we have to presuppose a singular evaluative perspective—, in what follows I shall try to anchor the study as to the nature of collective affective intentionality to the Heideggerian claim that our human way of being is essentially defined by *care* [*Sorge*].

4   Being-in-the-Same-World: Sharing Our Care-Defined Way of Being

We can, I think, begin to elucidate the nature of our ability to participate in collective affective intentional episodes by explicating the sense in which human intentionality may be said to essentially be shareable intentionality. In so doing, we shall come to appreciate, first, in which sense it can be claimed, drawing on Heidegger, that we human beings are, by and large, in the same world, and second, to which extent this being-in-the-same-world is a matter of our *having always already pre-thematically understood that we share a care-defined way of being*.

The basic intuition behind this suggestion is that certain ways of making sense of the concrete situations in which we encounter one another are common to us. This is an idea that can, in a first step, be explicated by appealing to a view widely shared among phenomenologists—a view that is central to Edmund Husserl's notion of an *intentional horizon*. According to this view, any perceptual experience of a given object could be taken to include a number of references not only to further aspects of these perceptual objects, but also to further possible objects and situations that may be said to be involved in any *meaningful experience* of the object at issue; references that are, thus, *essential* to that object's *appearing as the sort of object it is*.

Martin Heidegger seems to be elaborating on this idea when he points to the way in which the entities we encounter in everyday life quite often 'show up' as *ready-to-hand* [*zuhanden*] (1962 [1927], §§15–17), i.e. as something we immediately understand as 'equipment' to be used in the context of a practical project we are involved in. Our immediate (and pre-thematic) understanding of certain possibilities for dealing with these entities—our understanding of their mode of being—, Heidegger contends, is constituted by a series of 'involvements' that concern certain other entities, practices, activities, and purposes; by references the encountered entities 'make' by just appearing in the way they do in these situations.

Heidegger (1996 [1928/1929], §13) further develops this thought in such a way as to reveal our *mutual openness qua Dasein* by building upon a simple observation: We usually do not express our human co-presence by making thematic our mutual vicinity. Rather, we normally say that we are *with one another*. According to Heidegger, this way of thematizing our simultaneous presence makes it evident that we do not understand our encounters with other persons as encounters with entities that are spatially close to us and seem to *additionally* share our human nature. Rather, it is our sharing a particular mode of being that enables us to use the word 'with' in a meaningful way while describing the co-presence in question. The preposition 'with', Heidegger submits, does not indicate a particular spatiotemporal relation here, but a sort of *participation* (1996 [1928/1929], p. 85).

Heidegger continues this thought by arguing that it is our *comportment towards* other beings [*Verhalten zu* . . .] that reveals this participation. Concretely, it is the possibility we, in particular circumstances, have to be oriented towards *the very same* objects that makes visible that we are there with one another (pp. 89ff.). Insofar, however, as this being-with-one-another can be revealed by our comportment towards the same object even in those cases in which our individual acts are completely different in type, it must be our comportment *in purpose* towards the same object [*in Absicht auf Selbiges*], Heidegger contends, that ultimately discloses our being-with-one-another (p. 92).

Heidegger begins to explicate this suggestion by observing that we have to understand the *sameness* [*Selbigkeit*] in question here—the sameness of a shared intentional object—as something that is *relative to us* (p. 96). Otherwise, he thinks, we would not be able to make sense of the idea that this sameness reveals our being-with-one-another. He eventually claims that the sameness of those objects towards which we are oriented in purpose makes visible a basic and, in a way, shared sense of familiarity that underlies our practical engagement with them; this sameness, he writes, makes evident our 'being-alongside-things' [*Sein bei* . . .] (pp. 102ff.).[5]

---

[5]Stressing the idea of some sense of familiarity that usually accompanies our everyday engagement with other worldly entities, William Blattner recommends translating Heidegger's 'Sein bei' as 'being-amidst' (2006, p. 15).

The argument is a complicated one, and Heidegger elaborates on these thoughts in ways I cannot discuss here. But I think that one could take Heidegger to be arguing here that our having always already understood (in an at least non-thematic way) that certain ways of 'finding our way around' determinate situations *are common to us* (human individuals that are, or at least could be, involved in the situations at issue) is essential to, or is part of, our experiencing our world as a world that exhibits an objective character.

It is in this context that we could begin to elucidate the nature of collective affective intentionality (and of collective intentionality more generally) by conceiving of human intentionality in terms of an, in a weak sense, shared (i.e. not necessarily collective, but essentially shareable) orientedness towards worldly entities, which is grounded in our care-defined way of being. The idea being that our *having in common* this way of being allows us to have a shareable understanding of those situations in which we encounter each other, and our *pre-thematically understanding that we share a number of possibilities for dealing with other worldly entities* allows us to, in these situations, encounter each other *as an Other*—in the sense of 'another like myself'.

In what follows, I shall further develop this suggestion by discussing the role certain feelings may be said to play with regard to this care-defined way of being we share, i.e. by making clear in which sense 'ordinary' human intentionality may be taken to be, furthermore, *affectively enabled* shareable (and often shared) intentionality.

5   Feelings of Being: On Our Affectively Grounded World-Belongingness

Matthew Ratcliffe (2008) has recently rearticulated the Heideggerian idea that any concrete experience occurs against the background of an *affective attunement* to the world by pointing to a series of states that are frequently alluded to in everyday discourse. These are states that are usually referred to as 'feelings' and characterized, for instance, as a sense of 'belonging', 'familiarity', 'completeness', 'estrangement', 'separation', or 'homeliness' (cf. Ratcliffe 2008, p. 56). Since these affective states cannot be understood as emotional experiences intentionally directed towards particular objects, Ratcliffe proposes to regard them as 'existential background orientations' that shape our concrete object-directed experiences.

Arguing that these *existential feelings*, as he calls them, convey 'a sense of reality' to our everyday encounters with other worldly beings, Ratcliffe points to what we might call *a modifiable sense of world-belongingness*, which, as he observes, we usually take for granted when we experience or think about concrete objects. Referring to Husserl, Ratcliffe appeals to the idea of a 'pre-articulate conviction' (p. 4) concerning the real existence of the encountered beings, and suggests that this *felt conviction*, as we might call it, in a way *situates us* in a specific world.

Ratcliffe clarifies this idea concerning a distinct phenomenological role the states in question could be said to play—the role of situating us in a world—by explaining in how far this affective background may be understood as a *meaning-giving* background. He argues that these affective states allow things to always already have some sort of significance when we encounter them 'by revealing the world as a realm of practical purposes, values and goals' (p. 47). In this way, Ratcliffe suggests, existential feelings *set up* the world in which we can have specific and meaningful object-directed (affective and non-affective) experiences. This is a thought I would like to develop by appealing to the idea of some sorts of *disposing states* that may be taken to amount to our preparedness to have certain emotional experiences.

Ratcliffe himself seems to be conceiving of existential feelings in terms of such states when he refers to a remark Heidegger makes in his famous analysis of fear as a mode of attunement (1962 [1927], §30). In the relevant passage, Heidegger writes that fear 'has already disclosed the world, in that out of it something like the fearsome may come close' (1962 [1927], p. 180; cited from Ratcliffe 2008, p. 49). Following Jan Slaby (2007), we could further explicate this idea.

Referring to Heidegger's characterization of 'the fearing as such' [*das Fürchten selbst*], Slaby observes that objects or occurrences that might *in principle* be regarded as harmful are usually not experienced as fearsome if they are not understood as something that has some rather direct relation to us, i.e. as something that 'touches us' in our personal existence, in a way or another (2007, p. 97). In this context, he recalls an observation made by Heidegger, according to which the feeling of fear ultimately reveals our *fearfulness* [*Furchtsamkeit*] as a capacity for being threatened. Appealing to the idea of *a prior openness to the fearsome as such* [*das Furchtbare*] (Heidegger 1962 [1927], p. 180), Slaby provides an account of those situations in which we are in an affective state that lacks an identifiable target but clearly has the experiential quality of fear. He submits that these are situations in which the very possibility of being adversely affected by what one could encounter in the world becomes experientially actual in the form of an awareness of our capacity to be hurt, damaged, or otherwise negatively affected. So what this proposal suggests is that the preparedness in question here—our preparedness to have emotional experiences of certain sorts—should not be understood as a mere disposition to enter, under relevant conditions, into certain states that have a particular experiential character. Rather, this preparedness should be conceived of in terms of disposing states that *are already experiential in nature*.

In closing this section, let me make a remark that pertains to Ratcliffe's idea of a *modifiable* sense of world-belongingness. It is important to understand that *as far as our mere mutual openness is concerned*, we do not have to assume that we normally share a given background feeling. All we have to assume to be sharing (insofar as we are in-the-same-world) is our being always affectively attuned *in one mode or another* to the world. This being-affectively-attuned-to-the-world-in-one-mode-or-another is, however, not something we *merely have alongside each other*. For, as I have insisted, it is something we share in the sense of having always already understood (when we come to encounter one another) that this significance-disclosing way of being is something we have in common.

As I shall try to explain (in Sect. 6), this variability of our attunement to the world permits us to differentiate what Heidegger calls 'being-with' (i.e. our being-in-the-same-world) from our situation-specific being-*together*-in-the-same-world. In other words, it permits us to differentiate between merely shareable (or weakly shared) intentionality and genuinely collective intentionality by allowing us to make thematic a distinct mode of world-relatedness that is characterized by the *interdependence* of the way of being-in-the-world of the involved individuals.

In the remainder, I shall try to make plausible the idea that certain *pre-intentional* feelings may be said to set up, in the very same motion, the world we are *in* (in a given situation) and the character of *togetherness* some of our *intentional* affective experiences have.

6   Being-Together and Caring-With

In what follows we shall be concerned with a series of rather common experiences characterized by some sense of being *jointly* (i.e. collaboratively or cooperatively) engaged with concrete others in an act of emotionally motivated circumspection. These are experiences one normally has in the context of ongoing activities in which one is taking part as a member of a group. And these are usually groups that are distinguished for not being occasionally constituted or dissolved as a function of a momentary impulse. Take, as an example, some of the emotional experiences one may have while playing a decisive game with a volleyball team of which one takes oneself to be a part.

I think that we can begin to offer an account of these affective experiences by making an apparently trivial observation: One's failure to have these sorts of experiences in the relevant situations could bring oneself (and others too) to suspect that at this point one did not *really* understand oneself as a member of the group in question (despite one's taking part in these activities), i.e. that at this point, and for whatever reason, one was not really concerned with the 'wellbeing' and 'flourishing' of this group. This simple reflection, I think, brings us to see that the experiences in question here are phenomenologically defined by a felt conviction that we (the involved individuals) are *caring together about something*. A possible way to try to identify what might be at the base of these sorts of experiences consists, thus, in trying to understand what could ground our felt conviction concerning the collective character of our caring about something.

Appealing to some of the ideas discussed above (in Sect. 2), it may be maintained that we could in principle *give reason* for such a conviction by invoking some emotional responses of the relevant others, i.e. of those individuals with whom one takes oneself to be feeling together. And we could do this because, under the presupposition of a unified and for the most part rationally coherent evaluative perspective, some of their behaviors would be intelligible (considering some circumstances in which they could be explanatorily embedded) as emotional responses or actions out of emotion, i.e. as behaviors prompted by the subject's emotional assent to the import something has.

It is particularly important to understand that in saying that some feelings can prompt certain behaviors we are not just saying that we could presuppose certain emotions as *typical causes* for these behaviors. For at least concerning our actions out of emotion, which qua actions are aimed at some end, the appeal to certain emotional feelings, rather, is intended to make intelligible a concrete behavioral segment by referring to what *motivates* it. Helm observes in this respect that the evaluation implicit in the emotion is able to justify the action in question by presenting its end as something that is *worth pursuing* in the relevant circumstance (2001, p. 75).

Now, as we shall see below (in Sect. 7), at least some of these emotional responses and actions out of emotion are intelligible (and perhaps even exclusively so) as forms of finding something worth pursuing *for the sake of the relevant group*. And it is in view of this fact that I would like to suggest that what some emotional responses or actions out of emotion make visible is ultimately a mode of being-in-the-world that has its roots in our having come to share certain concerns with concrete others. I propose the notion of *caring-with* in order to refer to a mode of caring about something that is expressed in certain forms of circumspection that are characterized by a peculiar object of ultimate concern: a particular group.

We can begin to develop this notion of caring-with by observing that it differs from Heidegger's 'being-with' in that it refers to a *merely possible* and, in this sense, *circumstantially determined* way of being-in-the-world. Concretely, it refers to the situation-specific possibility of being-together-with-concrete-others, which qua possibility that can only be actualized when *concrete* others are involved contrasts with the essential being-with-one-another Heidegger takes to be proper to Dasein *as such*. Put another way, what justifies the introduction of the term 'caring-with' here is the relevant difference that exists between the discussed sense of being-in-the-same-world and what we could call the sense of being-together-in-the-same-world.

To understand what grounds this last distinction is absolutely fundamental. For the strategy I have been pursuing so far consists in trying to elucidate the nature of the phenomenon of collective affective intentionality by revealing some continuity to exist between our 'ordinary' affectively enabled, shared world-belongingness and genuine cases of collective affective intentionality. But revealing this continuity will advance our understanding of the relevant matter only if we are also able to specify the main difference that holds between these forms of world-relatedness. This difference, to have stated it, is the difference between the mere *sharing of our care-defined way of being* and *the sharing of concrete concerns that determine a particular way of being-in-the-world*.

Appealing to some of the ideas discussed above, so far I have only suggested that certain emotions may reveal a structure of shared concerns and a particular mode of caring-about, i.e. that they may make visible our being-together-in-the-same-world.[6] But the role feelings play in genuine cases of collective affective

---

[6]This suggestion, which I shall come to discuss below in some more detail, has been developed in different terms by Helm (2008) in an account to which the present paper owes much.

intentionality, I want to prompt further, is not exhausted by this capacity intelligible emotional responses have to make evident that we (the involved individuals) share a series of concerns. Recurring to the thought that our emotional feelings presuppose a preparedness to experience and make sense of concrete circumstances in certain ways—a preparedness that, as we have seen, may be said to already have some experiential character—, I want to introduce here a second notion: the notion of *feelings of being-together*.

What motivates me to introduce this notion is the intuition that some of the affective states listed by Ratcliffe are such that they might be had in certain situations only on the condition of having come to share certain concerns with concrete others. The suggestion being that these subspecies of existential feelings might serve in a situation-specific manner as experiential background structures that may allow us— prepare us—to experience and make sense of concrete circumstances as situations in which what goes on has significance for us as members of a group.

In the last section I shall try to elucidate in how far certain feelings might be understood as dynamic structures of experience whose emergence could be related to our having come to share certain concerns with concrete others.

7 Feeling and Coming to Feel Togetherness

Following Helm, it is possible to extend the idea that our emotions play a central role in constituting and disclosing the significance something has by addressing those cases in which one primarily cares about *someone else* (cf. 2008, pp. 29ff.). These are usually situations, Helm observes, in which we are concerned with the wellbeing and flourishing of another being *as a caring being*; situations, hence, in which we are caring about this other being in a particular respect, namely *as another being with whom we share our care-defined way of being*.

This simple analysis of what it means to care about another person *as a person* brings us to see in which sense we may come to be *secondarily* concerned with the 'wellbeing' of something while caring about the wellbeing of someone else. For, insofar as the wellbeing of the person in question is, to some extent at least, related to the 'wellbeing' of the objects she cares about, we usually come to care about what she cares about while caring about her. In a complementary way, and by virtue of our being rather passively involved (as objects of care) in situations such as normal child rearing practices, we may come to respond emotionally, in a more-or-less systematic manner, to some occurrences that have either in themselves or in view of further possible occurrences importance for certain others who care about us.

By means of these two sorts of processes, in the course of our repeated encounters with certain others we may come to respond simultaneously to some occurrences able to positively or negatively affect some possible objects of concern. In this way, we may begin to *have in common with these others* some concrete ways of being oriented in emotionally motivated circumspection towards a range of other worldly beings and occurrences.

It is, however, important not to overlook the asymmetry that characterizes the interpersonal relationships just described. For, although we can regard these processes as processes by virtue of which we become prepared to respond *simultaneously* to the significance something has for us (the involved individuals), we do not have to regard them as processes that prepare us to respond *together* to this significance. This is the reason why these situations quite often only instantiate the mode of caring Heidegger calls *caring-for* [*Fürsorge*] (1962 [1927], p. 157), and not the one I have called *caring-with*. In order to clarify the relevant difference, I shall address what we could call our *ultimate object of care*; what Heidegger calls *the for-the-sake-of-which* [*das Worum*] of our emotionally disclosed concern (p. 180).

Coming back to our example, we can begin to understand in how far we (the volleyball players) may be said to be affectively engaged with the world in a *completely different way* by emphasizing that in this case we would expect from one another to care about something *as members of a team we care about*. That is, we would expect from one another to be emotionally oriented towards something that, as Helm emphasizes, is worth pursuing *for the sake of our group* (2008). This simple specification allows me to provide a more precise characterization of the term 'caring-with' as a term that refers to a mode of caring that does not only involve more than one (ontic) subject of concern, but is, furthermore, characterized by the following particularity: the individuals involved in the relevant act can be said to be *caring with one another about something on behalf of a group they take themselves to constitute*.

We can begin to understand this idea by considering a situation in which someone is inclined to understand a certain behavioral segment as an emotional response, but unable to make sense of this behavior *as a genuine emotional response* in reference to the purely individual evaluative perspective of the behaving person. The idea being that a way in which the interpreting person could render intelligible this behavioral segment is by alternatively making reference to a concrete group as the for-the-sake-of-which of the emotionally disclosed concern—a group of which the behaving person can be said to be a constitutive part.[7] To illustrate the point, let me elaborate on Schmid's example of the successful first performance of a symphony.

Suppose that for Dania, who plays the oboe in the orchestra, this performance has a particular personal significance. For Professor Emerson, with whom Dania is hoping to continue her musical studies, is going to be in the audience. So the success of this concert is particularly important for her *with regard to the future actualization of certain personal possibilities*. In fact, she is not only concerned with the success of the orchestral performance in general, but also with achieving a

---

[7]The point is not that the mode of caring I am calling 'caring-with' has a for-the-sake-of-which that goes beyond the relevant subject of concern, as it were. Indeed, while caring-with-about-something we are not caring about this thing *for the sake of someone or something else*, but *for our own sake, insofar as we understand ourselves as members of the relevant group*; for the sake of a group *we constitute*.

more than satisfactory interpretation of a short solo passage she is going to play, and by means of which she expects to draw Professor Emerson's attention to her. This is, at least, the answer she gives when Frederic (another member of the orchestra who knows Dania sufficiently well) asks her why she looks so nervous.

But Professor Emerson abandons the theatre before Dania has come to play the solo passage. And this is something every member of the orchestra registers. After the concert, however, Dania looks satisfied with the general success of the performance. It is hard to doubt that she is participating in the joyful satisfaction that connects most members of the orchestra in this situation. And she definitively contributes with her expressed satisfaction to the joyful atmosphere that reigns this night at the theatre. Moreover, she credibly describes her own state as 'a sort of joyful satisfaction' when Frederic, who knows how important it was for Dania to impress Professor Emerson, asks her how she is doing.

In such a situation, I think, someone who, like Frederic, knows Dania sufficiently well may be inclined to interpret her emotional response as a response that makes evident that Dania is *ultimately* concerned with the success of this performance *as something that is important for the 'wellbeing' and 'flourishing' of the orchestra.* In this sense, Dania's emotional response may be said to make visible—not only to her, but also to certain others—the relatively higher import the success of this concert has for her *as a member of this group.*[8] What is more, someone who, like Frederic, takes himself to care about the 'wellbeing' and 'flourishing' of the orchestra could understand Dania's emotional response *as a response that expresses a form of caring that arises from an evaluative perspective they have come to share in the course of their having become members of this orchestra.*

Now, although an appeal to these sorts of emotional responses we have been discussing might *justify* someone's conviction that in the situations in question she and the other relevant individuals are feeling together the significance something has, from the perspective of a static phenomenological analysis, these affective states cannot be held to play the role of *setting up* these experiences marked by a sense of togetherness. To put it bluntly, these responses may warrant, but do not phenomenologically ground our experience of being there together. For according to the phenomenological perspective I am here alluding to (and endorsing), what opens us to the possibility of pre-thematically understanding a concrete situation as one in which we could take part in an emotionally motivated act of collective circumspection is not the *intentional* affective state that *interindividually* discloses our caring-with. Concretely, even if we can say with Helm that these (in a way, publicly evident) affective evaluations are constitutive elements of a pattern of evaluative attitudes that determine a shared evaluative perspective, what in a

---

[8]Of course, Dania could just have pretended to be satisfied. Moreover, even assuming that her emotional response was genuine, we could be inclined to understand it as the result merely of *emotional contagion*. This is the reason why I am appealing here to 'someone who knows Dania sufficiently well'; the point being that, depending on the rational consistency between this particular emotional response and other evaluative responses of Dania, this well-informed interpreter could feel entitled to rule out these two alternative interpretations.

concrete moment *sets up the situation for us* as one in which we *already have the possibility* of caring about something as members of a group is a state that belongs to the class of experiential background orientations Ratcliffe calls 'existential feelings'. It is in this order of ideas that I would like to suggest that our experiences of being-there-together are phenomenologically grounded in a class of feelings whose distinct role consists in defining certain circumstances as situations in which what goes on may positively or negatively affect us as a group. In other words, the class of affective states I have called 'feelings of being-together' is constituted by feelings that *open up the very possibility* of experiencing something as something that can affect us *collectively*.[9]

An additional consideration allows me to postulate this subclass of existential feelings. According to a view widely shared among phenomenologists, certain experiences may make possible and, furthermore, later prompt more complex types of experiences. The idea being that the structures that shape some of our everyday encounters with other beings may be said to be 'sedimented' structures of experience. In other words, certain aspects of our understanding of determinate situations could come to shape certain future experiences by virtue of their being 'always already pre-given' in these forthcoming experiences.[10]

The suggestion is, hence, that some situations, in which we repeatedly encounter each other as responding (in a rationally consistent way) to the significance of certain occurrences, might lead us to passively associate certain feelings with certain human constellations. As a result of such an association, some feelings may come to be elicited by certain forthcoming conditions in a circumstance-specific (but not object-directed) manner. These pre-intentional feelings could then operate as dynamic background orientations that may be claimed to amount to our preparedness to have certain sorts of object-directed experiences by situating us in a world in which what we encounter could be non-thematically understood as something that is worth caring about as members of a given group we constitute.

The key to understanding how it could be that coming to have a disposition to have certain feelings in the presence of a given group affects the content, as it were, of the relevant experiences (by 'bringing them to be' the experiences of something that is worthwhile for the group), consists in appreciating that two different types

---

[9]This last argumentative move, I am well aware, is particularly difficult to follow. The difficulty, I think, lies in the fact that, in endorsing this phenomenological view, we are radically changing our perspective and adopting a point of view that brings us to consider the issue in terms of a series of experience-constituting acts that frame and constrain the world in which we always already find ourselves when we come to encounter other worldly beings. This is the reason why Helm's (2001, §5.4) appeal to the idea of finding oneself *in the mood* to do certain things cannot offer a view on the matter comparable to the one I am recommending here. For the idea is not that the feelings in question here *modulate* some of our affective experiences. The point is, rather, that certain pre-intentional affective states may *open up a given space of experiential possibilities marked by a sense of togetherness*.

[10]This idea is at the base of what Husserl calls 'genetic phenomenology' as well as of a late development of Husserl's philosophy Anthony J. Steinbock (1995) calls 'generative phenomenology'.

of dispositions are involved here. First, the disposition to be attuned to the world in certain ways in the presence of a given group, and second, the disposition that these background affective states one is disposed to be in (in the presence of the relevant group) *in themselves constitute*; a disposition I have made thematic by appealing to the idea of a preparedness to have certain experiences which already has an experiential character. The point being that the experiences in question here should not be understood as experiences that have a peculiar phenomenal quality, but essentially the same content they would have, were we not disposed to find ourselves in certain ways in the presence of the relevant group. For, as I have insisted, the phenomenological role of the background structures I am appealing to here consists in situating us in determinate worlds in which certain experiences are likely and others not.

The suggestion is, hence, that many of the concrete situations that emotionally motivate us not only to pursue something, but furthermore, to engage in inter individually coordinated activities that have a common goal (or a series of common goals), are experienced in a particular way, namely as situations in which what is going on has significance for us as members of a group we care about. And I am proposing that this occurs on the basis of certain background orientations that in the course of different processes, by means of which we have come to share certain concerns with concrete others, have become part of the structure of some of our experiences.

So I am pointing to a thinkable variety of background feelings that may prepare us to experience and make sense of some circumstances as situations that are connected to something we value together (and as such motivate us to pursue a number of common goals) while referring to a series of feelings of being-together. And the idea is that these feelings of being-together could be at the heart of a particular sort of affective connectedness between beings that, in virtue of their nature, share a care-defined way of being, and in virtue of having taken part in different socialization and enculturation processes, have additionally come to share a number of concerns that constitute a sufficiently coherent shared evaluative perspective.[11]

References

Blattner, W.D. 2006. *Heidegger's being and time: A reader's guide*. London: Continuum.
Goldie, P. 2000. *The emotions: A philosophical exploration*. Oxford: Clarendon Press.
Heidegger, M. 1962 [1927]. *Being and time*. Trans. J. Macquarrie and E. Robinson. Oxford: Blackwell.

---

[11]The present chapter develops thoughts I have earlier argued for (cf. Sánchez Guerrero 2011). This work arose in the context of the project 'animal emotionale II' supported by a grant of VolkswagenStiftung. I am grateful to Rudolf Owen Müllan, Jan Slaby, and an anonymous reviewer for their valuable comments on previous drafts of this chapter.

Heidegger, M. 1996 [1928/1929]. *Einleitung in die Philosophie*. Frankfurt a.M.: Klostermann. Collected writings vol. 27.

Helm, B.W. 2001. *Emotional reason: Deliberation, motivation, and the nature of value*. Cambridge: Cambridge University Press.

Helm, B.W. 2008. Plural agents. *Noûs* 42: 17–49.

Ratcliffe, M. 2008. *Feelings of being: Phenomenology, psychiatry and the sense of reality*. Oxford: Oxford University Press.

Sánchez Guerrero, H.A. 2011. Gemeinsamkeitsgefühle und Mitsorge: Anregungen zu einer alternativen Auffassung kollektiver affektiver Intentionalität. In *Affektive Intentionalität*, ed. Jan Slaby, Achim Stephan, Henrik Walter, and Sven Walter, 252–82. Paderborn: Mentis.

Schmid, H.B. 2008. Shared feelings: Towards a phenomenology of collective affective intentionality. In *Concepts of sharedness: Essays on collective intentionality*, ed. Hans Bernhard Schmid, Katinka Schulte-Ostermann, and Nikos Psarros, 59–86. Frankfurt a.M: Ontos.

Schmid, H.B. 2009. *Plural action: Essays in philosophy and social science*. Dordrecht: Springer.

Slaby, J. 2007. Emotionaler Weltbezug: Ein Strukturschema im Anschluss an Heidegger. In *Gefühle – Struktur und Funktion*, ed. Hilge Landweer, 93–112. Berlin: Akademie-Verlag.

Steinbock, A.J. 1995. Generativity and generative phenomenology. *Husserl Studies* 12: 55–79.

Chapter 12
Joining the Background: Habitual Sentiments Behind We-Intentionality

Emanuele Caminada

Abstract How can the inner structure of we-intentionality be described? The early phenomenological account of Gerda Walther (Zur Ontologie der sozialen Gemeinschaft. In: *Jahrbuch für Philosophie und phänomenologische Forschung*, vol 6. Niemeyer, Halle, pp 1–158, 1923) offers interesting insights into the nature of human sociality: according to her we-intentionality is embedded in a network of intentional habits a network that shapes individual minds. She claims that the core of community is grounded in a concrete, intentional background that arises through a particular structure of affective intentionality: habitual joining.

In Walther's approach, the core of the We is pre-reflexive and non-thematic and it is formed in habits through a web of conscious and unconscious sentiments of joining. This us-background, a non-reducible basic level of community, is a necessary condition for actual we-intentionality. Common intentionality can therefore neither be understood as involving a unique super-individual bearer, nor simply as a habit shared by multiple individuals—it is a web of intentional relations between individuals with which several habits are linked.

In Walther's work we find no monological conception of intentionality, but a relational, interpersonal account of mind. A fresh look at her account could free the current debate from old prejudices concerning the phenomenological concept of intentionality. There is no preconstituted subjectivity that joins the community: in habitual joining, subjects and community reciprocally form each other.

E. Caminada (✉)
a.r.t.e.s. Graduate School for the Humanities Cologne, University of Cologne, Cologne, Germany
e-mail: emanuele.caminada@uni-koeln.de

A. Konzelmann Ziv and H.B. Schmid (eds.), *Institutions, Emotions, and Group Agents*,
Studies in the Philosophy of Sociality 2, DOI 10.1007/978-94-007-6934-2_12,
© Springer Science+Business Media Dordrecht 2014

1 Introduction

The task of this chapter is to present Gerda Walther's theory of community, and to situate it within the contemporary debate about collective intentionality. Gerda Walther (1897–1977) wrote *Zur Ontologie der Sozialen Gemeinschaft* in 1921 as a Ph.D. dissertation under the supervision of the Munich phenomenologist Alexander Pfänder. The text was published in 1923 in the phenomenological *Jahrbuch* edited by Edmund Husserl, for whom she also prepared the index of his *Ideas I* (Hua III/1, pp. 360–427), the work that ratified the "transcendental turn" of Husserl in the eyes of his students. Those who did not accept the transcendental frame of Husserl's constitution theory declared themselves *realistic* phenomenologists and rested on the project of descriptive ontology and psychology. Walther herself chose Pfänder as her supervisor because she felt more acquainted with his realistic approach than with the methodologies Husserl was still working out during her studies in Freiburg (Walther 1960, p. 244).[1] Walther's "unusually fruitful and suggestive" account (Spiegelberg 1994, p. 188) has only recently been discovered and discussed (Schmid 2005, 2009; Schmid and Schweikard 2009) thanks to the growing interest that realistic phenomenology has aroused in the last few decades within the research on the social frame of intentionality. After a century of mutual misunderstandings, we are finally seeing an exciting though not scorn-free rapprochement and exchange between the analytic and phenomenological traditions both in terms of thematic approaches and conceptual tools (De Monticelli 2011).

Within the reassessment of formal ontology and descriptive psychology spear-headed by the Seminar for Austro-German-Philosophy, an important bridge was built between the two traditions in the revaluation of Reinach's account of social acts through a comparison with contemporary speech act theory (Mulligan 1987). From both sides of the twentieth-century ideal "philosophical ocean", social ontology is nowadays recognized as being embedded in the tradition of early phenomenology (Salice 2011).

As collective intentionality analyses were for a long time limited to strictly practical and cognitive intentionality, the current rediscovery of empathy and affective states in cognitive sciences and philosophy of mind has brought renewed attention to the realistic phenomenological approach to emotional life and its relevance for both social cognition and social ontology (Thompson 2001; Zahavi 2001; Schmid 2005; Vendrell Ferran 2008). Concurrently, scholars who overcame firmly rooted prejudices about the role of embodiment and intersubjectivity in Husserl's constitution theory (Gallagher and Zahavi 2008) deeply enriched the frame of the "en-active approach" (Varela et al. 1991) integrating phenomenology and the cognitive sciences. In all these trends we are seeing a shift from an individualistic toward an embodied and socially embedded approach.

---

[1] In 1923, she also released an enquiry on mystics and additionally she published on psychiatry and parapsychology, being progressively ostracized by the scientific community because of her disconcerting interest in occultism (Lopez McAllister 1995).

Against this scientific background, I want to situate Walther's theory of community within the current debate on collective intentionality. Since the seminal works of Miller and Tuomela (1988) and Searle (1990), the core of the discussion has been the mereological value of collective intentionality. My claim is that Walther's tricky but fruitful strategy could represent a "Copernican Turn" in social theory (as cited in Schmid 2009, p. 43). But first we must clarify the *enhanced concept of intentionality* that phenomenology offers (Hua III/1, § 115). Despite the rigid division between realistic and Husserlian phenomenologies, we can profit from her account only if we understand it as mid-point between those of Pfänder and Husserl, i.e. in-between the analytic-realistic and the transcendental-constitutive approaches. Determining how to situate Walther's account among other theories of collective intentionality depends much more on the understanding of intentionality one endorses than the mereology one commits to.

It is a given that intentionality refers to the relation between mind and world. However, this still leaves open how one should describe intentionality. Both Pfänder and Husserl focused on the peculiar *directedness* of different ways of conscious life, developing the descriptive approach to intentionality initiated by Brentano (1874). If we live directed *toward* the world, i.e. in striving or in attentive perception or explicit thought, intentionality manifests itself as *centrifugal*. By contrast, we are subject to *centripetal* tendencies if we are *affected* by something, if we experience something as demanding our attention, and if we are guided by the implicit affordances of the environment. We can find centripetal and centrifugal intentionality in all three main classes of intentional life: the cognitive, the conative, and the emotive sphere.

Intentionality concerns, therefore, the whole experience of *directed life*, the driving and the driven one. What one grasps or is grasped by is not the content of an inner "intentional state" that is related to the outside, but rather the source or goal of this lived relation.

In phenomenological terms, there can be no succession of mental states without a motivational structure that links them. An abrupt noise motivates, for example, the shift of attention; its content can further motivate an attentive perception if one switches to a contemplative stance looking at the rain through the window; or a required problem-solving action if one realizes that the window is wide open; or, more cheerlessly a sentiment of begrudgement at the prospect of yet another dreary weekend. As this shows, a single intentional state can acquire its sense only within a framework of motivations. Despite this vividly differentiated account of mental life that Husserl shared with the phenomenological circles, since his "transcendental turn" he has often been accused of being a representationalist and therefore of falling victim to a monological, solipsistic account of intentionality. These striking criticisms emerged from amidst the misunderstandings and rivalries that increasingly took place within the phenomenological movement in the tragic times that began in 1914. They gave rise to interpretational problems that could only be eventually resolved through the careful study of Husserl's larger body of work in the elephantine edition of the Husserliana (Hua), that began 1950 and is still in progress. The aim of his lifelong research was the in-depth descriptive examination of intentional structures as *correlations* of thinking and thought, i.e. of experiencing subjectivity and experienced objectivity. In the *Logical Investigations* he had already begun an analysis of correlation structures of acts of representation and conceptual cognition. Step by step, the subject of this activity came to the fore. While at first logical structures were analyzed "monologically", i.e. in the inner speech of the cognitive subject (Hua XIX/1, p. 41), gradually the analysis reached the pre-categorical level and, finally, the intentional network that interweaves both intra-subjective and inter-subjective life (Zahavi 2001).

His transcendental turn, i.e. his tricky methodology of progressive reductions, was not conceived to escape reality and sociality, but to understand more deeply *how* we experience them within incessantly developing and never-ending differentiating intentional frames (Lohmar 2002).

For their part, realistic phenomenologists continued to describe different aspects of intentional reference to the world, focusing either on the psychological structure or the constant features of related intentional objects, without paying much attention to the dynamic interdependence of intentional correlations that obsessed Husserl (Hua VI, p. 169). Their psychological and ontological essays fell into obscurity and still remain like a "sunken continent", ready to be explored by both theoretical psychology and social ontology (De Monticelli 2000). The revaluation of this tradition is still in its infancy and can contribute greatly to the current debate. In this regard, no one has yet paid due attention to the relevance of Husserl's constitution theory for such topical questions as: How do we construct social reality? How can mind-dependent objects be better understood? To be sure, this research program reaches far beyond the limited aims of the present study. Nevertheless, as Husserl pointed out, in order to fulfill constitutional research within the intersubjective frame of the life-world, one needs a deeper analysis of the social web of intentional structures. This is what he called the way to constitutive analysis through the "new-born" (Hua XXX, p. 286) intentional psychology and sociology (Hua VIII, p. 108). If only one were to bracket the old, unfruitful polemic between realistic and idealistic metaphysics and provide a more sympathetic account of phenomenology as a (differentiated) whole then both analytic and phenomenological social ontology could be framed within Husserl's intentional analysis.

Bearing in mind this historical scientific background I will try to introduce Walther's work in terms accessible to contemporary readers, placing it between Husserl's constitutive approach and the realistic approach of Pfänder's psychology.

Walther's key concept is *"habitual joining"* (*habituelle Einigung*). In order to understand it properly, I shall first introduce Husserl's phenomenological under-standing of habits (Sect. 2.1) and present Pfänder's analysis of the act of joining (Sect. 2.2). It will then be possible to present the three ontological levels of Walther's theory: Non-thematic concrete background (Sect. 3.1), we-experiences against us-background (Sect. 3.2), and acts *in the name of* the community (Sect. 3.3).

2 Habitual Joining

Walther's understanding of intentionality is indebted to both Pfänder's and Husserl's accounts. She develops the concept of *habitual joining* on the basis of Pfänder's essays *Zur Psychologie der Gesinnungen* (1913/1916). Pfänder claims that there are three principal modes of being directed toward objects: in actual, potential, and habitual psychic experiences (*seelische Erlebnisse*). He complains that psychology entirely overlooks the potential and habitual modes in taking these simply to consist in hypothetically deduced nonconscious, pre-intentional dispositions to actual life (Pfänder 1913, p. 332). However, his own analysis of the act of joining did itself not go beyond the frame of actual-present joining (*aktuelle Einigung*). It was Husserl who, from 1917, began to develop an original analysis of *habitual intentionality* and who, in 1920, encouraged Walther to work on the concept of *habitus* (HuDok 3.2, p. 259).

2.1 Habitus in Husserl's Genetic Phenomenology

The concept of "*habituality*" is the key to Husserl's *genetic* account of phenomenology (Bernet et al. 1996, p. 185). The heart of the genetic approach consists in the methodological description of the ways in which intentional structures are acquired. It focuses on the dynamics through which every intentional network arises. Topics of genetic analysis are, for example: the cognitive operations that allow pairs and configurations to arise (*Paarung*); the way in which embodiment takes place in the simultaneous acquisition of bodily capabilities and the increasing enrichment of the environment as a horizon of affordances; or the complex intentional webs that emerge in the encounter with other subjects.

According to this genetic approach, every intentional act arises not only on the basis of an intentional "*horizon*" but also against a "*background*" of experience which produces intentional habits and provides the frames through which every new experience of the same type can be anticipated.

Saying that every intentional act is embedded in a *horizon* means that the mind has no atomic structure: every intentional experience implies a focus and a situated network of potential links that frame it. Thanks to this implicit holistic frame, the intentional content is meaningfully enriched. For example, depending on the implicit situation, one may be inclined to experience a shape *as* a real person (if one is entering the lobby of a hotel) or *as* a sculpture (if one is entering an art exhibition). Maybe in the hotel there is actually a hyper-realistic sculpture, but one does not *expect* it there. Anticipation is one strong shaping moment of the horizon: we experience much more than what we *actually presently* intend, since every intentional object is embedded in a network of potentialities motivated by the content and the modal quality of the act.

Every act further tends to leave behind meaningful marks of its execution in the form of *habitus*. The more one gets acquainted with typical structures of one's experience, the more one *feels familiar* with them (Husserl 1973, p. 123). The intentional network that frames every situation is not only shaped by attitudes and expectations, but also every experience leaves its mark. The expanding knot of meanings related to an intentional content develops into a framework through which every *token* of this *type* will be experienced. This meaningful framework is the intentional *schema* that configures every new encounter with similar objects or situations (Lohmar 2008, p. 103). Husserl calls such schemas "*types*" and the process of their development "*typification*". He defines types as a form of habitus, because, as any other habitual structure, types present an *enactive* moment, i.e. a punctual act that enacts this structure (*Urstiftung*), that is maintained in force and can be reenacted through endorsement or expire once it is given up. Mental life is therefore characterized as a never-ending dynamic of typification, i.e. sedimentation of experienced intentional networks in habitual structures that can be "aroused" in encounters with similar objects.

If I experience 'a cat on the mat', I apprehend it in a particular present perspective that is embedded in a network of potentialities relating to the content 'a cat on the mat'. Once I experience the cat on the mat, I enact the position: 'There is a cat on the mat'. If in the course of that same experience I come to judge that there is no real cat on the mat, but actually only a toy cat, it is because the later parts of the experience contradict the potentialities that were embedded in the intentional structures related to the matter of fact 'a cat on the mat', and force me to change the modal quality of my act from 'There is a cat on a mat.' to 'Is that actually a cat on a mat?'. I will move toward it, testing all the potentialities that should belong to 'a cat on the mat'. If new experiences are no longer meaningfully linked with 'a cat on the mat', i.e. are no longer embedded in its network of motivated potentiality, for example if the cat has a label with "made in China" written upon it, I will suddenly switch the whole intentional network: 'Aha! It isn't a cat, it is a toy!' The position of the state of affairs 'a cat on the mat' expires and another contrary one is enacted: 'a toy on the mat'.

It is important not to overlook the emotional dynamic linked to these processes: becoming acquainted with typical structures of the environment does not safeguard one from embarrassments. Once a sufficient number of types are sedimented, one is exonerated from the mental fatigue that every novel encounter requires. One can rely on one's habits and live in acquainted situations through routines. In the process of becoming acquainted one feels that mental fatigue is diminishing. To *feel familiar* with acquainted structures one has acquired therefore means that one is emotionally discharged from the tensions and distresses that come with unknown horizons. The explosion of an intentional network through the negation of an acquainted framework leads to emotional distresses and embarrassments. One has to be attentive to any sign that could recreate order, switching to another meaningful network re-enacting sedimented structures or trying to get acquainted with the new situation. All these processes are tied to emotional states and dynamics. In extreme cases, if an order can't be restored, it can also lead to panic or emotional disorders. To summarize, every act-fulfillment enlarges the domain of potentialities with new contents and every new experience enriches the *types* through which one can experience the *tokens* of the world. Actual experience brings into play these frames, not only in order to make a token's potentialities explicit, but also in order to structure its horizon through meaningful anticipations. The enrichment of these frames is a process of *habitualization* or *typification*: an intentional habit is a concrete knot of sedimented experiences that will guide each new apprehension of a similar type. Experiences do not simply disappear; they leave traces of their occurrence. These traces *sediment* themselves and become stable ground for further experiences, motivating fantasies, actions, or expectations that drive further perceptions, and so on.

Husserl and Pfänder describe the web of potential and habitual intentionality that surrounds every intended content as the "*background*" against which the subject experiences that content. The term 'background' refers not only to the formal structure of consciousness "*foreground/background*", which was explored by the *Gestaltpsychologie*, it also refers to intentional contents, since it describes the meaningful network of experiences sedimented in the subject's history. Intentionality is not only an actual state of the mind, it forms the subject itself; it is its very nature. It is its past in the form of habits in the background. It is its future, in the form of excitable potentialities that enact the affordances of its environment. It can be vividly experienced in fantasies and realized in actions. This *background* is therefore not a hypothesis about some non-intentional functions, it is an intentional structure articulated according to an intentional modality (*habituality*) that we can directly experience.

We do need a model of such a background in order to understand the mind but we can avoid reducing it to a neurophysiological desideratum as Searle does (1992, 1995). Certainly, the study of the background also involves what Husserl called the "nature-side" of the psyche: appetites, tendencies, drives (Hua IV). But all these phenomena can be experienced, and should be described as, lived ones, as embodied mental life, before one accepts the challenge to substantialize them, i.e. to naturalize them in the form of a causal mechanism.

In conclusion, thanks to the genetic approach to intentionality, phenomenology points out that subjectivity has two essential features:

- It is the intentional pole of centripetal *affection* and centrifugal *action*;
- It is the bearer of gradually evolving systems of *habitualized intentionality*, articulated in its background.

2.2   "*Joining" in Pfänder's Theory of Gesinnung*

So far, we have seen how the understanding of intentionality is enhanced in the tradition of phenomenology by the formal distinctions of actual, potential, and habitual modes of intentional life. These distinctions are related to the concepts of horizon and background and their inherent motivational structure. We saw these features at work in the process of typification that intentionality undergoes, according to Husserl. We also saw how the dynamics of acquaintance involve the emotional polarity of familiarity and befuddlement. These emotional states are side effects of the intentional cognitive operations of acquaintance, however they do not have an intentional character of their own. It is therefore important to contrast emotions with other kinds of feelings that do possess intentional features and play a central role in Walther's own account. We shall call them sentiments, as opposed to emotions.

The task of Pfänder's essays *Zur Psychologie der Gesinnungen* (1913/1916) was to give a systematic analysis of the structures of those feelings which were indicated by the German word *Gesinnung*. Lessing coined this term in order to translate the use of the French term *sentiment* in the eighteenth century, and it has had an impressive role in the German culture of the nineteenth and early twentieth century. It was used by Goethe, Kant, Herder, Hegel, and Fichte to describe a deep structure of personality, between will, sensitivity, and conviction, in opposition to caprice, sensible feelings, and mere opinions. Weber contrasted a deontological ethics of belief (*Gesinnungsethik*) with a consequentialist ethics of responsibility (*Verantwortungsethik*). The word *Gesinnung* became part of a slogan used for Nazi propaganda, and it has since fallen out of common use.

Hume's understanding of *moral sentiments*, which by the way stems from the same French root, has some kinship with the tradition of the German *Gesinnung*. Nowadays, the computational study of opinions, sentiments, and emotions in virtual statements (in social networks, user commentaries, etc.) is called "Sentiment Analysis" and explores some phenomena that were peripherally discussed by Pfänder. As we will see, sentiments tend to activate dispositional attitudes, but I would prefer to avoid translating *Gesinnung* either with "*dispositional sentiment*" or with "*dispositions*" (as is commonly done) in order to cover the broadest spectrum (i.e. to address actual, potential, and habitual sentiments) and to stress the intentional and rational features of this class of feelings, rather than their effects. For these reasons I translate *Gesinnung* as "*sentiment*".

According to Pfänder's definition, sentiments are not states, but *intentional feelings*. Their essential feature is manifested in their *positive* or *negative* polarity. Positive sentiments include for example love, friendship, sympathy, and favour; negative sentiments include hatred, enmity, antipathy, and disfavour.

The intentional structure of a fully developed sentiment has three different levels. From a developmental perspective each level *tends* to arise out of one of the more basic levels, but one can learn to control each autonomously. They are:

1. Affect (*Erregung*): Positive excitation/Negative excitation (positive/negative *Regung*);
2. Position-taking (*Stellungnahme*): Joining/Separating (*Einigung/Sonderung*);
3. Attitude (*Haltung*): Approval/Disapproval (*Bejahung/Verneinung*).

1. The first level is that of affect: it can be a positive or negative motion toward something or someone; for example a reactive expression of anger toward the car driver honking at me, or a feeling of sympathy for someone.

2. A centrifugal act of position-*taking* (*Stellungnahme*) toward the intentional object of the affect can arise if one follows it, moving to the object of sympathy, e.g. seeking contact with it. If one establishes contact, one *joins* it. Joining (*Einigung*) is an intentional sentiment of bonding, motivated by a positive affective disposition toward somebody or something. *To be* joined ("Einig*sein*") is not to be confused with *the feeling* of being bonded ("Einigungs*gefühl*"). On the other hand, if one establishes intentional contact with the object of a negative affect one will try to *maintain* or *increase the distance* from it through an act of *separating* (*Sondern*). In joining and separating, we bring our environment into affective relief, selecting relevant features which track ourselves and our character. Both of them model the background of the subject according to the intentional content and to the modal quality of the relation to it. Joining a mate, for example, who loves climbing doesn't mean that I will acquire his abilities, but it makes possible that, thanks to him, I will acquire some skills and some attitudes that could lead me to try to follow him in a climbing expedition. Through him I can learn to experience something which I never cared for before. Separating has positive effects, too. If I incline to separate myself from someone, I will avoid all those features which are tied together in the type that grew from the encounter with him. Furthermore, objects of joining or separating can be both persons (and animals) or inanimate objects, such as toys or luxury products, that can therefore acquire affective features (becoming animated) both in their individual and class character. Freud called "transference" the peculiar ability to transfer sentiments from one person to another, or from a person to an object. Since transferred sentiments seem to play a very important role in the development of infants' minds, because status symbols often define the social structure of adults, it remains an open task for phenomenology to analyze the intentional structure that links sentiments and transference (see Lohmar and Brudzinska 2011).

Joining and separating both influence the way my background develops, they model it constantly and, most of the time, they do so irrespective of my will. Acts of joining and separating can be divided into those which are conscious and those which are not. The intimate individuality of the person is given in the inner order of her sentiments: the less one is aware of one's sentiments, the more the background is responsive to their effects.

Through the affective relations of joining and separating one weaves one's social embedment: both joining and separating explain the relational character of the affective life that nourishes the social world. By taking a positive or negative position toward relevant phenomena of the affective environment, one reinforces the dialectical structures of relational life. Even refusing contact with someone leaves its mark upon the background of the one who is performing the separation. Refusals are carried into and influence individual life no less than fondness. Since in infancy personality is shaped within familiar sentiments, children are often told fairy tales that narrate the risks of growing up. Characters therefore are the representation in images of what children mostly live and fear: the bonding relations of caring, the fear of being refused, the monsters of loneliness, and their struggles for friendship and love. As one grows up and becomes a person, one is challenged by one's own past: the sentiments and fears that left their mark upon the background, the models one had, the refusals one suffered, and also the characters one heard about can become a rigid framework one cannot escape or the most intimate material one has to work out.

Sentiments manifest further peculiar modal qualities, as we know from novels and films, since one can differentiate, for example, between the amour-passion that consumes the whole life of the lover—ambivalent passions that switch between positive and negative qualities—and resentments, where separating replaces joining because of refusal. Of course, blind love and hesitating favor, cold or visceral hatred, given the same intentional object, do not mark the background in the same way.

As a result of joining and separating, one attunes one's affective life to one's social environment: we can therefore speak of a kind of "*affect attunement*" (Stern 1985, p. 140). Affects become modulated through the positions one takes toward their sources, they can be strengthened or partially stifled. Affects are shaped through the affective positions one takes: motions of sympathy can increase, for example, in the presence of a person one joins, toward whom one is well-disposed. In the opposite direction, a past act of separation can snuff out any positive motion. Through the habitualization of joining and separating one shapes one's own background according to the bonding relations in which one is involved. Joining and separating establish fields of relations that become part of the life of the subjects. By joining, one attunes oneself with these relational background fields, one *joins* them and embeds one's own background within a communal, joint one.

3. Finally, one can assume a personal attitude (*Haltung*) toward the object of joining or separating, respectively approving or disapproving of its existence and its values. Second order sentiments normally call for taking a stand on their objects, while endorsements or refusals involve an inner affective recognition or rejection of the affordances with which these sentiments are coupled. Sentiments of approving and disapproving are performed by the intimate "center" of the person: they become traits of her character. By taking a stand for someone, one implicitly commits oneself to care for him. Once one takes a stand for something, one implicitly assents to it as valuable, it becomes worth one's engagement. Sentiments give access to a particular domain of practical rationality: values are namely recognized via reflection on the state of affairs *qua* state of values as given through the affective relations that these higher order sentiments shape. This is an important point in the strictly phenomenological criticism of practical reason that cannot be further developed here, but it nevertheless has enormous implications for ethics and social theories.

For the purpose of this chapter we can therefore define joining as follows: *joining is a positive intentional sentiment of bonding, motivated by a positive affective disposition towards something or somebody.*

3   Walther's Ontology of Community

Following some of Husserl's suggestions, Walther developed the idea of joining by relating it to the process of habitualization. In her view, a community is essentially grounded in the joint background that arises through habitual joining.

She distinguishes three levels of community, according to three different steps of communal intentional structures:

1. Non-thematic concrete background;
2. We-experiences against us-background;
3. Acts in the name of the community.

3.1 Non-thematic Concrete Background

Walther radicalized Pfänder's account by stressing that if the object of joining (or separating) is another subject, habitualization takes the form of an (intentional) "other *in me*", through and with whom I can experience the world (Walther 1923, p. 71).

The solution that Walther's approach to we-intentionality proposes is tricky to understand and lies in the following intuition: beyond our active, actual conscious life, we carry in the background something like "others in me". What does it mean to live with others in the background?

She describes the way we-experiences operate as follows:

> [*M*]y experiences are actually lived in my I-Center, they stream toward it from my consciousness-background, from my Self, in which my I is embedded. Though in this embedment, in this background, from which these lived experiences arise, I am not alone as 'myself'—in the communal lived experiences—but I have taken the others inside into the background, I intentionally received them beyond my I-Center in my Self (or they grew up in it by themselves) and I feel myself at one, I feel myself joined with them (unconsciously, automatically or because of an explicit joining). (Walther 1923, p. 71)[2]

Following Pfänder, she describes subjectivity within the polarity of the "I-Center" and the "Self". Not every intentional motion has to be performed by the I-Center; on the contrary, the I-Center is the pole only of every *centrifugal* intentional act. Intentional motions and affects can arise peripherally in the background without involving the I-Center, but the I-Center is strictly embedded within its intentional background, which is therefore called the Self. Since every experience arises against the background, it somehow has its source in the Self. Nevertheless, not every experience has to be constitutively private. In the background the Self is not alone because it is embedded in its history, which is individuated by its affective relations. The background keeps track of all joining and separating acts. The Self is

---

[2] "[*M*]*eine* Erlebnisse vollziehen sich aktuell in *meinem* Ichzentrum, sie strömen ihm aus meinem Bewußtseinhintergrund, meinem Selbst, in das es eingebettet ist, zu. Doch in dieser Einbettung, in diesem Hintergrund, aus dem diese Erlebnisse hervorgehen, bin nicht nur ich allein als 'ich selbst'—bei dem Gemeinschaftserlebnissen—, sondern ich habe die anderen ja mit in ihn hereingenommen, ich habe sie hinter meinem Ichzentrum in mein Selbst intentional aufgenommen (oder sie sind von selbst hineingewachsen) und ich fühle mich eins mit ihnen (unbewußt, automatisch oder auf Grund einer ausdrücklichen Einigung)."

attuned to other subjects because it has sedimented its relations with them. These counterparts are *typificated* in the background as *relational types* that can be aroused in relevant situations thrown into similar forms of affective relief.

The "others in me" were *intentionally* taken into the background, as in every typification, but they restructure the intentional network in a very radical way. Through the typification of other subjects the intentional horizon is *extruded* into the social dimension. The relational fields become incorporated in the intentional horizon, carried in the background, and held in the potentialities of the network. The concrete background therefore manifests a peculiar form of sociality that Husserl called the intentional "being-one-in-the-other" (*Ineinandersein*). In the background one is "one-in-the-other" in such a way that one is attuned to intentional counterparts that co-determine the framework through which one experiences the world (Hua VI, p. 258). More than simply being "one-with-the-other" (*Mitsein*), as Heidegger stressed (as cited in Schmid 2005, p. 246), human sociality is characterized by this peculiar way of incorporating the social relations within one's own mind: being "one-in-the-other", one experiences a common world, extruding one's own environment into a social one. What Walther points out is that this extrusion only occurs via incandescent operations of joining and separating. Only affective life has the power to warm the background and to mold it radically.

One should not overlook Walther's intuition that the background can develop in relational fields despite the conscious life of the subject. Children, for example, experience the world largely through relevant counterparts who, without being thematized, enrich the environment with new intentional qualities. Daniel Stern calls these counterparts "regulators of the self" (Stern 1985, p. 76). Their presence in the background of the Self modifies the intentional structure of the experienced world. In relational life, backgrounds develop together in generative processes that lead to concrete (from *concrescere*, to grow with) sociality long before full conscious life develops. From the very beginning of early relational life, the background is marked by relevant counterparts who are not thematized. Some of them become familiar regulators of one's behavior, implicitly shaping habitual postures. They begin to be thematized only in fantasies and games, and not just in infancy. These counterparts can further be (partially) thematized in inner speech, referring to oneself through these intentional others in me. "It is constitutive to the human psyche to have *others in mind*", as Rochat keenly claims (2009, p. 17). The background is full of these "ghosts" that are sedimented through experience, related according to affective positions, such as joining and separating. Because of their strong emotive and affective relevance, they recur compulsively in our minds as soon as they are stimulated. In adult life, they are no longer *regulators* but rather *evaluators of the self*: the sentiments others bear toward us, the way they take or would take a stand, their judgments constantly drive not only our actions but also more deeply the cultivation of our desires and affects.

According to Walther's intuition the concrete background is the non-reducible basic level of sociality (Walther 1923, p. 69). In it, social relations are shaped: every act of joining or separating embeds the social positions one assumes in the background. The subject is therefore, from the very beginning, a bearer of habits that arise in relational, intersubjective affective interactions.

3.2 We-Experiences Against Us-Background

It is only against this concrete background that our actual we-experiences are possible. Individuals participate in them on the basis of their background and they are structured in mutual intentional interaction and common knowledge. The contemporary debate about we-intentionality tends to break down common knowledge into some form of iteration: in a predicative account of intentionality, it seems impossible to avoid a kind of *infinite regress* of mutual beliefs that are required in order to do something together. Walther points out that if a plurality of subjects experience something, these lived experiences do not become a *common* experience (a we-experience) by virtue of the different subjects simply knowing that everyone is experiencing the same object. She therefore switches from *having common knowledge* to *mutually joining common experience*. She describes this switch by analyzing the intentional structure of *actual-present we-experiences*. This theory of *we-experiences* has recently been partially criticized by Schmid (2005, pp. 132–138). However some of his critical remarks are moot if we understand Walther's theory in the frame of Husserl's concept of intentional background and Pfänder's psychology of sentiments. Here is the structure that Walther presents:

1. Experience of 'A', who is intentionally directed toward an object;
1a Experience of 'B', who is *similarly* intentionally directed toward the *same* object.
2. Empathic experience of 'A', who empathizes with the experience of 'B' (1a);
2a Empathic experience of 'B', who empathizes with the experience of 'A'. (1).
3. *Joining* act of 'A' with the act of 'B' (or with him) whom 'A' empathically experiences;
4. *Joining* act of 'B' with the act of 'A' (or with him) whom 'B' empathically experiences.
4a Empathic experience of 'B', who experiences that 'A' has joined his act (or him).

We already know that *actual-present* experiences are embedded in a background and tend to shape the background further in the form of *habitus*. When 'A' is intentionally directed toward an object, he does it in the way his habitual frames suggest to him and according to every new actual present experience. So does 'B'. Both of them are somehow acquainted with the object they are experiencing. Suddenly 'A' notices 'B', who is somehow similarly directed to the same object. 'A' is capable of empathy, he has already collected experiences with other people and can see that 'B' is interested in the same object as him. The same goes for 'B'.

In order to achieve (1–2), 'A' and 'B' already need to have a common background and to be acquainted with some typical structures that relate to the object they are experiencing. They have at their disposal a concrete background that already joins these intentional structures. Against it, they realize that they are both directed to the same object. They could remain in this situation of mutual recognition: in the rush of daily life we habitually notice that we are with other people doing similar things, waiting for the train or shopping, and so on. This usually happens without commitment: everybody gets off the train when they have to, without deliberating it with their fellow travelers, mutually knowing that they were plausibly all waiting for the same train. Thanks to typification it is possible to perform codified actions and cooperative endeavors that do not require an individual to go beyond his expected function: not only collective actions, such as daily commuting, but, for example, also working at an assembly line. Working together, one with the other, does not require a community if the work is standardized. On the other hand, fighting for workers' rights cannot be successful if the workers do not join together as a group and do not recognize themselves as part of it.

But let us return to the structure of actual we-experiences.

Let us now suppose that 'A' is backpacking, he is waiting on the platform and sees 'B' who is backpacking, too. They notice each other. 'B' is intrigued by 'A' and looks at her furtively. 'A' does likewise. Their eyes meet, they look around, their eyes meet again. They feel tension and embarrassment. Finally one of them smiles, the other smiles too. They turn to each other, mutually aware that the other is somehow friendly and well-disposed. They actually have something in common, they are in the same situation, they are both backpacking, and they know what it is like!

This example shows that a sentiment cannot be iterated in the way predicative knowledge can: if 'A' likes 'B' and 'B' likes 'A', 'A' surely likes that 'B' likes her and *vice versa*, rather they do not care how this statement can be iterated, they simply *join* themselves and like the fact that they are joining. The more they get acquainted the more their backgrounds interweave, the more their *actual-present* experience can stem from joint frames. If these joint frames become *habitual*, they will live through joint backgrounds, they will feel how bonded they are. They will act from reasons arising from this joint experience: they will live through their mutual "us in me", as they would say. Their joint background will be enriched: we can define it as the "us-background" against which they habitually live. When we-experiences become habitual, each member of this interaction can live through this communal rational structure even if other members are not actually present. Each member can therefore act according to communal reasons and experience the world and himself through the eyes of the relational *Us* that is interwoven in his background.

This common life is experienced by individual persons, but it streams from communal background-structures, which are sedimented in affective relations. Walther describes the *plural first person perspective* as follows:

> I live and experience at the same time through myself *and* through *them in me*, through 'Us'. Well *before* these experiences come to the fore of the I-point, before they are actualized, they are lived experiences of the community, because they already arise as motions from me *and* the others *in* me (Walther 1923, p. 71).[3]

Schmid's critical remarks on Walther's theory concern the suspicion that she remains restrained in the so-called Husserlian "monological" account of

---

[3]"Ich lebe und erlebe aus mir selbst *und* aus *ihnen in mir* zugleich heraus, aus 'Uns'. Schon *ehe* diese Erlebnisse in den Ichpunkt eintreten, in ihm aktualisiert werden, sind sie also Gemeinschaftserlebnisse, denn sie entspringen ja schon als Regungen aus mir *und* den anderen *in* mir."

intentionality (Schmid 2005, p. 136). Although the point of departure for her analysis of *actually present we-experiences* are acts in the mode of *I-intentionality*, we saw how they are embedded in a background that is from the very beginning socially attuned through acts of joining (and separating). If this us-background becomes a habitual one then a community arises: community (us-background) presupposes sociality (concrete background). Following Walther's ontology, the core of the *We* is pre-reflexive and non-thematic and it is tracked in habits through a web of conscious and unconscious sentiments of *mutual habitual joining*: it is the network of the us-background.

3.3   Acts in the Name of the Community

Thematizing their communal rational structure, members become capable of taking positions towards themselves and the world or towards the community itself. When its members thematize communal reasons the community reaches a further stage of complexity: its reasons directly become part of the process of motivations, and not only indirectly through pre-thematic us-background. Its members can now reflect on themselves *as members of* the community and can act accordingly. Finally, they can act or choose one that can act *in the name of* the community, representing it as a public person (Walther 1923, p. 104). Walther follows Reinach in order to conceptualize this further step of complexity, but she does not master his theory in its full richness (see Mulligan 1987). Be that as it may, it is important to stress that a reflexive and thematic *We* is necessary to give institutional form and functions to the community and that a thematic *We* is achievable only against the us-background.

4   Conclusions

Walther's original account is linked to two important issues in the phenomenological tradition that have fallen into obscurity: Husserl's intentional background theory and Pfänder's theory of sentiments. They both conceptualize subjectivity as an intentional pole of affection and action (or I-Center) and as a bearer of gradually developing systems of *habitualized intentionality*, articulated in its individuated background (or Self). Understanding subjectivity as a pole of affection and action does not mean giving an individualistic account of intentionality. Because Husserl calls this pole of intentionality "I", it is important to stress that this essential subjective polarity of intentionality is not to be confused with any form of "I-intentionality", in the sense that this expression has acquired in current debates. By "I-intentionality" one can mean both an individual embodiment, and a personal reference to the world. According to phenomenology, bodily intentionality is relationally shaped through acts of affect attunement. A personal level of subjectivity emerges within *intentional* attitudes that require the prior development of a background of affections and bodily actions. Walther shows how both personal I-intentionality and we-intentionality emerge from joint background and basic levels of concrete background: we-intentionality does not exclude subjective perspectives, but it occurs through common joint frames and against a common us-background. I-intentionality is always a matter of a socialized Self, since I reinforce *myself* in relation to my counterparts.

As the concretization of the background in its social embedment extrudes experience into a social level, habitual joining provides a new dimension: the dimension of we-intentionality against the us-background. Walther calls the switch to we-experience an "intentional somersault" (Walther 1923, p. 98): recognizing it as a scientific paradigm would mean a "Copernican turn" for sociology! Following Walther, the turn would consist in the enhancement of the description of social life and plural action through the phenomenological concept of background.

Far from being restrained by a monological account of intentionality, the tradition of phenomenology has provided a dynamic account of it by from the very beginning facing up to the challenge of social embedment. The description of subjectivity through the articulation of the respective roles of the I-Center, the Background, and the Self can open a path toward transposing the phenomenological account into the terms of our contemporary debate. The I-Center has the non-reducible character of the first-person perspective. Nevertheless, this egological life is embedded in the background of passive life. Each act performed by the subject tracks the background according to its intentional features. Thanks to the sentiments the background is enriched by relational fields that extrude the egological perspective into a socialized one, without suppressing it. That which lives against the background of the relational selves it carries is the I-Center. It is implicated in the intentional "being-one-in-the-other" (*Ineinandersein*) in a common social world (Hua VI, p. 258): it is the selves in the reciprocal backgrounds that are one-in-the-other. Knotted within these relational selves and their non-reducible embodied perspectives, the I-Center can acquire, through habitual positions and attitudes, a personal stance, that shapes a personal self. At the same time the I-Center can attune and share communal habits against the background of other selves.

Therefore, what is responsible for the mereology of collective intentionality is not the non-reducible egological character of intentionality, but the socialized background against which acts are performed. As Walther puts it, a common (or a group's) mind is a matter of a multipolar network of personal I-Centers and a concrete common relational background in which those I-Centers are embedded. Thus, in order to deny individualism in ontology and metaphysics we do not need to deny subjectivity as the concrete bearer of intentionality at all. There is no pre-constituted subjectivity that joins the community: in joining, subjects reciprocally form each other, long before they join a communal life in the further sense of a communal we-experience against an us-background. According to Walther the bearer of a community's own intentionality is not a unique super-individual subject, but a network of several habit systems. Its structure is not a subjective and polar one, as natural persons are, but a *multipolar* one.

In Walther's account we find no monological conception of intentionality, but a relational and interpersonal account of subjectivity that tries to describe how the irreducible modality of we-intentionality arises against a background of joint sentiments. She could therefore provide us with a paradigmatic turn in social ontology beyond both individualism and collectivism. Furthermore, a critical reception of her account situated in between realistic and constitutive phenomenology could free the current debate from old prejudices concerning Husserl's concept of intentionality.

References

Bernet, R., I. Kern, and E. Marbach. 1996. *Edmund Husserl: Darstellung seines Denkens.* Hamburg: Meiner.
Brentano, F. 1874. *Psychologie vom empirischen Standpunkte.* Leipzig: Duncker & Humblot.
De Monticelli, R. (ed.). 2000. *La persona: Apparenza e realtà.* Milan: Cortina.
De Monticelli, R. 2011. Phenomenology today: A good travel mate for analytic philosophy? *Phenomenology and Mind. The Online Journal of the Centre in Phenomenology and Sciences of the Person* 1: 18–27.
Gallagher, S., and D. Zahavi. 2008. *The phenomenological mind: An introduction to philosophy of mind and cognitive science.* New York: Routledge.
Husserl, E. 1973. *Experience and judgement: Investigations in a genealogy of logic.* Trans. J.S. Churchill and K. Ameriks. Evanston: Northwestern University Press.
Husserl, E. (Hua). *Husserliana: Edmund Husserl. Gesammelte Werke.* The Hague: Springer.
Husserl, E. (HuDok). *Husserliana: Edmund Husserl—Dokumente.* The Hague: Springer.
Lohmar, D. 2002. Die Idee der Reduktion: Husserls Reduktionen – und ihr gemeinsamer, methodischer Sinn. In *Die erscheinende Welt: Festschrift für Klaus Held*, ed. H. Hüniand and P. Trawny. Berlin: Dunker & Humblot.
Lohmar, D. 2008. *Phänomenologie der schwachen Phantasie.* Dordrecht: Springer.
Lohmar, D., and J. Brudzinska (eds.). 2011. *Founding psychoanalysis phenomenologically: Phenomenological theory of subjectivity and the psychoanalytic experience.* Dordrecht: Springer.
Lopez McAllister, L. 1995. Gerda Walther. In *A history of women philosophers*, vol. 4, ed. M.E. Waithe, 189–206. Dordrecht: Kluwer.
Miller, K., and R. Tuomela. 1988. We-intentions. *Philosophical Studies* 71: 223–265.
Mulligan, K. (ed.). 1987. *Speech act and Sachverhalt. Reinach and the foundations of realist phenomenology.* Dordrecht: Martinus Nijhoff.
Pfänder, A. 1913/1916. Zur Psychologie der Gesinnungen. In *Jahrbuch für Philosophie und phänomenologische Forschung*, vol. 1, 325–404 and vol. 3, 1–125. Halle: Niemeyer.
Rochat, P. 2009. *Others in mind: Social origins of self-consciousness.* Cambridge: Cambridge University Press.
Salice, A. 2011. Social ontology as embedded in the tradition of phenomenological realism. In *Proceedings of the inaugural meeting of the European network on social ontology*, ed. B.S. Kobow, H.B. Schmid, and M. Schmitz. Dordrecht: Springer.
Schmid, H.B. 2005. *Wir-Intentionalität: Kritik des ontologischen Individualismus und Rekonstruktion der Gemeinschaft.* Freiburg: Albers.
Schmid, H.B. 2009. *Plural actions: Essays in philosophy and social science.* Dordrecht: Springer.
Schmid, H.B., and D. Schweikard. 2009. Einleitung: Kollektive Intentionalität. Begriff, Geschichte, Probleme. In *Kollektive Intentionalität: Eine Debatte über die Grundlagen des Sozialen*, ed. H.B. Schmid and D. Schweikard, 11–65. Frankfurt a. M: Suhrkamp.
Searle, J.R. 1990. Collective intentions and actions. In *Intentions in communication*, ed. P.R. Cohen, J. Morgan, and M.E. Pollack, 401–415. Cambridge, MA: MIT Press.

Searle, J.R. 1992. *The rediscovery of the mind*. Cambridge: MIT Press.

Searle, J.R. 1995. *The construction of social reality*. New York: The Free Press.

Spiegelberg, H. 1994. *The phenomenological movement: A historical introduction*. Dordrecht: Kluwer.

Stern, D. 1985. *The interpersonal world of the infant. A view from psychoanalysis and developmental psychology*. New York: Perseus.

Thompson, E. 2001. Empathy and consciousness. *Journal of Consciousness Studies* 8(5–7): 1–32.

Varela, F.J., E. Thompson, and E. Rosch. 1991. *The embodied mind: Cognitive science and human experience*. Cambridge, MA: MIT Press.

Vendrell Ferran, I. 2008. *Die Emotionen: Gefühle in der realistischen Phänomenologie*. Berlin: Akademie Verlag.

Walther, G. 1923. Zur Ontologie der sozialen Gemeinschaft. In *Jahrbuch für Philosophie und phänomenologische Forschung*, vol. 6, 1–158. Halle: Niemeyer.

Walther, G. 1960. *Zum anderen Ufer: Vom Marxismus und Atheismus zum Christentum*. Remagen: Otto Reichl.

Zahavi, D. 2001. *Husserl and transcendental intersubjectivity: A response to the linguistic-pragmatic critique*. Athens: Ohio University Press.

Chapter 13
Collective Intentionality and Recognition from Others

Arto Laitinen

Abstract This paper approaches questions of collective intentionality by drawing inspiration from theories of recognition. After making some remarks about "recognition" and "groups" the paper examines whether the kind of dependence on recognition that holds of individual agents is equally true of group agents. In the debates on collective intentionality it is often stressed that the identity, existence, ethos, and membership-issues of the group are up to the group to decide. The members collectively accept (recognize) status functions, goals and beliefs for the group. This paper asks whether this thesis of "forgroupness" should be re-evaluated: could the status functions, goals and beliefs be in some significant sense "for others" as well? Can the group be dependent on others' takes?

1 Introduction

In the debates on collective intentionality it is often stressed that the identity, existence, ethos and membership-issues of the group are up to the group to decide.[1] The members collectively accept or recognize status functions, goals and beliefs *for the group* (see Tuomela 2007, p. 15). This exploratory paper asks whether this thesis of "forgroupness" should be re-evaluated: can the status functions, goals and beliefs be in some significant sense "for others" as well? Can the group be constitutively dependent on others' takes?

---

[1]By "debates on collective intentionality and social ontology" I refer to the debates where for example the following have played a formative role: Bratman 1999, 2007; Gilbert 1989, 1996, 2000, 2006; Lagerspetz et al. 2001; Lewis 1969; Miller 2001; Pettit 1993, 2001; Pettit and List 2011; Searle 1995, 2010; Tuomela 1984, 1995, 2000, 2002, 2007.

A. Laitinen (✉)
Department of Social Sciences and Philosophy, University of Jyväskylä, Jyväskylä, Finland
e-mail: arto.laitinen@jyu.fi

A. Konzelmann Ziv and H.B. Schmid (eds.), *Institutions, Emotions, and Group Agents*,   213
Studies in the Philosophy of Sociality 2, DOI 10.1007/978-94-007-6934-2_13,
© Springer Science+Business Media Dordrecht 2014

This paper approaches questions discussed in the debates about collective intentionality by drawing inspiration from theories of mutual recognition.[2] After some conceptual remarks about "recognition", the paper asks whether the same points that can be said about the dependence of individual thinkers or agents or persons on recognition apply to group thinkers or agents as well.

Thus the paper focuses on whether group agents need recognition from outside. And if they do, do they need it more specifically in order to exist at all, or to have recognized deontic statuses, or to have a functioning "relation to self"? The idea of a group's relation-to-self derives from an analogy with individuals: it is often stressed that for individuals, respect from others is necessary for self-respect, esteem from others enhances self-esteem, and so on (Honneth 1995). This paper suggests that a group's implicit relation-to-self can be said to consist of the "attitudinal climate" among its members, but the group also has an explicit "realm of concern", "intentional horizon" and an "ethos" (Tuomela 2007, p. 15). It will be examined below whether and how these implicit and explicit self-relations depend on recognition from outsiders.

It is perhaps worth pointing out that the paper leaves out of discussion various other relations of recognition such as recognition between the members, or recognition between the group and its members, and the paper does not elaborate on the nature of groups as recognizers. The focus will be on how "ordinary" collective intentionality might depend on recognition *from outside* the relevant group, whose intentions or beliefs or other attitudes are at stake.

2 "Recognition" in the Relevant Sense and Why It Matters

In one meaning of the word, recognition can mean mere *identification* and re-identification of anything as the thing it is, or the kind of thing it is. This can be a purely non-normative usage (see Ricoeur 2005; Ikäheimo and Laitinen 2007).

There are three further usages that are normatively loaded, and which are of interest to the debates on collective identity. These differ on whether the target of recognition is a normative entity (a principle, a reason, a value, a rule, a right, a duty etc.), in which case recognition is not a matter of merely identifying the normative entity, but a matter of taking the principle, value, or reason as *valid*. We can reserve the word *acknowledgement* for this usage. The principles so acknowledged may include moral principles, which according to moral realists are valid whether or

---

[2]E.g. Hegel 1807; Brandom 2007; van den Brink and D. Owen 2007; Deranty 2009; Gutmann 1994; Fraser and Honneth 2003; Honneth 1995, 2007; Ikäheimo and Laitinen 2011; Pinkard 1994; Pippin 1989, 2008; Redding 1996; Ricoeur 2005; Schmidt am Busch and Zurn 2010; Siep 1979; Taylor 1992; Thompson 2006; Wildt 1982; Williams 1997.

not so acknowledged. It is a substantive debate between realists and constructivists whether the existence of all reasons, principles and normative entities depends on acknowledgement.[3]

By contrast, what John Searle (1995, 2010) and Raimo Tuomela (2002, 2007) call collective "recognition" or "*acceptance*" concerns *institutions*. There is significant consensus on the fact that institutions are in one way or another made by humans. What such collective acceptance or recognition involves is a matter of debate, and one can perhaps approach it in a roundabout way: acceptance or recognition in this sense refers to those kinds of "taking and treating" which collectively bring institutions into existence and sustain them in existence. Searle (2010, p. 8) has recently stated that he prefers the word "recognition" as it does not suggest that "approval" is necessarily involved. As this paper distinguishes between several meanings of "recognition", the term "acceptance" can be reserved for the kind of acceptance or recognition relevant to the existence of institutions. Everyone agrees that institutions result in some way from human activity and thought, but it is debated whether they result precisely from collective acceptance (or whether their emergence can be explained without reference to collective intentionality at all). Typically, creation of new institutions at the same time creates new normative demands and rights, and for that reason "acceptance" of an institution is intimately related to "acknowledgement" of these demands and rights as "valid, if the institution exists". But there are arguably also pre-institutional normative demands and rights to be acknowledged. So, for example, it is possible to hold that moral rights are valid independently from acknowledgement, but that legal and institutional rights depend on collective acceptance for their existence. So, for example, it is possible to hold that moral rights are valid independently from acknowledgement, but that legal and institutional rights depend on acceptance for their existence (Laitinen 2011).

There is finally the important sense of "recognition" where the recognized ones are recognizers themselves: individual persons or possibly groups.[4] This is the central sense of recognition used in such slogans as "mutual recognition" or "struggles for recognition". It goes beyond mere identification, and may partly consist of acknowledgement of claims (say, rights), including claims dependent on institutional acceptance. Respect, esteem and concern for other persons are central forms of recognition in this sense. They are "recognitive attitudes", or ways of taking and treating others more or less adequately in light of their normatively relevant features. All persons are worthy of respect, or claim respect from others, based on the mere fact that they are persons. Recognizing others in the sense of respecting them, is partly a matter of acknowledging the validity of the normative claims that the others' personhood generates. Further, their merits make them worthy of esteem from others. (Such merits may concern for example service in an institutional role, which nicely illustrates how adequate recognition of persons takes

---

[3]Ikäheimo and Laitinen 2007; Laitinen 2011.
[4]Honneth 1995; Brandom 2007; Ricoeur 2005; Ikäheimo and Laitinen 2007.

place in the context of institutions, which in turn depend on acceptance in the sense given above). As needy, vulnerable beings capable of well-being or suffering, human persons call for care or love or empathy from each other—and it has been suggested that mutual concern is an emotional form of mutual recognition. It is this sense of recognition between persons (or groups), respect, esteem, concern (in contrast to mere identification of anything, or acknowledgement of validity, or acceptance of institutions) that is centrally at stake in the philosophy of mutual recognition.[5]

Being recognized in this relevant sense as a responsible agent, capable of autonomy, or as a possessor of merits, or as one of "us" *matters* to people's lives in many ways. Here are five claims that will serve as the background for this paper:

Recognition from others is, first of all, arguably *constitutive of personhood*. Many theories claim that being recognized by others is a necessary condition of personhood, and thus essential for anyone's *existence* as a person. Even if some rival theories of the nature of persons do not make this claim, it is however familiar, and quite widely held by theorists from different (from Hegel 1807 to Dennett 1978).

Secondly, recognition is relevant for one's deontic or normative statuses. Persons usually have deontic statuses which depend on them being recognized: for example, being granted a citizenship, or a role or an office is a matter of being recognized, and it brings with it new rights and normative statuses. Additionally, persons may have some basic moral and normative status based on e.g. human dignity, which creates *requirements* for others to recognize them—and such a basic status need not be dependent on being recognized. Whether or not it is, recognition of someone as a citizen or role-holder can bring with it new deontic or normative statuses on top of the basic status as a person.

Thirdly, recognition from others is intimately dynamically (causally and intelligibly) intertwined to an agent's *relations to self*. Respect from others affects one's self-respect, esteem from others affects one's self-esteem *et cetera*. This seems to be a deep fact about the human psychology, and it is understandable why it is so.

Fourthly, recognition from others is a feature that affects one's agentic capacities or competences *via* such self-relations. One can be paralyzed or dysfunctional when one lacks the courage to say "no" to others or when one suffers from a sense of inferiority to others: that is, without sufficient self-respect or self-confidence one may cease to function as an agent.

A fifth point worth stressing is that recognition from others is *not* directly constitutive of self-relations. The views of others (about the agent, or about anything else for that matter) do not directly constitute the agent's views—it is crucial that the agent's views and other's views are ontologically separate and in principle *can* conflict and be a source of tensions and struggles. Despite the intimate connection and influence, the relationship is not a direct constitutive one. In the following, I will examine whether these five claims on recognition apply to groups as well. To be able to do so, I will first make some remarks on the nature of groups.

---

[5] Schmidt am Busch and Zurn 2010; Thompson 2006; Ikäheimo and Laitinen 2011.

3 Groups

Groups come in many shapes and sizes. In order for a collectivity to be capable of collective intentionality, it must be "an integrate" *group agent*, i.e. have some decision-making or opinion- and will-formation mechanism, not merely "an aggregate", i.e. a factual subset of agents that form the extension of some intensional definition (say, the lefthanded males born in Boston), nor merely a socially (externally) constructed or labelled "grouping", e.g. a race.[6]

One issue is whether group agents can be group *persons*. That of course depends on what is meant by personhood. A reason for not regarding group agents as persons is that they are not full blown moral persons in the sense of having a serious right to life (Tooley 1972). Accordingly, I will here assume the more moderate claim that groups are *agents* with no separate mind of their own, but with collective intentions that allow them to function in a way that is sufficiently organized to have responsibility ascribed to them. Therefore, they may even be moral agents, and they may have a moral standing of some sort (e.g. they may have various rights), but not the significant standing of being a person (e.g. they do not have a serious right to life).

It is possible that two different group agents have exactly the same members. This is so because groups *qua* agents have not only members, but also *a constitutive structure* (related to its ethos), and *historical and modal properties*, which serve to distinguish two groups with exactly the same members. For example, the members of a hiring committee of a company might also form a jazz band in their free time. Although they have the same members, the hiring committee and the jazz band cannot be identical entities, as they have a different ethos, typically different historical properties (they were created at different times) and different modal properties (the committee can remain in existence even if the jazz band is dissolved). What is it then that determines a group's identity? One could think that as sameness of members does not settle the issue (which can also be seen from the fact that a group can remain the same even if its members change, in the same way that an organism can remain the same even if it is composed of different matter—different atoms—at different points of time[7]), it must be the ethos (the central goals and commitments of the group) that is the group's constitutive structure—analogously to the structure of an organism that remains the same and guarantees the organism's sameness despite changes in the matter that it is composed of.

Things are, however, complicated by the fact that a group as a "continuant" may change at least some elements of its ethos and yet remain the same group (a sports club can be the same club even if it adds new kinds of sport to its repertoire, and drops off others). Furthermore, it is possible that different groups have similar ethos but different members, such that they cannot be the same group

---

[6]See e.g. Pettit 2001; Tuomela 2007; Gilbert 1989; Pettit and List 2011.

[7]See e.g. Wiggins 2001; van Inwagen 1990. Interestingly, van Inwagen illuminates the ontology of biological organisms with an analogy to an institutional entity, an empire (pp. 170–81).

agent (any seemingly two things must necessarily be qualitatively indiscernible for them to be candidates for being numerically one and the same thing). As an interesting borderline case, one may ask whether there could be two groups with the same ethos and the same members. This depends on how the notion of "ethos" is cashed out in more precise terms. Say, the Finnish national soccer team and the Finnish national soccer team for under 21 year olds might in principle have the same members and a qualitatively similar ethos, but nonetheless they would differ in their modal properties: the former could in principle include older players but the latter could not. Their "constitutions" differ in the things that they rule out (although realistically speaking, this is bound to be reflected in their "ethos".) This example serves to highlight the fact that modal and historical properties may need to be invoked, in keeping track of the numerical identity of the group. Concerning the ontology of material beings, it has been argued that even if a lump of bronze and a statue constituted by it may share the same spatio-temporal location, they differ in their historical and modal properties: the lump can survive flattening, but the statue cannot, and the lump typically is older than the statue (Baker 2000). Similarly, two groups (such as the two football teams discussed above) with different histories and different modal properties are indeed two different entities, even if they would have the same members and share the same ethos.

In any case, to be a group agent a group needs to have more than only members (and modal and historical properties); it needs to have a particular ethos, consisting of the set of its central goals and commitments. More precisely, we can follow Tuomela (2007, p. 15) and say that a group agent has a "realm of concern", "intentional horizon", and an "ethos".

I understand these notions by Tuomela so that the "realm of concern" consists of the *questions* (including practical matters) of interest to the group. By contrast, the group's "intentional horizon" consists of the *answers* collectively accepted in the name of the group—the group's official views as it were. The ethos consists, roughly, of the central elements of the group's realm of concern and intentional horizon—of its central goals and commitments (below, a closer look at how "ethos" relates to the realm of concern and to the intentional horizon will be taken).

Given this distinction we can see that group agents are partly individuated by their *realm of concern* that determines what kind of group agent is in question. Thus, the library committee and the hiring committee, in spite of having the same members, are different groups in virtue of having different realms of concern. The fact that they have same members does not turn them into the same group, as they are groups for different purposes: one has the task of deciding and finding information about issues relevant to the library, the other about issues relevant to hiring. The groups can further be distinguished by their *intentional horizon*, by the answers they accept to the questions—typically political parties may share their realm of concern with other political parties but differ in the kinds of answers they accept and the kinds of views they hold.

The "realm of concern" of individuals is not constitutive of their numerical identity (although it is constitutive of their "thick self" or practical identity).[8] Furthermore, the "realm of concern" of individuals is not constitutively limited by collective acceptance, or by anything else for that matter: they can in principle have views about *anything*. There may be a limit to how complex things they can understand (and these limits can be stretched by studying etc.), and there may be normative limits, issues that are "none of their business" (for reasons of privacy etc.). Now *groups*, being constructed for some purpose or another, or being multi-purpose groups for sharing most aspects of life, do have a *constitutive* realm of concern. There is some appeal in the idea that some group *cannot* (officially) have views on a totally unrelated subject matter—that there are some normative constitutive bounds. But then again, perhaps the realm of concern simply broadens when a group successfully forms views on some matters.

In the literature it is typically assumed that the realm of concern, intentional horizon and ethos are self-constructed by the group. Below, we will take a closer look at the ways in which concern, horizon and ethos might be shaped in "dialogical" relations of recognition. Moreover, we will examine how the (unofficial) "attitudinal climate" among group members may also be shaped by recognition from outside.

4 Recognition from Outside and the Existence of Groups

Insofar as there are group agents, we can ask whether recognition from outside is similarly constitutive of group agency as it is constitutive of individual personhood. We can start with issues of *existence*. Can there be group agents devoid of any recognition from outside at all? Whatever plausibility the claim concerning the necessity of recognition has concerning individuals, it seems to lose it completely concerning groups. Secret societies, for example a secret society of stamp collectors (Tuomela 2007, p. 21), provide a knock down argument against the view that groups cannot exist without recognition from outside. All it takes is that the members relate to each other in certain ways, have an ethos and a realm of concern, and can function as members of the group. No one else, no support *from outside*, is needed. It is thus rather obvious, then, that there are *independent unrecognized groups*, secret societies being a clear case in point.[9]

---

[8] See e.g. Laitinen 2008.

[9] Could the whole of humanity be a group agent that is not recognized from the outside? To the extent that it is a group agent, it could, in a very interesting sense—otherwise it is a mere grouping or "aggregate" and not of interest to this paper as it does not have collective attitudes. But in principle it could also happen that the group including all humans would be recognized by some subgroup whose members are humans. Perhaps there could even be two groups which both have all humans as their members, but which have a different ethos and serve a different purpose. These two groups could recognize each other from the outside—as the groups would not be each other's members, their views would not come from within the group—and even send letters to one another.

Individual human beings are not born with fully formed capacities, but group agents seem to be. The group supervenes or depends upon its members, who have a variety of capacities and abilities. The group agent is, in a manner of speaking, a capable adult agent since day one. For example, it can be said to master a natural language, or several, because its members do so. It needs no socialization from outside, like human individuals do—who in getting socialized acquire rich relations of recognition to others. A group can come to exist without any such relations to others—relations between its members suffice for its existence. (There are, to be sure, puzzles about the collective intentional states that count as the group's states. One puzzle is *the problem of the first belief*: a newly constituted group does not have any commitments when it comes to existence. Then it is somehow supposed to make its first commitment, without any background of prior commitments. The puzzle is whether we can make sense of a believer with only one belief.)

Such independent unrecognized groups provide a clear case of pure "forgroupness". Any of the group's matters are up to the group, for the group to decide, including the decision whether to keep on existing or not. The division of labour or authority within the group is a matter of internal relations of recognition, but no recognition from outside is needed.

For the purpose of drawing a contrast with other kinds of cases we can compare these independent groups to the main character (Descartes) in a joke. Descartes is sitting at a bar, so the joke goes, when the bartender asks whether he'd like another drink. Descartes responds "I think not", and vanishes into thin air.

Of course, the joke does not get Descartes' philosophy right, but it might get some theories about groups right: these theories make it seem like the existence of groups depends solely on whether the group (often the relevant members of the group) keeps thinking, or collectively accepting, that the group still exists.

However, a closer look will suggest that not all groups fit this picture. There are *externally* dependent groups, whose existence depends on recognition: nothing is a group *of that kind* without it being duly recognized from outside. For example, nothing is an independent sovereign state without recognition from other states. Nothing is a business corporation, a registered association, or a married couple without being recognized by some relevant authority. Groups of this kind do not come to existence or cease to exist merely by the relevant members thinking so: affirmation *from outside* is needed.

To *be* a group of that kind is not only to be it "for the group", it is, and constitutively so, to be it "for others" as well. Switzerland is a state not only for the Swiss; Heikki and Ming-Chen are a married couple for others as well, and not only in their own minds; the Finnish philosophical society is recognized at least by some registrar of the Finnish state; and Nokia is recognized as a business corporation by various countries.

Cf. Wiggins's (2001, p. 35) example about one officer sending a letter to another, even if both roles happen to be occupied by the same human being. (I thank an anonymous referee for the question.)

Legally recognized associations cannot come to existence or cease to exist on their own will—at least the relevant kind of notice to the registrar is needed. A group can be dormant, but still in existence, for example if the relevant registrar still legally recognizes its existence. (The registrar may for example come to think that an attempt to cease to exist has failed, because the association has not carried out some obligations it may have.)

Thus we have independent groups on the one hand, and externally dependent groups on the other. There may also be interesting intermediate cases, such as groups, which come to existence as independent groups, and then take on various duties, obligations and responsibilities towards other parties. Because of these responsibilities, they owe it to the other party that they fulfill them—and it would be wrong of them to decide to cease to exist without fulfilling the responsibilities. It is possible to argue that as long as the responsibilities are recognized by the outsider party, and the group continues to be capable of functioning as a group agent, the recognized normative role keeps the group in existence. Human individuals cease to exist when they die in the biological sense, but groups cease to exist on the basis of intentional and social factors. Thus, there is room to argue that also an initially independent group may be kept in existence by the recognition from outside, if the group has by its deeds given the outsider party some "normative say" or "normative power" concerning the matter—and one form which this normative power can take is the power to determine whether some obligation, duty or responsibility is satisfactorily fulfilled, so that the outsider party no longer has a claim against the group. Thus, continuous recognition of an unmet moral responsibility might be sufficient to keep an otherwise dormant group in existence.

Another kind of intermediate case could be a group which is an externally dependent group to begin with, but then the outsider party grants the group independence. After that, it is up to the group to decide whether to continue in existence. We will return to such cases below, when we discuss other core aspects of the group phenomena, over and above the issue of existence.

Before moving on, it is worth noting that even though the "forgroupness" principle does not hold concerning the existence of externally dependent groups (such as business corporations, registered associations, married couples), there is typically a broader context, a group or a society where a constitutive rule is accepted: "something is a married couple only if ...", "something is a business corporation only if ..." and so on. Thus, the "forgroupness" feature may hold concerning this wider society, but within it, the smaller unit in question (say, a married couple) is dependent on recognition from outside.

5 Recognition from Others and Deontic Statuses

Let us turn next to normative issues of deontic status. Typically there are not only constitutive rules accepted in the wider society but also *regulative* rules concerning how to treat such smaller groups as married couples. For example, concerning marriages, the members of the society in their relevant dealings and expectations recognize a couple as married and thus refrain from certain kinds of interpersonal relationships (e.g. refrain from romantic interludes out of respect for the marriage) and engage in others (e.g. invite couples to events together); and the married couple is also recognized by the state which sees marriage as making a difference for the rights and responsibilities of the individuals. In these cases there are regulative rules of how to take and treat others—and cases of treating them in these ways are importantly cases of recognition. Taking such cases into account enables us to see how such group items as married couples are multiply recognized by others in the social context.

This kind of recognition of the "deontic statuses" (rights and responsibilities) of groups makes a huge difference to the practical relevance of these statuses, but may also be necessary for the group even to have the deontic statuses in question. Moral realists argue that individual persons have a moral status independently of whether others recognize it. We can grant that here in order to draw a contrast: it is much more doubtful whether groups have such a moral standing, or any deontic statuses, independently of recognition, or of instituting or granting them —at least acquiring institutional rights is a matter of being recognized. Perhaps there is an independently valid demand for others to respect a group's ethos, which derives from the demand to respect the members' autonomy. But it is an open possibility that groups have deontic statuses only by them being recognized.

Furthermore, independently of how the deontic statuses have arisen, it is a contingent issue whether such statuses will in fact be sufficiently respected by others. Thus, recognition from others will make a difference to how the deontic statuses actually work.

While secret societies were the prime example of independent groups (and independence seems to have a positive connotation—independence certainly sounds good), here one of the crucial downsides of secrecy comes to the fore. Others cannot be in a position to respect a secret group's ethos. (Note that known, but formally independent groups *can* have such a status—such as a stamp collectors' club which is not secret, but retains all the normative say concerning its own matters). Norms of how to take and treat a group concern *others*, *outsiders*, and their ways of regarding the group in their practical reasoning and more immediate—they are norms of recognition. In many contexts, deontic status of this kind is the most important way in which recognition from outside matters to groups.

6 Self-Understandings of the Group and Recognition from Outside: The Attitudinal Climate, the Realm of Concern, the Intentional Horizon and the Ethos

Having discussed so far issues of existence and deontic status (the first two ways in which recognition matters mentioned in Sect. 2 of this Chapter), let us next turn to issues of self-relations and self-definitions (points 3 and 4 in Sect. 2 of this Chapter).

As mentioned above, the self-related attitudes of individual persons, e.g. their self-esteem and self-respect, depend on attitudes of esteem and respect from others. Moreover, the self-related attitudes seem to affect a person's agentic competences in social surroundings (Honneth 1995).

Concerning the self-directed attitudes of groups let me first point out that the way outsiders perceive the worth of a group's activities affects the (private) attitudes of the members towards their group. Particularly, it affects their motivation to function as members of *this* group in the face of obstacles, difficulties and conflicts. The level of commitment, identification or solidarity of the members may depend on how highly others think of the group. Such informal "for-otherness" can be highly relevant to both formally independent and dependent groups. The attitudinal climate among members depends in understandable ways on recognition from outside.

Among the members, there is an attitudinal climate concerning the importance of the group (how vital is it from the viewpoint of the daily life, well-being or meaning of life of the members? does it have a special mission or calling in realizing certain values or functions for wider society or humanity?), the capabilities of the group (what kinds of power does the group possess? what kind of power-in-common do the members have? will they be able to "stick together" in their pursuit of demanding or important goals?), the evaluative qualities that the group may have and the members and others may want it to have (how just, respectful towards the rights of all members and internal minorities, democratic, well-organized, pleasant, solidaristic, internally divided *etc.* is it?). Similarly, there is an external attitudinal environment concerning the importance, capabilities and evaluative qualities of the group—and this external attitudinal climate consists of the environment of recognitive attitudes directed at the group in question. As in the case of individuals, it seems that the implicit self-understanding of the group is dependent on recognition from outside, from those who are not part of the group.

So the first claim I make is twofold: (i) The functioning of any group depends on its "morale" or "group spirit", i.e. the attitudinal and motivational climate among the members with regard to the group's importance, capabilities and evaluative qualities. (ii) The "morale" or "spirit" of the group is dynamically affected by recognition from outside concerning the importance, capabilities and evaluative qualities of the group.

The second matter of importance with regard to self-directed attitudes of groups is their "realm of concern" (Tuomela 2007, p. 15), consisting – as already mentioned—of the questions (including practical matters) of interest to the group.

Here, too, the difference between dependent and independent groups is relevant: the realm of concern is not always for the group to determine. Think of a committee whose tasks are fixed before its members are chosen, and whose members do not have the normative say over the tasks of the committee. Such a committee is dependent on how such tasks are defined from outside. By contrast, other groups, such as the secret stamp collectors' club can be free to make up and revise its realm of concern.

Again, we can ask whether in the case of dependent groups, the idea of "forgroupness" can be held concerning a larger group: say, the larger organization which sets the tasks for its library committee, and its hiring committee. Such a move seems possible, but it does not seem to threaten the idea that, the library committee and hiring committee are nonetheless genuine cases of externally dependent groups— they are real groups and not merely aspects of the larger group.

Here, the intermediate category of a group which starts as a dependent group but acquires independence by being recognized as an independent group seems relevant: the group may gain some more normative say over its own realm of concern, if the external group recognizes its independence.

Our third concern is accounting for the group's "intentional horizon". Perhaps surprisingly, the intentional horizon is categorically very different from the realm of concern when it comes to recognition. An intentional horizon consists of the *answers* (including intentions) the group accepts to the questions of its "realm of concern", the actual stand it takes on its issues. For example, the library committee may prefer some option X to some option Y. Here it seems that a categorical stand is available: to be the group's views, they *have* to be accepted by the group itself (via its members or representatives); not from outside. Interestingly, all group agents must in this respect be independent groups, if they are to have views at all.

Theories of recognition concerning individuals concur on this point: A's views are sometimes in tension, or in struggle with B's views, so there cannot be a direct constitutive connection. The connection between the adopted views, and views of outsiders may be very intimate, but it cannot be a *constitutive* relation. (See point 5 in Sect. 2 of this Chapter.)

The fourth matter to be addressed is the ethos of the group. Can group ethos be externally dependent? Here one may in fact expect a clash of intuitions among theorists: their considered opinions may remain divided, if we accept the sharp difference that the previous two points create between the "realm of concern" and the "intentional horizon". On the one hand, it makes good sense to assume that the group's ethos is a subset of its intentional horizon and that a group can define its ethos only itself. Indeed, if ethos is a subset of the intentional horizon, and intentional horizon is always self-defined by the group, then ethos is also self-defined. On the other hand, it also makes sense to assume that the central questions of the realm of concern, the tasks that provide the *raison d'être* of the group, are a crucial constitutive part of the group's ethos. And then, in the case of committees whose tasks have been defined from the outside, part of the ethos of the committee has been defined from the outside. Defenders of the first view may hold that the committee acquires an ethos only when its members collectively accept the externally defined realm of concern, and decide to affirm and take on the tasks posed from outside (to give a contemporary example from Egypt or Libya: an army unit which rebels against tasks given from outside defines its ethos by itself, and so its ethos has not been defined from outside.) But the defenders of the second view may say that in many cases we cannot draw such a distinction: each member may accept the given tasks when he or she is nominated to the committee, and no collective acceptance need take place before the ethos is fixed "by default" as it were. All in all, equally good arguments seem to suggest both, that group ethos is a subset of a group's intentional horizon, and that group ethos includes a group's realm of concern (which may be defined from outside).

Thus, discussing the issues of self-understandings of groups from the viewpoint of recognition yields somewhat surprising conceptual results: the realm of concern is sharply different from the intentional horizon when it comes to possible dependence from outside recognition. This is so even though both of the notions are intimately related to the notion of the *ethos* of the group. These three notions (realm of concern, intentional horizon, ethos) comprise the group's official self-understandings, and on top of them, any group will have an informal attitudinal climate, which is indirectly relevant to the group's capacity to act.

7 Conclusions

The paper has explored whether and in what ways recognition from others plays a role for collective intentionality and the ontology of groups. The conclusion is that recognition from others is functionally relevant for all groups, and constitutively relevant for the dependent and the intermediate groups.[10]

The distinction between independent and externally dependent groups proved to be central, particularly with regard to the issues of *existence* and the *realm of concern*. The very fact that there are externally dependent groups challenges the idea of pure "forgroupness", but that idea can perhaps be preserved by pointing out that in these cases there is always a broader context or wider society in which the questions of the existence and realm of concern of a group are determined. Whereas the issue of the *deontic statuses* of the group is primarily "for others" and not "for the group", the *intentional horizon* is always self-determined, and primarily "for the group"— even though it is for others as well in the sense that others may respect the group's views and ethos in their behavior and attitudes. The informal *attitudinal climate* among the members is always more or less open to influences from outside—and this climate makes a big difference to how motivated the group members are to act for the group reasons created by the ethos of the group.[11]

---

[10]Finally, it could be asked (indeed, an anonymous referee did ask) whether one must adopt a non-reductive view of groups to accept the claims of this paper. Or could a reductive account defend the same set of claims? It seems that most of my claims are independent of claims about the ontological status of groups. The only clear exception is the ontological issue of coming to exist and ceasing to exist. If one holds the view that groups do not literally exist, then their coming to exist and ceasing to exist do not literally take place either, so recognition cannot make a difference in that respect.

[11]I would like to thank the participants of the *Collective Intentionality VII* conference at Basel 2010, August 23–26, as well as Raul Hakli, Matti Heinonen, Onni Hirvonen, Heikki Ikäheimo, Byron Kaldis, Kaarlo Miller, Pekka Mäkelä, Mikko Salmela, David Schweikard, Maj Tuomela, Raimo Tuomela and an anonymous referee for their comments.

References

Baker, L.R. 2000. *Persons and bodies: A constitution view*. Cambridge: Cambridge University Press.

Brandom, R. 2007. The structure of desire and recognition. *Philosophy and Social Criticism* 33(1): 127–150.

Bratman, M. 1999. *Faces of intention*. Cambridge: Cambridge University Press.

Bratman, M. 2007. *Structures of agency*. Oxford: Oxford University Press.

Dennett, D. 1978. Conditions of personhood. In his *Brainstorms*. Cambridge: MIT Press.

Deranty, J.-P. 2009. *Beyond communication—A critical study of Axel Honneth's social philosophy*. Leiden: Brill.

Fraser, N., and A. Honneth. 2003. *Recognition or redistribution. A philosophical-political exchange*. London: Verso.

Gilbert, M. 1989. *On social facts*. London: Routledge.

Gilbert, M. 1996. *Living together: Rationality, sociality, and obligation*. Lanham: Rowman and Littlefield.

Gilbert, M. 2000. *Sociality and responsibility: New essays in plural subject theory*. Lanham: Rowman and Littlefield.

Gilbert, M. 2006. *A theory of political obligation: Membership, commitment, and the bonds of society*. Oxford: Oxford University Press.

Gutmann, A. (ed.). 1994. *Multiculturalism. Examining the politics of recognition*. Princeton: Princeton University Press.

Hegel, G.W.F. 1977 [1807]. *Phenomenology of spirit*. Oxford: Oxford University Press.

Honneth, A. 1995 [1992]. *The struggle for recognition. The moral grammar of social conflicts*. Cambridge, MA: MIT Press.

Honneth, A. 2007. *Disrespect. The normative foundations of critical theory*. Cambridge: Polity Press.

Ikäheimo, H., and A. Laitinen. 2007. Analyzing recognition. In *Recognition and power*, ed. B. van den Brink and D. Owen, 33–56. Cambridge: Cambridge University Press.

Ikäheimo, H., and A. Laitinen (eds.). 2011. *Recognition and social ontology*. Leiden/Boston: Brill.

Lagerspetz, E., et al. (eds.). 2001. *On the nature of social and institutional reality*. Jyväskylä: SoPhi.

Laitinen, A. 2008. *Strong evaluation without moral sources*. Berlin: De Gruyter.

Laitinen, A. 2011. Recognition, acknowledgement, and acceptance. In *Recognition and social ontology*, ed. H. Ikäheimo and A. Laitinen, 309–348. Leiden/Boston: Brill.

Lewis, D. 1969. *Convention*. Cambridge, MA: Harvard University Press.

Miller, S. 2001. *Social action*. Cambridge: Cambridge University Press.

Pettit, P. 1993. *The common mind*. Oxford: Oxford University Press.

Pettit, P. 2001. *A theory of freedom*. New York: Oxford University Press.

Pettit, P., and C. List. 2011. *Group agency. The possibility, design and status of corporate agents*. Oxford: Oxford University Press.

Pinkard, T. 1994. *Hegel's phenomenology. The sociality of reason*. Cambridge: Cambridge University Press.

Pippin, R. 1989. *Hegel's idealism. The satisfactions of self-consciousness*. Cambridge: Cambridge University Press.

Pippin, R. 2008. *Hegel's practical philosophy*. Cambridge: Cambridge University Press.

Redding, P. 1996. *Hegel's hermeneutics*. Ithaca: Cornell University Press.

Ricoeur, P. 2005. *The course of recognition*. Cambridge, MA: Harvard University Press.

Schmidt am Busch, H.-C., and C. Zurn (eds.). 2010. *The philosophy of recognition – Historical and contemporary perspectives*. Lanham: Lexington Books.

Searle, J. 1995. *The construction of social reality*. New York: The Free Press.

Searle, J. 2010. *Making the social world: Structure of civilization*. Oxford: Oxford University Press.

Siep, L. 1979. *Anerkennung als Prinzip der praktischen Philosophie: Untersuchungen zu Hegels Jenaer Philosophie des Geistes*. Freiburg: Karl Alber.

Taylor, C. 1992. The politics of recognition. In *Multiculturalism: Examining the politics of recognition*, ed. A. Gutmann. Princeton: Princeton University Press.

Thompson, S. 2006. *The political theory of recognition. A critical introduction*. Cambridge: Polity Press.

Tooley, M. 1972. Abortion and infanticide. *Philosophy and Public Affairs* 2(1): 37–65.

Tuomela, R. 1984. *A theory of social action*, Synthese library. Dordrecht/Boston: Reidel.

Tuomela, R. 1995. *The importance of Us*. Stanford: Stanford University Press.

Tuomela, R. 2000. *Cooperation: A philosophical study*. Dordrecht: Kluwer.

Tuomela, R. 2002. *The philosophy of social practices: A collective acceptance view*. Cambridge: Cambridge University Press.

Tuomela, R. 2007. *The philosophy of sociality*. Oxford: Oxford University Press.

van den Brink, B., and D. Owen (eds.). 2007. *Recognition and power*. Cambridge: Cambridge University Press.

Van Inwagen, P. 1990. *Material beings*. Ithaca: Corness University Press.

Wiggins, D. 2001. *Sameness and substance renewed*. Cambridge: Cambridge University Press.

Wildt, A. 1982. *Autonomie und Anerkennung. Hegels Moralitätskritik im Lichte seiner Fichte-Rezeption*. Stuttgart: Clett-Cotta.

Williams, R. 1997. *Hegel's ethics of recognition*. Berkeley: University of California Press.

Chapter 14
The Conditions of Collectivity: Joint Commitment and the Shared Norms of Membership

Titus Stahl

Abstract Collective intentionality is one of the most fundamental notions in social ontology. However, it is often thought to refer to a capacity which does not presuppose the existence of any other social facts. This chapter critically examines this view from the perspective of one specific theory of collective intentionality, the theory of Margaret Gilbert. On the basis of Gilbert's arguments, the chapter claims that collective intentionality is a highly contingent achievement of complex social practices and, thus, not a basic social phenomenon. The argument proceeds in three steps. First, Gilbert's thesis that certain kinds of collective intentionality presuppose joint normative commitments is introduced. Second, it is argued that, on this view, individual commitments can only constitute the relevant kinds of collective intentional states if there are socially shared "principles of membership" that connect the force of individual commitments to a shared content. Third, it is shown that strong collective intentionality depends on the practical acceptance of shared norms and on the establishment of authority relations through mutual recognition.

1 Introduction

A large part of contemporary debates about social ontology is primarily concerned with two questions about collective intentional states: (i) are there any collective intentional states, i.e., do we have to refer to collective intentionality in the best possible account of social reality; and, (ii) if we have to, what exactly are collective intentional states and how are they connected to individual intentionality? Although these questions are, of course, reasonable and important, they tend to encourage a view of collective intentionality in abstraction from other social phenomena.

T. Stahl (✉)
Department of Philosophy, Goethe Universität, Frankfurt, Germany
e-mail: stahl@em.uni-frankfurt.de

A. Konzelmann Ziv and H.B. Schmid (eds.), *Institutions, Emotions, and Group Agents*, 229
Studies in the Philosophy of Sociality 2, DOI 10.1007/978-94-007-6934-2_14,
© Springer Science+Business Media Dordrecht 2014

The most extreme result of looking at the question of collective intentionality from this perspective is the attempt to understand it as some brute "given", as an ability which humans possess naturally (Searle 1995, pp. 23ff.), or as an ability which is fundamental in at least the sense that it does not require any further social preconditions to be met in order for (fully developed) individuals to be able to attempt to exercise it.

As an alternative to this view, it can be argued that ascribing collective intentional states to groups of persons is part of a complex general social practice of ascribing to the verbal and non-verbal behaviour of groups a specific *status*, namely the status of this behaviour *counting as* intentionally governed by collective beliefs, desires or other intentional states. If we adopt this perspective, other questions become more important: what conditions must a society fulfil in order for its members to be able to describe themselves and others in intentional terms? And are there any specific conditions to be met for them to be able to describe themselves as being engaged (or trying to engage) in *collective activities* and as having *collective beliefs* in a strong sense?

In other words, by adopting this perspective, it might turn out that there are very specific and demanding social conditions which have to obtain in a community of speakers for them to be able to attribute certain collective intentional states to each other. To appreciate this point, at least a certain form of collective intentionality—not only in individual instances but in regard to its very possibility—should be understood as an *achievement*, as something which not only needs to be examined with respect to how it can be explained, but also with respect to how it is possible at all.

To provide some arguments in favour of this perspective, it is helpful to focus on the specific normative role that ascriptions of collective intentional states play in social life. For this purpose, the following discussion focuses on Margaret Gilbert's account of collective intentional phenomena (Gilbert 1989). According to Gilbert's approach, collective intentional states necessarily involve *joint normative commitments*, either of a plural subject or of the members of some group.

This chapter will argue that Gilbert's concept of joint commitment, which she takes to be central for at least certain kinds of collective intentionality (Sect. 2), cannot be understood without noting that the very possibility of the relevant kind of joint commitment depends on the social institution of *inferential rules*—that is, rules that govern what follows from such joint commitments for individuals—which give joint commitments practical significance. This claim is justified by discussing two objections against Gilbert's account of joint commitment (Sect. 3). The chapter then shows that if one accepts her description of joint commitments, the relevant collective intentional states cannot be understood in abstraction from the social practices in which these rules are instituted (Sects. 4 and 5). In particular, the chapter argues that the kinds of social practices that must be presupposed to make sense of strong forms of collective intentionality should be understood as instances of those inferential practices which Robert Brandom analyses in his "normative pragmatics" (Sect. 6). Finally, it is suggested that this amounts to understanding strong collective intentionality as dependent on an underlying structure of mutual recognition (Sect. 7).

2   The Centrality of Normative Commitments for Strong Collective Intentional States

Descriptions of social phenomena in terms of collective intentional states try to capture those features of social reality which cannot be explained by mere descriptions of how persons *influence* each other's individual intentional states, but only in virtue of them *sharing* certain intentions, attitudes or beliefs in a *strong sense*.

Of course, you and I can share an intention to push a car up a hill individually, in the sense that we both have the intention individually. We might even know of each other's intentions, might individually intend to make the intention of the other person effective, and might recognise that the effectiveness of the other person's intention is a condition for the realisation of our own intention. However, according to some accounts in contemporary social ontology (Gilbert 1989, pp. 161f.), there is still a difference between such cases and the case where, in an emphatic sense, we do something as *our* project. This difference is spelled out as follows. For a goal to become "our" goal in the strong sense of being the object of a collective intention, each of us must not only be individually bound to our (suitably related) individual intentions, we must be bound to a goal *as a group*. We do not need to look as far as to patriotism or class solidarity to find examples of this phenomenon: if a friend and I jointly intend to push a car up the hill, a possible failure of either of us (or even a mutually known simultaneous failure of both of us) to act on this intention would not just be a failure to realise our individual intentions, but would amount to us— collectively—*failing a joint project* in the sense of an enterprise with a joint goal (Gilbert 1989, pp. 163, 421ff.). Furthermore, insofar as collective projects in this strong sense also establish mutual obligations between group members or shared normative commitments to act in a certain way, these obligations and commitments cannot be understood as just individual obligations, but are rather *obligations that we have together* (in other words, obligations of the group as subject), and *joint commitments*. In participating in a collective project, one could say, we jointly accept a goal together and thus are collectively responsible for its attainment.

This strong notion of collective intentionality, which has mainly been developed by Margaret Gilbert and Raimo Tuomela, presents a challenge to individualist theories of social ontology. Since individualist theories often assume that collective intentionality supervenes on individual intentional states and phenomena on the one hand, and on certain non-normative relations between these states or between the individual agents on the other hand, they are at a loss to explain how the collectivised normativity described above—beyond the normativity involved in individual intentional attitudes—comes into play (cf. for example Bratman 1999).

There is more than one way to describe the normative features of collective intentional states: Raimo Tuomela, for example, identifies the "reproachability" induced by the existence of joint commitments as one of the core conceptual dimensions of strong collective notions (Tuomela 2007, p. 37). A very similar notion of joint commitment is central to Margaret Gilbert's theory on which this paper will focus.[1] The most concise summary of Gilbert's view is that "genuine [acting] together involves rights and duties that are something other than moral rights and duties" (1989, p. 162), and that the same feature holds for collective beliefs. Putting the question aside whether all kinds of collective intentionality depend on such joint commitments, she at least claims that *certain* kinds of collective intentional states—which I will call "strongly collective intentional states"—involve normative commitments. According to Gilbert, such commitments are clearly to be distinguished from both general moral duties and, more importantly, from the "personal" normative commitments we can undertake via individual intentionality.

As evidence for this claim, Gilbert cites the fact that we intuitively feel entitled to "punitive criticism" of fellow members of those groups with which we share collective beliefs and intentions. Whenever those members act inconsistently with collectively shared attitudes, we feel entitled to rebuke them (1987, 1990). We take such reactions to be appropriate, according to Gilbert, because the joint acceptance of a proposition or goal necessarily involves a joint commitment as a body or *as* one (Gilbert 1996, p. 8). A shared commitment is, furthermore, not a genuinely joint commitment if the parties to the commitment are only committed individually—which would imply that they could leave or abrogate the commitment as individuals—but only if they are committed in such a way that they can only rescind the commitment *together* (Gilbert 1999, pp. 152f.). Because this relation of the commitment to the group as a whole is typical for strongly collective intentional states, Gilbert assumes that such joint commitments are necessary to make groups of individuals into strongly collective subjects ("plural subjects", cf. Gilbert 1989, p. 163), or into group agents in a sense that supports diverse explanatory projects.

3 Two Objections against Joint Commitment Accounts

If we are interested in the conditions that make it possible to ascribe intentional states to groups in a way that is not just metaphorical, Gilbert's claim that strongly collective intentional states must be understood as necessarily involving joint commitments, or commitments of plural subjects, is a useful starting point. But as two kinds of objections raised to this claim show, it is defensible only if we understand such commitments as being made possible by the existence of a complex social structure. Firstly, the idea of a joint commitment seems to leave us with a *paradox of constitution* in regard to its subject, since joint commitments are taken to be at the same time *constitutive of* plural subjects and a state of *already given* plural subjects. Secondly, it is unclear how the collective obligations deriving from joint commitments can become effective obligations of individual group members.

---

[1] I accept Gilbert's claim to the effect that strong collective intentional states have the relevant normative features. This claim is contested—for an overview about the normativity question, see Tollefsen (2004); for more specific arguments for a normative view, see Meijers (2003).

In regard to the first objection, the obvious dilemma we face when talking about joint commitments is that the subject of a joint commitment does not exist independently of the commitment itself. Joint commitments are not commitments of individuals, but are rather commitments of "plural subjects". However, plural subjects do not exist independently of their relevant joint commitments but are rather *constituted* by such commitments (Gilbert 1996, p. 348). Although it can subsequently undertake additional joint commitments, the emergence of a plural subject in Gilbert's sense requires an initial joint commitment. But who undertakes this initial joint commitment? A plural subject cannot emerge through individuals undertaking a joint commitment, since, by definition, individuals are *the wrong kind of subject* to undertake such commitments. Thus, plural subjects and joint commitments must emerge simultaneously, as part of the same process. But how do we have to understand this process?

According to Gilbert, a joint commitment emerges whenever two or more persons *express their readiness to be jointly committed* to each other and their doing so becomes common knowledge among them (Gilbert 2002a, p. 65, 2006, pp. 138f.). Yet this explanation is somewhat puzzling: if an individual expresses a readiness to be jointly committed, she might thereby commit herself *individually* to undertake (a part of) a joint commitment. If there is common knowledge about such commitments within a group, then she can also acquire information about the respective individual commitments of others. But this does not explain *what* she has committed herself to be *a part of*. In other words, if one expresses one's readiness to be jointly committed, one is *individually* committed to undertake a joint commitment. But one is not yet *jointly committed*. One is only jointly committed if one is not only ready but *actually undertakes* a joint commitment and does not fail to do what one has expressed oneself to be ready to do. The readiness to join a joint commitment, in other words, cannot itself already be the joint commitment, for the joint commitment is the commitment of a plural subject whereas the readiness expresses the commitment of an individual subject. But if it is necessary for a plural subject already to exist in order for there to be a joint commitment (Gilbert 2002b), then the account of individual readiness does not provide a satisfying explanation of the emergence of plural subjects.

The second objection to Gilbert's account starts from the observation that, in her view, joint commitments become effective in governing the behaviour of social agents by way of individual commitments that "flow" from joint commitments. Such derived individual commitments are not "personal" (i.e. "normal", non-derived) commitments of an individual person because they have a special feature that they do not share with non-derived personal commitments; they cannot be abrogated unilaterally (Gilbert 1999, pp. 145ff.). Gilbert explains this feature by pointing out that joint commitments are commitments of a group and that, consequently, an individual is not in a position to abrogate them because they are not her *own* commitments. Accordingly, by virtue of being a member of a plural subject, an individual is also not in a position to abrogate those of her individual commitments that are derived from joint commitments of this group.

Gilbert thus introduces individual commitments that are derived from joint commitment as a special class:

> Though it is clearly not appropriate to speak of the parts of a joint commitment, each of the parties to a joint commitment is committed through it. It is therefore tempting to refer to the parties' 'individual commitments'. (1996, p. 11)

And similarly:

> Though no one of them independently constitutes the subject of their joint commitment, each of the committed persons is committed through it. Each is bound at least in the way a personal intention binds its subject: each has sufficient reason to act in a certain way. Bearing this in mind, one might speak of the parties' derived or associated 'individual' commitments. (2006, p. 136)

Kenneth Shockley (2004) argues convincingly that this explanation puts Gilbert's account in a dilemma. If joint commitments are commitments of a plural subject which can be distinguished from the corresponding set of individuals insofar as this subject can have obligations which the individuals do not have as a mere set, it is necessary to explain how individual commitments "flow" from this joint commitment. Such an explanation is required because individual agents seem to have no obvious reason to adhere to the commitments of *another agent* (the group). In other words, how can derived commitments be at once the individual's *own* commitments (insofar as she has reason to let her actions be guided by them) and *not her own* commitments (insofar as she is not in a position to abrogate them)?

Furthermore, not only does the joint commitment of a group seem to fail to provide individual members with *reasons* to conform to them, it also fails to put individuals in a *position to rebuke* their interaction partners for non-compliance, because, as individuals, they are *the wrong sort of subject* to take the joint commitment as a reason for action. In absence of a convincing explanation of how joint commitments can become relevant for the individuals which are not their subjects, the introduction of joint commitments cannot do the work required in Gilbert's account.

Intuitively, Shockley argues, we would think that if persons are party to the commitments of groups, they are so in virtue of some aspect of their *membership* in those groups. What we need to find then are facts establishing the right kind of membership that can provide the necessary link between joint and individual commitments, and that can explain how individuals can come to be bound by the commitments of the group.

In other words, we must find facts which make it the case that individuals have individual commitments derived from the commitments of the group. Shockley (2004, p. 552) calls this condition a "principle of membership" (M):

> (M): If Group A is (jointly) committed to X and B is a member of Group A, then B is (individually) committed to Y.

(M) is a different way of describing what has to be the case in order for Gilbert's account of joint commitment to be plausible. If there is anything that can make this principle true, it has to be the *relation of membership* which binds individuals to groups. But what kind of relation does the truth of (M) depend on? (M) must either be true in virtue of a *relation between the individual and other individuals* or in virtue of a *relation between the individual and the group as plural subject*.

Shockley subsequently argues that Gilbert's plural subjecthood account rests on an equivocation between these two possible truth-conditions. While (M) might seem plausible because we hold each other responsible *as individuals* for failing to fulfil shared commitments, the other possible relation, described by the part-whole sense of (M), is—according to Shockley—not only *mysterious* but *unnecessary* to understand our intuitions about the truth of (M). However, Gilbert seems to rely on this second interpretation of the truth conditions of (M) in order to justify her introduction of joint commitments as commitments of "plural subjects".

If we come to accept the plausibility of the first interpretation of (M), Shockley argues, we can relinquish the talk of plural subjects and joint commitments and acknowledge that the normative character of collective intentionality depends on non-collective, inter-personal commitments alone. This solution, however, would also mean giving up Gilbert's plural subject account of collective intentionality.

4   Two Kinds of Commitment

It remains to be determined whether the two objections just described can be answered. The following arguments will try to show that there is at least one way to think about the social preconditions for the possibility of plural subjecthood that makes sense of the thought that the truth of the principle of membership might be given by a relation between the individual and the group in a non-mysterious way.

Even though Shockley convincingly argues that it is unnecessary to introduce the concept of a plural subject in order to understand the force of the interrelated commitments of group members, this argument does not show that we can dispense with the concept of joint commitment in analysing collective intentionality. Even though we can and should understand the *force* of the basic commitments in virtue of which members of groups hold each other accountable—and on which collective intentionality consequently supervenes—as established by commitments between (individual) persons, an analysis of the *content* of these commitments may still license or even require the concept of a plural subject (for the distinction between normative force and normative content, see Brandom 2009, p. 71). In other words, individual-individual relations may be sufficient to establish *that* group members are committed to each other, but these relations might be insufficient to fully understand *to what* they are thereby committed.

In order to appreciate this point, it is useful to distinguish between two possible ways of analysing collective intentional states in terms of individual commitments. The first option is to analyse a *collective intention to do A* as a *joint commitment to do A*, which is in turn constituted by *individual commitments to do A* between group members, possibly in combination with other individual commitments.

On this account, joint commitments are at least partly constituted by individual commitments *with the same content* (or at least with a content that can be derived from the content of the joint commitment by understanding what the group has committed itself to). On this account, whenever a group is collectively committed to doing A or believing B, and one understands what A and B mean, one does *not need any further knowledge* or interpretation to know what the individual members have committed themselves to via their membership in the group.

The second option is to analyse a joint commitment to do A in terms of individual commitments with a *different content*. In this case, the question of *what* individuals are *individually committed* to as members of a joint commitment to do A cannot, in normal cases, be answered without engaging in some interpretation of what it *means* for them to collectively do A or believe B. On this account, a joint commitment to do A may essentially involve *distinct* individual commitments to do C. In most cases, a joint commitment of a group ("to take a walk") in some specific social context will involve individual commitments to *accept criticism* for behaviour that violates some shared standard of social behaviour which may or may not be derived from the object of the joint commitment. A joint commitment to take a walk together might, in some social context, involve distributively shared commitments to wear hats, because there is a socially shared rule "taking a walk with others is incompatible with not wearing a hat". This can be true even in cases in which this standard is *not entailed* by the concept of taking a walk.[2] While we may then perfectly understand what the group has jointly committed itself to, we might—according to this understanding—not know the full extent of what the individual members are *individually* committed to (if, for example, we are not familiar with the rule that the membership in a group which is jointly taking a walk is incompatible with not wearing a hat or that persons become open to criticism if they do not wear hats while taking a walk with others).[3]

Thus, the content of a joint commitment does not straightforwardly entail the content of individual commitments, *even if the binding force of the joint commitment can be fully explained by a particular structure of individual commitments.*

Rather, the content of the individual commitments is only *indirectly* connected to the content of the joint commitment through a *shared understanding of the meaning of the joint commitment*. So, if we want to know what a group collectively intending to take a walk entails for its members, we have to take account of it being an open

---

[2]It is implausible to claim that the content of the derived individual commitment can always be straightforwardly derived from the content of the joint commitment without further information about the social context (Gilbert 2006, p. 136). Firstly, there are types of collective commitments that do not have the promotion of a goal as their content, and secondly, the individual commitments flowing from the joint commitment to a goal need not be commitments to promote that goal, although functional constraints usually guarantee that they do not diverge too far.

[3]In the case of an individual intention, fully understanding a person's intention entails understanding what this intention commits her to. In the collective case, however, even a full understanding of the collective intention leaves open the *further* question of what *individual* commitments one has to accept to count as a member of the relevant group.

question (within some boundaries) what its members are individually committed to—and this holds true even if we understand perfectly what the group is collectively committed to.

On this second account of the connection between individual and joint commitment, the concept of a plural subject is irreplaceable because the individual commitments involved in a joint commitment can only be understood in their relation to a joint commitment with some *content of its own*. The reference to this joint commitment cannot be eliminated and replaced with a reference to individual commitments. In this case, it must be the commitment of *another subject*, namely, the group.[4]

As Gilbert's walking-together example suggests (Gilbert 1990), the content of this connection between individual and joint commitment is highly contingent: in different social settings or in different cultures, we might expect different standards of what is appropriate when walking together, and consequently of what minimal set of individual commitments is constitutive of two people counting as collectively taking a walk together. In general, we can only say that whenever there are individual commitments between persons to criticise and accept criticism according to some standard that is inferentially connected to a collective action type, they fulfil one of the conditions for attributing to them a joint commitment to the content of the relevant collective intentional state, and thereby for an ascription of the collective intentional state to a plural subject constituted by these persons.

5   The Social Constitution of Plural Subjects

Having answered one of the two objections to Gilbert's account of collective intentionality, the argument for the claim that strongly collective phenomena are not basic (if they have the normative structure that Gilbert describes), but depend on complex social preconditions, can be spelled out. Plural subject phenomena involve *two types* of commitments whose contents are not analytically connected (in the sense that there is no open question whether the connection is true), namely: (1) the individual-individual commitments of group members; and (2) the joint commitment of the group as a whole. The existence of the appropriate set of elements of the first type is constitutive for the *force* (and, thus, the very existence) of the second, but the *content* of the individual commitments between the members involved in the first element is to be fully understood only in relation to the (separate and non-trivially related) content of the joint commitment of the group as a whole. If the content of individual and collective commitments is independent in this way,

---

[4]As Philip Pettit (2003) notes, we can attribute to groups minds of their own if they collectivise reason in an appropriate way. Thus, the individual commitments necessary for plural subjecthood could be understood as commitments to collectivise reason without it being necessary for the participants to be personally committed to the result of this process.

and if some individual commitments with some content constitute the force of any collective commitment, then the relation between specific individual and joint commitments cannot be assumed to be given *a priori*, but must rather be understood as *socially created*.

Taking note of the significance of the *socially shared standards* that regulate what joint commitments entail for the commitments of individuals helps us to better understand the role of the "principle of membership". An analysis of the membership of individuals in a group requires both, an understanding of how individual commitments acquire their content from a shared interpretation of what membership in a group with a specific joint intention requires, *and* an understanding of how these individual commitments, if they are undertaken, establish the force of the joint commitment and constitute the plural subject. While the interpretation of the "principle of membership" given above is not supposed to spell out the full significance of the relation of membership in all its aspects, it can still serve the more limited function of establishing a relation between joint and individual commitments. To do so, it must express the (contingent, non-analytical, socially established) connection between individual and joint commitment in both these dimensions: it is only possible for a group of individuals to form a plural subject with this commitment, if there is some socially accepted principle of membership which specifies the connection between some specific individual commitments and some specific joint commitment.

To put it more technically, principles of membership can be described as parts of *constitutive rules* (cf. Searle 1995, p. 28) that define *what kinds* of social groups with *which properties* count as plural subjects exhibiting *which collective intentional state or attitude*. The general form of such a constitutive rule is:

A group of persons with properties Y counts as a plural subject with the strongly collective intentional state or attitude S in context C.

Because principles of membership as discussed here do not necessarily exhaust the properties and context that are constitutive for plural subjects, the fact that such principles are accepted should only be taken as a necessary condition for their constitution. Thus, we get at least a necessary part of the relevant constitutive rule:

A group of persons counts as a plural subject with the strongly collective intentional state or attitude S only if it displays a structure of mutual interlocking commitments to accept criticism and criticise each other according to some set of normative standards N.

This general rule is only a "template" for the relevant parts of more specific constitutive rules: each socially instituted collective action type or attitude type depends on the social acceptance of some concrete constitutive rule, that is, on a socially accepted inferential connection between some N and some S in regard to plural subjects.

As these parts of constitutive rules specify that for any plural subject, each of its members must accept their respective part of a structure of individual commitments obliging them to accept criticism and to criticise according to some set of standards of what counts as correct for members of this plural subject, these rule parts thereby also acquire a regulative-normative dimension. In other words, the rule parts connect the status of membership to the individual acceptance of certain obligations and entitlements.

If Gilbert's account is reformulated in this manner, it can answer Shockley's objection: even if joint commitments supervene on a structure of individual commitments in regard to their *force*, we still need plural subjects, because we can understand the *content* of the individual commitments only in terms of plural subjecthood. That is, the normative status instituted by the principle of membership can only be understood as being the status of a group that is committed as a plural intentional subject.[5]

This answer also lays the foundation for the beginnings of a solution to the first problem, the problem of the constitution of plural subjects. If the acceptance of a principle of membership is a precondition of plural subjecthood, and insofar as the principle of membership specifies that a specific structure of interrelated individual commitments constitutes a plural subject, individuals just displaying their readiness to enter into a joint commitment is insufficient to constitute this commitment. Rather, each individual must independently undertake the required individual commitments in order to create a specific plural subject, but they can do so only given a background of an already socially accepted principle of membership. Consequently, the fact that all initial joint commitments are created by the individual commitments of their prospective members does not mean that the *content* of these joint commitments is derivable from the individual intentions to undertake such individual commitments. Rather, it means that undertaking individual commitments is a precondition of *some* joint commitment acquiring normative force, the content of which can only be inferred if one knows the relevant socially shared background rules. That means that the joint commitment can acquire its content only on the condition that there is a socially accepted constitutive rule which specifies that a group with some structure of individual commitments *counts as* a plural subject with commitments of its own.

Thus, a specific structure of individual commitments is necessary for the constitution of a plural subject and for its having a certain joint commitment. This structure can also plausibly be said to be constitutive for something further; namely, for the type of *relation* between the individual members and the plural subject that is sufficient to establish an obligation of the individual members towards the plural subject.

In other words, we can neither deny the significance of the individual-individual nor the significance of the individual-collective relationship, although the normative individual-collective relationship (the commitment of the members to the plural subject) derives its normative force from the standards that are instituted by the individual-individual relations.

---

[5]Of course, nothing keeps us from only talking about the individual membership commitments (as part of an explanatory story, for example). But we will miss the point of these commitments if we do not see that they socially institute the group as a plural subject.

6   An Intersubjectivist Model of Joint Commitments

To summarise the argument so far, there is at least one possible answer to both
objections that have been made against the joint commitment theory of Gilbert.
It involves the claim that the relation between individual commitments and strong
plural subjecthood can only be usefully understood if we assume that there is
a socially accepted background of principles of membership that specify which
structures of individual commitments can legitimately be counted as establishing
strong plural subjects of some kind.

What then are some of the social preconditions which must obtain in a community in order for its members to be able to enter into collective intentional
states? First of all, there must be some established standards that define the *content*
of the individual commitments that form the structure constituting a plural subject.
In the normal case, these will be commitments to criticise and accept criticism for
the violation of the socially accepted inferential properties of a given collective
intentional state. These rules define, for example, the socially shared understanding
of which individual behaviour is appropriate for you if you are member of a group
that has the intention to take a walk together, or if you are a member of a group that
collectively believes that a poem is beautiful. Without such standards, the relevant
principle of group membership will be empty.

However, we should not understand these standards as themselves instituted by
some sort of collective or individual *belief*. This would either, in the collective
case, lead into an infinite regress or, in the case of individual beliefs, undermine
the justification for the claim that joint commitment has an independent normative
force. We should rather understand the background standards as a part of the implicit
"institutional fabric" of a community.[6]

Understanding background standards in this way means, however, that strongly
collective intentionality can not be understood as a simple, basic building block
of institutional reality. It rather depends on the existence of other social facts,
particularly on the implicitly shared acceptance of relevant normative standards.
One necessary precondition of strongly collective intentionality is therefore a social
practice in which certain normative standards are implicitly instituted.

But how should we understand this precondition? Fortunately, the extended
discussion of the Wittgensteinian problem of rule-following has already produced
useful ways of examining this question, of which Robert Brandom's (1994) normative pragmatism is perhaps the best known. In the case of individual intentionality
Brandom argues that we can understand the ability of rational agents to follow
explicit rules, that is, to regulate their behaviour according to normative constraints,
only if we presuppose forms of *shared, implicit, practically instituted* propriety
(1994, pp. 18ff.). By taking this implicitly governed, practically instituted ability to

---

[6]This argument connects to a point frequently made by Tuomela: collective action types have to be
available for members of a community in order for concrete collective actions to be possible. This
issue is also discussed in Stekeler-Weithofer (2002).

correctly undertake, evaluate and ascribe normative commitments as fundamental, we can, according to Brandom, get a grip on the issue of intentionality: we have to understand the ascription of intentional content as the attribution of a specific normative status, of a commitment to a position in the "space of reasons", the significance of which is defined by collectively instituted inferential rules that lay out the further entitlements and commitments connected to this position.

Without going into the details of his model, I propose to extend Brandom's programme of understanding intentionality as the ascription of a normative status from individual to (strongly) collective intentionality. Just like we can treat an individual as an intentional agent by attributing to her intentional states that can be spelled out as the entitlements and obligations that follow from the status of having undertaken a certain kind of commitment, so we can also treat collectives (in the strong sense) as intentional agents by taking them to be able to undertake and successfully act on joint commitments.[7]

There is, however, an important difference between the individual and the collective case. In the individual case, we attribute, for example, a belief to a specific person by ascribing a complex normative status to *the same* person. Roughly, we might say that we take her behaviour to be governed by an obligation that does forbid her from assenting to any proposition that is incompatible with the attributed belief-content, or to anything that entails such a proposition, an obligation to provide reasons for her belief when challenged, an entitlement to commit herself to the consequences of her belief (and so on). According to Brandom, even the very idea of a subject can be understood as the reference point for the ascription of such normative commitments which need to be consistently integrated with one another (Brandom 2009, pp. 48f.).

The collective case, in contrast, both establishes a *new* kind of subject position (a plural subject) and builds upon an *already established individual* subjectivity. When there is a strongly collective intentional state, there is, similarly to the case of individual subjects, a commitment attributed to the (plural) subject of the intention or belief, as being a subject with a "mind of its own". This plural subject is taken to be governed by norms prescribing, for example, that the inferential consequences of the relevant beliefs and intentions be rationally consistent. There is, however, another set of norms. In the case of strongly collective intentionality, there are also norms that specify commitments of the individual *members* of the plural subject, prescribing what they ought to do or to believe in their institutional role as group members.

To take up Gilbert's example once again, if two persons jointly intend to take a walk together, there is *one* set of norms that apply to them jointly: They cannot without any further reason stay at home and play chess without inviting doubts about their (perhaps professed) joint intention. But there is also a *second* set of norms that apply to them *individually*. As individuals, they must not, for example, run away

---

[7] This approach is very similar to Tollefsen's (2002) analysis, which describes the ascription of collective intentional states from the perspective of Dennett's and Davidson's "interpretationism".

from the other person without a reason, and they have to conform to a huge number of culturally and socially implicit requirements to count as members of a group that intends to jointly take a walk. These two sets of norms have not only different content but also different subjects, whereby the subject of the first set is constituted by the individuals being in social relations which are defined by the second set.

It is essential to distinguish between these two sets of norms in order to avoid the pitfalls of either reductive individualism or strong collectivism. If we assume that the inferential properties of the social status attributed in the course of the ascription of collective intentional states and the resulting commitments are strictly congruent with their equivalents in the individual case, then we have either to attribute *all relevant commitments* to the individual members of the group, rendering the talk of a plural subject unnecessary but also missing the normative consequences of strongly collective intentionality, or we have to attribute all relevant commitments *only* to the plural subject and not to the individual members, making the reality and effectiveness of joint commitments mysterious.

The question which has been asked at the beginning of this chapter can now receive a tentative answer: If we do not assume that strongly collective intentional states are to be explained as simple building blocks of institutional reality, but rather as an achievement of practices of the ascription of normative statuses that turn out to be rather complex, we can say more about their social preconditions. Strongly collective intentional states presuppose—as a necessary condition, though certainly not as a full explanation—the existence of certain social practices of attributing both individual and joint commitments. More specifically, they presuppose social practices which incorporate shared rules and understandings about the connection between collective and individual commitments, and shared rules and understandings concerning the conditions of membership in plural subjects with certain types of strongly collective intentional states. This formulation does not in itself tell us everything we need to know about collective intentional states, as it is compatible with a wide range of theories. However, it does establish constraints that any plausible theory of strongly collective intentional states must satisfy.

7   Recognition as the Condition of Possibility of Collective Commitment and Collective Self-Governance

If collective intentionality presupposes socially instituted implicit principles of membership, then collective intentionality is not a simply given, free-standing feature of social reality. The ability of individual persons to enter into joint commitments, their ability to be subjects of strongly collective intentional states, depends on the existence of shared inferential rules—or principles of membership— which establish a shared understanding of the connection between collective and individual commitments. The existence of such an understanding is—as I have attempted to show—constitutive for the possibility of strongly collective intentional states.

To present a slightly more concrete picture, it might be appropriate to comment further on the social preconditions of strong plural subjecthood—even if these remarks are somewhat speculative.

If the practical proprieties which establish shared inferential rules are necessary preconditions for collective intentional states, then the practical interactions (assessments, sanctions and so on) which establish their normativity must be underwritten by some kind of *authority* for these rules to be in effect in any meaningful sense. Thus, being strongly jointly committed to a goal requires that the participants accept the authority of their co-members regarding their conformity to those rules which are the inferential consequences of the collective acceptance of that goal.

The ability to enter into a strongly joint commitment thus presupposes an attitude of the potential participants towards their prospective co-participants that attributes to them the entitlement to judge the behaviour of their fellow (potential or actual) group members and, if necessary, to respond to it with criticism. But this authority ascription only covers the *application* (again, the *force*) of certain shared rules and not their meaning (content). One does not have to accept the reactions of others as the last word on the *meaning* of the shared rules. Rather, the meaning of these rules and standards depends on the acceptance of the relevant principles of membership, which in turn get their meaning from more widely shared understandings of a linguistic or cultural community. These principles therefore involve acceptance of the authority of a large number of *other* persons (the relevant community) which normally includes the more limited number of those persons with whom one enters into a joint commitment. Thus, we can understand normative commitments in both the narrow sense in which they are necessary for collective intentionality and in the wider sense in which they are fundamental to the shared understanding of membership rules as presupposing structures of *mutual authority ascription*.

These structures of mutual authority ascription are *recursive* and *defeasible*. They are recursive insofar as being a co-member of a collective intentional state not only requires me to authorise you to evaluate my actions according to some rule which we both accept, and which defines what follows from our being jointly committed; I must also accept your evaluation of my *interpretation* of that rule according to some further linguistic or interpretative rules that we both share with a larger community. The authority is defeasible insofar as the acceptance of a person's authority—her recognition by others as a fellow member of a "we"— accords her not an indefeasible and absolute but only a *standard authority*, which is usually kept in check by rules governing exceptions. Being party to a joint commitment as well as being a member of a social practice entails having to accept evaluations by co-members, but this obligation can always be overridden by an *a priori* unspecified number of exceptions. Strongly collective intentionality thus supervenes on structures of *pragmatic, defeasible authority ascription* which can be called—in line with the neo-Hegelian theory of language and mind proposed by Brandom, Pippin and others—"mutual recognition".

As the individual preconditions of joint commitments are always only intelligible in their embedding into this whole structure of recognition, the theory of collective intentionality cannot be reduced to a project concerned only with an analysis of

244   T. Stahl

the phenomenal properties of collective intentional states in terms of relations or properties of individuals; rather, it must attempt to achieve an understanding of these properties in the context of systems of social practices. If we understand the possibility of collective intentionality as an achievement of recognitive communities, collective intentionality theory must not be conducted as a mere extension of the philosophy of mind but at least to the same degree as social analysis.

References

Brandom, R. 1994. *Making it explicit*. Cambridge: Harvard University Press.
Brandom, R. 2009. *Reason in philosophy. Animating ideas*. Cambridge: Belknap/Harvard University Press.
Bratman, M. 1999. Shared intention. In *Faces of intention*, 109–129. Cambridge: Cambridge University Press.
Gilbert, M. 1987. Modelling collective belief. *Synthese* 73(1): 185–204.
Gilbert, M. 1989. *On social facts*. London: Routledge.
Gilbert, M. 1990. Walking together: A paradigmatic social phenomenon. *Midwest Studies in Philosophy* 25: 1–14.
Gilbert, M. 1996. *Living together. Rationality, sociality and obligation*. New York: Rowman and Littlefield.
Gilbert, M. 1999. Obligation and joint commitment. *Utilitas* 11(2): 143–163.
Gilbert, M. 2002a. Acting together. In *Social facts and collective intentionality*, ed. G. Meggle, 53–72. Frankfurt a. M: Dr. Hänsel-Hohenhausen AG.
Gilbert, M. 2002b. Considerations on joint commitment: Responses to various comments. In *Social facts and collective intentionality*, ed. G. Meggle, 73–10. Frankfurt a. M: Dr. Hänsel-Hohenhausen AG.
Gilbert, M. 2006. *A theory of political obligation: Membership, commitment, and the bonds of society*. Oxford: Oxford University Press.
Meijers, A. 2003. Can collective intentionality be individualized? *The American Journal of Economics and Sociology* 62(1): 167–183.
Pettit, P. 2003. Groups with minds of their own. In *Socializing metaphysics*, ed. F. Schmitt, 172–175. New York: Rowman and Littlefield.
Searle, J. 1995. *The construction of social reality*. London: The Penguin Press.
Shockley, K. 2004. The conundrum of joint commitment. *Social Theory and Practice* 30(4): 535–557.
Stekeler-Weithofer, P. 2002. Zur Logik des 'Wir'. Formen und Darstellungen gemeinsamer Praxis. In *Kultur – Handlung – Wissenschaft*, ed. M. Gutmann, D. Hartmann, and W. Zitterbarth. Weilerswist: Velbrück Wissenschaft.
Tollefsen, D. 2002. Organizations as true believers. *Journal of Social Philosophy* 33(3): 395–410.
Tollefsen, D. 2004. Collective intentionality. *Internet Encyclopedia of Philosophy*. http://www.iep.utm.edu/coll-int/. Accessed 19 Sept 2011.
Tuomela, R. 2007. *The philosophy of sociality*. Oxford: Oxford University Press.

Part III
Collective Reasons and Group Agency

Chapter 15
Acting over Time, Acting Together

Michael E. Bratman

Abstract In temporally extended agency, past, present, and (normally) future thought and action are tied together in distinctive ways. In shared intentional activity, the thoughts and actions of the participants are tied together in distinctive ways. My conjecture is that a fundamental ground of these human capacities for temporally extended and shared intentional agency are human capacities for planning agency. The conceptual, metaphysical, and normative resources in play in our planning agency provide a backbone of our temporally extended and shared intentional agency.

1

I want to focus on two inter-related features of human agency, and a conjecture about their common ground.

The first feature concerns ways in which action is related to time. It might be that an agent persists over time and acts in the present in ways that influence the future and are to some extent shaped by the past, and yet these actions do not involve that

---

This essay is based on my presentation at the August, 2010 Collective Intentionality Conference, Basel, Switzerland; in this final version I benefited from helpful comments from an anonymous referee for this volume. Sections 1, 2, and 3 are mostly taken, with the kind permission of the American Philosophical Association, from my "Agency, Time, and Sociality," *Proceedings and Addresses of the American Philosophical Association* 84:2 (2010): 7–26. © American Philosophical Association. Throughout (and especially in Sects. 4 and 5) I draw from (Bratman 2014); see that monograph for further developments, complexities, and references.

M.E. Bratman (✉)
Department of Philosophy, Stanford University, Stanford, CA, USA
e-mail: bratman@stanford.edu

agent's own grasp of the larger temporal arc of his activity and the guidance of his activity by that grasp. The actions are goal-directed, but nevertheless primarily a reaction to present conditions. In contrast, in many cases of human agency the agent's present activity involves her grasp of how it is embedded in what she has earlier been doing and what she is on her way to doing.[1] Her grasp of the larger temporal arc of her activity is a central element in her guidance of that activity both at that time and over time. And this grasp is central to our understanding of her activity.

Think about building a hut. If we were gods perhaps we could simply will "let there be a hut!"—and then, there it is. But, of course, our agency is not like that. For us, building a hut takes time, and it is crucial—both to the agent's guidance of the activity and to our understanding of her activity—that at various stages along the way the agent herself understand and guide her activity then in part by way of her understanding of and commitment to its relation to earlier and, if all goes well, later activities. Call this *temporally extended* agency. One striking feature of human agency, as we know it, is that it is quite frequently temporally extended.

Consider now ways in which an agent's actions are related to the actions of other agents. Agents frequently act in a context that includes other agents in the vicinity, where each agent is aware of what the others are doing. In such contexts the actions of each of the agents might be mutually responsive: each adjusts to the actions of the others who are adjusting to each. And this might be out in the open, public. This is what happens, for example, when strangers in a crowd manage to walk together down the street without colliding. In contrast—and as Margaret Gilbert has emphasized—sometimes agents walk together in an importantly stronger sense (Gilbert 1990). They each see their own activity as embedded in what *they* are doing together, and this understanding of their individual activity as embedded in their shared activity is a central element both in their guidance of that activity and in their and our understanding of what they are doing. Call this *shared intentional* activity. One striking feature of human agency, as we know it, is that it is many times a part of such shared intentional activities.

These reflections support the thought that among the important practical capacities involved in human agency are capacities both for temporally extended and for shared intentional activity. A human life that did not significantly involve these capacities would be impoverished and difficult to understand. But what are these capacities, and how are they related to each other?

In temporally extended agency, past, present, and (normally) future thought and action are tied together in distinctive ways. In shared intentional activity, the thoughts and actions of the participants are tied together in distinctive ways. We need to understand what these ties are, and what they tell us about human agency.

In each case our concerns are conceptual, metaphysical, and normative. We seek conceptual resources that help us in our theorizing to cut up these phenomena at their joints. We want to understand what there is in the world that constitutes these forms of agency. And we need to understand central normative elements.

---

[1] For a similar contrast see Ferrero (2009).

I can now state my conjecture: A fundamental ground of these human capacities for temporally extended and for shared intentional agency are human capacities for planning agency.[2] In saying that these planning capacities are a fundamental ground, I mean that the proper exercise of these planning capacities, given relevant contents of the plans, relevant contexts, and relevant inter-relations with past, future, and others, will realize phenomena of temporally extended and/or shared intentional activity. In this sense the conceptual, metaphysical, and normative resources in play in our planning agency provide a backbone of our temporally extended and shared intentional agency.

In saying this I do not mean directly to address larger, institutional forms of shared agency, such as, perhaps, law or democracy. My target is small scale shared intentionality, in the absence of institutional authority relations. It is a further question how such small scale and larger scale cases are related. I also do not mean to claim that the exercise of planning capacities is the only possible form of temporally extended or shared intentional activity. My conjecture concerns important forms of temporally extended and small scale shared intentional activity, without being a claim to uniqueness. Nevertheless, this conjecture helps us answer basic questions about these phenomena.

2

Planning agency is a distinctive kind of goal-directed agency, one that involves attitudes of intention that are at least in part future-directed. These intentions settle relevant practical matters and are normally embedded in larger plans. These larger plans normally have a hierarchical, end-means structure; and these plans will typically be partial in the sense that they do not yet specify all the steps needed for each intended end.

Intentions are plan states. Though they are subject to revision, these plan states nevertheless have a characteristic stability over time. And these plan states normally adjust in the direction of intention-belief consistency and means-end coherence of plans at a time. They are responsive to pressures for consistency of the many different things one intends with each other and with what one believes; and they are responsive to pressures to fill in hierarchically structured partial plans as needed with specifications of means and the like. These tendencies toward diachronic stability and synchronic consistency and coherence correspond to associated rationality norms, ones whose at least implicit acceptance is at work in the psychic functioning of a planning agent.

Given the rational pressure to fill in partial plans to avoid means-end incoherence, prior plan states tend to pose problems for further deliberation, problems of means

---

[2]I offer a framework for thinking about our planning agency in my *Intention, Plans, and Practical Reason* (1987).

and the like. Given my intended end of writing this essay, for example, I am faced with a problem about how to do this. And given the rational pressure for consistency, these plan states tend to filter out from practical reasoning options intending which would not be consistent with one's other intentions and beliefs. Given that I already plan to teach my seminar on Tuesdays, for example, my plan for writing my essay is under rational pressure to be compatible with that—though I might, of course, instead change my seminar. And when the time for action is recognized to have arrived, these plan states are set to guide and control relevant conduct.

These roles and associated norms help distinguish intentions from ordinary desires and beliefs. Roughly, and partially: Ordinary desires are not subject to the same rational pressures for consistency. Desiring things that are not by our lights co-possible is all too human. And a belief that one will be doing something later—in contrast with an intention to do it—need not require that one settle on means to doing it; just think of your prediction that you are about to trip.

If all goes well, planning structures induce cross-temporal referential connections that are both forward and backward looking. My present plan to go to Basel next week at least implicitly refers to my later, then-present-directed intention to go by getting on the airplane; and my later intention at least implicitly refers back to my earlier intention. Further, the normal stability of such intentions over time helps support a coordinated flow of activity over time. These cross-temporal constancies and referential inter-connections help support a temporally extended structure of partial plans that can provide a background framework for further deliberation aimed at filling in these plans as need be and as time goes by. In these ways, a planning agent's purposive activity over time is typically embedded within interwoven structures of partial, referentially interlocking, hierarchical, and more or less stable plan states, and in modes of further deliberation and planning that are motivated and framed by these plan states.

Now, the capacity for temporally extended agency is the capacity to guide and control one's activities in light of one's grasp of their location in a larger, temporally extended structure of what one has been doing and what one is committed to doing. And the important point now is that the psychic economy of a planning agent will realize this capacity for temporally extended agency. The inter-woven, referentially inter-locking, and more or less stable structures of partial and hierarchical plan states will normally guide and control present activity as an element in larger activities favored by these plan states; and it will normally involve an explanatorily relevant grasp on the part of the agent of salient relations between temporally larger activities and their temporal sub-parts.

So this planning psychology is a realization of the capacity for temporally extended agency. And this will come as no surprise. When we reflect on why we bother with planning—why we do not just cross our bridges when we come to them—the commonsense answer will appeal to the way in which it supports the cross-temporal organization of our agency. What we have briefly explored is the deep structure of this way in which the human mind supports this cross-temporal organization.

I can now turn to shared intentional activity.

3

When I noted Gilbert's example of walking together, I drew a contrast with a case in which there is not, in the relevant sense, shared intentional activity even though there are publicly interdependent intentional activities of each—as when you and a stranger walk down the street without colliding. But there is also a second contrast we need to draw, this time with a case in which you and I exchange promises that we will each walk with the other, thereby incurring mutual obligations to perform. Such exchanges, and their associated obligations, are not sufficient for shared intentional activity: just think of a case in which each promises insincerely and has no intention in favor of a shared walking. Nor are such promises necessary, as Hume observed about those who row the boat together "tho' they have never given promises to each other" (Hume 1968 [1739–1740], p. 490).

What we want is a model of shared intentional activity that threads a path between walking with strangers and a web of promissory obligations. And here I propose to appeal again to our planning agency.

We begin with planning agents. We give their plan states contents of a sort that are characteristic of shared intentional activity. We locate these agents in a context in which their relevant plan states are appropriately inter-related. And we describe central ways in which these inter-related intentions of each inter-dependently work their way through to joint action. We try thereby to provide a plan-theoretic construction that is sufficiently rich to be a realization of shared intentional activity.[3]

Let me sketch how I would proceed with such a plan-theoretic construction.

Suppose that you and I are going to Basel together, and that this is a shared intentional activity. What plan-theoretic construction can realize what is essential here?[4]

My proposal appeals primarily to five ideas. First, there is the idea that each of us intends not just *to* go to Basel, but *that we* go to Basel.[5] Second, there is the idea that each intends that we go to Basel in part *by way of* the *other* person's intention that we go. Third, there is the idea that we each intend that we go to Basel by way of sub-plans of each of us that *mesh* in the sense of being co-compatible. Fourth, there is the idea of *interdependence* in the persistence of these intentions of each. And fifth, there is the idea that these intentions of each lead to our going to Basel by way of *mutual responsiveness* of each to each, mutual responsiveness that tracks the intended joint activity.

I proceed to reflect briefly on this quintet of ideas.

First: I intend *that we* go to Basel, and so do you. It is not just that I intend to go while expecting you to go. But must this appeal within the content of my intention

---

[3]Though I do not argue that this is the unique realization.

[4]The answer that follows is drawn in part from my quartet of essays on this subject in my *Faces of Intention* (1999), "Shared Agency" (2009a) and "Modest Sociality and the Distinctiveness of Intention" (2009b).

[5]My initial thinking about this idea was aided by comments from Philip Cohen.

to *our* activity involve the very idea of our shared intentional activity? No, it need not. The concept of our activity, as it is involved in the content of my intention, can be a weak concept that includes cases like that of strangers walking together down the street without colliding. We then depend on the appropriate explanatory role of relevant, inter-dependent intentions to distinguish between such a weak form of acting together and shared intentional activity.

But can I really *intend* our activity? Isn't what I can intend limited to my own actions? Well, if we use the infinitive construction—intend to—then we are limiting what is intended in this way. But we also have the idea of intending *that*. And I can, normally, intend that *p* if I believe that whether or not *p* will depend on whether or not I so intend.

But we are supposing that *each* of us intends that we go to Basel. How can *both* of us sensibly think that whether *we* go is dependent on *his* intention? The answer looks ahead to our fourth idea: interdependence in persistence. Each can think that our going depends on his own intention in part by way of the support that intention provides for the persistence of the other person's intention that we go, where our going also depends on that intention of the other person.[6]

This brings us back to the second idea, that each intends that we go to Basel in part *by way of the intention of the other*. There is, within the content of the intention of each, reference to the role of the intention of the other. This contrasts with a case in which each intends that we go to Basel by way of throwing the other into the trunk of his car. The intentions characteristic of shared intentional activity, unlike such "mafia" intentions, referentially interlock with each other. The intentions of each refer to each other in ways that parallel the semantic interconnections over time of the intentions of an individual planning agent.

Third—and again in contrast with the mafia case—each intends that there be the cited *mesh in sub-plans*. This does not mean that there is yet such a mesh, only that each has a plan-like commitment to there being such mesh, where achieving that mesh may require relevant bargaining or shared deliberation. And such interlocking intentions in favor of mesh in sub-plans can motivate and frame such further bargaining or shared deliberation.[7]

These second and third ideas appeal to inter-relations between the intentions of each that are built into the contents of those intentions. The final two ideas— interdependence in persistence, and mutual responsiveness that tracks the intended joint activity—concern ways in which these intentions actually interact in their functioning. This interaction in functioning is related in complex ways to the cited contents of the intentions of each. In particular, the interaction involved in mutual

---

[6] In these last two paragraphs I am responding to challenges posed by, among others, Baier (1997b), Stoutland (1997), Velleman (1997). For further discussion, see my "I Intend that We *J*" in Bratman (1999). And see also Baier (1997a).

[7] These complex contents of relevant intentions need not be explicitly conscious (though of course they may). Instead, these contents may be implicit in relevant, underlying dispositions of tracking, adjustment, and responsiveness in thought and action—dispositions that are grounded in the agent's plan states.

responsiveness will be in part explained by the contents of the intentions of each. It is because I intend that we go in part by way of your intention that we go, that I will adjust my relevant activity so as to help support the efficacy of your intention. And vice versa. Further, and as we have seen, it is in part because there is believed to be the cited inter-dependence in persistence that the intention of each in favor of the joint activity is itself coherent.

There is more to say. In particular, I would want to add that this structure of inter-related intentions is out in the open: that is why the participants can engage together in reasoning that uses the premise that *they* intend so to act together. But here let me just highlight the initial quintet of ideas. A basic conjecture is that these interdependent and interlocking intentions of each will, in responding to the rational pressures involved in individual planning agency, function together in ways that, if all goes well, constitute shared intentional activity.

In partial support of this conjecture recall that if you and I are involved in such an inter-personal planning structure, I do not just intend to do my part while expecting you to do yours, as I might intend to walk to my left knowing that the stranger is walking to my right. Rather, I intend that we act in part by way of your analogous intention and meshing sub-plans of our intentions; and intending is not merely expecting. This means that the rational pressure on me to make my plans means-end coherent and consistent—pressure built into individual planning agency—ensures rational pressure on me to mesh with and, as needed, support *your* relevant plans. And vice versa. This will frequently involve rational pressure on each of us to help the other, if such help is needed. In this way, rational pressures on the *individual* planning agents—given suitable contents of, and inter-relations between their plans—induce rational pressures in favor of forms of *social* coherence and consistency that are characteristic of shared intentional activity. These pressures of social rationality depend on the presence of relevant intentions of each participant, intentions whose continued persistence is supported, though not ensured, by pressures for stability. And there will be these normative pressures even when—as is common—each participates in the shared activity for different reasons.

Suppose that we can in this way articulate a plan-theoretic construction that realizes an important form of shared intentional activity. Such a construction would bring to bear conceptual resources drawn broadly from the domain of individual planning agency[8] and argue that these conceptual resources are adequate to the task of theorizing about small scale shared intentionality. It would aim to see the metaphysics of shared intentional activity as a construct of metaphysical resources already in play in the case of individual planning agency. And it would aim to see basic normative pressures characteristic of shared intentionality as rooted in normative pressures central to individual planning agency.

Now, we can see shared intentional activity as joint activity that is explained by relevant shared intentions. In our shared intentional walking together, for example, we walk together because we intend to walk together—where talk of what we intend

---

[8]Though questions remain about the idea of being out in the open.

is talk of our shared intention. And according to our plan theoretic construction, what makes it true that we intend to walk together is, roughly, a complex of inter-locking and interdependent intentions of each in favor of our walking by way of meshing sub-plans.[9]

Our plan-theoretic construction uses as its basic building block intentions of the sort that are central to individual planning agency, though intentions that have distinctive contents and inter-relations. This contrasts with a view like that of John Searle's according to which the kind of intention of individuals that is needed for shared intentionality is not ordinary intention with a special content, but a fundamentally different attitude: a so-called "we intention" (Searle 1990). Our plan-theoretic construction can draw directly from what our theory of individual planning agency tells us about the nature of intending, while also bringing to bear appeals to special contents, contexts, and inter-relations. But if we see the building blocks of shared intentionality not as ordinary attitudes of intending with special contents, but rather as distinctive attitudes of we-intending, then it is not clear that we can do this.

Another contrast returns us to mutual obligation. Our plan-theoretic construction ensures that rational pressures for social coherence and consistency apply to shared intention and shared intentional activity. But it does not say that it is essential that the parties have distinctive obligations of performance *to* each other, obligations grounded in the specific shared activity.[10] Nevertheless, we can expect such obligations to be extremely common given that there will quite frequently be, in shared intentional activity, forms of assurance, intentional creation of expectation, or—as Facundo Alonso (2009) has emphasized—intentionally reinforced reliance that ground relevant moral obligations. And when the parties are guided by their recognition of those obligations there will be a corresponding increase in the stability of the sharing.

This plan-theoretic proposal highlights conceptual, metaphysical and normative continuities between the individual and the shared case, continuities that depend on a rich model of individual planning agency. Both Searle and Gilbert take a different tack. They each see the step from individual to shared agency as involving a basic new metaphysical resource. In Searle's view what is needed is a new attitude of we-intention. In Gilbert's view what is needed is a new relation of "joint commitment" between the participants, a relation that necessitates mutual obligations (Gilbert 2009). And both philosophers then try to understand larger institutions in large part in terms of the new element that they cite as central to small scale shared agency (Searle 1995; Gilbert 2006). In contrast, my plan-theoretic approach begins by distinguishing, in the individual case, between simple goal-directed agency and planning agency. Once individual planning agency is on board, the step to small scale sociality need not involve a fundamental discontinuity—though this is not to

[9]A *caveat* is that, as indicated earlier, we have not precluded the possibility that shared intention and shared intentionality are multiply realizable. To keep the discussion manageable, I put this qualification aside here.

[10]Here I am disagreeing with Margaret Gilbert (see Gilbert 2009).

say that all planning agents have the capacity for shared intentional activity.[11] But this planning approach leaves it open how best to move from small scale shared intentional activity to larger institutions.

4

The step from goal-directed to planning agency supports, then, important forms of both temporally extended and shared agency. This is part of the *fecundity of planning structures*. This fecundity is both theoretical and practical. It is theoretical in providing resources—conceptual, metaphysical, and normative—for understanding broad aspects, both descriptive and normative, of our human agency. It is practical in highlighting ways in which our planning capacities support aspects of our lives that we highly value.

Let's reflect further on central aspects of this planning approach to shared agency.

On this approach, shared intentional agency, at least in a theoretically central case, consists in the inter-connected planning agency of the participants. The participants have the appropriate planning attitudes, where these include intentions of each in favor of the joint activity. These intentions are to be understood by way of the theory of individual planning agency. And these intentions are appropriately inter-connected. They are referentially interconnected: each intends that the other's intentions be effective in the joint activity and that there be mesh in sub-plans of both. And these intentions are interdependent in their persistence, where this interdependence potentially involves causal and rational adjustment of each to each, and where this interdependence (or at least beliefs about this interdependence) is central to the very coherence of each intending that they act. Further, the way that these intentions of each work their way through to joint activity involves mutual responsiveness that tracks the joint activity, mutual responsiveness that is itself rationally supported by the intentions of each.

The idea that such shared intentional agency involves inter-personal inter-connections is in the spirit of one aspect of Gilbert's view. As noted, Gilbert sees shared agency as essentially involving joint commitment, where joint commitments essentially involve mutual obligations. Her view is not that shared agency involves *beliefs* on the part of the participants that they have obligations to each other. The view, rather, is that shared intentional activity involves *actual obligations* of each to the other. These obligations are actual, normative relations between the participants.

An underlying idea here is that shared intentional agency involves, at the ground level, basic inter-relations between the parties. And this underlying idea is shared by the planning approach I have been sketching. The difference is that the planning approach aims to understand these inter-relations by way of resources

---

[11] So my theory is compatible with Michael Tomasello's conjecture that the great apes are planning agents who nevertheless do not have a capacity for shared intentional activity (see Tomasello 2009).

from the theory of individual planning agency and without an essential appeal to the relational normative phenomena to which Gilbert alludes.

So, while Gilbert and I disagree about what the inter-relations are, we agree that shared intentionality involves basic inter-relations. In this respect we both disagree with John Searle's apparent view that what is essential to shared intentional agency is exhausted by certain attitudes in the heads of the participants.[12] The planning theory agrees with Searle that certain intentions of the individuals are central—though, in contrast with Searle, the planning theory seeks to understand these intentions primarily in terms of the resources of the theory of individual planning agency. But the planning theory also emphasizes, in partial agreement with Gilbert, that certain inter-relations are also central.

I have said that the planning theory does not make an essential appeal, at the ground level, to the relational normative phenomena highlighted by Gilbert's account of joint commitment. But we need to understand this contrast with care. It would not be accurate simply to say that the planning theory eschews appeal to the normative. After all, it is central to the planning theory that there are norms of individual intention rationality—including norms of consistency, coherence, and stability. And it is a basic claim of the planning theory that within relevant structures of interconnected planning agency these norms induce associated norms of social rationality. Instead, the relevant issue between the planning theory and Gilbert's theory is best described as the issue of what specific normative features are essential. According to the planning theory, what are essential are norms of individual intention rationality—though of course shared intention will in fact normally interact with other domains of normativity, including especially morality.

Why might one think—as Gilbert does—that, in addition, mutual obligations of each to each are essential? Well, return to cases of mere concatenation of activities with mutual tracking and adjustment. We can suppose that such cases take place within a context of common knowledge. It is, for example, common knowledge, between me and the stranger, that we are walking near to each other and in the same direction and at roughly the same pace down the street. And that is why we keep an eye out to avoid collisions. But ours is not a case of shared intentional activity. Why not? It is not a matter of the absence of knowledge of each about each. Instead, in the case of shared intentional activity there is a distinctive practical tie— a practical, social "glue". And this is a practical tie that is not ensured by further, merely epistemic conditions. But what could this practical tie be? And here it is tempting to say: these are, at least in part, ties of *obligation* of each to each.

---

[12]Searle writes: "all intentionality, whether collective or individual, could be had by a brain in a vat..." (1990, p. 407). Strictly speaking, this is not yet to say that shared intentional activity is solely a matter of what could be had by a brain in a vat. But since Searle's entire theory of "collective intentionality" is a theory of the we-intentions that could be had by a brain in a vat, it seems that he at least implicitly endorses this stronger thought. And it is this stronger thought that Gilbert and I reject. (John Hund makes a related point (See Hund 1998, p. 129). [Thanks to Facundo Alonso for this reference.])

This last step supposes that if the practical ties are not merely an epistemic matter then they are, at least in part, a matter of mutual obligation. But what the planning theory helps us to see is that our philosophical options are richer than this. In particular, once we have on board the planning theory of individual agency we have the resources—conceptual, metaphysical, and normative—to characterize, without appeal to mutual obligations, both intentions with distinctive contents and distinctive practical ties of interlocking, intended mesh, and interdependence between these intentions of the participants. Granted, when there are relevant mutual obligations—as there very commonly are—their recognition will normally contribute to the standard functioning of shared intention. Nevertheless, the conjecture of the planning theory is that, given its resources, we can characterize these fundamental practical ties without essential appeal to such mutual obligations.

5

In individual planning agency there is an individual who is both the agent of the activity and the subject of relevant intentions. What about shared agency? Is there a group agent? A group subject?

Consider Jane who, alluding to her partner Sue, says:

1. We are painting the house together as a shared intentional activity, and
2. we intend to paint the house together.

According to the planning theory, 1. and 2. are true if there is an appropriate social-psychological web, one that connects up in the right way to action: Jane intends that they paint; Sue intends that they paint; these intentions interlock and favor meshing sub-plans; these intentions are mutually inter-dependent; this all leads in the right way to their painting; and so on. But what is the reference of 'we', as it appears as the grammatical subject in 1. and 2.?

Well, the concept of 'we' that is involved in the contents of the relevant individual intentions of Jane and Sue concerning their painting can be a merely distributive notion—it can be merely the concept of a collection of the two individual agents. But we can still go on to ask whether, if 1. and 2. are true, there *is* a group agent of the action in 1. and/or a group subject who has the intention in 2.

I think—and here I have benefitted from work by Björn Petersson—that the planning theory can and should allow that when 1. is true there is a weak sense in which a group, one involving Jane and Sue, is the agent of the cited action (see Petersson 2007).[13] As Petersson emphasizes, the relevant idea of a group

---

[13]Petersson discusses this idea of a group causal agent within the context of a purported criticism of my account of the contents of the intentions central to shared intentionality. In my *Shared Agency* (forthcoming) I explain why I do not think this criticism works. Here, however, I just want to draw on Petersson's positive proposal of the idea of a group causal agent.

agent is simply that of an internally structured complex of individuals, where this structure supports the ascription of certain causal powers and effects to that group. In Petersson's example, a swarm of bees can be a group agent in this sense: after all, it may be true that the swarm frightens the sheep. And in the case of Jane and Sue there is also a structured complex, though in this case—in contrast with a swarm of bees—this structure is induced by inter-connected planning psychologies. So we can allow both that 'we' in 1. can in fact refer not simply to the distributed collection of Jane and Sue but, rather, to the group (which consists of the social-psychologically organized structure involving Jane and Sue), and that this group is the agent of the shared action.

Now, this group (unlike a swarm) is the agent of an action that is, in particular, a shared intentional action. And what makes this a shared *intentional* action is the role of the shared intention reported in 2. Should we say then that 'we' in 2., when 2. is true, refers to a group that is the *subject* of this shared intention?

I think that this is not in general true: in shared intentionality there need not be a group subject of the shared intention. To talk of a *subject* who intends is to see that subject as a center of a more or less coherent mental web. The idea of a subject who intends X but has few other intentional attitudes—who intends X in the absence of a mental web of that subject in which this intention is located—seems a mistake. This is a lesson we can learn from Donald Davidson's work on the holism of the mental (Davidson 2001b).[14] But in shared intentionality the sharing will typically be partial and limited: Jane and Sue might have no other shared projects, and might significantly diverge in their reasons for participating in this shared project. The sharing can be quite transitory. And the sharing can cross-cut: Jane might paint with Sue while singing with Bob. These features of the sharing need not block the idea of a group causal agent of a shared intentional activity, an agent that is limited in its causal impacts and, perhaps, quite temporary. But the minimal holism of the mental distinguishes this idea of a *causal agent* of a shared intentional activity from the idea of a *subject* of a shared intention. Being the agent of the shared action can come apart from being the subject of the shared intention, even given that the shared action is explained by the shared intention.

I have attributed to Davidson the idea of a minimal holism of the mental. The idea, roughly, is that we make sense of ascriptions of contents to attitudes of the same person in ways that require that these contents and attitudes more or less hang together in ways that are partly constitutive of the mental. We also owe to Davidson the idea of a tight connection between being an agent and being a subject of a holistic mental web. In his essay "Agency," Davidson ties agency to intentionality; and his background theory of the intentionality of action sees such intentionality as, roughly, relevant explainability by the agent's attitudes (Davidson 2001a, esp. p. 46). But, according to Davidson, these attitudes must be embedded in a more or less consistent and coherent mental web. According to Davidson, then, to be an

---

[14]See also Rovane (1998). Some of my remarks in this paragraph draw from my Bratman (2009b, p. 163).

agent involves being an *intentional* agent, and so a *subject* of a holistic web of attitudes.

Following Petersson, I have tried to make room for a weaker notion of agency, one not tied so tightly to intentionality. But even when we focus in particular on *intentional* agency, what we have seen to be problematic is a straightforward extension to the case of *shared* intentional agency of the Davidsonian tie between individual intentional agency and individual subject-hood. On the Davidsonian model, the individual agent of intentional activity is the subject of a holistic web of attitudes, some of which are part of the explanation of that activity. But when we turn to shared intentional agency this tight connection between intentional agency and subject-hood does not survive—which is not to deny that there may be special cases in which it is plausible to talk of a Davidsonian group subject (see Rovane 1998; List and Pettit 2011).

Now, a central theme of this essay has been that our planning agency is a ground of both our temporally extended and our social agency. In each case our planning agency characteristically involves cross-intention referential interconnections. It is important to note that in the case of individual planning agency, these cross-intention referential interconnections are among the relations across time that a broadly Lockean theory would see as fundamental to personal identity over time.[15] And we have been exploring a parallel between such cross-temporal Lockean ties in the individual case and the interlocking referential ties between the intentions of the participants in cases of shared intention. Nevertheless, even given this important parallel, we should not infer from the fact that there is a *subject* of an individual planning agent's intentions over time, that there is a *subject* of the shared intention. And, indeed, we have seen reason to reject the idea that there is, quite generally, such a subject of a shared intention.

Is this in conflict with Margaret Gilbert's claim that in shared intentional activity there is always a "plural subject"?[16] Well, it depends on how we are to interpret Gilbert's talk of a plural subject (Gilbert 2000, pp. 19 and 22).[17] On an ambitious interpretation, Gilbert's talk of a plural subject is closely analogous to our talk of an individual subject. In particular, such a plural subject involves a minimally holistic mental web.[18] And I have argued that there need not be a plural subject, in this ambitious sense, for there to be shared intentionality. On a modest reading, Gilbert's talk of a plural subject is only a shorthand for talk of a collection of persons who are jointly committed to a specific joint action. The metaphysics of shared intentionality lies entirely in such joint commitments—commitments that

---

[15] See my "Reflection, Planning, and Temporally Extended Agency" in Bratman (2007).

[16] My remarks in this paragraph draw from my 2009b (pp. 163–4).

[17] J. David Velleman alludes to this interpretive issue in his (1997, p. 201). Velleman himself seeks a theory in the spirit of the first, more ambitious interpretation.

[18] Pettit and Schweikard (2006, p. 32) interpret Gilbert in this way.

can be quite local and quite limited.[19] So interpreted, Gilbert is not claiming that there is a plural subject over and above specific joint commitments, in the way in which there is an individual subject over and above specific intentions of that subject. On this modest interpretation, the appeal to the idea of a plural subject itself does no further philosophical work in Gilbert's theory. In particular, it does not—contrary to what we may have hoped—add to our understanding of what constitutes the *jointness* of joint commitment. On this interpretation of her view, then, Gilbert and I are not disagreeing about the need for a plural subject in shared intentionality; our disagreement is, rather, about how best to understand the interpersonal interrelations that constitute specific cases of shared intentionality. And the key here, as I see it, is the network of conceptual, metaphysical and normative resources provided by the planning theory, and the associated ways in which our planning agency supports both our activities over time and our shared activities with each other.

References

Alonso, F. 2009. Shared intention, reliance, and interpersonal obligations. *Ethics* 119: 444–475.

Baier, A. 1997a. *The common mind*. The Paul Carus Lectures, presented at the 1995 eastern division meetings of the American Philosophical Association. Chicago: Open Court.

Baier, A. 1997b. Doing things with others: The mental commons. In *Commonality and particularity in ethics*, ed. L. Alanen, S. Heimnämaa, and T. Wallgren, 15–44. Basingstoke: Macmillan.

Bratman, M. 1987. *Intention, plans, and practical reason*. Cambridge, MA: Harvard University Press. [Reissued 1999. Stanford: CSLI Publications].

Bratman, M. 1999. *Faces of intention*. Cambridge: Cambridge University Press.

Bratman, M. 2007. Reflection, planning, and temporally extended agency. In *Structures of agency: Essays*, ed. M. Bratman, 21–46. New York: Oxford University Press.

Bratman, M. 2009a. Shared agency. In *Philosophy of the social sciences: Philosophical theory and scientific practice*, ed. C. Mantzavinos, 41–59. Cambridge: Cambridge University Press.

Bratman, M. 2009b. Modest sociality and the distinctiveness of intention. *Philosophical Studies* 144: 149–165.

Bratman, M. 2010. Agency, time, and sociality. *Proceedings and Addresses of the American Philosophical Association* 84(2): 7–26.

Bratman, M. 2014. *Shared agency: a planning theory of acting together*. New York: Oxford University Press (in print).

Davidson, D. 2001a. Agency. In *Essays on actions and events*, ed. D. Davidson, 2nd ed, 43–62. Oxford: Oxford University Press.

Davidson, D. 2001b. Mental events. In *Essays on actions and events*, ed. D. Davidson, 2nd ed, 207–224. Oxford: Oxford University Press.

---

[19]In correspondence (December, 2008) Gilbert noted her preference for this second reading, citing her *A Theory of Political Obligation* (2006, pp. 144f), where she says: "It is useful to have a label for those who are jointly committed with one another in some way. I have elsewhere used the label 'plural subject' for the purpose and shall use it that way here. To put it somewhat formally: A and B (and …) (or those with feature F) constitute a plural subject (by definition) if and only if they are jointly committed to doing something as a body—in a broad sense of 'do'."

Ferrero, L. 2009. What good is a diachronic will? *Philosophical Studies* 144: 403–430.

Gilbert, M. 1990. Walking together: A paradigmatic social phenomenon. *Midwest Studies in Philosophy* 15: 1–14.

Gilbert, M. 2000. What is it for us to intend? In *Sociality and responsibility*, ed. M. Gilbert, 14–36. Lanham: Rowman & Littlefield.

Gilbert, M. 2006. *A theory of political obligation*. Oxford: Oxford University Press.

Gilbert, M. 2009. Shared intention an personal intentions. *Philosophical Studies* 144: 167–187.

Hume, David. 1968 [1739–1740]. Book III, Part II, Section II "Of the origin of justice and property". In *A treatise of human nature*, ed. L.A. Selby-Bigge. Oxford: Oxford University Press.

Hund, J. 1998. Searle's construction of social reality. *Philosophy of the Social Sciences* 28: 122–133.

List, C., and P. Pettit. 2011. *Group agency: The possibility, design, and status of corporate agents*. Oxford: Oxford University Press.

Petersson, B. 2007. Collectivity and circularity. *Journal of Philosophy* 104: 138–156.

Pettit, P., and D. Schweikard. 2006. Joint action and group agents. *Philosophy of the Social Sciences* 36: 18–39.

Rovane, C. 1998. *The bounds of agency: An essay in revisionary metaphysics*. Princeton: Princeton University Press.

Searle, J. 1990. Collective intentions and actions. In *Intentions and communication*, ed. P.R. Cohen, J. Morgan, and M.E. Pollack, 401–415. Cambridge, MA: MIT Press.

Searle, J. 1995. *The construction of social reality*. New York: The Free Press.

Stoutland, F. 1997. Why are philosophers of action so anti-social? In *Commonality and particularity in ethics*, ed. L. Alanen, S. Heimnämaa, and T. Wallgren, 45–74. Basingstoke: Macmillan.

Tomasello, M. 2009. *Why we cooperate*. Cambridge, MA: MIT Press.

Velleman, J.D. 1997. How to share an intention. In *The possibility of practical reason*, ed. J.D. Velleman, 200–220. Oxford: Oxford University Press.

Chapter 16
How Where *We* Stand Constrains Where *I* Stand: Applying Bratman's Account of Self-Governance to Collective Action

Joseph Kisolo-Ssonko

Abstract Certain theories of collective action claim that collective intentions can have a direct normative power over individuals. This chapter seeks to make sense of the relationship between this and the assumed autonomy of individual agents. It is argued that a modified version of Michael Bratman's "self-governance" account of the normative force of individual intentions can be applied to collective intentions. Doing this gives a distinct way to understand the normative interplay between the individual and the collective. It changes the way we must see the universality of the normative force of collective intentions and it emphasises the importance of the individual's agentive identity being entangled with the agentive identity of the collective.

1 Setting the Scene

Accounts of collective action that are collectivist, in the sense defined below, present us with an as yet unresolved task, understanding how a collective intention can normatively constrain the actions of an autonomous individual. In this article I argue that we can shed light on this issue by comparing it with its individual analogue, i.e. understanding how individual intentions can normatively constrain the actions of an autonomous individual. To fully explicate this endeavour I must first set out its background. So let us begin with a scenario, versions of which will be very well-known to those who are familiar with the recent discussions concerning collective action:

> **The argumentative walkers**: A couple are engaged in a long walk to the top of a high hill. As time drags on one of them becomes bored and announces to the other that they intend to abandon the endeavour. "You can't give up", the other reacts, "*We* said *we* would walk to the top!"

J. Kisolo-Ssonko (✉)
Department of Philosophy, Sheffield University, Sheffield, UK
e-mail: j.kisolo-ssonko@sheffield.ac.uk

A. Konzelmann Ziv and H.B. Schmid (eds.), *Institutions, Emotions, and Group Agents,* 263
Studies in the Philosophy of Sociality 2, DOI 10.1007/978-94-007-6934-2_16,
© Springer Science+Business Media Dordrecht 2014

Here, the way in which the keen walker expresses their complaint suggests that it is not grounded on the errant walker's expressed intention being in conflict with their own intention as such (though it may well be in conflict). Rather, the keen walker's complaint appears to be grounded in the conflict between the errant walker's expressed intention and an intention that they *collectively* hold, namely, their intention *as a couple* to walk to the top of the hill. At least, this is how we are invited to read such situations by theories of collective action, which propose that collective intentions can be distinct from the mere sum of the intentions of the individual members of the collective and also propose that they can, nevertheless, impact on the rational deliberation of those individuals.

Margaret Gilbert, from whom the example of the walkers originates,[1] is in this interpretive camp. This does not mean that she believes that collective intentions are instantiated by some mysterious, ontologically distinct, social entity; rather just that she believes they can have a content that is distinct from that of the individual intentions held by the members of the collective. In the case of our two walkers this means that their having the collective intention "We intend to get to the top of the hill", is not just a matter of each personally having the intention "I intend for both of us to get to the top of the hill." Neither does it necessitate that each have such an intention.

Rather than being mere sums of individual intentions, Gilbert believes that collective intentions are formed by individual group members 'joining forces' and 'pooling' their wills to form a 'plural subject' that holds those intentions.[2] This happens by means of it being common knowledge that each individual is willing to form a plural subject on the condition that others are also willing in this way. This process is an *essentially* collective one—individual group members engage in a collective process of generating an intention that holds over them *as a collective*. As Gilbert (1996) says, when the relevant conditions are fulfilled, " . . . all wills are bound simultaneously and interdependently" (p. 185). The fact that this is an essentially collective process opens up the possibility of the collective intention being distinct from the sum of individual intentions and thus the possibility that the collective intention can, potentially, be in conflict with these individual intentions.

The example of the walkers, Gilbert believes, shows that, when there is dispute between that which is required by the collective intention and that which is required by the individual's own intention, an individual can be rebuked if they act on their personal intention against the collective intention. Such a rebuke is legitimate because it is a response to that individual's transgression of what Gilbert calls their "obligation not to act contrary to the shared intention" (Gilbert 2000, p. 17). Now the term 'obligation' carries with it a strong moral flavour. However Gilbert wants us to see this obligation as akin to that which an individual has towards their own individual intentions. That is, just as an individual who intends to *f* has an obligation

---

[1] Gilbert's (1996) example has a slightly different form but illustrates the same point (pp. 177–94).

[2] Gilbert develops these terms from suggestive metaphors into technical terms of art across her work. An early comprehensive exposition can be found in Gilbert (1992), particularly pp. 146–236.

to act in such a way as to bring about *f*, a member of a collective that intends to *g* has the same kind of obligation to act in such a way to bring about *g*. In this way, when Gilbert speaks of forming a collective intention as involving 'joint commitment', she does not mean to indicate any external obligating force, moral or otherwise. Instead she means to indicate a *commitment of the will*, albeit a joint rather than individual one.[3]

Importantly, a difference between collective commitments of the will and individual ones is that while we understand individuals as normally able to absent themselves from the duties imposed by their own personal commitments through merely rescinding them, this is not the case with collective commitments – for just as a collective intention is instantiated collectively, it can only be rescinded collectively. On this model then, the errant walker is reprimandable *directly* because what his declared individual intention demands of him (i.e. to give up on the walk) conflicts with what the intention he holds collectively with the other walker demands of him (i.e. to continue to the top of the hill). Moreover, he cannot absent himself from this criticism by merely abandoning the collective intention; for the collective intention can only be rescinded jointly with the other walker.[4] In this sense I shall speak of collective intentions as normatively constraining individuals.

This then is the departure point for the discussion that follows. It can be summed up in the following two claims:

1. The intentions of a collective can both fail to correspond with, and conflict with, the personal intentions of the members of that collective.
2. An individual faces normative pressure to act in line with the intentions of a collective (that they are a member of), even where this conflicts with what their own personal intentions would have them do.

These conditions, taken together, define what I shall refer to as the 'collectivist model of collective intention'.[5] These proposals are far from uncontroversial and, although Gilbert goes to great lengths to set up her examples such as to exclude any indirect explanation for the obligations,[6] one might think that whatever the descriptive advantages, accepting that an individual can be directly normatively constrained in their action by intentions, other than their own personal intentions, is itself too high a price to pay. Such an objection gains its plausibility from the rather

---

[3]See Gilbert (2000, p. 21) for a comparison between 'personal commitments' and 'collective commitments'.

[4]Gilbert (1996) refers to the requirements of being able to explain these two points as the 'obligation' and the 'permission' criteria (p. 180).

[5]There is some dispute and ambiguity about what makes a theory 'individualist' or 'collectivist'. For my current purposes I do not mean to imply anything more by the term 'collectivist' than that it fits with the two conditions expressed here.

[6]In particular, Gilbert (1996) sets up her example so as to avoid the possibility of the obligations just being "moral" or "merely a matter of prudence or self-interest" (p. 184). The possibility of alternative explanations is also well countered by Abraham Roth (2004) who looks in particular at an explanation based on exchanged promises (pp. 364–69).

fuzzy, but nonetheless intuitively forceful idea that to allow practical motivation to arise from a location external to the individual agent is counter to the fact of individual autonomy.[7]

The plausibility of the intuitions that lie behind such an objection can be seen in the following modification of the walkers' scenario:

> *The presumptuous walker*: Suppose that in her rebuke the keen walker had made reference to her own personal intention rather than to that of the collective—"But you can't stop," she might have said, "I intend for us to walk to the top!"

Now there are *indirect* ways in which this kind of phrase might sometimes be an appropriate, even if rather rudely put rebuke, for example, if the errant walker had promised to do whatever the keen one wanted. However, suppose that we try to account for it in the same way that the collectivist account proposes that we account for the rebuke attached to the collective intention. That is, suppose that we propose that the rebuke is legitimate because one individual can be *directly* normatively constrained by the individual intentions of another. Against such an explanation it appears fair to complain that the individual's autonomy is not being taken into account. Indeed, one might wonder if we have not reduced the agent who is constrained by the intention of the other into a mere puppet controlled by that other.

Now, this case is clearly not completely analogous with that where the keen walker invokes a shared collective intention. Whereas the errant walker is a part of the collective that holds the collective intention, in contrast, he plays no equivalent part in the constitution of the keen walker. It is not immediately clear, however, that this difference makes the concern about autonomy disappear. One might argue that, just as in the presumptuous walker example, the individual has become a puppet of something external to them, in this case a puppet of the collective.

Perhaps we might counter these worries by stipulating that, as a basic fact of being social creatures, we *just can* be directly constrained by the intentions of others. We might think that such a possibility is ignored only because of a prejudicial attachment to a sort of theoretical individualism, a mode of thought that Hans Bernhard Schmid (2009) scathingly calls the 'Cartesian Brainwash' (pp. 29–42). Schmid suggests, *contra* to this theoretical bias, that our actual social experience is of routinely acting directly on the intentions of others without seeing this as being problematic. He gives the simple example of one agent moving aside on a park bench to fulfil the intention of the other to sit down (p. 19). Schmid proposes we label acceptance of this possibility as 'Motivational Heterarky' (p. 19). In a similar vein, Roth (2004) suggests that we accept what he, perhaps more informatively, calls 'Practical Intimacy'. He defines this as the idea that "[i]t is possible for one individual to take up and act on the intention formed by another without re-issuing the latter's intention" (p. 383).

---

[7] I mean to use 'autonomy' here in its broadest sense, rather than in a more demanding sense that might require such things as political freedom, rational desires and the like.

How do these proposals sit with our current concerns? Well, Schmid (2009) believes that there is no reason to think that they pose any challenge to autonomy, for an individual can still be fully autonomous even when acting on the intentions of others, because it can still be 'up to them' whether they act or not. For example, in the case of one agent, A, moving aside on a park bench in order to fulfil the intention of another agent, B, to sit down, "[i]t is not that B somehow acts *directly* through A's behaviour, bypassing and displacing A's agency (. . .). Rather, A's behaviour still instantiates A's own action" (p. 19). Unfortunately such a reply does not quite address the concern about autonomy as I have presented it here, for as Roth points out in his discussion of Gilbert's walkers, the issue is precisely that in these cases it is *not* up to the errant walker whether the collective intention has authority over them. The problem is that the collectivist model proposes that individuals who have formed collectives are thus normatively constrained by the particular intentions of that collective, whether or not, in that instance, they want to be.[8]

So where does this leave us? Schmid and Roth may be right in their insistence that the mere possibility of acting on the intentions of others does not run counter to agentive autonomy. However we need to go further than this if we are to get to grips with the concern about normative constraint by intentions that are not solely one's own. In what follows I want to suggest that the fuzzy idea of agentive autonomy does not provide quite as clear-cut an objection to normative constraint by collective intentions as it might first appear. Straightforwardly we might think that agentive autonomy is compromised by allowing an agent's free choices to be normatively constrained at all. However, we need to note that free agents can, un-problematically, be normatively constrained by their own intentions. We can pose the question; "why is an autonomous agent not free to merely act as they please rather than being constrained by their intentions?" I want to suggest that answering this question can both give us a model that we can apply to understanding normative constraint by collective intentions and also bring to light the necessary limitations of this constraint.

Michael Bratman (1987), with his 'planning theory of agency', provides us with a potential answer to this question. His theory aims to tell us not just why constraint by one's own intentions does not conflict with autonomy but also why it is fundamental for being an autonomous agent at all. Given that collectivist theories propose that we should understand the constraint of collective intentions as being of the same type as the constraint issuing from individual intentions, there seems to be clear motivation for attempting to apply an explanation that mirrors Bratman's account of individual intentions to collective intentions.[9]

---

[8] Roth's (2004) own solution to this problem rests on the idea that in certain circumstances one agent can have authority over the actions of another (pp. 391–97).

[9] This is not a use to which Bratman, as far as I am aware, has attempted to put his theory of (individual) intentionality. This should not surprise us, as Bratman rejects the collectivist account of collective intentionality. In contrast he believes, roughly, that collective intentions require the existence of interlocking of conditional personal intentions which have the same orientation towards the collective act, and thus does not allow the possibility of conflict between

2   Constraint by Intentions and Self-Governance

Bratman starts from the fact that intentions pervade our practical lives. Such intentions come in various guises; some are very short term (such as my intention to finish typing this paragraph before I pause for a rest); others are longer (such as my intention to finish the whole chapter by the end of the day); and others much longer (such as my intention to write more chapters this year than I did last). As Bratman (2000) notes, the holding of intentions is part of us seeing "...ourselves as agents who persist over time, who begin, develop and then complete temporally extended activities and projects" (p. 35). Having such intentions means that we do not have to treat each moment as one where we must decide what to do, instead we can follow the path our preformed intentions set for us. We might say then that intentions act like the scaffolding supporting the construction of a bridge, for, just as the scaffolding once erected constrains the bridge's developing shape, intentions once formed provide stable platforms from which we can construct our practical lives. This metaphor is apt, for, stretched just a little further, it brings us to Bratman's second key insight: just as scaffolding can only facilitate the construction of a bridge if once erected it is rigid enough to hold the relevant materials in place, our intentions can help us structure our practical lives only if they constrain the valid choices available to us.

This point can be further elucidated by comparing intentions with desires. On one level intentions and desires are similar; both contain descriptions of certain sets of affairs, and both can be said to motivate us towards those sets of affairs. So, a desire to keep fit has the same aim as an intention to keep fit, and either, if held by me, would motivate me towards exercise. In this sense both are, to use Donald Davidson's (1963) terminology, 'pro-attitudes', that is, they are attitudes that put us in a positive relation to some set of affairs. However, while our desires do motivate us to live in certain ways, unlike our intentions they do not normatively constrain our actions. Thus it is not the case that an agent who desires to x behaves incorrectly if they do not act in such a way as to bring about x. This is not just because we generally hold a host of conflicting desires, though it makes such persistent plurality conceptually understandable. Rather, it is because even where a desire is more strongly held than all conflicting desires, it still fails to structure our options in the way that intentions do.

Being constrained in this way by intentions is of much instrumental value. It is, as Bratman (2004) notes, a "more or less all-purpose, universal means" to any end (p. 1). This is true, firstly, because you cannot usually just make it the case that what you intend just comes about—you need to do those things that are needed to bring it about, in order to bring it about. Moreover, if you do not want to be at cross purposes, to bring about things other than that which you wish to bring about,

---

the collective's intentions and the individual's personal intentions (see Bratman 1999, pp. 93–142). Nor should it preclude us from attempting to do so, for his non-collective account of collective intentionality does not directly or necessarily follow from this account of individual intentions.

holding conflicting intentions will frustrate you in achieving your aim. Given this instrumental value we might give the following explanation of the normative force of intentions:

> ***Instrumental explanation***: Intentions have the power to normatively constrain an agent's actions because of the instrumental benefit of the effect of this constraint for said agent.

Does this explanation hold up? It certainly explains why it is reasonable to expect a sensible agent to let themselves be guided by their intentions. However, it does not necessarily follow, from the fact that being constrained by intentions is useful for achieving our ends, that an agent must stick to these rules in *every particular case*. As John Broome (1999) notes, intentions appear to be 'strict' normative relations; that is, they require that those who have them act appropriately, rather than 'slack' normative relations, that is relations that merely recommend that they do (p. 409).[10] Or as Bratman (2009) puts it, intentions appear to have a "... noninstrumental normative significance in the particular case, a significance that is distinctive in the sense that it is not merely a matter of the promotion of your particular ends" (p. 418). This is most clear in cases which involve intentions that have bad ends. So, for example, I might intend to push over an old lady (which would be morally reprehensible), or I might intend to cut myself (which would have a negative effect on my health). In both of these cases, the fact that objectively speaking we probably should not positively value the intended ends does not appear to change the fact that if I intend them and yet fail to be constrained by those intentions, then (in some sense) I am in error.[11] We can say that the power of intentions appears to be universal in that it applies in each particular case.

So, what then provides this distinctive non-instrumental reason for abiding by our intentions?[12] Bratman's answer is that "... our reason for conforming to these norms of practical rationality derives in part from our reason to govern our own lives" (2009, p. 412). At first this might seem odd; following the rules that append intentions constrains our practical deliberation—how can something that constrains us make us more able to govern our own lives? Isn't autonomy freedom from constraint? Bratman's response takes inspiration from the work of Harry Frankfurt in

---

[10]Thanks to an anonymous referee for pointing out the relevance of Broome's work on this point.

[11]While it seems clear to me that the idea that evil intentions constrain us fits with the natural folk experience of the situation, those coming to action theory via a concern with the foundations of ethical action, often find it problematic for us to be normatively constrained to commit bad ends. Bratman (2009) admits that in the past he tried to avoid the conclusion that we can have such constraints (p. 443n.75), but he (2009) now admits that they do exist as there is an intrinsic reason for self governance even where "... self governance involves volitionally necessary bad ends" (p. 443).

[12]Bratman (2009) accepts that it is possible to reject the idea that there is a distinctive non-instrumental normative force. He calls theories that do so 'Myth theories'. However, given that the norms of practical reasoning do present themselves to us as compelling, he believes that one should only accept a myth theory if one cannot give a compelling account of the power of these norms (pp. 418–19).

proposing that being able to govern one's own actions requires more than merely being free to act as one pleases;[13] it requires that we can identify the process that brings about our action as being governance by our very selves. As we shall see, Bratman believes that being constrained by our own intentions is a necessary part of us being the kind of agents who can do this. His position can be summed up as follows:

> *Self-governance explanation*: Intentions have the power to normatively constrain an agent's actions because of the necessity of the structure such constraint provides, for said agent to be able to govern their actions.

Understanding Bratman's self-governance explanation starts by noting the complexity of human psychology: our beliefs, desires, memories and other psychological states change as time passes, and, even in any one particular moment, we will hold a diverse array of mental states, some of which may even be contradictory. However, even though our psychological content is heterogeneous, when any part of it causes us to act, we consider our actions to be those of a single unified agent. This is most apparent at times when we do not feel we have truly governed our acts, as in the example of smashing an inkpot that David Velleman (2000) quotes from Sigmund Freud. In this example Freud notes that as he sat down to write at his desk he moved his hand in "... a remarkably clumsy way" and knocked an inkstand to the floor (p. 2). Freud's explanation for this was that his sister had recently remarked that the inkstand was ugly, and that by sweeping it to the floor he was carrying out the execution of the condemned inkstand. Here, although the behaviour seems motivated by a part of Freud's psychology (his urge to get rid of the now unwanted ink stand) it is not something he wants to say *he* did. In a similar vein, Frankfurt (1997) gives an example of an unwilling addict, who finds himself injecting a drug even feeling as if he is being controlled by an alien force (p. 49). In both these cases something is missing, something that would make us more ready to say that the behaviours could be characterised as authentic actions.

So we see ourselves as having the potential to act as single unified agents, yet this possibility appears to require something in addition to the mere fact that behaviour comes about as a result of elements of our psychic stew. Frankfurt's (1997) solution to this quandary, with which Bratman agrees, is that our actions must arise from a standpoint that we can identify with. As Bratman (2009) notes, "... it is only if there is a place where you stand that *you* are governing in the corresponding domain, for in self-governance where you stand guides relevant thought and action" (p. 431). How though do we move from our heterogeneous psychological content to having the potential to act from a standpoint that is authentically ours? Or to put the question another way, what makes the diverse set of mental attributes into something that is both unified and the causal effects of which are identifiable with governance by ourselves as agents?

---

[13]Frankfurt (1971) says being able to do whatever one desires, though it captures an element of freedom, "... misses entirely ... the particular content of the quite different idea of an agent whose will is free" (p. 14).

Bratman's answer stands in a Lockean tradition in that it seeks to explain the unity of the self in terms of psychological continuities bringing about "... cross-temporal organization and integration of thought and action" (Bratman, 2009, p. 430). While he acknowledges that we can be united by mental links of many types (such as memories and the like), he believes that intentions provide an especially strong kind of bond, a bond that has the power to make a standpoint not only united *but also governing*. Intentions not only unify an agent but give them a 'where I stand' from where their actions can be governed. They can do this because of the way in which they structure future rational deliberation. If we did not see intentions as necessarily structuring our future reasoning in this way, then they would not be the kind of thing that has the power of speaking for us and they would thus have the same status as desires. We can have inconsistent desires without this devastating where we stand because desires, by themselves, are not enough to determine where we stand. Here, my earlier comparison, between an agent who merely desires to keep fit and one who intends to, is germane. If an agent has the desire to keep fit, but not the intention, then if she fails to keep fit, she, other things being equal, commits no error. However, if she has an intention to keep fit then this frames what she ought to do—we can say that it frames her standpoint.

In summary then, the explanation for the normative force of the rules that append intentions in every particular case, is that seeing these rules as obligatory is a necessary element in the metaphysics of self-governance, that is, in making oneself into a united agent capable of governing.

3   Constraint by Collective Intentions and Collective Self-Governance

Let us now return to the main topic of the chapter, collective intentions. Recall that we are starting from the assumption that collectivist accounts of collective intentions are correct, and further, that these accounts see the normative constraint issuing from collective intentions as having the same kind of character as individual intentions. Within this framework it makes sense to suppose that collective intentions structure the practical choices of collectives, just as individual intentions structure those of individuals. This can be seen in the example of our walkers; they have the collective intention to walk to the top of the hill and it is as natural to suppose that they would be constrained by this, as it is to suppose that they would be constrained by their own individual intention to walk to the top of the hill—if they collectively intend to walk to the top of the hill then they cannot rightly also intend to abandon the walk half way up, nor can they rightly intend not to wear down the path to the top of the hill if we know that walking to the top of the hill will require this. Further, their collective intention to walk to the top of the hill structures their practical lives; for example, it settles the practical questions of what they should do as they progress past different landmarks (i.e. keep going until they reach the hill's summit) thus allowing them not to have to deliberate at each stop.

Given the above, we should be able to take Bratman's account and simply plug collective intentions into the place occupied by individual intentions. This results in the following:

Collective self-governance explanation: Collective intentions have the power to normatively constrain because of the necessity of the structure such constraint provides, for the collective to be able to govern its actions.

From here, it appears to follow that collective intentions can play the same part in constructing a where-we-stand as individual intentions play in constructing a where-I-stand; i.e. that they can give us a collective standpoint. Moreover, it then follows that we can say that it is only if there is a place where *we* stand that *we* are governing in the corresponding domain. That this seems to hold in the collective case, as in the individual case, can be seen in the following example: imagine that our walking couple are setting out on their hill climbing adventure on a particularly hot day. Let us suppose that there are two ways to get to the start of the hill. One is short and quick and best facilitates starting the hill climb, the other is much longer and requires wading through a river. It seems that in such a situation, just as Freud's subconscious desire to smash his ink pot could lead him to do so, our walkers might have unexpressed desires to get wet in order to cool off, and these could lead them to take the longer path without individually realising or collectively expressing their motives. While the walkers' collective act of ascending the hill is something that they can lay full authoritative claim to as being their action, something that they truly *do* as a collective, conversely this is not the case with their diverting along the path that takes them through the river. There is a need for an authentic collective standpoint for us to achieve collective action, just as there is need for an authentic individual standpoint for us to achieve individual action.

Given the above, the argument can therefore progress as it did in the individual case. Just as an individual not seeing her own intentions as normatively constraining undermines her own ability to act from a standpoint she can identify with herself, the members of a collective not seeing their collective intentions as normatively constraining also undermines their ability to act from a standpoint they can identify as *their* own collective standpoint. In the case of our walkers, this means that if they do not see their collective intentions in general, and their collective intention to climb to the top of the hill in particular, as normatively constraining upon them, they will fail to form a collective agent capable of the intentional act of collectively walking to the top of the hill.

One possible objection to this line of reasoning is that just because a collective fails to be an agent this does not necessarily mean that it will fail to be a collective per se. There may be other ways in which we can identify the collective as a coherent whole, for example, that its members have common characteristics or certain physical relationships between each other and such like. Alternatively, we might consider it to be a single entity because of its legal or conventional status as one. This is correct; however, these facts do not blunt the force of the argument above, just as the following similar point does not blunt the argument regarding individual intentions. One could still identify an individual who failed to be bound by their own intentions as being a unified thing *of some sort*; this could be achieved by reference to their physical properties, to their social position, or their legal standing and so on. However, whilst being a united thing of some sort, this person would fail to be an agent united in a way that made her capable of governing her own actions. The same holds true for the collective; it is not what it takes to be a united object of any sort that is relevant, but rather what it takes to be united as a possible agent of actions.

4   The Relationship between Individual Self-Governance and the Necessity for Collective Self-Governance

Assuming that the above argument is sound, i.e. that there really is a correspondence between that which explains the unity of the individual standpoint and that which explains the unity of the collective standpoint, then, just as individual intentions have force over the individual, collective intentions have force over collectives. Unfortunately, this does not yet quite get us where we need to be as it is not yet completely clear what is at stake for the individual in the collectives achieving agentive action.

The intrinsic reason that each individual has for their own self-governance cannot be straightforwardly transposed onto the collective case. In the case of the individual, the agent cannot abandon their own perspective—they have no other perspective to fall back on. Conversely, in the case of an agent's attachment to the collective perspective, we might wonder why that agent cannot simply abandon the perspective of the 'we' and retreat back to the perspective of the 'I'. What we are justified, at this juncture, in making is the conditional claim that if an agent does want to see their actions as part of a collective action then they must see the intentions of that collective as normatively constraining, for it does not make sense for an agent to see their actions as part of a collective action if they fail to be able to rightly see the collective as acting. Accepting this gives us the following:

Conditional collective self-governance explanation: Collective intentions have the power to normatively constrain because

1. the agent sees their individual action as part of a collective action,
2. (1) requires that the collective can act,
3. collective intentions being normatively constraining provides the structure necessary for the collective to be able to govern its actions and thus to act.

This explanation does appear to show how collective intentions can be strict normative relations, in Broome's sense, for, if an agent wants to see their action as part of a collective action then this does not merely recommend that they see the collective intentions as normatively constraining, rather it requires it. However, it might be complained that the conditionality of this argument nullifies the force of what I set out as the second criteria of collectivist accounts; namely that an individual faces normative pressure to act in line with the intentions of a collective (that they are a member of), even where this conflicts with what their own personal intentions would have them do. There now appears to be an easy way for the agent to escape from those normative pressures, i.e. they can just stop seeing their actions as part of the collective action. Keith Graham (2007) appears to mark this point when he suggests that "[p]recisely because we are individuals whose existence is not exhausted in the social relations we participate in and the groups to which we belong, questions can arise about whether to identify with or dissociate from collective agencies of which we are members" (p. 8). Thus, in the example of our walkers, the errant walker appears to be free to dismiss the keen walker's rebuke on the grounds that it is inappropriate because they simply reject that they are part of a collective actor.

What is to stop our errant walker doing this? Well, seeing actions as collective does have its pragmatic advantages. It allows us to navigate a social world which is populated by a vast number of different individuals without having to consider each individual as such. We can engage rather with collectives. Being able to consider practical questions from a collective perspective also seems to solve problems of the rationality of co-operation in 'prisoner's dilemma' type cases as co-operation is indisputably the most rational choice from the collective standpoint.[14] Clearly, not being able to understand the world in terms of collective action has many disadvantages. This gives us a forceful pragmatic reason to be able to understand the collectives we are part of as potential agents of collective actions. However, if this reason is only pragmatic then why is it not easily trumped by the other pragmatic demands of an agent's own standpoint? As we have already seen, the move from general rules to particular norms is difficult. Whilst we might have a *general* reason to maintain the identity of collective agents in this way, this does not necessarily give us a reason *in each particular case*.

This is not to say that an individual cannot perform actions that involve others merely for pragmatic reasons. Take Bratman's (1999) own example of interaction that falls short of collective action; suppose that I am a gangster and that, "I intended that we go to New York together as a result of my kidnapping you and forcing you to join me" (p. 100). Imagine that I gave you a choice; either you act as if we are travelling together or I have your parents murdered. You would have a strong pragmatic reason to go along with my scheme and take part in what, to onlookers, may appear to be a collective act. This would be an interesting kind of social interaction but it would not be authentic collective action. One could consider us to be a unit of sorts, united by our physical proximity, our interdependence or perhaps our mutual goal. However, we would not be bound *as an agent*. Thus we would not be entangled with a collective will and both of us would be free to act contrary to the mutual goal (of travelling on the plane together) without being concerned about this destroying the potential of our collective to act, although of course you would rightly be very concerned about maintaining the fiction of our collective act so that I did not carry out my threat.

---

[14]For example, see Hollis (1998) for an elucidation of what he calls the 'team work' solution to problems of the rationality of cooperation (particularly pp. 137–42).

Most social situations, however, are not like that of being kidnapped. In more typical social situations we do not conceive of ourselves as merely pragmatically interacting with others. Rather we *do* see ourselves as involved in authentically collective acts. Further, we do not stand outside of each instance of social interaction and at each moment choose whether to engage in collective action—rather we find ourselves *already bound up in* many ongoing social projects. This can be seen by moving from our hill climbers to an example of some real life climbers found in the following quote: "When asked who reached the summit of Everest first, Hillary and Tenzing have always insisted that they climbed it together and that there is therefore little point to that question—after all, *they* did" (Ebert and Robertson 2010, p. 102). Here, it seems to me, the climbers are noting that as they have already understood their endeavour as collective they cannot now, post-hoc, reconceptualise it as an individual feat. Graham (2007) seems to be noting a similar point in saying that "[s]ome of the things that people do gain their significance from being part of some collective action" (p. 60).

My argument is, then, that we can assess our reason for sustaining the collective's potential to act in two parts; firstly, prior to doing so and secondly, post doing so. We can say that, given the general utility of collective action, each of us has a general reason to engage and enable it (a slack normative relation). However, following this, we can say that once we have done so, continuing to do so becomes necessary, because if we do not then we will not be able to fully make sense of our contributory actions as the type of actions we intended them to be (a strict normative relation). We set up our actions to be contributions to social agency because it is beneficial to do so. Once we have done so, we can only continue to understand our contributory action as the kind of thing we set it out to be if we are able to see the collective as an agent capable of governing our collective actions, and because this requires its intentions to constrain, we must see them as doing so. Post-hoc reconceptualising our contributions is logically possible but seems to be a kind of inauthenticity for that is how, at the moment of our actions, we set them out to be.

This account has the form of a two-part transcendental argument, for it starts with people's experience and says that our social lives are such that we feel ourselves to be part of collective actions. It then presents (firstly) the existence of a collective capable of governing its own actions as necessary for us to have this experience, and (secondly) the constraint of individuals by collective intentions as conceptually necessary for the existence of the collective as an agent. From this it concludes that collective intentions must constrain individuals.

Transcendental collective self-governance explanation: Collective intentions have the power to normatively constrain because

1. as a contingent, but actual and beneficial, fact an agent is engaged in collective action.
2. given (1) the agent must understand their individual action as part of a collective action.
3. (2) requires that the collective can act.
4. collective intentions being normatively constraining provides the structure necessary for the collective to be able to govern its actions and thus to act.

To return to our hill walkers, on such an account, they have a general pragmatic reason to start walking together, given the importance of such collective actions. This pragmatic reason does not force them to engage in collective action. They may, for instance, feel that walking up the hill as individuals, perhaps individuals under contract to help each other if needed, is just as individually beneficial as fully-fledged collective action. If they do so they will not be constrained by the normative constraints of a collective intention although they may face other normative pressures, such as fulfilling their contracts to each other. However, if they do decide to engage in collective action then, once they are doing so, their understanding of their own contributory action will be bound up with the existence of the collective act. This will require them to continue to see the collective as capable of governing its action. This in turn means that they must see themselves as having to abide by the norms that append the collective intention to walk to the top of the hill, because failure to do so will result in failure for them to be able to understand their contributive behaviour as such, and thus failure to fully understand what they are doing.

We can conclude, then, that an individual's reason for seeing themselves as constrained by the intentions of a collective of which they are a member is both similar to and different from that which they have for being bound by their own intentions. It is similar in that it is a matter of securing a unitary standpoint which can be the authentic agent of actions. However, it is different because the securing of this standpoint is not an a priori necessity for the individual. Rather, it becomes a necessity only after the fact of social interaction.

Modifying Bratman's account allows us to understand collectivist accounts of collective intention, such as Gilbert's, as rightly saying that collective intentions are projects of constructing binding collective commitments. However, it does so only if we accept that for the members of these collectives the strictness of these commitments is conditional on the extent to which their understanding of their own actions is entangled with the agency of the collective act. Given their entanglement in various plural agencies the socially situated autonomous individual is faced with a choice: (1) accept the normative constraint of the collective intention or (2) abandon the possibility of collective self-governance. Unlike abandoning the possibility of individual self-governance the latter option is not completely barred to the agent, for the agent can fall back onto their own individual agency. However this option is not without cost, for, given our contingent but actual social experiences, our own sense of self is bound up with our sense of belonging to and acting as part of a collective.

References

Bratman, M. 1987. *Intentions, plans, and practical reason*. Cambridge, MA: Harvard University Press.
Bratman, M. 1999. *Faces of intention: Selected essays on intention and agency*. Cambridge: Cambridge University Press.

Bratman, M. 2000. Reflection, planning and temporally extended agency. *Philosophical Review* 109(1): 35–61.

Bratman, M. 2004. Shared valuing and frameworks for practical reasoning. In *Reason and value*, ed. R.G. Wallace, P. Pettit, S. Scheffler, and M. Smith, 1–27. Oxford: Oxford University Press.

Bratman, M. 2009. Intention, practical rationality and self-governance. *Ethics* 119: 411–443.

Broome, J. 1999. Normative requirements. *Ratio (new series)* XII: 398–419.

Davidson, D. 2001 [1963]. Actions, reasons and causes. In *Essays on actions and events*, 3–20. Oxford: Oxford University Press.

Ebert, P., and R. Roberson. 2010. Mountaineering and the value of self-sufficiency. In *Climbing—Philosophy for everyone*, ed. S.E. Schmid. West Sussex: Wiley-Blackwell.

Frankfurt, H. 1971. Freedom of the will and the concept of a person. *Journal of Philosophy* 68(1): 5–20.

Frankfurt, H. 1997. The problem of action. In *The philosophy of action*, ed. A. Mele, 42–52. Oxford: Oxford University Press.

Gilbert, M. 1992. *On social facts*. Princeton: Princeton University Press.

Gilbert, M. 1996. *Living together: Rationality, sociality and obligation*. Lanham: Rowman & Littlefield.

Gilbert, M. 2000. *Sociality and responsibility: New essays in plural subject theory*. Lanham: Rowman & Littlefield.

Graham, K. 2007. *Practical reasoning in a social world*. Cambridge: Cambridge University Press.

Hollis, M. 1998. *Trust within reason*. Cambridge: Cambridge University Press.

Roth, A.S. 2004. Shared agency and contralateral commitments. *Philosophical Review* 113(3): 359–410.

Schmid, H.B. 2009. *Plural action: Essays in philosophy and social science*. Dordrecht/Heidelberg/London: Springer.

Velleman, D. 2000. *The possibility of practical reason*. Oxford: Oxford University Press.

Chapter 17
Team Reasoning and Shared Intention

Abraham Sesshu Roth

Abstract "Team reasoning"—understood as fundamentally different from individual instrumental reasoning—has been proposed as a solution to a problem of strategic interaction discussed in game theory. But this form of reasoning has been deployed recently in philosophical discussion about shared agency and joint action, in particular to characterize the special "participatory" intention an individual has when acting with another. The main point of the chapter is that constraints on intending raise some challenges for this approach to participatory intention. If team reasoning rationally yields a participatory intention to A, it would require a belief or presumption on the part of the agent regarding what fellow participants will do—namely, that they or enough of them will also employ team reasoning. But what warrants this assumption? I contend that some ways of defending it are incompatible with what originally motivates team reasoning as a solution to a problem of strategic interaction. I will argue that if, as its proponents insist, team reasoning is to be fundamentally distinct from individual instrumental reasoning, then it must invoke a notion of a rational yet non-evidential warrant for belief. The distinctiveness of team reasoning would require, in general, that a team reasoner's belief or expectation that other participants are also team reasoners is rational, but not acquired in the way that rational belief as it is usually understood should be acquired, that is, on the basis of evidence.

What, if anything, distinguishes the intention I have when acting on my own from what we might call the *participatory intention* I have when acting with another? Some say that my participatory intention in what is variously called *shared activity* or *joint action* is an ordinary intention but with special collective content; others

A.S. Roth (✉)
Department of Philosophy, Ohio State University, 350 University Hall, 230 N. Oval Mall, Columbus, Ohio, 43210 USA
e-mail: roth.263@osu.edu

A. Konzelmann Ziv and H.B. Schmid (eds.), *Institutions, Emotions, and Group Agents*, Studies in the Philosophy of Sociality 2, DOI 10.1007/978-94-007-6934-2_17,

contend that the attitude itself is somehow primitively collective. My focus here is a recent suggestion that points instead to the distinctive form of reasoning that is said to issue in the intention. This "team reasoning"—understood as fundamentally different from individual instrumental reasoning—has been proposed as a solution to a problem of strategic interaction discussed in game theory. I will not attempt any detailed discussion of the theory of team reasoning itself; though I raise some questions about it, much of it will be taken for granted here. The focus, rather, is the theory's deployment in philosophical discussion about shared agency and joint action. My main point is that constraints on intending make it difficult to understand just how team reasoning might be used to characterize the participatory intentions essential for shared activity. If team reasoning rationally yields a participatory intention to A, it would require a belief or presumption on the part of the agent regarding what fellow participants will do—namely, that they or enough of them will also employ team reasoning. But what warrants this assumption? I contend that some ways of defending it are incompatible with what originally motivates team reasoning as a solution to a problem of strategic interaction. I will argue that if team reasoning is to be fundamentally distinct from individual instrumental reasoning, then it must invoke a notion of a rational yet non-evidential warrant for belief. The distinctiveness of team reasoning would require, in general, that a team reasoner's belief or expectation that other participants are also team reasoners is rational, but not acquired in the way that rational belief should be acquired, that is, on the basis of evidence.

1 The Basic Problem of Participatory Intention

What one is up to when, in the relevant sense, one is acting together with another is quite different from what one is up to when acting on one's own. For example, going for a stroll with a friend is different from walking in proximity to a stranger whose path on a city street happens to converge with yours. And this is so, even if your walk is coordinated with the stranger's insofar as the two of you keep some appropriate distance and don't run into each other.[1] Now, if what one is up to is a matter of one's intention (or the intentions with which one acts), then the distinction between shared activity and merely coordinated actions of individuals is at least in part a matter of the intentions of the individuals involved: there's something about my intention when I walk together with a friend that makes it a participatory intention, distinct from my intention when I walk in proximity to and in some coordination with a stranger. What, then, is the difference?

---

[1] Gold and Sugden (2007) give examples of individual actions that are coordinated (in the sense of being in Nash equilibrium), and yet intuitively do not count as shared activity. See also Bratman (2009) in this regard. But the difference is not just a third-personal fact about the nature of the coordination between individuals; it is also reflected in how it is for each participant, which is what the *what one is up to* locution is meant to capture. There is, moreover, the normative difference between the cases emphasized by Gilbert, who introduced this example. For recent discussion, see her 2009. I discuss the normative issue in Roth (2004).

One thought is that in shared activity what I'm up to involves more than just my own actions; I intend the entirety of our activity, J.[2] My intention concerns, for example, our walking together. For Bratman, this has to involve the idea of the intention that we J. This locution serves to highlight parallels Bratman sees between intention and the propositional attitude of belief. But if one finds this way of talking awkward, think of it alternatively in terms of an intention of the form: I intend to J with you. Either way we construe it, the proposal runs up against a number of plausible conditions on intending. For instance, many think that one can only intend one's own actions.[3] Even if we try to take advantage of the alternative locution and insist that my J-ing with you is my own action, it is unclear whether I have the control or authority to settle or conclude that I will do it with you. Indeed, if I am in a position to form an intention and settle what we all do (or settle that I do this with you), then this suggests that I have authority or control over fellow participants—hardly compatible, it would seem, with the activity being shared.[4]

Why not then attribute to a participant something more modest? The intention to do one's *part* in shared activity does not encompass the actions of fellow participants. Thus, it doesn't run afoul of the own action condition and entails no problematic authority over others.[5]

But this doesn't capture what it is that I'm up to in acting with you. Take the case of walking together. If we suppose that my part is simply to walk at a certain pace, then the proposal would be that I have an intention to walk at that pace. The problem becomes evident when we consider what happens when you stumble and fall. If my intention is simply to walk at some pace, I could very well continue walking and leave you in the dust, without stopping and helping you up. Indeed, my intention of walking at some standard pace is entirely consistent with attempting to trip you or otherwise undermining your contribution to what we're doing. So, the intention understood in this thin sense doesn't capture what the agent is up to. Even if nothing happens that would prompt me to leave you in the dust, etc., and our actions are coordinated without a hitch, the point is that on this thin understanding, the intention that is to represent what I'm up to in acting with you fails to rule out doing things entirely incompatible with shared or even merely coordinated action.[6]

---

[2]Searle (1990), Bratman (1992), and Velleman (2001). Bratman (1993) makes clear that a commitment on everyone's part to the entire activity makes sense of the coordination; it would not be reasonable to rely on others the way we do in shared activity unless there is some such commitment. And the thought is that this commitment can be understood in terms of intention.

[3]For a defense against this challenge, see Bratman (2014). See also Roth (2013).

[4]In the end, I don't think that such an authority is incompatible with shared activity. See Roth (2013).

[5]See for example Tuomela and Miller (1988), Kutz (2000). Tuomela's (2005) addresses criticism of his earlier statement.

[6]What about the intention not merely to walk at a certain pace, but to keep pace with you, where keeping pace is cooperatively neutral? It's not clear that this captures what I'm up to when acting with you. Stalking involves the intention to keep pace with someone, and yet what one is up to when stalking someone is far from what one is up to in walking with them.

One might object that I'm not taking seriously the idea of doing one's part in shared activity. So suppose we avail ourselves of a more robust conception of *part*, so that each participant intends to do his part in shared activity as such. This would appear to rule out attempts to undermine a partner's contribution, and offers the prospect of capturing what an agent is up to in shared activity. But it creates another problem. It's not clear that I can actually will my part so understood, if your contribution is not forthcoming.[7] My intention would seem to require that your contribution and our J-ing be a settled matter; but when was this settled? Doesn't your being settled on it depend on my being settled?[8] How then could I rely on your being settled in order to form my intention? The intentions of the participants are supposed to settle the matter; but it seems that each of those intentions presupposes what they are supposed to accomplish.

To sum up: We understand what one is up to in shared activity in terms of one's intentions. An intention concerning the entire activity does capture what I'm up to when acting with another, but seems to entail an authority over others incompatible with the activity being shared. We might instead opt for the strategy that appeals to the intention to do one's part. But this strategy leads to a dilemma. Either we have a thin understanding of 'part', in which case we don't account for what one is up to in shared activity. Whereas, a robust conception of part presupposes shared activity/intention in taking as settled the activity that the intention was supposed to establish. We might call this the Settling Problem, since a participatory intention seems to entail settling what another will do in a way that is incompatible with shared activity, or else problematically presupposes as settled the contributions of fellow participants.[9]

Before proceeding, we might wonder whether participatory intentions could be understood in terms of the even more modest *intention to do A in the hope that others will also join*. That is, one intends to do A with the *aim* that we J, or as part of an attempt at getting us to J. But such an intention also fails to capture what I'm up to as a participant. An analogy might help illustrate the sort of point I want to make. Suppose that I'm making a rude gesture in your direction, and that you are facing me and see it. Then I'm offending you, and my intention is to do so. If I know you are facing away and can't see it, then my intention would be not to offend you, but perhaps to let off some steam. It seems that there isn't a common intention across the two cases.[10] One way to try to make sense of the rude gesture case (where I'm

---

[7] This is over and above the worry that such a specification of the intention threatens circularity. The circularity worry is that an account in terms of the robust intention presupposes an understanding of the concept of shared activity which, if not the very notion we're trying to elucidate, is awfully close (Searle 1990, p. 405).

[8] I don't mean to suggest that nothing can be said to address this problem. For example, perhaps I can form the intention because I *predict* your contribution. See below. I discuss my concerns with the predictive strategy more fully elsewhere.

[9] See Velleman (1997).

[10] My intention to move my arm just so, when prompted by the intention of offending you, is quite different from my intention of moving my arm the same way when prompted by the intention to let off steam.

not sure which way you're facing) denies, for example, that I'm intending to offend you, at least in the sense of intending according to which I can settle the matter. Rather, what I'm doing is at best a prelude to offending you. I'm taking a preliminary step, seeing whether what happens is that you'll be offended, or that I'll merely let off some steam. But taking this preliminary step to see what happens is hardly a commitment to what turns out to happen, hardly, for example, to will the offense. It's quite different from what I'm up to when I make the gesture right in your face.

This point also applies to shared activity. Part of the problem here is that the project is that of defining or articulating the intention *constituting* the individual's contribution to shared intention, and his or her involvement in joint activity. An intention that doesn't settle for me my involvement, that I see as something that may or may not lead to intention and activity that's shared, hardly fits the bill. I suppose the thought is that the commitment to the activity comes from intending something that is aimed at the activity, where aiming doesn't entail settling in the way that intention does. I worry that this doesn't suffice for commitment, for one might aim at two different and incompatible ends, for example when one seeks to marry X, and also Y, thinking that this increases the chances of marrying only one.[11] To adapt the example for the shared case: X and I make plans to get married. I aim to do my part in X and myself getting married. But Y and I also make plans to get married. I likewise aim to do my part in that. I can aim for both of these things. But in aiming at these incompatible things, what I'm up to in either of the activities is fundamentally different from what I'm up to in intending and committing to only one of them.

2   Team Reasoning

But perhaps there remains a way of characterizing the intention to do one's part that doesn't presuppose shared activity as settled, but which captures the appropriate attitude the participant has to the activity. The approach I'd like to investigate appeals to the aforementioned theory of team reasoning emerging from a recent strand of the literature on strategic interaction. At least on some versions of this approach, nothing in the form and content of the participatory intention distinguishes it from an ordinary individual intention. What makes this sort of intention distinctive (and a candidate for capturing the difference between shared activity and merely coordinated individual behavior) is the special team reasoning that leads to it. We find this approach in Bacharach (2006), and taken up in Gold and Sugden (2007). Thus,

> team reasoning was originally introduced to explain how, when individuals are pursuing collective goals, it can be rational to choose strategies that realize scope for common gain. But it also provides an account of the formation of collective intentions ... it is natural to regard the intentions that result from team reasoning as collective intentions. (Gold and Sugden 2007, p. 126; see also pp. 110, 121)

---

[11] Bratman (1987).

Table 17.1 The Hi-Lo game

		You	
		A	**B**
Me	**A**	10, 10	0, 0
	B	0, 0	1, 1

But what is this team reasoning in terms of which we're to characterize participatory intentions? Consider the sort of scenario that has been used to motivate it, the two-person case of Hi-Lo (Table 17.1). In this game, each of the players has two options, A and B. For example, A could be the strategy expressed by the player as "I pick the King of Hearts", and B the strategy expressed by "I pick the Three of Spades". Each gets a prize if both pick the same option, but in one case (both adopt the same strategy A of picking a King of Hearts, say) the prize is much greater than the other (both adopt the same strategy B of picking a Three of Hearts). No prize is awarded if they don't pick the same option. All this, and the rationality of each player (in the sense of maximizing individual expected benefit), is common knowledge.

Intuitively, the upper left box is the uniquely rational option. But the best reply reasoning of standard game theory does not favor this outcome over the lower right, which is also a Nash equilibrium. According to ordinary individual instrumental reasoning, one should act in such a way as to maximize one's expected benefit, given one's beliefs—among which are expectations about what others (in this case, you) will do. Thus, given that I believe that you (will) play A, I should play A; this would be my best reply to what you do. However, the same line of reasoning could be made in favor of playing B: given that I believe that you (will) play B, my best reply would be to play B. Thus, we don't capture the intuition that both of us playing A is the *only* rational outcome of our interaction.[12]

But why on earth would you play B? Isn't it obvious that you should play A? Well, yes. But this is something that a theory of rationality is supposed to explain or

---

[12]Unless, as Gold and Sugden (2007) point out, we supplement standard game theory with assumptions regarding imperfect rationality (see also Bardsley 2006, p. 147). E.g. I think you are as likely to play A as to play B, so maximizing leads me to pick A. But it's odd to have to appeal to the idea that you're so irrational as to be as likely to pick A as you are to pick B. A further thought would be that I remain entirely agnostic about what you will pick (as was suggested by a referee). Wouldn't maximizing expected benefits then point me to pick A? No, because I wouldn't have any expected benefit. If I'm truly agnostic about what the other person will do, then I should be agnostic about what the expected benefit will be.

account for. And an account in terms of individual rationality would be presupposing what it is meant to explain if it relies on the assumption that the other player would opt for A because it is obviously the rational thing to do.[13]

So the upper left box is what we should rationally opt for, and it seems that ordinary instrumental rationality doesn't secure that result. How then are we to explain the rationality of choosing in such a way that the upper left box is the outcome?[14]

Team reasoning takes up this challenge. The basic thought is that the individual asks himself not

What is best for *me* given what you do?

but

What is best for *us* or the group as a whole?

This shift or enlargement of deliberative perspective leads to choosing the upper left box, in the sense of ranking it the highest.[15,16]

For the purposes of this discussion, we can grant that the team-reasoning theorist is correct about the rationality of this choice in Hi-Lo.[17] Now, Bacharach reasons that it is *not* possible for me to intend or, as he puts it, implement this choice (2006, p. 63). That would be to settle more than I'm entitled to, since what I've chosen involves your actions as well as mine. What I've selected in answer to the question of what we should do leads me, rather, to intend my component or part of our action in the upper left box; in this case, it would lead me to intend to A. This intention concerning my own A-ing counts, in this scenario, as the collective option for me, i.e., it reflects what I'm up to in doing something with you. The intention's status

---

[13] See Bardsley (2006, p. 147).

[14] Actually, one figure in the team reasoning literature, Sugden, doesn't seem to argue for the rationality of team reasoning. See Sugden's editorial note 22 in Bacharach (2006, p. 141), where he rejects Bacharach's interpretation of him.

[15] We need to understand the team reasoning approach correctly. If it is to address the problem of how individuals can come together to share an intention and act jointly, the team reasoning approach has to be addressed to the individual: it's an account of how the *individual* reasons toward the intention that might represent her commitment to shared activity. Some presentations of team reasoning occasionally sound as if the question, *what should we do?* is entertained not by an individual but by the entire group or group-like entity comprising the individual participants, where it's unclear what implication this is supposed to have for the rationality of each of those participants.

[16] There are different views about how this shift occurs, e.g. whether it's voluntary or not, an object of choice, etc. Gold and Sugden catalog several views—such as those of Hurley (1989), Bacharach (2006), and Anderson (1996).

[17] Regarding the assumption of rationality: in the philosophy of action, intentional action is tied to rationality; intentional action is understood as acting for reasons and explained in terms of reasons (Anscombe 1963; Davidson 1963). Given this tradition, the goal is to understand shared activity as a form of rational action. So it wouldn't do us any good if selecting the cooperative option weren't rational. It would, in this tradition, be problematic if shared activity and interrelated structure of intentions couldn't be rationally willed.

as collective and reflecting what a participant is up to stems from how the intention was arrived at. The act was rationally chosen in this situation because it generates the best outcome for everyone (Pareto optimal), as represented on the matrix, and that it was chosen by the individual as a response to the question of what we should do (what would be best for us).[18] The fact that an individual is to think in this team perspective—to see the options in this way, and to act accordingly—captures the sense in which the intentions that result are participatory intentions, which serve to distinguish shared activity from individual agency.[19]

3   Does Team Reasoning Resolve the Settling Problem?

We're investigating whether participatory intentions can be understood as the product of team reasoning. Now, does the attitude described as 'that which issues from my team reasoning' count as settling some relevant practical matter? It is important to ask this question because otherwise the attitude would not be the right intention, or not even count as an intention at all. Either way, the proposal would fail to account for what one is up to in shared activity, given that what one is up to is understood in terms of one's intention.[20]

It *appears* that we have an intention here. Through team reasoning, I am able rationally to opt for A-ing. Further, as the matrix suggests, it seems that A-ing is something I am able to do irrespective of what you do. On the team reasoning view, when it comes to forming the intention after one has engaged in team reasoning, one just intends one's own action (e.g. the A-ing that I would do in our both A-ing).

---

[18] I leave open the question of circularity, of whether the proposal smuggles in the notion of collectivity by invoking some robust conception of parthood that presupposes the concept of joint or shared activity.

[19] This might be understood as providing a relatively concrete sense to the sort of we-mode attitude in Tuomela (2007), or Searle's notion of collective intention (1990).

[20] The line of criticism to be pursued here is in the tradition of those given by Tuomela and Bratman, each of whom also draws on the distinctiveness of intention in questioning the team reasoning proposal. Tuomela (2009) focuses on schema 4 from Gold and Sugden (2007, see Sect. 5 below) as encapsulating the team reasoning proposal. He points out that the *pro tanto* considerations serving as premises in the schema are not strong enough to establish the all out conclusion needed for an intention in the conclusion of the schema.

Even if we set aside Tuomela's worry and assume some sort of all things considered judgment can be secured by reasoning along the lines of Schema 4, it's still not clear that the resulting judgment corresponds to an intention. My participatory intention might be to J, even though the value judgment via team reasoning regarding what we should do is some J' distinct from J. To take an example from Bratman (Shared Agency), weak willed lovers might through team reasoning judge it best *not* to elope. But they elope regardless, each intending his/her part in it. The judgment not to elope may reflect what is best for us. But we nevertheless elope, and do so together, and we each have the corresponding participatory intention to elope. In assuming that valuing most the option of not eloping is or directly converts to the corresponding intention (of not eloping), the team reasoning proposal fails to appreciate how intending is distinct from valuing.

The point is that I have control over what I do, so am able to settle that. This is what ensures that the settling condition is satisfied. Thus, my intention to A is rational and reflects what I'm up to in a way that appears not to run into the Settling Problem.

But I think that the problem here is that the matrix offers a misleading picture of how it is possible that I may be settled on A-ing (where A-ing is my part, or what I do, in the shared activity). If the other person doesn't join in, then often there simply is no A-ing for one to do. Think of a case where A-ing is lifting my end of a heavy sofa that I could not budge by myself. Or, to draw on a cliché, think of dancing the tango. One can't dance one's part of a tango if the other person declines. One might go ahead and dance by oneself. Then again, one might perhaps skulk off to get a drink. Whatever one does, it is something that one does *instead* of acting on the original intention to do one's part. That's because what each of us does in the tango or the sofa-lifting (as the case may be) is interdependent with what the other does, and hence my intention to lift this end of the sofa or my intention to dance my part of the tango is interdependent with your corresponding intention. Dancing one's part is not something I can settle (or be settled on) independently of you.

Although the table representing possible outcomes in Hi-Lo might suggest the possibility of A-ing in situations when others don't join in as well as when they do, this is misleading. There may be a sense in which this is true in the card case of picking either a King or a Three.[21] But it's not always true. As Bratman has emphasized in recent discussion, what intention one has often depends on the intentions of one's partners.[22] In many scenarios for which we might construct the sort of table of options that we have for Hi-Lo, the *intention* to play the Hi strategy (A) is not guaranteed to be available to me. Without knowledge or assurance that you have the corresponding intention, I am not in a position to form mine. So even though A-ing is my own action, whether I'm in a position to A is not entirely up to me to settle. One cannot intend A if it's not something that one can thereby settle.

A clarification before proceeding. When I speak of the intention to A being interdependent with those of fellow participants, I don't mean to deny the possibility of error, where I form the intention but my presupposition that you intend likewise and will join in turns out to be false. As with representational states generally, there is the possibility of things going wrong. Compare the case where I intend to drive to the store, but don't realize that my car is broken: I have the intention, but its conditions for success are unsatisfied. Of course, once I learn that the presupposition is false and that you aren't joining in or that my car is broken (as the case may be), I will revise the intention. But until I discover this, my intention to A in the

---

[21] In the case of the cards, it does seem that I can pick and intend to pick the King, irrespective of what you do. However, it is not clear that I can pick and intend to pick the King as part of each of us picking the King, or as a way of carrying out the intention to pick the same card as you (unless I have some reason to think that you'll pick it as well). *Picking the King because you are also picking it* is not something I can do or intend without information about you also picking it.

[22] See Bratman (2014) on enabling interdependence.

context of shared activity is the same as the intention to A when there is no shared activity, except that the latter won't succeed. In light of this, the initial point about interdependence should be understood as one about what one can rationally intend: I cannot rationally maintain my intention if I lack sufficient warrant for holding that the conditions for its success are in place.

Returning to the main thread, we might wonder what to say about some A-ing that differs from the tango or sofa-lifting insofar as it is possible for me to A even if others don't joint in. Might we say that at least in these cases, team reasoning successfully addresses the Settling Problem? To see that a problem remains, note that the nature of the interdependence of intentions is usually not merely that of satisfying an enabling condition on what's intended. There is also the thought that often there is no point to acting this way unless someone else is also participating. Take Bratman's case of intending to leave town prompted by a desire to elope. Part of the point of my running away is that I am doing it with you. I do intend to A in the case where you join in, but I would intend no such thing if you don't come along.[23] And this is typical of cases that are taken to demonstrate the need for team reasoning. Team reasoning doesn't seem to address this sort of interdependence. If so, this would be a significant limitation for this way of characterizing participatory intention.

There are of course cases where one would intend to A irrespective of whether others will join in. For example, I'd be happy to go to the farmer's market with you, but I'm fine going by myself if you're too busy with other errands: I plan/intend on going in any case. Thus, some intentions are pitched at a sufficient level of abstraction that they will count as being acted on irrespective of whether others join in. Why, then, couldn't the team reasoning strategy be used to arrive at some more abstract intention that could serve to capture participatory commitment?

One worry with this view is that it seems that not all cases of reasoning toward shared intention and joint action involve first formulating an intention and only subsequently figuring out whether to do it on one's own or with someone else. Our walking together is not always an implementation of some prior or higher order individual or cooperatively neutral intention. (One might assume that there is always a more general intention because one subscribes to a picture of practical reasoning that has it starting with the most general ends, which are then rendered more specific.) But let us grant for the sake of argument that in the present case I do have an intention, for example, to go to the market, but have not yet filled in the details—including whether I'll do it with someone or on my own. The second worry, then, is that if this is the sort of intention that's defined by the team reasoning approach, then it's not at all obvious that it depicts what I'm up to in shared activity. The picture, after all, is of an intention where I have not yet decided or committed to act with another. To address the settling problem by appealing to an intention that can be implemented irrespective of whether or not one acts with others is precisely what ensures that the intention won't account for the "what it is that I'm up to" in

---

[23]See Bratman (2014), on *reasons-for* interdependence.

acting with you. To get to the right sort of intention, one would have to so to speak descend to an intention more specifically implementing joint activity. But this was what couldn't be settled by the individual.

So in many instances where others do not join in, either I would be unable to do my part or there would be no point in doing my part. Although there is a sense in which A-ing is up to me, A-ing-only-in-the-context-where-you-join-in is not something that I can settle. And it's the latter attitude that is supposed to be the output of team reasoning, and which is needed to capture what I'm up to when I'm acting with someone. So if the team reasoning approach cannot handle the settling aspect of intention, then it hasn't accounted for participatory intention.

The point might be put this way. By engaging in team reasoning, one is led to rank highest a certain cooperative outcome (the upper left box on our table). According to Bacharach (2006, p. 63), this will (rationally) lead one to intend one's component in that highest ranked box. But the claim about intention formation does not follow from the claim about ranking. Bacharach (p. 136) argues that willing the outcome that's best for the group requires that one will one's actions that that outcome entails. That would seem to be so if the Means-End Coherence Principle is true. But it's not clear that one is in a position to will the outcome of the group, rather than just rank it the highest. Ranking it highest doesn't entail willing one's part in it. There are many states of affairs that I value, but if I don't think I can settle the matter and bring it about, then I'm not rationally required to intend means to bringing it about. The Means-End Coherence/Instrumental principle does require one to intend necessary means, but this only applies to *intended* ends, and not to some state of affairs that I rank the highest but for one reason or another do not intend.

4 The Distinctiveness of Team Reasoning

In this section, I consider two natural responses to the Settling Problem in light of the interdependence of intentions. I conclude that these responses are unavailable to the team reasoning approach because they each would undermine the case for team reasoning in the first place.

The first response is to think of participatory intentions as a kind of conditional intention. On this view, I intend our activity, or my part in it, conditional on you also so intending. This would avoid the Settling Problem, because such an intention does not presume to settle what others will do, nor does it presume that what they will do is settled.

But such a proposed amendment would not be welcomed by the advocate of team reasoning. To see this, consider the Hi-Lo scenario that motivates team reasoning in the first place. One thing that might plausibly be said about it is that each individual has a conditional intention to pick Hi (A, in the table above) so long as the other does as well. But of course, this would be an incomplete description because presumably each also intends to pick Lo (B) so long as the other does as well. Thus, interdependent conditional intentions do not offer an account of how one decides and settles the matter of what to do in the Hi-Lo scenario; at best it merely re-describes a problem situation that the team reasoning is meant to resolve. It is not surprising, then, that Bacharach explicitly criticizes such an approach.[24]

Another familiar and natural response to the Settling Problem suggests that one's participatory intention that we J (or that I J with you) is founded on a *prediction* about what others will do, or would do given how one acts. Now, one might think that this would be of use to the advocate of team reasoning. After all, things won't go well for me when I use team reasoning and you don't. If I could predict that you would choose Hi then I can be reassured in using it myself. However, this solution threatens to collapse team reasoning into ordinary individual instrumental reasoning, whereby I choose Hi based on my prediction that you will choose Hi, and my belief that this would maximize expected benefit. The Hi-Lo scenario is meant to motivate team reasoning as something distinct from ordinary individual instrumental reasoning. If it is to do so, then presumably we cannot merely on the basis of experience predict what the other person will do.[25] Otherwise, the rationality of picking Hi is accounted for in terms of ordinary individual instrumental reasoning. Thus, Bardsley (2007, p. 149) says "proponents of team reasoning explicitly deny that coordination is based on expectations about others' actions." He cites Sugden (1993, p. 87): "It is because players who think as a team do not need to form expectations about one another's actions that they can solve coordination problems."

Somewhat puzzling, however, is the position of Bardsley and, it seems, Sugden, regarding one's belief or assumption that the others are also team reasoners. Sugden requires that "each member … has reason to believe that each other member endorses and acts on team reasoning … " (Gold and Sugden's conclusion in Bacharach 2006, p. 168; see also Sugden 1993). Bacharach refers to this requirement as "Sugden's Proviso" (p. 141). In an editor's note to Bacharach's text (p. 153, note 22), Sugden makes clear his own view that "If it is common knowledge that all members of the relevant group conceive of rationality in terms of group agency … then it is rational for each member to act according to the prescriptions of team reasoning." Presumably, we may add: whereas, if there is common knowledge that each makes use of individual instrumental reasoning, then one should not be engaging in team reasoning. The point is that an expectation or belief about others being team members and engaging in team reasoning is crucial for team reasoning. In the same vein, Bardsley says:

> For the intention [generated by team reasoning] to arise the agent must expect that the requisite circumstances obtain. The key circumstance for collective intention is that the agents constitute a team, implying that the other agents are fellow team members with reciprocal beliefs about the membership of the relevant others. That involves viewing them as disposed to act on a plan to bring about some goal, without making this conditional on

---

[24]Bacharach (2006, pp. 137–41). There are issues regarding whether such interdependent conditional intentions really count as intentions, even apart from whether it would be endorsed by advocates of the team reasoning proposal. See my 2004.

[25]That's why team reasoning points to a solution even when what we have is a one-off interaction with individuals with whom we have not interacted previously.

the others' actions, or else we are back into a coordination problem, but rather conditional on their team membership. (Bardsley 2007, p. 153; see also pp. 145, 150)

But it's not at all clear why the belief that others are team reasoners is any less problematic for the advocate of team reasoning than the belief that others will act by doing A (picking Hi). After all, what good is the belief that another is a team reasoner if one cannot conclude that they will act on it and choose Hi? Whether it concerns how the other will act or whether the other is a team reasoner, the belief that would seem to be necessary for team reasoning to go through is the belief that the other will play Hi. But such a belief would render team reasoning otiose. For with the belief that the other will play Hi, or that the other is a team reasoner (and so will play Hi), one can simply apply individual instrumental reasoning in order to generate the response that we all think is intuitively rational—picking Hi.

Consider Gold and Sugden's proposed schemas to articulate the rationality of team reasoning (at least on behalf of Bacharach). Their Schema 4 is meant to represent team reasoning from the perspective of an individual participant:

1. I am a member of S.
2. It is common knowledge in S that each member of S identifies with S.
3. It is common knowledge in S that each member of S wants the value of U to be maximized.
4. It is common knowledge in S that A uniquely maximizes U.

I should choose my component of A.[26]

How are we to understand the premises in this schema? Gold and Sugden say, "Our basic building block is the concept of a schema of practical reasoning, in which conclusions about what actions should be taken are inferred from explicit premises about the decision environment ..." (Gold and Sugden 2007, p. 121). This makes it sound as if an individual reasoner establishes the premises independently of and prior to engaging in the inference. But then the worry is, again, that the premises involving common knowledge might warrant the conclusion on the basis of ordinary individual reasoning; there would be no need to appeal to some special form of team reasoning.[27]

5   Non-evidential Warrant

Suppose we agree with the advocate of team reasoning and think that this reasoning is distinct from individual instrumental reasoning, and necessary to account for what we think would be rational to do in the Hi-Lo situation. Then we need to take the

---

[26]Gold and Sugden's use of 'A' differs from mine in that for them it denotes the shared act, rather than just one's component in it.

[27]This is especially so if we modify premise 3 as Tuomela (2009, p. 299) rightly insists we should. See note 20 above.

same attitude toward the belief that the other is a team reasoner as we do toward the prediction that the other will play Hi. That is, we must deny that either of them is available as an *independent resource* for solving the Hi-Lo problem. Otherwise, the problem will not demonstrate the need for team reasoning as opposed to individual instrumental reasoning.

What should be evident now is the peculiar or distinctive character of the belief concerning fellow participants that's presupposed in team reasoning (the belief, that is, they are also team reasoners and hence will opt as one does for Hi). The presupposition cannot be an ordinary belief or expectation, based on evidence, if team reasoning is to be distinct from individual instrumental reasoning. But if the presupposition is not an ordinary belief, how should we understand it?

One possibility is that the presupposition is a belief, but not one based on evidence; it's just a brute fact of our psychology that we form such an expectation in response to certain situations. This might be suggested by Bacharach's talk of framing, where depending on the situation one is triggered to see oneself as acting alone, or together with others.[28] Gold and Sugden remark that "whether the individual reasons as an individual or as a member of some larger group and, if the latter, which larger group she reasons as a member of are matters of psychological framing, not rationality" (Gold and Sugden, in Bacharach 2006, p. 164). But if we leave it at that, it's not clear that we have vindicated the *rationality* of team reasoning. Rationality is normative, concerning what one in some sense should or ought to do; and this goes beyond a mere description of the psychological facts. It might be suggested in response that we can understand the missing normative element by understanding the psychological framing of a situation on externalist or reliabilist grounds.[29] For example, the tendency to frame the Hi-Lo situation so as to prompt team reasoning and the choice of Hi might be rationally vindicated simply by the fact that the players one generally encounters also see it this way, with the consequent favorable outcome. On this view, one's belief that others are team reasoners receives a favorable epistemic assessment, even though one doesn't have any reason or justification for it. Whether and how reliabilism handles a purported rationality constraint on knowing is a contested matter.[30] But even if something along these lines can be made to work, it's not clear that what would be vindicated is team reasoning to the exclusion of ordinary individual instrumental reasoning, which after all could make use of the same externalist/reliabilist strategy to solve the Hi-Lo problem.

So how are we to regard the presupposition that others will also engage in team reasoning? It won't turn out so well if one engages in team reasoning when others don't cooperate. But I take it that if team reasoning is a valid form of reasoning

---

[28] See for example Bacharach (2006, p. 137) who refers to a theory of entification involving framing as psychological, drawing a contrast with a normative theory of rationality.

[29] See Bacharach (2006, pp. 143–44) for suggestive remarks here.

[30] For this concern about reliabilism, see Bonjour (1980). See Burge (1993) for a view that addresses this concern in the case of testimonial warrant.

that is distinct from individual instrumental reasoning, then it can be rational to adopt the cooperative intention even before it is settled in any ordinary evidential sense what one's partner(s) will do. Of course, if the balance of evidence is that one's partners won't cooperate, one should not proceed. We might put the point as follows: team reasoning itself offers an answer to why we have the defeasible non-evidential expectation we do about the other parties: it's a presupposition of a manifestly rational way of thinking (viz., team reasoning) that the other also thinks this way.[31]

If team reasoning is a distinctive form of reasoning, the reasoner's expectation regarding what others (or a significant element thereof) will do is just a matter of the rationality of the individual posing the question of what *we* should do in the situation and answering it by choosing Hi. But the latter is the central claim of the team reasoning proposal. That's to say that the expectation regarding what the others will do is not independent of team reasoning.[32]

So, the rationality of team reasoning is itself the answer to why one is non-evidentially warranted or entitled to the presupposition that fellow participants are team reasoners, and thus why one is in a position to form the relevant participatory intention. This will not impress those who are convinced that there is no need to modify standard game theory by revising the assumption of ordinary individual instrumental reasoning. But if you are amongst those who find compelling the arguments that traditional individual instrumental reasoning fails to account for the rationality of choosing Hi in the Hi-Lo scenario, you will also have to maintain that one's (defeasible) entitlement to presuppose team reasoning in one's fellow participants is part and parcel of the rationality of engaging in team reasoning and choosing Hi. We couldn't engage in this manifestly rational reasoning and behavior unless we're entitled to the (defeasible) presupposition that others will also reason, intend, and act this way.

***

To recap, the strategy of thinking of intentions as concerning one's own action will not solve the Settling Problem that confronts accounts of participatory

---

[31]It's not as if we have positive evidence for thinking that the other is a team reasoner; rather, it's a presupposition that might be defeated. In contrast, the predictive view doesn't seem to be committed to any thought about the rationality of fellow participants (although perhaps it may—in which case it would have to explain the rationality). That is, on the predictive view, one can base the requisite prediction on *whatever* evidence one may have about fellow participants, irrespective of whether one takes them to be rational or irrational. For example, maybe it's just a matter of habit that the other person tends to behave as she does, and this is something I come to know through experience in observing her.

[32]Contrast the status of prediction for e.g. Bratman, where the warrant for prediction is based on one's experience of what the other does. Bratman works in a different literature and doesn't feel that we need to build our account of joint action around the special case of Hi Lo. Whereas, the team reasoning view thinks of this special case as definitive of shared agency, and thus having a significance that extends to cases where this sort of reasoning is not necessarily required for coordination.

intentions in shared activity. And the team reasoning approach, at least as it has usually been presented, is no exception. This becomes clear once we recognize that normally in shared activity you only form participatory intentions when others would do so as well. So even if one is only intending one's part and not what we all are doing, given this interdependence of intentions, how could one get into a position to intend? We've seen that the appeal to conditional intentions doesn't solve the problem. And the appeal to the predictive strategy undermines the distinctiveness of team reasoning.

Team reasoning presupposes a belief that fellow participants are team reasoners. If we have any conclusive *evidence* for believing that they are, then we don't need team reasoning. I conclude, instead, that if the rationality of team reasoning is manifest, then this should be demonstration enough of a *non*-evidential yet defeasible entitlement or warrant to think that fellow participants are team reasoners.

References

Anderson, E. 1996. Reasons, attitudes, and values: Replies to Sturgeon and Piper. *Ethics* 106: 538–554.

Anscombe, G.E.M. 1963. *Intention*. Ithaca: Cornell University Press.

Bacharach, M. 2006. *Beyond individual choice*. Princeton: Princeton University Press.

Bardsley, N. 2007. On collective intentions: Collective action in economics and philosophy. *Synthese* 157(2): 141–159.

Bonjour, L. 1980. Externalist theories of empirical knowledge. In *Midwest studies in philosophy 5: Studies in epistemology*, ed. P.A. French, T.E. Uehling Jr., and H.K. Wettstein, 53–73. Minneapolis: University of Minnesota Press.

Bratman, M. 1987. *Intentions, plans, and practical reasoning*. Cambridge, MA: Harvard University Press.

Bratman, M. 1992. Shared cooperative activity. *Philosophical Review* 101: 327–341.

Bratman, M. 1993. Shared intention. *Ethics* 104: 97–113.

Bratman, M. 2009. Modest sociality and the distinctiveness of intention. *Philosophical Studies* 144: 149–165.

Bratman, M. 2014. *Shared agency: A planning theory of acting together*. Oxford: Oxford University Press (in print).

Burge, T. 1993. Content preservation. *Philosophical Review* 102: 457–488.

Davidson, D. 1963. Actions, reasons, and causes. *Journal of Philosophy* 60: 685–700.

Gilbert, M. 2009. Shared intention and personal intentions. *Philosophical Studies* 144: 167–187.

Gold, N., and R. Sugden. 2007. Collective intentions and team agency. *Journal of Philosophy* CIV(3): 109–137.

Hurley, S. 1989. *Natural reasons: Personality and polity*. New York: Oxford University Press.

Kutz, C. 2000. Acting together. *Philosophy and Phenomenological Research* 61: 1–31.

Roth, A.S. 2004. Shared agency and contralateral commitments. *Philosophical Review* 113: 359–410.

Roth, A.S. 2013. Prediction, authority, and entitlement in shared acitiviity. *Noûs* 47(3): 1–27 DOI: 10.1111/nous.12011.

Searle, J. 1990. Collective intentions and actions. In *Intentions in communication*, ed. P. Cohen, J. Morgan, and M. Pollack, 401–415. Cambridge: MIT Press.

Sugden, R. 1993. Thinking as a team. In *Altruism*, ed. E.F. Paul, F.D. Miller, and J. Paul. Cambridge: Cambridge University Press.

Tuomela, R. 2005. We-intentions revisited. *Philosophical Studies* 125(3): 327–369.

Tuomela, R. 2007. *The philosophy of sociality: The shared point of view*. New York: Oxford University Press.

Tuomela, R. 2009. Collective intentions and game theory. *The Journal of Philosophy* 106(5): 292–300.

Tuomela, R., and K. Miller. 1988. We-intentions. *Philosophical Studies* 53: 367–389.

Velleman, D. 1997. How to share an intention. *Philosophy and Phenomenological Research* 57: 29–50.

Velleman, D. 2001. Review of faces of intention by Michael Bratman. *The Philosophical Quarterly* 51(202): 119–121.

Chapter 18
Collective Intentionality and Practical Reason

Juliette Gloor

Abstract In this chapter I am interested in the conceptual relation between the claim that practical reason just is or reduces to instrumental reason (I will call this position "instrumentalism about practical reason") and the claim that the real problem of instrumental rationality is not its instrumentalism about practical reason but its "individualism about goals". I understand this to mean that the problem of instrumental rationality is not its consequentialist aspect that agents have preferences only over outcomes (but not over actions) but its individualist implication about motivation: that agents can be motivated only by their own desires. According to such an interpretation of the problem of instrumental rationality, collective intentionality is seen as providing the solution: it frees instrumentalism from its individualism while preserving its consequentialism. That is, the sort of normativity characteristic of collective intentionality will still be instrumental normativity. My aim in this chapter is twofold: I will first argue that instrumentalism about practical reason has fundamental difficulties in showing how reasons can be guiding for self-conscious rational beings. From there I depart to show, second, that this has to do with the fact that the instrumentalist concept of human self-relation as instrumentally normative fails to show how human agency can be what it must be in order to function well, i.e. to be unified. Therefore the sort of normativity characteristic of collective intentionality cannot be instrumental rationality.

1

Hans Bernhard Schmid (2009, p. 242), to my knowledge, is the only philosopher working on collective intentionality who explicitly expresses the idea that the real problem of instrumental rationality is not its instrumentalism about practical

J. Gloor (✉)
Department of Philosophy, University of Basel, Basel, Switzerland
e-mail: juliette.gloor@me.com

A. Konzelmann Ziv and H.B. Schmid (eds.), *Institutions, Emotions, and Group Agents*, 297
Studies in the Philosophy of Sociality 2, DOI 10.1007/978-94-007-6934-2_18,
© Springer Science+Business Media Dordrecht 2014

reason—the claim that practical reason is identical with or reduces to instrumental reason—but its "individualism about goals". The idea seems to be that there remains nothing problematic about instrumentalism once it has been made compatible with the claim that agents can be motivated by other people's desires or by desires that they share with others. If desires can be shared with others, the deliberation of others does not merely function as a further fact in one's own deliberation but must be taken into account as part of one's shared deliberation with those others.

So Schmid (2009, esp. ch. 7 and 8) challenges individualism about ends by motivating the two claims that people can be moved to act by other people's intentions and desires *directly* (i.e. without those desires having to be based, ultimately, on one's own desires), and that people can deliberate and intend together without treating each other as mere means. I am very sympathetic to attempts to show how desires, intentions, and their objects can be shared.[1] What I want to question in this chapter is rather whether instrumentalism about practical reason can really be made more plausible by challenging its individualism about ends. I will argue that there is something about instrumentalism about practical reason that makes it ill suited for the idea of sharing reasons.

I think that other philosophers can be interpreted as sharing an important implication of Schmid's claim that instrumentalism about practical reason is not the problem but rather its individualism about ends. The implication of this claim, as I understand it, is that the kind of normativity constitutive of collective intentionality is the same kind of normativity that is constitutive of individual intentionality, namely instrumental or means-to-end rationality. Postema (1995, p. 48), for example, argues that instrumental rationality is not a special mark of the singular or individual perspective compared to the plural perspective, which seems to bring him close to Schmid's view—for if instrumental rationality is not what essentially distinguishes the singular from the plural perspective, it certainly cannot be what makes the singular perspective problematic compared to the plural perspective. Rather the difference between the singular and the plural perspective consists in, according to Postema (ibid., p. 48), "the respective conceptions of the deliberative unit of agency". To deliberate from the plural perspective is to deliberate from the perspective of an integrated whole of which both one's own deliberations and those of the other agent(s) are internally related parts.

Other philosophers, most notably Michael Bratman, seem to accept Schmid's conclusion that instrumental rationality is the kind of normativity essential for collective intentionality. Bratman (2004, p. 10) emphasises that plans can be shared without sharing non-instrumental reasons, i.e., merely "by way of bargaining and compromise" for which instrumental rationality is constitutive.

---

[1] Note that sharing intentions differs from sharing desires in that intentions are subject to stronger constraints of rationality than desires are, as Bratman (1987) has shown. As a unified rational agent one cannot intend to do something which one is sure that one cannot do or which conflicts with the realisation of other intentions. Consequently sharing intentions requires more work of coordination and structuring between distinct agents than does the sharing of desires.

Of course one difficulty here is that much depends on how exactly we are to understand the position of instrumentalists about practical reason, and the literature on the topic is anything but homogeneous or uncontroversial. I will try to give the least contentious description of the main claims of this position possible. Instrumentalism about practical reason has it, firstly, that practical reasoning is exclusively a matter of means-to-end reasoning, that is reasoning about sufficient means to one's ends, but not a matter of reasoning about ends themselves. Practical reason, according to this view, can help us figure out the instrumentally rational means to our ends, but it cannot tell us anything about the rationality of the ends themselves. It is important to note, secondly, that what the instrumentalist about practical reason denies is *not* that if one intends to do *A*, one has to take oneself to have a reason to do *A*. What she does deny is that the ultimate reasons for action are grounded in practical reason itself. According to the instrumentalist, reasons are grounded in desires. The fundamental problem here is that it is anything but clear what the instrumentalist means by claiming that reasons are grounded in desires, and so what the correct description of the view of the instrumentalist's *opponent* is. In the next section I am going to raise some preliminary doubts concerning what might seem at first glance a straightforward view about the normative scope of practical reason.

2

The instrumentalist's position receives its force from a worry that relates to their claim of the nature of reasons, but is seldom clearly stated. I suggest that this worry, as outlined in the following, can be generalised to the notion of shared ends, when it comes to the question of *collective* practical reason. For, as previously shown, instrumentalists investigating the normative character of shared or collective ends do not see instrumentalism *as such* threatening the analysis of collective practical reason, but only its individualism about ends. I shall therefore assume that the instrumentalist's worry concerning reasons applies to both, individual and collective practical reasoning. Accordingly, the term "agent" will be used to refer to both individual and group agents, and the term "end" to both individual and shared ends.

The instrumentalist's worry is that having an end does not necessarily give the agent a normative or justifying reason to take the means to her end, because reasons defined in terms of desires might well be reasons for a bad or stupid end. From this, the instrumentalist seems to infer that our ends, insofar as they are motivating forces, can only give us instrumental but not normative reasons for action, since rationality cannot prescribe which desires we ought to have. An argument along these lines is given by John Broome (1999) who distinguishes between reasons-relations of "narrow scope" and of "wide scope". "Wide scope" reasons-relations provide agents with merely instrumental but no normative reasons. The "wide scope" instrumental reasons at work in practical reasoning are considered somehow akin to requirements of rationality that do not tell us what we ought to do (hence the term "wide-scope").[2]

Accordingly, the instrumental principle that tells us to take the means to our ends is understood as a disjunctive requirement of rationality with which the agent can comply *either* by realising her (part of the shared) end *or* by giving up her (part of the shared) end. All that the agent has to make sure is that her pattern of mental attitudes satisfies this requirement of rationality.[3] Whether she gives up her (part of the shared) end or whether she actually realises her (part of the shared) end does *not* affect her status of rational agent, as long as she has the right combination of mental attitudes.

However, on this conception of practical reason, it is not clear how reasons can actually *guide* the agent's behaviour. The advice that one should *either* keep one's end and then realise it *or* give it up is no real guidance at all with respect to the primary question whether to keep the end or to give it up. It becomes instrumental guidance only once the agent has decided (but on what grounds?) to keep her end: *then* she is rationally required to take the means to her end.

So the worry that our desires and ends need not give us normative reasons for action is expressive of the instrumentalist assumption that practical reason cannot tell us anything about the ends we should have since rational deliberation about ends is not possible.

3

The instrumentalist's motivation for thinking that practical reason can tell us nothing about the ends we rationally ought to choose may have to do with the instrumentalist's assumption that the 'ought' of practical reason merely refers to the fact that one should satisfy the desires of one's actual or given motivational set. A central controversy is what status these desires or motives are supposed to have.

Hume and some of his instrumentalist followers may be read as arguing that in order to avoid an endless regress with regard to action explanation one must posit

---

[2]Cf. Schmid's (2009, pp. 53–54) brief discussion of Broome's idea of requirement of rationality in the context of collective intentionality.

[3]The fact that instrumental consistency of one's mental attitudes can conflict with *practical coherence* indicates that instrumental rationality may not be the fundamentally interesting concept for practical rationality. Consider the following example: the means one takes to realise one's ambition to make a career in a certain profession are sensitive to how this affects one's other values and ends, for example the value of integrity. Perhaps one realises that pursuing a specific career requires actions of a kind that one cannot reconcile with one's self-conception as a person of integrity. Even though one's mental attitudes would be consistent if one pursued an end by way of a non-justifiable means this does not mean that one's action would also be coherent. It is not coherent for an agent to violate deep-seated personal commitments by so acting. So it seems that it is coherence rather than means-to-end consistency that enables an agent to act as one, or in a non-conflicted way.

some natural psychological (or physiological) state as regress stopper. Such ultimate and unmotivated psychological states are typically, and quite understandably, considered to be non-cognitive types of desires. This construal is the root of the instrumentalist's worry that having an end does not give us a normative reason for action. If our ends are ultimately based in some non-cognitive psychological or physiological state, then, so she argues, they surely cannot give us normative reasons for action. The agent will just have them without any possibility of further justifying them.

Now this brings us to the heart of the problem I want to discuss. If desires are non-cognitive forces mostly not under our control in any interesting sense, how are they liable to *explain* actions done for reasons?[4, 5] If desire is understood in terms of something like an orectic state or physiological disposition, then surely our giving reasons in explaining action gets mystified if our action explanation bottoms out in an historical development of desire. I think that the Humean tradition of letting chains of action explanation bottom out in "unmotivated desires" is particularly sensitive to this kind of criticism. The most plausible way to understand the notion "unmotivated desires", so it seems, is to understand it in terms of non-cognitive desires. But if this is right, then the instrumentalist position seems to collapse, since it undercuts the claim that reasons are desires, and with it the support of the claim that the norms of practical reason do not pertain to ends.

Basically, I see two challenges arising from this for the instrumentalist. First, how does she distinguish between different sorts of *non-cognitive* desires, desires that are (the ultimate) stable features of the agent's basic motivational set, on the one hand, and desires that arise from fleeting but perhaps recurring bodily changes, on the other hand? Second, how does she explain the emergence of cognitive desires from ultimate non-cognitive ones? Unless desires are potentially cognitive in the sense of being reason-responsive, it is not clear how they can serve as reasons for action.

Sometimes the instrumentalist tries to clarify her claim that desires are reasons by contrasting her view with that of her[6] opponents, who may be broadly referred

---

[4]Unmotivated desires are not the sort of thing we should accept as natural regress stoppers for action explanation since if unmotivated desires explain some behaviour at all they do not explain it in the right way, i.e. in such a way as to pick out the behaviour as an action instead of a mere reaction or an effect of a cause. This is why I think that the behaviour of Davidson's (1963) famous mountain climber who lets go of her fellow climber as a result of a nervous fit caused by the desire to let go should not be described as an action.

[5]Here I merely wish to draw our attention to the important fact that actions done for reasons are unlike other things we do, such as digesting food or perceiving that the cat sleeps on the mat. Of course we can cite perceptual beliefs that are not really under our control in the explanation of things that we or intelligent animals do. But my point is that when we hold such a perceptual belief it is not under our control in the sense that we do not really hold it for reasons and therefore are not responsible for it in the same way we are responsible for beliefs that we hold for reasons such as e.g. "I believe that my father cheats on my mother".

[6]In what follows I will use the feminine pronoun to refer to the instrumentalist, and the masculine pronoun to refer to her Kantian opponent. This is merely a technical device of presentation, i.e. of clearly keeping the two accounts separate, and carries no meaning in itself.

to as 'Kantians'. According to the instrumentalist, 'Kantians' regard reasons as desire-independent principles prescribing an action directly without referring to the agent's desires or interests. Reasons so understood are thus grounded in *reason itself*. Kantians are particularly known to hold this view with regard to the domain of moral action and reasoning. Instrumentalists interpret it in the sense that the agent of a moral action must not be motivated by the action's content or the end for which it is done, but *solely* by the moral worth (that is, out of respect for the law) of doing it. Obviously, this seems to be too strong a requirement for a general theory of practical reasoning since not all practical reasons are moral reasons. Moreover, this makes it seem as if reasons in the Kantian understanding were wholly disinterested. Reasons so conceived, the instrumentalist argues, are external and have nothing to do with the agent's own motivations and desires. I think this construal of the opponent's position should be rejected because it forces us to choose between two extreme views of reasons that are equally implausible. The choice is, so it seems, between reasons whose normative force renders their motivational force incomprehensible (the Kantian *externalist* position) and reasons with an exclusively motivating force whose binding force must as a result remain a mystery (the instrumentalist *internalist* position).[7]

Barbara Herman's (1996) analysis of desires offers a way out of this dilemma between desire-dependent reasons on the one hand and desire-independent reasons on the other hand by showing in what sense reasons or rational motives are both internal (desire-dependent) and external (desire-independent). More precisely, Herman proposes that desires should not be understood as non-cognitive and unmediated internal passions or psychological states one just has, but rather as states potentially open to *evaluative regulation and transformation by practical reason*. From the fact that practical reason must be unconditional, it does not follow that the agent's motives for action must themselves be entirely "extramaterial" and "in complete separation from the empirical life of the human agent" (Herman 1996, p. 43). In other words, even though the *authority* of our will is unconditional this does not mean, as Herman (1996, p. 43) puts it, that our *effective* motives have to be morally unconditional or good, as well. So if we think of desires (and emotions) more in the sense of calm passions that are potentially open to regulation by reason, the opposition between motivation grounded in desires and motivation grounded in reason itself is undercut.

If this is correct then the instrumentalist's concern with her opponent's construal of moral motivation can be dispelled. Christine Korsgaard (2008, pp. 216–29)

---

[7] Internalism about reasons is a metaphysical position about the conceptual link between reasons and motivation. A consideration is a reason in the internalist sense for a particular person to do *A* if the consideration is a reason for the agent to *A* and it being a reason depends on its ability to potentially motivate the agent to *A*. Something is an external reason if being a reason does not depend on its ability to motivate the agent to *A*. Although I cannot show this in detail here I think we must give up such a divided view of reasons in favour of understanding reasons neither as wholly internal nor as wholly external but as both internal and external.

demonstrates in more detail how this can be done. The instrumentalist's concern is, as we have seen above, that the Kantian takes an agent as acting morally well *only* if she is motivated by the moral worth (or respect for the moral law) of performing this action *rather* than by the action's content or the end for which it is done. Korsgaard convincingly argues that these two kinds of motivation do not exclude one another: morally good action and rational action in general involve *both* being moved by love or desire *and* being moved by one's awareness of the goodness of one's motivation, i.e. the awareness that doing a certain act for the sake of a certain end is also worth doing for its own sake.[8] An action is worth performing for its own sake if one can will a certain act as a means to a certain end for its own sake.[9]

Consider the description of Jill's possible action "I will take a week off from work in order to help my sister". We can understand Jill wanting to take a week off from work in order to help her sister, both because she loves her sister and because she thinks that helping her sister justifies taking a week off from work. Taking a week off from work in order to help one's sister is good for its own sake or at least permissible (under favourable circumstances).[10] Good action by its very nature is neither motivated merely by awareness of what is worth doing for its own sake nor merely by the end that the action serves or the action's content (Korsgaard 2008, p. 226).[11]

How does this help us reassess the position of the instrumentalist's opponent? I think we should understand his denying that reasons are desires in the first place as denying that reasons exclusively refer to the psychological or purely subjective inner world of an agent's mind. Reasons, he might argue, need to be shareable. Therefore, they cannot be confined to an agent's states of mind. On the other hand, an agent's desires must certainly play an essential role in his being motivated to act. How can these two constraints on reasons be reconciled? The following example may help answer this question. Suppose I think that it is a good thing that a city is friendly to cyclists, i.e. that it provides a sufficient number of safe routes for

---

[8]Good action differs from right action in that it not only requires that the action is right, i.e. as duty demands (the notorious example is that of keeping a promise), but also good in that the agent who does it does it with a good motive, namely for its own sake, and therefore does it virtuously.

[9]An anonymous referee has pointed out to me that the instrumentalist can accept the form of words here, even though the instrumentalist will hold that awareness of the action's being worth doing for its own sake amounts to just recognizing it as the object of a telic or non-cognitive desire. But this is exactly what the Kantian rejects as incomprehensible: how can such clearly reason-responsive recognition be the object of a non-cognitive desire?

[10]Note that it is the whole means-to-end maxim that is a candidate for being good for its own sake (i.e. taking a week off in order to help one's sister), and not just the end of helping one's sister.

[11]My reply to an anonymous referee who argued that we should cite the desire in response to *why*-questions (instead of what someone did, i.e. what act she performed for the sake of what end) is this: I contend that in the paradigmatic case, there is no difference between action explanation and action justification. We cite the end (which the agent would not pursue unless she had a desire for it) that the action serves and the (moral or non-moral) value the agent thinks her action has as a whole. Cf. also Korsgaard (2008, pp. 218–27).

cyclists (all else equal). This is my reason for supporting a referendum that tries to achieve this aim. It seems that the instrumentalist would have to describe my reasoning here in the following way[12]: (1) "I want that my city becomes friendly to cyclists and their concerns. (2) The referendum is a means to satisfy my desire. (3) Therefore, I will support the referendum." Assuming that my desire just is my reason to support the referendum, however, the instrumentalist would have to say that the fact that I want my city to become cyclist friendly is my reason to support the referendum. But this seems a wrong description of my reason. Describing someone as taking *the fact that she wants something* as a reason for supporting the referendum depicts her as implausibly self-centered. The mere fact that I want something does not seem the best of candidates for marking some consideration out as a reason. Importantly, the same holds for shared desires if one assumes that practical reason just is instrumental reason or that desires just are reasons. In that case, the fact that we want our city to become cyclist friendly is our reason to support the referendum. This is why I think that introducing shared ends does not help making instrumentalism about practical reason more plausible. Introducing shared ends merely pushes egoism to another level, namely that of the collective.

Moreover, the instrumentalist's view of reasons makes it seem as if one finds something good or valuable *because* one desires it. But surely this cannot be right: We do not find something good, when we find it good, because we desire it—we desire many things that we acknowledge are *not* good—but we desire something because we think it is good (for us).

Taking this relation between values and desires into consideration, the instrumentalist's opponent has the resources to account for the guiding force of reasons. His position, properly assessed, is to hold that we desire something because we consider it good (and not the other way around). Thus, his accounting for the agent's reasoning in the scenario of the cyclists' planning a referendum is far more plausible than it appears in the instrumentalist version: (1) "It is a good thing that a city is friendly to cyclists and their concerns. (2) Because of (1), I desire it to be the case that my city is friendly to cyclists and their concerns. (3) The referendum is a means to that end. (4) Because of (2) and (3), I will support the referendum." Thus, it is the fact expressed in clause (1) that establishes a good reason for me or for us to support the referendum. More precisely, it is the fact that this is *important* or *matters* to me or to us that motivates our supporting the referendum.

Whence does this mattering-relation, as I will call it, receive its justification? That is, why does having a cyclist friendly city matter? It matters to the people of the city because it is expected to make the city safer for cyclists and further people's health if they are thereby encouraged to go by bicycle rather than by car.

---

[12]The following example is in the spirit of Schueler (2003, pp. 59–60). See also Korsgaard (2009, p. 210).

What is more, pollution may be reduced by people changing their driving habits. Of course whether the city will *actually* become safer for cyclists when more cyclist routes are constructed is largely an empirical question. Nevertheless, the important philosophical point remains intact: *voting for the referendum in order to promote safety for cyclists, to further people's health, and to reduce pollution* is an action maxim whose end(s) are, to put it with Richardson (1997, p. 55), "appropriately regulating the manner and extent of the pursuit". In other words, the maxim "I will vote for the referendum in order to promote safety for cyclists, to further people's health, and to reduce pollution" is considered good or justifiable as a whole.

This is the sense in which reasons are desire-independent: rather than expressing an agent's desires they point to an agent's relation to a fact she values and that therefore matters to her. This value relation, or "mattering-relation", can be expressed in a principle of action. Although the maxim "I will do act *a* for the sake of end *e* because it is good as a whole" depicts the instrumental or means-to-end *structure* inherent in intention and action,[13] it also provides the structural resources for the evaluation and explanation of action. That is, for an action to be considered good or intelligible, the entire means-to-end relation—in our example voting for the referendum in order to promote safety for cyclists, to further people's health, and to reduce pollution—must be justifiable in some sense. This is the way in which reasons are external or desire-independent: the relation they express is desirable or valuable *not because* I or we desire it but because the relation's parts, i.e. the means (or act) and end (or purpose), are related in the right way, i.e. as good for its own sake or as justifiable in some sense.[14] By this, however, I do not mean that the relation has *intrinsic* worth independently of the agent. This brings us to the sense in which reasons *are* desire-dependent for the Kantian non-instrumentalist, even though he denies the instrumentalist claim that reasons reduce to desires. In this *other* sense of desire-dependency, *reasons can matter only* for sentient beings with desires (in our example, desires for health and an intact environment), for beings to whom things can matter, that is, who can take interest in things.

We can now further characterise this twofold nature of reasons with Korsgaard (2009, p. 105 and pp. 122–24) who argues that a practical reason is never just an incentive alone, but a *conjunction* of an incentive and a principle of choice in the following sense. (i) A reason is an incentive because a reason must respond to our sentient nature as animals with desires. It is under the aspect of incentive that the agent is presented with an action that she might perform since her desires or inclinations reach out for incentives, so to speak, or features that make an object

---

[13] By this I merely wish to repeat Anscombe's (1963) insight that the structure inherent in action is a teleological or means-to-end structure. But the instrumental order inherent in action does not serve as an independent argument for restricting the normative scope of practical reason to instrumental reason.

[14] Cf. Korsgaard (2008, pp. 227–28).

attractive and desirable. (ii) A reason is a principle of choice because it is with regard to such a principle that the agent eventually chooses to do the action—when she chooses it. As a principle of choice a reason is an action description expressed by the form 'I will take the means m to the end e for its own sake'. More specifically, we can understand this not merely instrumentally normative principle that is constitutive of good action along the lines of Korsgaard's (2008, p. 217) Aristotelian idea of the "*orthos logos*": "A good action is one that embodies the *orthos logos* or right principle: it is done at the right time, in the right way, to the right object, and (. . .) with the right aim." In my view, if all of these parameters are satisfied the action can be willed or valued as good or justified *for its own sake*. If only some of the parameters are fulfilled, I would say that the action may still be permissible or intelligible in some sense: then it can be willed as justifiable but not as right or good for its own sake.[15] In a nutshell, we can say that to endorse a desire as a reason is to consider the desire's end or object as rightly or at least justifiably regulating how the means are pursued. So my disagreement with the instrumentalist can be boiled down to the following two considerations.

First, a reason understood as a justifying or mattering-relation concerns the question, roughly, whether the end justifies the means, whereas the instrumentalist-relation, as we might call it, is concerned with the question what the sufficient means are to realise the given (shared) end. The difference between the Kantian asking whether the end justifies the means and the instrumentalist asking whether the means is sufficient for the given end is that citing the sufficient means for effectively achieving the end need not make the whole action intelligible (let alone, good)—after all, the end may not support the act. As we shall see, it is really this different focus of the instrumentalist who takes the end as given, that renders it unintelligible how reasons can be shareable.

Second, contrary to what the instrumentalist argues rational deliberation about ends—deliberation that is not merely concerned with how to *effectively* realise some given end but with *what* ends we should pursue—is possible if one assumes that ends can more or less appropriately regulate means where such appropriateness involves more than considerations of instrumental efficiency, namely something of the Aristotelian idea of acting well.

---

[15]Thus, an action is right and not merely justified if it is justifiable *for its own sake*. This helps us see how the action principle described here can be regarded as the intermediate link between the fact of pure practical reason (rightness) and social norms (justifiability) as it draws our attention to the conceptual distinction between rightness and justifiability. One could e.g. argue with Heath (1997, p. 469) that an action is right only if it is justifiable now with respect to a system of shared social norms and "if it would *remain justified* under any *improvement* of this system". The improvement of the system could then be spelled out in terms of something like a democratic procedure, as Heath suggests, that draws our attention to the rational quality of the principles of choice by which we determine social norms.

4

I think there is one last reply by the instrumentalist to challenge my argument. She could argue that she in fact concurs with me that desires are not identical with reasons in the sense that desires are treated *as* reasons. That is, the instrumentalist would thereby agree that we need *some* action principle or law to guide our actions but she could deny that this is the moral law or some principle of the sort of the *orthos logos*.

This means that the issue now is *not* the familiar one against the Humean instrumentalist who seems to fully allow her desires to determine what she does *without* treating them as reasons for action. Unlike the Humean instrumentalist, our instrumentalist is assumed to grant some sort of *endorsement* of the agent with her desires as reasons or principles. The interesting question now is *what kind* of action principle the instrumentalist can be said to endorse and what guiding force such a principle can have for the agent. From all that I know, I think there is only one way to understand it, namely as some version of the principle of prudent self-love: "I will satisfy my prudent desires, i.e. those which have the best consequences."

The first thing that strikes us here is that by accepting some such principle, the instrumentalist seems to *tacitly* assume a substantive theory of rationality, namely one that tells us that acting rationally means pursuing those ends or satisfying those desires that promote the best consequences in the long run. If this is correct, however, then the instrumentalist cannot *also* argue that practical reason just is or can be reduced to instrumental reason.[16] Instrumental reason alone tells us nothing about which ends we should pursue. So the instrumentalist is faced with something like a dilemma.

On the one hand, if she stays true to her instrumentalist claim that practical reason just is instrumental reason, then she *cannot* say that in the pursuit of our (shared) ends we desire what we think are *good* ends, in the sense of rational ends, because she has no standard by which she could judge which end is good or rational and which is not. To reply that we in fact desire what is rational or good for us would be question-begging.

On the other hand, if the instrumentalist wants to account for the guiding role of desires as reasons, then she no longer is a true instrumentalist, as we have seen, because now she actually defends some substantive view about what one has good reason to do, that is, what ends or objects one has good reason to pursue— for example those that maximise satisfaction of one's prudent individual or shared desires.[17]

---

[16]For such an argument see Korsgaard (2003).

[17]The instrumentalist adheres to a normative theory of rationality to the extent that she has a view about what it is rational to want. For example, taking drugs would not belong to those things that it is rational to want, according to the instrumentalist.

Our discussion so far suggests that when Schmid claims that the problem of instrumentalism is its individualism about ends, what he *actually* means is that something like the principle of prudent self-love as the paradigmatic action principle should be rejected by showing that ends can be shared. But I tried to show that unlike the Kantian, the instrumentalist cannot account for the nature of good action (and therefore, as we shall see, she cannot show how reasons are shareable) and merely pushes its self-centered element to the level of the group.

But there is still the option for Schmid to show how instrumental rationality can accommodate the idea of agents deliberating together or sharing ends such that instrumentalism is no problem. In the next two sections I will examine this option in more detail. More precisely, I will critically discuss Schmid's (2009, pp. 242–44, 2011) claim that the way in which individuals are normatively related to themselves when pursuing an end or to each other when sharing an intention or a desire is purely instrumental.

5

Schmid (2003, 2009, 2011) has convincingly argued that the problem of instrumental rationality is that it instructs us to treat others and their deliberations as mere means or restrictions to our own deliberations. Not unlike Postema (1995), Schmid argues in favour of regarding human instrumental reasoning as capable of integrating other people's perspectives without treating each other as mere means. In other words, Schmid argues that in sharing an end with you, I do not treat you as a mere tool to *my* interests, because my interests, just like yours, are part of *our* interests. By sharing ends with you, I do not treat you and your deliberations as mere constraints on my own since your deliberations and actions are part of what enables *us* to achieve the shared end.

Schmid's point is that you are not used by me as a means to an end that *you share with me* for the same reason that you do not *treat yourself as a means simply by pursuing your own end*. I am very sympathetic to this line of reasoning.

What I consider to be problematic is that Schmid goes on to argue that it remains nevertheless true that I am interested in your reasons—we are members of the same group sharing an intention or desire—merely as instrumental reasons, i.e., in their role as means to realise our shared end. When agents pursue shared ends, they are concerned with each other's instrumental rationality, just as they are concerned with their own instrumental rationality when pursuing individual ends (Schmid 2009, p. 243). In the interpersonal or social case you and I are normatively connected to each other in virtue of our sharing an end, while in the intrapersonal case I and my future self are normatively connected to the individual goal, that is, here one must take one's own will as normative for oneself (Schmid 2011, p. 50). Nevertheless, the normative expectations either towards oneself or towards others are first and foremost instrumentally normative (Schmid 2011, p. 51).[18] It is this claim that I want to challenge here.

I will show that it makes little sense to ascribe to an animal in general instrumental or efficacious rationality as the primary relation in which it stands to itself and others, without being clear about what the underlying ascription of *non-instrumental normativity* is. With regard to *human* animals, my point is that the primary relation the agent has to herself and to others is the mattering-relation and not the instrumentalist-relation. The ascription of failures in a human agent's efficacy depends for its intelligibility on what one thinks counts as her own behaviour in the first place.[19]

6

What I want to say is that an animal's practical irrationality does not reduce to failures in efficacy. Without some knowledge about *what the animal ought to do, as the animal it is*, we cannot say anything about the efficacy of such an animal's behaviour. Human animals have in common with non-human higher animals[20] that they do not have to learn that physical and psychic sensations of pleasure and pain are good or bad sorts of things for them. However, unlike non-human animals, *self-conscious* human animals have to learn to act for good reasons, that is, for considerations about whether some end justifies taking the means to it. That is, we have to learn which instances of good sorts of things are good and which are not. Such learning, however, wouldn't be possible if none of our desires were reason-responsive where 'reason' means more than 'instrumental reason'. Non-human animals, whose ends are largely given to them by their instincts (or by training), do not need to be able to rationally deliberate about ends. I think that is why they cannot, unlike human animals, share ends.[21] For ends to be shareable, the human agent must be capable of regarding the end not as given but as part of a mattering-

---

[18]Thereby I take Schmid to think that he has demonstrated that instrumentalism is not a problem after all, but only its individualism about ends.

[19]My argument here is greatly indebted to Korsgaard's thinking about autonomy and efficacy in her 2009 book *Self-Constitution*, pp. 81–108.

[20]By "higher" or "intelligent" animals I mean animals that are endowed with intelligence such that they can cognize the world, that they can make experiences in the world, and can learn from them. Such an animal can put together cause and effect, generalise from particulars, and it can pursue the means that she has learned or instinctively knows will bring about the desired end (most reliably).

[21]Of course non-human animals or insects are "social" or organized in such a way that they automatically fulfil their function in a colony or some sort of community (think of bees building a honey comb together or of wolfs hunting in packs). Although I cannot argue for this here, sharing an end and engaging in joint intentional action is an essentially different thing with respect to self-conscious human animals because they are aware of what they have in common with others of their kind.

relation that can be the object of her *principled* choice, that is, of a choice whose object is an entire means-to-end maxim that the agent can, as a result, share both with herself and others. Actions that are chosen in the sense described above are inherently open to participation by other self-conscious animals since they are, as Korsgaard (2009, pp. 163 and 146) puts it, "for the good of the whole" instead of "for its own good". I take this to mean that desires considered by themselves, without any relation to non-instrumental practical reason, are really for their own good in the sense that they compel the agent to satisfy each one of them. Desires lack the power to unify.[22] Since desires by themselves, whether shared or not, cannot unify, freeing instrumentalism from its individualism about ends will not render instrumentalism more plausible.

Now we can better understand what it means to say that there is a sense in which reasons are grounded in reason itself rather than in desires. Since reason itself is directed at the good for the whole, desires themselves alone cannot properly guide an agent since guidance requires unification. To repeat, to act for reasons on the Kantian view is not to treat one's ends as settled by one's given desires but as open to rational deliberation that is not just concerned with taking an instrumentally sufficient means to some end but with the whole action description, i.e. the means-to-end relation that describes the action. Not surprisingly, it turns out that whole actions (and not just ends) must be the objects of agents that must act as one or as a unified person.

Instrumentalism about practical reason that is only concerned with taking the instrumentally rational means to one's ends is therefore ill-suited to accommodate the idea of sharing reasons since it cannot account for the idea of good action that incorporates both means and end. We can also see this by considering the following: The way in which one can be right or wrong as far as instrumental rationality is concerned is that one can either achieve one's ends or one can fail to achieve one's ends. Success or failure in this case need be of no concern for others apart from the agent herself. Of course, it *may* be of others' concern if they share an end with the agent, the success of whose realisation partly depends on the agent and her contribution to the shared end. The decisive point is that, on the purely instrumentalist view of practical reason, others are not necessarily *committing a wrong* if they decide that the respective agent's contributions to the shared end are no longer needed and upon a carefully performed cost/benefit analysis exclude her from their community. This is an illustration of the way in which instrumentalism is not good for the whole. On the conception of practical reason that I have attributed to the instrumentalist's opponent, however, the agent would have a claim not to be treated in this way even if she didn't share a particular end with the other members of the community. Excluding a person from a community on the grounds that her

---

[22]The Kantian, as I understand him, is not saying that the desires we can treat as (potential) reasons for action are themselves arrived at by reasoning. What he says is that guidance in action requires the power of practical reason that is not identical with instrumental reason: desires must be open to rational evaluation that is not exhausted by concerns about instrumental efficacy.

contribution to the shared end is not needed (all else equal) counts as unjustifiable since thereby the person would be treated as a mere means. These considerations lead me to agree with Kratochwil (1989, p. 148) who argues that

> [I]t is our common conception of the freedom and responsibility of moral agents that *precedes*, and has to be logically prior to, any attainment or utility of goals that agents choose to undertake, singly or in conjunction.

I understand this as another way of saying that the primary way in which human beings are related to themselves and to each other cannot be instrumental normativity.[23] The concept of human agency is not intelligible unless the concept of moral responsibility is logically prior to that of instrumental rationality. But if this is correct then the authority of a human agent's will cannot be primarily instrumentally normative as Schmid seems to suggest.

The notion of responsibility finally leads us to explain the sense in which the normativity entailed in human agency is *not merely natural* compared to that entailed in animal agency more generally (cf. Korsgaard 2011). Here the fact of pure practical reason comes in. Perceptions of a creature that is not only sentient but also *self-conscious* with an evaluative self-conception will naturally have moral feelings besides bodily and perceptual feelings.[24] These moral feelings have their origin in the feeling of respect for the moral law, which is a law about how the animal *should be related to herself and to others*, namely as unified or good for the whole. Self-conscious animals must bridge the gap that self-consciousness confronts them with in order to act for reasons; to act for reasons ("Can I endorse this desire as a non-instrumental reason?"), in a way, is to act as a unified whole, i.e. to act *with oneself.* So what primarily holds the agent together when she acts for reasons is not an instrumental relation that connects her to her end, as Schmid seems to argue, but a mattering relation to herself and others.[25] The feeling of respect for the moral law is a feeling of responsibility. So the human animal stands in a mattering-relation to herself and others which is not naturally good but normatively good,

---

[23] Another way to demonstrate that instrumental rationality is not an independent form of rationality is to ask what it could mean to say that some action is instrumentally virtuous. While it makes perfect sense to speak of intellectual and moral or practical virtue, it is not clear what instrumental virtue by itself could mean. This is because within a certain range of practicability we can simply take *any* means to *any* ends.

[24] Here, I refer to the kind of self-consciousness that only gradually develops in human beings and that non-human beings lack. Self-consciousness so understood is not exhausted by the animal recognising her own attitudes but involves the animal's awareness of how her attitudes influence her own actions, which allows (or rather, makes necessary) that the animal forms an attitude towards the fact that she is being moved in a certain way. Here lies the potential for moral awareness, the awareness of right and wrong. Cf. Korsgaard (2007, p. 21).

[25] So other people's reasons are not normative for me insofar as they share some particular end with me, as Schmid claims. They are normative for me because as sentient moral beings they have certain moral claims on me whether or not they share some end with me. Cf. also Korsgaard (2009, pp. 201f.).

that is, *conferred* by the animal on herself. After all, the moral law is one that the self-conscious animal gives to herself.

If my argument is on the right track, we can conclude that pursuing a shared goal, *pace* Schmid, cannot transform an otherwise solitary relation into a socially normative one. It is not clear how collective intentionality in the form of social normativity can be constructed out of otherwise solitary relations. Human self-relation must be inherently shareable. As a consequence, there is no *principled* distinction between a rational animal's individual ends, i.e. the ends she can share with herself, and the ends she can share with others. Thus instrumentalism cannot be saved by introducing the concept of shared ends. Rather, the solution must lie in abandoning the idea that instrumental reason is all that practical reason amounts to and with it the instrumentalist concept of human self-relation, since it fails to show how human agency can be what it must be in order to function well: it must unify the agent with herself and others.

References

Anscombe, E. 1963. *Intention*. Oxford: Blackwell.
Bratman, M. 1987. *Intention, plans, and practical reason*. Harvard: Harvard University Press.
Bratman, M. 2004. Shared valuing and frameworks for practical reasoning. In *Reason and value: Themes from the moral philosophy of Joseph Raz*, ed. R.J. Wallace et al., 1–27. Oxford: Oxford University Press.
Broome, J. 1999. Normative requirements. *Ratio* 12(4): 398–419.
Davidson, D. 1963. Actions, reasons, and causes. *The Journal of Philosophy* 60(23): 685–700.
Heath, J. 1997. Foundationalism and practical reason. *Mind* 106(423): 452–474.
Herman, B. 1996. Making room for character. In *Aristotle, Kant, and the Stoics: Rethinking happiness and duty*, ed. S. Engstrom and J. Whiting, 36–60. New York: Cambridge University Press.
Korsgaard, C.M. 2003. The normativity of instrumental reason. In *Ethics and practical reason*, ed. B. Gaut et al., 215–254. Oxford: Oxford University Press.
Korsgaard, C.M. 2007. Human nature and the right. From an unpublished lecture series collectively entitled *Moral Animals*, delivered at the University of Oklahoma as the David Ross Boyd Lectures in 2007. http://www.people.fas.harvard.edu/korsgaar/CMK.MA2.pdf. Accessed 28 Dec 2011.
Korsgaard, C.M. 2008. *The constitution of agency*. Oxford: Oxford University Press.
Korsgaard, C.M. 2009. *Self-constitution*. Oxford: Oxford University Press.
Korsgaard, C.M. 2011. Natural goodness, rightness, and the intersubjectivity of reason: Reply to Arroyo, Cummiskey, Moland, and Bird-Pollan. *Metaphilosophy* 42: 381–394.
Kratochwil, F.V. 1989. *Rules, norms, and decisions*. Cambridge: Cambridge University Press.
Postema, G.J. 1995. Morality in the first person plural. *Law and Philosophy* 14: 35–54.
Richardson, H. 1997. *Practical reasoning about final ends*. Cambridge: Cambridge University Press.
Schmid, H.B. 2003. Rationality-in-relations. *American Journal of Economics and Sociology* 62(1): 67–101.
Schmid, H.B. 2009. *Plural action*. Dordrecht: Springer.
Schmid, H.B. 2011. The idiocy of strategic reasoning. *Analyse & Kritik* 33(1): 35–56.
Schueler, G.F. 2003. *Reasons and purposes*. Oxford: Clarendon.

Chapter 19
The SANE Approach to Real Collective Responsibility

Sara Rachel Chant

Abstract In this paper, I offer an argument for the existence of 'real collective responsibility' and the beginnings of an analysis of it. 'Real collective responsibility' refers to the responsibility that is borne by a group of individuals, but which is not reducible to the responsibility of each individual in the group. The approach I take is to draw an analogy between the uncontroversial way in which an individual's moral responsibility may be mitigated when her behavior is coerced, and the way in which group dynamics may exert pressure constraining the behavior of each member of a group. This sort of consideration suggests that real collective responsibility may occur when a group finds itself in a highly stable, accessible Nash equilibrium, which I refer to as the SANE condition for real collective responsibility.

1 Introduction

The claim that a group bears collective moral responsibility for its action has both a trivial and a non-trivial reading. On the trivial reading, the claim that a group is morally responsible for an action is merely shorthand for the claim that every individual in the group is morally responsible for her contribution to the action. For instance, if a set of bank robbers is morally responsible for a bank heist, we may mean only that each individual robber is morally responsible for her contribution to the robbery. This claim is widely assumed to be unproblematic.

The non-trivial reading is that the group may bear moral responsibility above and beyond the responsibility borne by the individual members. On this reading, the group of bank robbers is morally responsible in some sense that does not reduce to the responsibility of each robber. In contrast to the first sense of 'collective moral

S.R. Chant (✉)
Department of Philosophy, University of Missouri-Columbia, Columbia, MO, USA
e-mail: chants@missouri.edu

A. Konzelmann Ziv and H.B. Schmid (eds.), *Institutions, Emotions, and Group Agents*, 313
Studies in the Philosophy of Sociality 2, DOI 10.1007/978-94-007-6934-2_19,
© Springer Science+Business Media Dordrecht 2014

responsibility', the latter reading is extremely contentious in at least two ways. First, there is no consensus as to whether there are such cases at all; second, even those authors who have argued for it have not agreed on how this sense of 'collective moral responsibility' is to be analyzed.[1]

I shall refer to this former sense of 'collective moral responsibility' as 'distributive' because the responsibility of the group is distributed to the members, with nothing 'left over', so to speak. I shall refer to the latter sense as 'real collective responsibility'. In this paper, I argue for the existence of real collective responsibility, and I offer the beginnings of an analysis of it. The strategy I shall take is to draw an analogy between cases of real collective responsibility and ordinary cases in which an individual's moral responsibility is mitigated or excused by the fact that she was coerced into performing the action. Although coercion is not typically brought into discussions of real collective responsibility, I shall argue that coercion is relevant. This is because cases of real collective responsibility are ones in which (at least part of) each individual's moral responsibility has been mitigated by some situational feature, despite the fact that this mitigating feature fails to mitigate the responsibility of the group as a whole. This mitigating feature may be understood in analogy to coercion. According to the argument I shall offer below, real collective responsibility is to be understood entirely in terms of such mitigating features.

I shall begin by rehearsing an uncontroversial set of cases in which individuals are excused of (at least part of) their moral responsibility for their actions. These are cases in which the person is coerced into action on the force of a credible threat. Thus, I shall begin in the first section with Harry Frankfurt's famous arguments concerning (what he calls) the 'doctrine that coercion excludes responsibility' in his paper, 'Alternate Possibilities and Moral Responsibility' (Frankfurt 1969). Although there is a lively debate about the status of the broader so-called 'principle of alternate possibilities' which is the target of Frankfurt's analysis, it will not be necessary for me to become involved in those larger issues. Instead, I shall focus entirely on the uncontroversial cases which Frankfurt uses to motivate his main argument. In the second section, I examine an argument due to Joel Feinberg (Feinberg 1991), in which he argues that there is such a thing as (what I call) real collective responsibility, as well as some theoretical results in judgment aggregation due to Christian List and Philip Pettit (List and Pettit 2004), which have been interpreted to show that at least some facts about collectives are not reducible to facts about its members (as in Pettit 2004; Copp 2006). Although I shall conclude that the arguments from Feinberg and the impossibility results of List and Pettit cannot establish the existence of real collective responsibility, I will argue in the third section that they do point the way to a general account. That section contains an equilibrium account of real collective responsibility, which I argue provides the basis of a satisfactory account. I expand upon this account in the fourth section, where I offer the beginning of an analysis of the concept of real collective responsibility.

---

[1]There is a wide literature on the subject of collective responsibility, including Copp (2006), Feinberg (1991), Lewis (1991), May (1990), May and Hoffman (1991), Mellema (1988), Miller (2001), Narveson (2002), Sverdlik (1987), Pettit (2007).

2   Coercion Excludes Responsibility

My main argument in favor of the existence of real collective responsibility is that the dynamics that give rise to collective action are sometimes relevantly similar to cases in which individuals are coerced into performing actions that they would normally be unwilling to perform. Because cases of individual coercion are ones in which the individual's moral responsibility is mitigated or eliminated entirely, it is possible for group dynamics to have the same mitigating effect on the responsibility of the members of the group. In this way, any moral responsibility for the group's collective action must attach to the group *qua* group, without being distributed to the group's members.

Cases of individual coercion are often not discussed in detail in the literature on moral responsibility or collective action. Instead, the focus is typically on more difficult questions concerning moral responsibility and related concepts. However, individual coercion was one focus of 'Alternate Possibilities and Moral Responsibility' (Frankfurt 1969). In it, Frankfurt attacks the so-called 'principle of alternate possibilities' (hereafter, PAP), according to which an individual does not bear moral responsibility for her action if she couldn't have done otherwise. Frankfurt's argument against PAP takes the form of a single counterexample, the notorious Jones-4 case. In it, Jones-4 performs an immoral action of his own volition, but could not have done otherwise because another agent, Black, would have forced him to decide to perform the action if Jones-4 had wavered in his decision. Thus, Jones-4 bears responsibility for his action (presumably because the action was a result of his own motivations and was brought about 'in the right way') despite the fact that he couldn't have done otherwise (because Black would have ensured that he decide to perform the action in any event).

Given the tremendous intuitive plausibility of PAP, Frankfurt bolsters the Jones-4 counterexample by arguing that PAP gains its plausibility from a previously unquestioned assumption that it is relevantly similar to another principle, which Frankfurt takes to be unproblematic and uncontroversial. This is the principle that a person is not morally responsible for her action if she has been coerced into performing that action. According to Frankfurt, the so-called 'principle that coercion excludes moral responsibility' is sound, but PAP illicitly gains its plausibility from the assumption that PAP underwrites it. However, on closer examination, Frankfurt concludes that the relationship between coercion and moral responsibility does not depend on PAP after all.

For our purposes here, it is useful to rehearse Frankfurt's discussion of the relationship between coercion and moral responsibility. This discussion highlights a few uncontroversial features of coercion, which I will rely upon to motivate the SANE approach to real collective responsibility.

In his discussion, Frankfurt leads the reader down a garden path of cases, in which various agents are subjected to forces that are intended to constrain their choice of action. These cases lead Frankfurt to note that, although people may be under the same threat, some may be genuine cases of coercion, while others are not. For example, Jones-1 has decided to perform some action, and is subsequently issued a threat from someone intending to coerce him into performing that very same action. But Jones-1, due to his peculiar psychology, is completely unmoved by the threat—he would have performed the action in any event, and the threat is completely irrelevant to him. So when he performs the action, he is fully responsible for having performed it, and so the threat does not count as constituting coercion at all.

On the other end of the spectrum, Jones-2 is 'stampeded' by the threat. Once the threat has been issued, no previous decision or intention of his is relevant at all. Thus, when Jones-2 carries out the action, it is entirely because of the threat. Thus, in contrast to Jones-1, we would say that Jones-2 is *not* responsible for the action. His responsibility is mitigated (or even excused entirely) because he is coerced.

Of course, when we say that coercion excludes moral responsibility, we are not typically thinking of cases that are as extreme as those of Jones-1 and Jones-2. Because Frankfurt is most interested in understanding why we treat coercion this way in ordinary cases, he goes on to consider one last case of coercion before examining PAP. In this penultimate case, Jones-3 has similarly decided before the threat is issued that he will perform a particular action. Subsequent to this decision, he is given the same threat that Jones-1 and Jones-2 were given. However, Jones-3 is a reasonable person who recognizes that the threat is credible, and so the consequences of failing to carry out the action are figured into his decision. That is, he is not (like Jones-1) impervious to threats, nor is he stampeded by them (like Jones-2). Rather, he rationally figures the consequences of inaction into his deliberations. Recognizing that the threat is credible, and that the consequences are severe, Jones-3 performs the action.

At this point, Frankfurt admits that the case might not provide a clear counterexample to the principle that coercion excludes moral responsibility. This is because Jones-3 had already decided to perform the action prior to being given the threat, and so it is difficult to attribute his action to either the threat or to his prior decision. The Jones-4 case, in which Black has the power to directly cause Jones-4 to decide on a particular course of action, is structured the way it is because it eliminates the ambiguity in attributing the origin of the action to either the prior decision of the agent or the influence of Black. But for the purposes of the present paper, we need not take a stand on whether Jones-3 has performed the action because of the threat or because of his prior intention. For the present discussion, we need only consider cases that are clearer; in particular, we can restrict our attention to cases in which an individual has not previously formed an intention to perform the action, but her decision is swayed by a sufficiently severe and highly credible threat. If we hold—as I think we should—that a rational person with an ordinary level of willpower and self-determination could be swayed by a credible threat, then we can have cases in which the person's moral responsibility is at least mitigated, and perhaps eliminated entirely. In short, the principle that is easily motivated by an example like Jones-3 is that:

> An ordinary person, with an ordinary level of autonomy or self-determination may have her moral responsibility at least mitigated by a credible threat of sufficiently serious harm.

Later, I will argue that this uncontroversial principle is relevantly similar to another principle that underwrites the existence of real collective responsibility. In short, my argument will be that there are cases in which every individual in a group is under a coercive threat which emanates from the entire group as a whole; this distinctive type of coercion mitigates the moral responsibility of the individuals in the group, but does not excuse the group itself of its moral responsibility. But before I can give this argument in detail, we must examine some other principles that have been taken to imply the existence of real collective responsibility.

3   Ought Implies Can and the Discursive Dilemma

Attempts to argue for the existence of real collective responsibility fall broadly into two categories. The first category consists of attempts to deploy the 'ought implies can' principle to show that real collective responsibility exists. The second sort of attempt uses structural features of the group to show that the group— but not the individuals—bears moral responsibility. These two strategies are not entirely unrelated. But although both are contentious, and neither of them yield clear examples of real collective responsibility, together they point the way toward a better strategy. In this section, I will briefly discuss each strategy in turn.

The first strategy, that of deploying the 'ought implies can' principle, has a simple logical form. We begin by arguing that there is collective moral responsibility in some case, while leaving open the question as to whether it is merely distributive moral responsibility or whether it is 'real collective responsibility'. We then argue that there is some aspect of the case for which there is moral responsibility, but which no individual could have prevented. If so, then the principle that 'ought implies can' will entail, by a simple *modus tollens* argument, that no individual bears responsibility for that aspect of the example. Therefore, because there is moral responsibility that is borne by no individual in the group, we conclude that the group *qua* group must be the bearer. So such a case must be one of 'real collective responsibility'.

Examples of this argumentative strategy go back at least to Joel Feinberg's paper, 'Collective Responsibility' (Feinberg 1991). This paper centers around a particular example that Feinberg takes to be a clear instance of real collective responsibility. In the example, a train is robbed by Jesse James. The robber is well-armed, and the passengers aboard the train are not. Although Jesse James is clearly morally responsible for the robbery, Feinberg specifies the example so that the passengers also bear responsibility for having been robbed. According to how the case is stipulated, no individual passenger is capable of preventing the robbery (since Jesse James is armed and the passengers are not); any attempt of any single passenger to fend off the robber will be unsuccessful. However, Feinberg stipulates that if the passengers were to rise up together, they could collectively fend off Jesse James at no risk to themselves.

Feinberg argues that if the passengers fail to do so, then they are collectively responsible for being robbed (at least, they bear a portion of the responsibility). If we accept the principle that 'ought implies can', then according to Feinberg, we have to excuse each individual passenger—after all, the example stipulates that no individual could have done anything to prevent the robbery. Thus, if there is responsibility, it must attach to the entire group of passengers as a whole, for only the group *qua* group could have done anything to prevent the robbery from occurring.

Although I shall argue below that the Jesse James case turns out to be quite close to the kind of case that is required, Feinberg's diagnosis of it is not compelling. The major difficulty with the case is that Feinberg explains it by appealing to the 'ought implies can' principle, and his argument depends upon the pair of assertions that the group could have repelled the robbery, while no individual could. There is at least a tension in holding both that:

1. No individual passenger could have risen up to stop the robbery, and
2. the group as a whole could have risen up to stop the robbery.

After all, if (2) is true, then its truth entails that all of the individuals could have stopped the robbery, since the group is simply composed of the individuals. But if so, then the truth of (1) entails that (2) is false. To put the point another way, because the group's behavior supervenes on the behavior of the individuals, it is difficult to so cleanly separate the possible behavior of the group from the possible behavior of the individuals; if it is possible for the group to act in a particular way, then it must be possible for the individuals to act correspondingly. We may put the argument more generally, in the following way. First, we assume that the behavior of a group supervenes on the behavior of the individuals who compose it, in the sense that if the individuals all behave in a particular way, then this fully determines the collective behavior of the group. Thus, if it is possible for the group to perform an action, then this entails that it is possible for the individuals to perform the component actions upon which the group action would supervene. So if the group is judged to have the power to perform a particular action, then we must say of the individuals that they each have the power to perform the corresponding individual actions. Therefore, examples of the form specified by Feinberg cannot be stipulated.[2]

A more subtle approach to the question of real collective responsibility has been used, which depends upon a set of impossibility results originating with Kenneth Arrow's (1950) seminal work on rational preferences, and extended in important recent work by Christian List and Philip Pettit (List and Pettit 2004). These results show that there are situations in which the judgments of a group have logical properties that are in a sense 'disconnected' from the judgments of the individuals. In particular, they show that no method of aggregating the judgments of individuals can guarantee logical consistency, even if the judgments of every individual in the group are logically consistent.

---

[2] I am grateful to Kirk Ludwig for pressing me on this point in an earlier draft of this paper.

Table 19.1 Alice, Bob, and
Carol's beliefs about global
warming

	(1)	(2)	(3)
Alice	True	True	True
Bob	False	True	False
Carol	True	False	False
Total	True	True	False

To take a simple example, suppose that a committee of three people, Alice, Bob, and Carol, are charged with writing a report on global warming. They are to decide on the truth or falsity of each of three propositions:

1. Human carbon dioxide emissions have reached a particular threshold.
2. If human carbon dioxide emissions were to reach that threshold, then this would cause global warming.
3. There is global warming.

Let us assume that each of these propositions is open to reasonable disagreement among rational, well-informed people. However, there is one set of beliefs that would be irrational; namely, if someone were to believe (1) and (2), then it would be irrational not to believe (3), because it is simply the logical consequence of the first two propositions. Any other combination is rational (or so we shall stipulate). Now suppose that Alice, Bob, and Carol have the following opinions about (1)–(3):

- Alice believes that all three propositions are true.
- Bob believes that (1) is false. However, he does believe that (2) is true. Thus, because he does not accept the antecedent of (2), he is not rationally required to accept (3). And indeed, Bob does not believe that (3) is true.
- Carol also believes that (3) is false. However, she has different reasons. She believes that (1) is true (thus, disagreeing with Bob), but she does not believe that this level of carbon dioxide emission is sufficient to cause global warming (2).

We may represent their beliefs in the chart in Table 19.1. The relevance to collective responsibility comes into the picture when we consider how their judgments would be combined. To make the example more vivid, suppose that the committee has been charged with writing a report on global warming, divided into three sections corresponding to the three questions above. It may appear to be a reasonable plan for the committee members to vote on the conclusions to be asserted in each section. Suppose that they agree to do so, thereby deploying what List and Pettit refer to as a 'premise-centered' approach to judgment aggregation. When they vote on the first question, there is a majority in support of the claim that human emissions of carbon dioxide have reached the critical threshold, with only Bob dissenting. Accordingly, their report will assert that the first question has a positive answer. The same holds for the second question (with only Carol dissenting), and so they would write in their report that this level of emissions would be sufficient to cause global warming. But when they turn to the conclusion of the report, they vote that global warming does not exist, despite the fact that they have collectively agreed to a set of conditions that logically entails that there is global warming. Thus, they collectively believe an inconsistent set of propositions, despite the fact that no member of the group does.

It has been suggested that in a case of collective judgment that is structured like this one, moral responsibility may attach to the group without any of the individuals bearing responsibility (Copp 2006). For if irrationality is a morally culpable fault, then it attaches to the group as a whole, but not to any individual member of the group.

More generally, such phenomena in judgment aggregation, preference aggregation, and the so-called 'discursive dilemma' show that the behavior and judgment of individuals may come apart from the behavior and judgment of the group. To put the point another way, although the collective judgment of the group supervenes on the judgments of the group's members, the rationality of the group judgment is not entailed by the rationality of the individuals' judgments. An argument for real collective responsibility says that when the moral responsibility of the group is tied to the rationality of the group, then so too, the moral responsibility of the group can come apart from the moral responsibility of the members. This sort of case is a much more substantive argument for the existence of real collective responsibility because it allows us to deny any version of the premise that caused problems for Feinberg's case. That is, in Feinberg's case, the fact that group actions supervene on individual actions makes it difficult to conclude that we have a genuine case of real collective responsibility. But the formal results due to Arrow and to List and Pettit show that the rationality of a group does not supervene on the rationality of the individuals. And this fact opens up the possibility that group rationality and individual rationality may come apart, thereby creating the possibility of real collective responsibility.

The argument does face a different challenge, however. This challenge is to point out that in order for no individual to bear moral responsibility, the example must be specified in such a way that there is no individual upon whom we can blame the failure of the judgment aggregation procedure. For example, if a committee were in danger of falling into the sort of situation faced by Alice, Bob, and Carol, then one might reasonably argue that it would be the responsibility of each of them to seek a way to avoid that outcome. Perhaps, for instance, each could have proposed a new method of aggregating their judgments—one that would not have yielded such paradoxical results. Or suppose, for instance, that the committee was charged with their task by the president of their university, who also required that they aggregate their judgments by voting on each question separately. Then it would be reasonable to lay the moral fault at the feet of the president, since it was at least foreseeable that the group would fall into this logical trap.

But suppose that there was, in fact, no way for any of the individuals to have foreseen or taken steps to avoid the situation that Alice, Bob, and Carol found themselves in. If so, then it seems that the group necessarily found itself in this judgment aggregation paradox. But if that is the case, then it is difficult to see how the group could have failed in any meaningful way to have met its responsibilities. For the principle that ought implies can would seem to imply that, because there was no way for the group to avoid its collective irrationality, then that failure cannot be a failure to meet any moral obligation.

4   Equilibria and Real Collective Responsibility

The failures of the previous cases to provide a clear-cut example of real collective responsibility do not show that the task is hopeless. On the contrary, I think that we learn a few important lessons that help us see how to construct a genuine example. In this section, I shall draw out those lessons and argue for the existence of real collective responsibility. The class of examples I shall develop will point the way toward a general account of this phenomenon.

Recall that in the Jones-2 case, we excuse Jones-2 because he faces a credible threat of serious harm. In examining the first three of the Jones cases, we are led to the common-sense conclusion that a reasonable human being may be excused of moral responsibility for at least some (otherwise) immoral acts if she faces such a threat. Furthermore, it is not required that the person be 'stampeded' into performing the action. Rather, a person can be in control of her rational faculties and simply perform the required action because she properly understands the risk to herself if she refuses. Of course, a person could still refuse on general principle. But we would typically say of such a person that she acted heroically, and that her refusal to perform the action was supererogatory, not morally required. For instance, if a person is ordered to rob a bank under threat of being killed by a bomb, and the threat is credible, then only a hero would refuse the request. Any reasonable person would comply, and we would ordinarily excuse the person of any moral responsibility for robbing the bank, despite the possible existence of such heroic individuals.

Of course, such cases do not concern *collective* moral responsibility—they are merely cases in which individual responsibility is mitigated. However, as I have mentioned above, there is a substantive link between mitigation of moral responsibility and real collective responsibility. This link is that real collective responsibility occurs if there is moral responsibility, but every individual's responsibility has been mitigated to a sufficient degree by a credible threat of serious harm.

The second lesson is from both Feinberg's 'ought implies can' case, as well as from the judgment aggregation case of List and Pettit. What both of these purported examples have in common is that they rely on some structural feature of the group to support the claim that there is real collective responsibility. That is, real collective responsibility is to be explained by the fact that the individuals' actions are somehow constrained by the dynamics the group finds itself in. In the Feinberg case, the relevant dynamic is that in order to successfully stop the robbery, everyone on the train would have to act together, and this coordination is difficult to achieve. In the judgment aggregation case, the dynamic is that the group must aggregate its judgment according to a specific procedure that is vulnerable to the judgment aggregation problem that arises. If either of these dynamics were changed, it would be much more difficult to maintain that there is real collective responsibility. For example, if it were easy for the passengers on the train signal to each other that they should all rush the robber at the same time, we would probably be far less likely to excuse the individuals of their moral responsibility. Similarly, if each member of the committee had the power to suspend their voting procedure and call for a new procedure to be developed, then we would also be far less likely to say that this is a case of real collective responsibility.

Combining these two lessons, we are led to consider whether there are cases in which each individual in the group faces a credible threat constraining her individual action, but in which that threat is due to a structural feature of the group that no individual can evade.

But this set of conditions is quite familiar. It describes cases in which a group has an equilibrium behavior, where that equilibrium is highly suboptimal, but in which deviation from that equilibrium will be severely penalized. In the following section, I will explain this condition in more detail, and argue that it both motivates the existence of real collective responsibility, while also explaining some of the most plausible features of that form of responsibility.

5 The SANE Approach

The equilibrium concept I shall use here is due to John Nash, from his seminal paper, 'The Bargaining Problem' (Nash 1950). To understand the Nash equilibrium concept, we consider a set of agents, each of whom faces a choice between two or more actions. In order to be non-trivial, the situation should be a *strategic game*, meaning that each individual will be rewarded or penalized based not only on her own choice of action, but also upon the choice of action of the others. We say that a set of players is in a Nash equilibrium if each player has no incentive to switch strategies, provided that nobody else switches. Put in a slightly different way, each player is getting as high a payoff as possible, given the strategies of the other players.

Perhaps the most widely discussed such game is the so-called 'Prisoners Dilemma', which also happens to be relevant to the present discussion. In this game, each individual has a choice between a cooperative and a non-cooperative action, typically labeled C (for cooperation) and D (for defection). The game is characterized by the fact that the sum of their payoffs is highest when both players cooperate, despite the fact that each player is better off by defecting, no matter what the other player does. It is therefore a dilemma in the sense that the agents jointly prefer to both cooperate, but each individual has an incentive not to cooperate. A payoff matrix for the game is given in Fig. 19.1.

The Prisoners Dilemma is a particularly clear case for illustrating the Nash equilibrium concept because it is so easy to see that (D,D) is the unique equilibrium. For suppose that a player is playing C. No matter what the other player does, it would be best to switch from C to D, for either her payoff would improve from 4 to 5, or from 0 to 2. Because both players face exactly the same choice, they must both play D, and so that is the unique Nash equilibrium. This is notwithstanding the fact that their combined payoff would have been better if they had both played C (with a combined payoff of 8 if they both cooperate, but merely 4 if they do not).

Fig. 19.1 The Prisoners
Dilemma. The row player's
payoff is first in each pair,
and the column player's
payoff is second

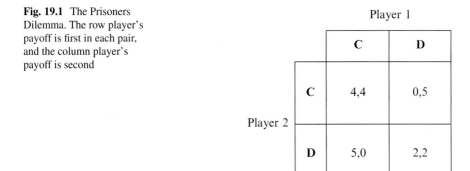

Of course, I am not arguing that any simple formal condition such as an equilibrium will fully characterize real collective responsibility. However, with appropriate additions, the Nash equilibrium concept goes a long way toward understanding it.

Recall the Jesse James train robbery case advanced by Feinberg. With some appropriate specifications, it is reasonable to interpret the situation as a sort of Prisoners Dilemma. Suppose that it would not be necessary for every single passenger on the train to collectively rise up and prevent the robbery, but that it would take many of them to do so. If sufficiently many people cooperate to stop the robbery from happening, there would be only a small risk to any of them, but there is no risk whatsoever to those passengers who just sit passively and allow themselves to be robbed. In this situation, every passenger prefers that a sufficiently large number of them work together to stop the robbery; but each passenger prefers to sit passively and let others take the risk of doing so. Thus, the passengers will be in a Nash equilibrium if they all sit passively allowing themselves to be robbed. For if we assume that everyone else is sitting passively, there is no incentive (indeed, there is a powerful disincentive) to try to stop the robbery from occurring.

With the example respecified in this way, consider what we would say about the moral responsibility of the passengers. Let us suppose, with Feinberg, that there is moral responsibility borne by the group for failing to prevent the robbery. If we agree that a person's moral responsibility can be mitigated by a credible threat of serious harm, then each passenger's moral responsibility is mitigated here as well; for the example stipulates that even if a sufficient number of passengers cooperates to stop the robbery, each individual who does so is still taking a serious risk. Thus, if there is moral responsibility in such a case, there must be real collective responsibility.

Note that this argument does not depend upon the principle that ought implies can. In fact, we have stipulated that the individuals can rise up, individually and collectively, to stop the robbery. But they can do so only in the sense that a heroic person could do so. And the group of passengers is collectively capable of doing so only insofar as it is possible for the train to contain a large number of heroic individuals. What mitigates each individual's moral responsibility is not that they *cannot* stop the robbery, but that it is very *risky* for them to stop the robbery.

324   S.R. Chant

Another case will help clarify important differences between Feinberg's argument and the argument I am advancing here. Let us suppose that global warming will occur unless a sufficiently large number of people recycle their trash. However, no individual's recycling their trash will have any positive effect at all. Now suppose—realistically enough—that given these facts, nobody recycles their trash and global warming occurs. What are we to say of each individual's responsibility for global warming?

On Feinberg's account, we must say that we are collectively, but not individually, responsible for global warming. This is simply because it is not possible for any individual to make any positive impact by recycling her own trash. Thus, if Feinberg were right to deploy the 'ought implies can' principle, then we are each excused of any moral responsibility for global warming.

I think this is not a reasonable conclusion to draw about our moral responsibility. Rather, we each surely bear some, perhaps small, responsibility for our contribution to global warming. If anything is a clear example of distributive moral responsibility, it is when each person knowingly contributes to the production of a serious harm, despite the fact that each person's contribution is fully voluntary, and there is no risk for refusing to contribute to the harm.

5.1 Relevance of Equilibria to Real Collective Responsibility

The Nash equilibrium concept is useful for understanding real collective responsibility because it concisely expresses an important way in which the behavior of rational individuals is constrained by the structure of the group and the decision problem the group faces. It shows that a group may find itself trapped in an undesirable pattern of behavior because each individual is constrained by the collective behavior of everyone else in the group, despite the fact that the individuals may find this collective behavior to be quite undesirable.

Here, it is useful to consider coercion once more, and how coercion excuses or at least mitigates an individual's moral responsibility. Suppose I put a gun to your head and order you to perform an action that is morally repugnant. If you justifiably believe that I will fire the gun if you refuse, then you are surely excused for performing the action. And this is true even if the situation is less than life-threatening. If I 'merely' threaten to shoot you in the leg if you refuse, then only a hero would be expected to stand her ground. You are surely not blameworthy for failing to behave heroically. In this way, the blame is properly refocused on me, because I coerced you into performing the action.

In some situations, an entire group of individuals may face an equally unattractive choice—it may be the case that every member of a group faces a similar threat of serious harm if they fail to behave in a particular way. Clearly, these considerations apply without serious modification if someone is literally holding a gun to the head of every member of a group. But what the Nash equilibrium concept shows us is that the threat may be directed at each member of the group *by every other member of the group*.

To see this, consider the following example. Suppose that in a particular country, it is difficult for individuals to survive economically unless they invest in a dubious financial scheme. Worse yet, as resources are diverted into it, there is less left over for those who refuse to take part, making it more difficult for people to exit the scheme. If the threat of serious harm is great enough, it is only reasonable to judge that the individuals who are involved in the financial scheme are 'trapped', and the consequences are dire enough that we would largely excuse them for failing to take a principled stand against it. Suppose that as a result, there is an economic crisis and serious harm ensues. If we take seriously the analogy between individual-level coercion (as in the Jones cases) and group-level coercion, then we should conclude that the moral fault lies with the source of the coercive force. In this case, the coercion came from the group of investors as a whole, and the coercion was directed at the very individuals who compose the group. Accordingly, the group bears moral responsibility, while the individuals in the group do not. In other words, this is a case of real collective responsibility.

5.2   Beyond Formal Considerations: Stability and Accessibility

Of course, no substantive moral claim will be fully understood in terms of a purely formal concept such as that of a Nash equilibrium. For example, suppose that a terrible consequence can be averted if a large enough number of people contribute one penny to a charity. If nobody contributes to the charity, and the terrible consequence ensues, then the individuals are in a Nash equilibrium. To see this, note that no individual has an incentive to contribute a penny to the charity, on the assumption that nobody else does; for by stipulation, no single individual's contribution will avert the disaster. So each person faces a choice between contributing a penny and not contributing a penny, with the disaster occurring regardless of their choice (assuming that nobody else is contributing). Each person therefore prefers to keep their penny, so this is a Nash equilibrium.

Obviously, it is too much to simply excuse everyone of their moral responsibility if the disaster could have been averted with only a trivial contribution from enough people. In other words, the threat of losing a penny is not sufficient to constitute a credible threat of serious harm of the severity that normally excuses an individual in cases of coercion.

In game-theoretic terms, the severity of the threat—or more generally, the strength of the penalty for deviating from the equilibrium—is often characterized as determining the 'stability' of the equilibrium. The motivation for referring to this as the equilibrium's 'stability' is that although deviations from equilibria are virtually always possible, deviations are less likely to occur if the penalty for deviating is very great. For this reason, the equilibrium will be more likely to persist in such a case. On the other hand, if the penalty for deviation is very small—as in the case where it only costs a penny to behave out of equilibrium—we would be much more likely to see the group move away from the equilibrium behavior.

The fact that the stability of an equilibrium comes in degrees fits well with our pre-theoretic attributions of real collective responsibility, as well as with our intuitive judgments about coercion. After all, we are less likely to excuse a person of moral responsibility if they were 'threatened' with some trivial harm than we would be if they were threatened with a more serious harm. Clearly, mitigation of moral responsibility comes in degrees, regardless of whether we are considering the actions of an isolated individual, or the actions of a number of individuals in a group. Because the degree of moral responsibility is at least partially determined by the severity of the threat, the equilibrium account of real collective responsibility coheres well with our pre-theoretic notions.

It is also worth considering a second way in which the equilibrium concept highlights an important feature of real collective responsibility. We may think of stability as a measure of how likely or unlikely it is that a group will leave an equilibrium state once that equilibrium has been reached. But there is also a question of how likely it is that a group will enter an equilibrium state in the first place. This is not answered merely by citing the stability of the equilibrium, since an equilibrium may be highly stable and yet difficult to reach, owing to a variety of possible features of the situation. To take a timely example, it may be the case that there is a set of financial and economic reforms that would be very efficient and therefore highly stable if those reforms were ever enacted. But because of various political obstacles, it may be very unlikely that such reforms would ever be enacted, despite the fact that there is widespread agreement that the reforms are quite desirable. Let us refer to this property of an equilibrium as its 'accessibility'.

Accessibility comes in degrees, just as stability does. On one end of the spectrum, the equilibrium may simply be the *status quo*, the state the group immediately finds itself in. This is the case in Feinberg's description of the Jesse James robbery case. Presumably, when the robbery begins, the passengers are not particularly organized, and there is no mechanism in place for them to coordinate their actions with each other. This feature, despite the fact that it is only implicit in Feinberg's description of the case, lends plausibility to the assertion that the passengers, in some sense, could not have coordinated a response to the robbery. If, for some reason, the passengers had been in a highly organized state—perhaps if they were all members of the same organization and they frequently are called-upon to coordinate their actions—we would be more likely to find them morally blameworthy.

On the other end of the spectrum, it may be the case that a group goes through a lengthy and deliberate process to place itself in an equilibrium state. For example, once the bank robbery has begun, it may be true that each robber has a strong disincentive to stop performing their part of the robbery—for instance, it may increase their chance of getting caught if any of them stopped doing their part. In this way, the robbers may be in a very strongly stable equilibrium. But we do not normally excuse the individuals of their moral responsibility in such a case. This is because, despite the fact that they are in an equilibrium, that equilibrium state was not very accessible insofar as it took a significant and deliberate effort to place themselves in that state to begin with.

The proposal, therefore, is that real collective responsibility exists in a situation to the extent that the group acts as a result of finding itself in a Stable, Accessible, Nash Equilibrium. In a slogan, this is the SANE approach to real collective responsibility.

6   Conclusion

Real collective responsibility is a particularly difficult concept because there are intuitively compelling arguments both for and against its existence. For instance, we frequently speak as if there is real collective responsibility—as when we say of a corporation *qua* corporation that it is guilty of a crime. Thus, common usage seems to militate in favor of the existence of real collective responsibility. However, it is equally intuitively compelling that if a group is morally blameworthy, then there must have been some failure at the individual level which accounts for it. After all, we are used to thinking of the actions of groups as determined by the actions of the individuals, and this habit makes it reasonable to think of real collective responsibility along the same lines.

For this reason, it is extremely difficult to motivate the existence of real collective responsibility by giving intuitively compelling examples, or by relying on simple moral principles such as 'ought implies can'. But conversely, there is no obvious reductive argument establishing that real collective responsibility must supervene on individual responsibility, especially given the judgment aggregation results showing that other group-level predicates such as rationality are not necessarily a function of the corresponding individual-level predicates.

Thus, I have attempted to take a different tack in this paper. Rather than directly examining purported cases of real collective responsibility, I have argued that such cases are specific instances of a more general class of cases. These are ones in which an individual (or group of individuals) has their moral responsibility mitigated or excused entirely. In such cases, the moral responsibility is transferred, as it were, to the agent who is the source of the coercion. Once we have adopted this perspective, it is clear that there are cases in which every member of a group is coerced, but this coercive force comes from the group itself. Such cases are all too common. We may understand a large variety of collective action problems, moral hazards, economic inefficiencies, and instances of systemic social corruption in these terms.

Despite the fact that real collective responsibility is not fully explicable in mathematical or other formalisms, there is a family of theories that may be quite valuable for describing these examples. As we might hope, the theory of Nash equilibria, which has proven so useful for studying group behavior, can also be pressed into service here. Cases in which the group exerts a coercive force on its own members turn out to be a subclass of Nash equilibria. The concept of a Nash equilibrium proves its worth in this context in much the same way as in economic contexts. That is, despite the fact that it is not the 'end of the story' for explaining either real collective responsibility or group behavior in general, it does provide an extremely useful framework, which highlights the most important ways in which the analysis must be expanded.

In the case of real collective responsibility, additional questions are relevant. For example, we want to know about the relative strength of the coercive force that the group exerts on its members, and how likely it was the group would find itself in that equilibrium. It is an important virtue of the present approach that these additional factors do not need to be added in any *ad hoc* manner. Rather, these factors are naturally described in ways that cohere well with each other within the equilibrium framework. This has led us to the SANE approach—that real collective responsibility exists when the group is in a stable, accessible, Nash equilibrium. No doubt there are other features that will turn out to be relevant to a fuller understanding of real collective responsibility. The present account will be judged to be successful to the extent that these other features cohere equally well within the equilibrium framework.

References

Arrow, K. 1950. A difficulty in the concept of social welfare. *Journal of Political Economy* 58(4): 328–346.

Copp, D. 2006. On the agency of certain collective entities: An argument from 'normative autonomy'. *Midwest Studies in Philosophy* 30: 194–221.

Feinberg, J. 1991. Collective responsibility. In *Collective responsibility: Five decades of debate in theoretical and applied ethics*, ed. L. May and S. Hoffman, 53–76. New York: Rowman & Littlefield Publishers.

Frankfurt, H. 1969. Alternate possibilities and moral responsibility. *The Journal of Philosophy* 66(23): 829–839.

Lewis, H. 1991. Collective responsibility. In *Collective responsibility: Five decades of debate in theoretical and applied ethics*, ed. L. May and S. Hoffman, 17–33. New York: Rowman & Littlefield Publishers.

List, C., and P. Pettit. 2004. Aggregating sets of judgments: Two impossibility results compared. *Synthese* 140: 207–235.

May, L. 1990. Collective inaction and shared responsibility. *Nous* 24: 269–278.

May, L., and S. Hoffman. 1991. *Collective responsibility: Five decades of debate in theoretical and applied ethics*. New York: Rowman & Littlefield Publishers.

Mellema, G. 1988. Causation, foresight, and collective responsibility. *Analysis* 48(1): 44–50.

Miller, S. 2001. Collective responsibility. *Public Affairs Quarterly* 15(1): 65–82.

Narveson, J. 2002. Collective responsibility. *The Journal of Ethics* 6(2): 179–198.

Nash, J. 1950. The bargaining problem. *Econometrica* 18: 155–162.

Pettit, P. 2004. Groups with minds of their own. In *Socializing metaphysics*, ed. F. Schmitt, 167–193. New York: Rowman & Littlefield Publishers.

Pettit, P. 2007. Responsibility incorporated. *Ethics* 117: 171–201.

Sverdlik, S. 1987. Collective responsibility. *Philosophical Studies* 51(1): 61–76.

Chapter 20
Are Individualist Accounts of Collective Responsibility Morally Deficient?

András Szigeti

Abstract Individualists hold that moral responsibility can be ascribed to single human beings only. An important collectivist objection is that individualism is *morally* deficient because it leaves a normative residue. Without attributing responsibility to collectives there remains a "deficit in the accounting books" (Pettit). This collectivist strategy often uses judgment aggregation paradoxes to show that the collective can be responsible when no individual is. I argue that we do not need collectivism to handle such cases because the individualist analysis leaves no responsibility-deficit. Harm suffered in such situations can have only two sources. Harm is either due to culpable wrongdoing by individuals. Harm is then redressed by holding these individuals responsible. Or harm does not result from culpable wrongdoing. Such harm may have to be redressed too, but not because anyone is responsible for it. Therefore, the charge of moral insensitivity against individualist accounts can be rejected. Furthermore, in the last section of the chapter I will show that collectivist talk about moral responsibility can be used for ethically questionable purposes as well. Collectivists cannot claim the moral high ground.

1 Introduction

Individualism is here defined as the view that moral responsibility can be ascribed to single human beings only. In particular, no collective *qua* collective is a proper addressee of responsibility-ascriptions. More specifically, individualist accounts of collective responsibility hold that when we allocate responsibility for an outcome brought about by some group, we can either ascribe individual responsibility to

Work on this article was made in part possible by support from the Hungarian Innovation Office (formerly NKTH)/MAG Zrt. research project "What is it to be human?" (BETEGH 09).

A. Szigeti (✉)
Department of Philosophy, Lund University, Lund, Sweden
e-mail: andras.szigeti@fil.lu.se

A. Konzelmann Ziv and H.B. Schmid (eds.), *Institutions, Emotions, and Group Agents*, 329
Studies in the Philosophy of Sociality 2, DOI 10.1007/978-94-007-6934-2_20,
© Springer Science+Business Media Dordrecht 2014

individual members of that collective and/or ascribe joint responsibility to individual members for their contribution to the collectively brought about outcome. Once responsibility has been ascribed to individual members of the collective, however, there is nothing more to allocate in terms of backward-looking moral responsibility.[1]

Collectivism is the opposite view which holds that the responsibility of a group is in some cases not reducible to the responsibility of individual members of that group. In these cases, the collective *qua* collective is a proper addressee of responsibility-ascriptions.

The debate between individualists and collectivists about responsibility is being fought on two fronts. First, there is the theoretical clash concerning the nature of action and its metaphysical foundations. Thus some individualists doubt that collective responsibility is *metaphysically* possible believing that collective responsibility presupposes collective agency, but only individual human beings (if anybody) meet the conditions of agency.[2]

But, second, there is a normative, or more narrowly, ethical motivation to engage with the issue of collective responsibility as well. In late modernity it has become clearer than ever that the existence of collectives can crucially impact on human lives. By being associated with other people we become sources of special types of harm (and benefit) to others (Kutz 2000, pp. 1–3). It is hoped that getting a grasp on collective responsibility will enable us to place the blame (or praise) where it belongs. This ethical interest creates the second scene of battle between individualists and collectivists. Specifically, what many collectivists fear is that many familiar types of wrong (and good) happening to us may remain unaccounted for without a robust notion of collective responsibility.

The agent-theoretical and the ethical interests are obviously not independent from one another.[3] Ultimately, what one is to think of the overall prospects of the

---

[1] It should be clear that the notion of responsibility I talk about here is robust, desert-based, backward-looking moral responsibility which is commonly thought to be presupposed by a distinct range of reactive attitudes (e.g., guilt, resentment, blame, etc.) and normative consequences (e.g., punishment, sanctions, reparation, etc.). Pettit, for example, makes it quite clear that this is the notion of responsibility he has in mind when talking about the responsibility of collective agents (see Pettit 2007, p. 174).

[2] Haji (2006), among others, shows how to run such an argument, although he stops short of drawing a definite anti-collectivist conclusion. See also Miller and Mäkelä (2005, p. 646n15) for such metaphysically-oriented anti-collectivist arguments. McKenna (2006) is an interesting mixed case. McKenna argues that while some collectives meet the conditions of agency, they do not meet the more exacting conditions of morally responsible agency. McKenna also adds (2006, p. 29) that his is an empirical claim and should not be taken to entail that as a matter of metaphysical impossibility there could not be morally responsible collective agents.

[3] For example, some believe that the (allegedly) unproblematic attributability of moral responsibility to collectives can be taken as evidence for the metaphysical possibility of collective agency. Or, conversely, some think that the metaphysics of collective agency is unproblematic, and since the metaphysics of collective agency is unproblematic, we have no reason not to acknowledge the attributability of moral responsibility to such collective agents (see French 1979). And then there are some who put forward independent but in their conclusions converging collectivist (or anti-collectivist) arguments in both areas (e.g., Pettit 2007).

opposing positions will depend on one's assessment of their respective contributions in both "theatres of war". In this chapter, however, I will focus only on the ethically-motivated collectivist worry that individualism is *morally* deficient because it leaves a normative residue. Without attributing responsibility to collectives *qua* collectives, there remains a "deficit in the accounting books" (Pettit 2007, p. 194; see also French 1979, p. 207; Kutz 2000, p. 113; Copp 2006, p. 216, etc.). Nobody will be called to task for many kinds of harms, the source of which appears to be the existence of collectives—so especially (but not exclusively) for the harms brought on by corporations, governments, international organizations, and other organized collectives. Therefore, it is concluded, the individualist account is morally inferior to collectivist approaches.

I will argue in this chapter that there is no such responsibility-deficit. If harm[4] is the result of culpable wrongdoing, it will be possible to account for it by ascribing responsibility to individuals. I will grant that there may be other types of harm suffered in the kind of situations the collectivist focuses on. It will become clear, however, that these other types of harm are not the result of culpable wrongdoing and so no responsibility can be ascribed for them. This is not to say that victims of these other types of harm can raise no legitimate claims for redress under certain circumstances. But if they can raise such claims, it is not because they have been the victims of culpable wrongdoing. In short, either some individual is responsible for the harms suffered or no one is. If that is correct, the charge of moral insensitivity levelled at individualist accounts can be rejected.

Further, as I will show at the end, collectivist talk about moral responsibility can be used for ethically questionable purposes as well. Collectivists cannot claim the moral high ground.

2 Irreducible Collective Responsibility and Paradoxes of Judgment Aggregation

The wrongs collectivists typically worry about are such that (i) they are brought about as a result of the actions of several individuals, and (ii) these individuals themselves do not appear to be culpable at all, or (iii) if even they are culpable to some extent, it is not clear that their culpability would add up to the sum total of culpability for the wrong which the given case involves, and finally, (iv) if the wrong in question had been done by an individual, we would not hesitate to hold that individual responsible (provided she is fit to be held responsible for that action of course, but that is another matter).

For example, each typical inhabitant of the metropolis upstream seems only marginally culpable for her contribution to polluting the river (after all, typically her contribution to pollution is neither necessary nor sufficient for the environmental

---

[4]In the following, I will only discuss responsibility-ascriptions for wrongdoing, setting aside the issue of praiseworthy actions.

damage). Yet the pollution is a serious wrong suffered by the inhabitants of the village downstream. If the pollution had been brought about by a single individual, we would not hesitate to hold her responsible. But if there is no given individual to be held responsible for the pollution, should we just refrain from holding anyone responsible? Should we refrain despite the fact that the pollution is indisputably a collectively brought about outcome and so there is an obvious candidate for the ascription of responsibility, namely the collective itself?

There are different types of cases for which collectivist arguments have been made in this style: first, cases of collective omissions (Petersson 2008, etc.), second, cases of marginal individual contributions to collective harm (as in the pollution example above) (Kutz 2000, etc.), third, outcomes causally overdetermined by individual contributions (Kutz 2000, but cf. Parfit 1984), and fourth, cases which involve aggregations of individual judgments.

From here on, I will focus *only* on the fourth type of case here. I limit my inquiry to this type not only for reasons of space and not only because the most original collectivist arguments have been put forward in this area, but also because if the collectivist analysis of this fourth type of case is correct, collective-level responsibility for wrongdoing can be entirely autonomous from the responsibility of individual members of the collective.[5] The collective can be culpable even if none of the members are. Therefore, the individualist could be guilty of creating a particularly large gap in the accounting books by not attributing responsibility directly to the collective. As a result, the argument from normative residue seems particularly forceful in this type of case.

As noted already, such cases involve complications of judgment aggregation. Here is my slightly modified version of a celebrated example (which was first introduced in Bovens and Rabinowicz 2006; see also List 2006; Copp 2006, 2007; Pettit 2007, etc.).[6]

---

[5]In the first three types of case, individual contributions may be said to be culpable to some extent because even if not necessary they constitute at least marginal contributions to the collectively brought about wrong or at least amount to some other sort of (non-causal) complicity in that wrong (see Kutz 2000). As we will see, no such complicity can be made out in the fourth type of case.

[6]Note that Bovens and Rabinowicz (2006) use the Tenure Committee example to focus on epistemic features of aggregation procedures. My version of the Tenure Committee case is probably closest to Copp (2007). However, it differs in important ways from how the case is presented there. In Copp's version of Tenure Committee, the committee's decision is taken in two stages, each of which involves a different decision procedure. The ground for complaint in Copp's version is that the respective outcomes of these two procedures conflict *and* the candidate is made aware of the results of both procedures. According to Copp, this two-stage decision raises a legitimate expectation in the candidate that she will receive tenure after the first stage which expectation is then frustrated after the second stage. But if *this* was the problem in the Tenure Committee case, then it could be easily fixed, namely by telling the candidate only about the final outcome after both stages have been concluded. If the collectivist argument is to get off the ground, then the Tenure Committee type case must involve some deeper flaw. I believe my version brings out what this deeper flaw may be, how it may serve as the basis for the collectivist argument, and why nevertheless that collectivist argument fails. I thank Kirk Ludwig for pressing me to make the difference between Copp's version and mine clearer.

Table 20.1 Tenure Committee

	Research?	Teaching?	Service?	Tenure?
A	No (−p)	Yes (q)	Yes (r)	No -(p&q&r)
B	Yes (p)	No (−q)	Yes (r)	No -(p&q&r)
C	Yes (p)	Yes (q)	No (−r)	No -(p&q&r)
A&B&C	Yes (p)	Yes (q)	Yes (r)	Yes (p&q&r)

Three members of a university's tenure committee have to decide whether to award tenure to Ms Borderline. The university's standard for tenure states that excellence in the three areas of research, teaching, and service is required (and is sufficient) for tenure. In the case of Ms Borderline, in each of the three areas, a majority of the committee votes that she has achieved the required standard of excellence (i.e., the committee uses the so-called premise-based decision procedure). So they award tenure despite the fact that individually each member of the committee is against awarding tenure given that they each judge that Ms Borderline fails to meet one of the three required criteria (Table 20.1).

Now, the university administration or another candidate for tenure, call her Ms Secondbest, may challenge this result. The complaint appears to have some ground. After all, no member was in favor of awarding tenure! But who, if anyone, is responsible for the decision? Only the Tenure Committee as a whole can be responsible—after all, to repeat, no member was in favor of awarding tenure!

So let us retrace how the collectivist argument runs here. If the complaint is legitimate, then somebody must have wronged Ms Secondbest. But we can only charge the Tenure Committee with wronging Ms Secondbest. No individual member has done anything wrong. Furthermore, it is not simply that the members did *not* intend the collectively brought about outcome. Each member individually intended its opposite and cannot have foreseen the outcome! So *they* certainly cannot be charged with culpable wrongdoing.

But if only the Tenure Committee did wrong, then there will clearly be a responsibility-deficit unless we attribute responsibility to the collective directly.[7] Moreover, attributing responsibility collectively to the Tenure Committee will eliminate the responsibility-deficit because the culpable wrongdoing at issue was done by the Tenure Committee, and the Tenure Committee only, i.e., not by the Committee's individual members or anyone else for that matter.

---

[7] Of course, as already noted, there are other necessary conditions for the attributability of moral responsibility. The addressee of the attribution must be fit to be held responsible. A number of conditions need to be met for this to be the case. In general, it is commonly thought that only *agents* are fit to be held responsible. So if collectives *qua* collectives are responsible, they must be agents *qua* collectives (see Copp 2006, pp. 216–7). Among others, Pettit argues that many groups meet these necessary conditions (Pettit 2003, 2007; Pettit and Schweikard 2006).

3   Some Individualist Responses Considered

Let me repeat that I set aside here the various individualist objections which are based on the thought that collective responsibility presupposes collective agency, but collective agency is impossible for *metaphysical* reasons. I will just assume here for the sake of the argument that the collectivist can establish that the group is a rational agent in a sufficiently demanding sense, namely in the sense of satisfying the conditions that any agent has to satisfy in order to be fit to be held responsible.[8]

It is worth noting too that collectivists could also use the individualist's idea in reverse as it were, arguing that since Tenure Committee type cases show that there is robust collective responsibility, there must be robust collective agency too (see esp. Copp 2006, p. 216). So in any case, it is essential to evaluate the moral argument in favor of collectivism on its own merits.

As for ethical considerations, I think there is an individualist response to Tenure Committee type cases which should be rejected as well. This individualist response would be that if the Tenure Committee's actual decision is indeed morally objectionable, then this shows that the rule applied in the decision-making procedure is flawed, and so moral responsibility must lie with the individuals who adopted those rules in the first place.

This individualist response should be rejected. However, it should be rejected not because of what some collectivists say, which is that the rule-adopting individuals could not have foreseen the outcome and therefore have a legitimate excuse for adopting what in the end turned out to be a faulty rule (pace Copp 2007, p. 380).[9] As will be seen shortly, even if the rule-adopting individuals could have foreseen the outcome, they could not have opted for a rule that was more likely to yield a better outcome. If blamed, they should plead lack of a better alternative, not ignorance. In short, this individualist response should be rejected for the right reason. This reason is that there is no alternative rule that would be in the relevant sense faultless (*pace* Miller 2007, p. 405).[10]

But in what sense exactly is the decision procedure flawed? The peculiarity of the decision in the Tenure Committee case as described above is that the decision

---

[8]As a matter of fact, I do not think that the collectivist can establish this. But that is a topic for another paper.

[9]Here is what Copp says in the passage referred to above: "Let me also stipulate that the Borderline case arose long before paradoxes and problems of voting procedures came to be widely known and to be studied in universities. Given these stipulations and given the familiar technical problems in designing voting procedures, it would be unreasonable to hold that someone in the university must be blameworthy for the faultiness of the university's rules." This collectivist argument misses the point about there not being less "faulty" alternative decision procedures available (this is probably due to the misleading presentation of the crucial example, see footnote 6 above).

[10]Miller's individualist response in (2007) to Copp fails, I think, precisely for this reason. If there is no alternative decision procedure available which would not be equally "flawed" in the relevant respect, then there cannot be a valid obligation, *pro tanto* or all-things-considered, to adopt another one, and so nobody is culpable or blameworthy for deciding in the way they have.

reached is not supported individually by *any* of the members. As we have seen, it is on these grounds that Ms Secondbest could challenge the Tenure Committee's decision in that version of the case. The paradoxical result that the decision reached is not supported by any given committee member individually is indeed generated by the specific (premise-based) decision procedure used to aggregate the members' judgments in this particular case.

It is however not only the specific decision rule the Tenure Committee happened to use in the above case which yields such a paradoxical result. For example, the Tenure Committee could have an alternative rule in place whereby each member reaches her decision by individually considering each of the relevant criteria and each member votes only on one question, namely whether or not to award tenure to Ms Borderline (this is the so-called conclusion-based procedure). Since each member judges that Ms Borderline fails to meet one of the three required criteria, the Committee would not award the tenure to her.

But now Ms Borderline may challenge this result. After all, a majority of members judged that she did meet *each* of the required criteria! The problem is that there is decisive support in the Tenure Committee for both the decision objected to by Ms Secondbest and the decision objected to by Ms Borderline.[11] Which will carry the day depends only on whether a conclusion-based or premise-based aggregation rule is used. If that is true, then there will always be a way to challenge the collective's decision. The result of the conclusion-based decision procedure can be challenged by appealing to the group's vote on individual criteria (the premises). The result of the premise-based procedure can be challenged by appealing to the aggregate of each member's individual judgment on whether to award tenure or not (the conclusion).

In fact, this problem is quite general and not restricted to the premise-based and conclusion-based procedures. We find a growing number of impossibility theorems for judgment aggregation in the literature. Common to these is the negative conclusion that there exists no aggregation procedure which could satisfy a limited and intuitive set of rationality criteria (provided the number of propositions to be decided upon and the number of group members is both larger than 2) (List and Pettit 2002). To put the same point in somewhat more technical terms, the paradox of collective judgment aggregation, as demonstrated in the pertaining impossibility theorems, consists in the fact that there exists *no* collective judgment aggregation procedure which for any (rational) profile of individual judgments will *both* (i) guarantee responsiveness to the views of members on each of the issues involved, *and* (ii) yield collective judgments on these issues which are themselves consistent and complete (List and Pettit 2002). This is why it cannot be guaranteed that for any distribution of judgments held by rational individual members of a group the respective outcomes of the premise-based and the conclusion-based procedures will be the same.

---

[11] In fact, the decision against Ms Borderline, the result of the conclusion-based procedure, would have unanimous support. But this difference is not what the collectivist is worried about, as we will see shortly.

It is essential to keep in mind that the possibility of challenging the decision procedure, which the collectivist makes so much of, is based on this "flaw" rooted in the paradox of judgment aggregation. As already noted, several different versions of Tenure Committee can be found in the literature. The original version (Bovens and Rabinowicz 2006), for example, involves only two criteria of tenure to be voted upon. Because only two criteria are used, it will no longer be true that there is no overlap between any of the individual member's view and the final outcome of the premise-based procedure. By contrast, in my version, the outcome of the conclusion-based procedure is unanimously supported and so there will be no overlap between the collective view and that of the individual members. This difference, however, does not alter the basic structure of the paradox that creates the possibility of challenging the decision in both versions of Tenure Committee. It will still be true in the two-issue version too that the decision can be challenged because it cannot be guaranteed that the respective outcomes of the premise-based and the conclusion-based procedures are going to coincide.

4 How the Individualist Should Really Respond

Again, when assessing the collectivist argument we should not lose track of what the basis for the complaint is in cases such as Tenure Committee. In general, there are of course a great variety of other reasons why a decision taken in a collective by means of a formal decision procedure could be challenged or complained about. Let us consider some of these briefly in order to see that these are *not* the kinds of challenges the collectivist has in mind in cases of the Tenure Committee type.

The basis for one important type of complaint is that the decision procedure was substantially unfair, i.e., that for some reason the playing field was not level. And, no doubt, procedures for decision-making can be faulted for substantial deficiencies in many cases: personal bias, prejudice, sloppiness, failure to consider all the relevant facts can all skew decisions taken by a group. In such cases, ascriptions of individual responsibility may be apposite. The wrong involved in adopting a faulty decision procedure in such cases is indeed due to culpable wrongdoing by one or more individuals, e.g., those who opted for the faulty decision procedure, say, in the hope of personal gain. Holding these individuals responsible—and consequent upon the ascription of responsibility, punishing them, criticizing them, calling upon them to apologize or make reparation or whatever response seems appropriate in the given situation—is the way to redress the harm caused in such cases.

But, of course, such substantial unfairness is not what the collectivist argument under scrutiny builds upon. The collectivist's problem is not that the playing field would not be level in Tenure Committee type cases.

There can also be other, more subtle epistemic and moral reasons to challenge a given decision procedure used for aggregating judgments as well. Specifically, it may be argued on the basis of various epistemic or moral criteria that the premise-based and conclusion-based procedures are not equally suitable for the aggregation of judgments. This may be due to the particular circumstances of situations in which judgments have to be aggregated and/or due to general differences between the two decision procedures.[12]

For example, it has been argued that the premise-based procedure is under most circumstances a better "truth-tracker" than the conclusion-based procedure (Pettit and Rabinowicz 2001; Bovens and Rabinowicz 2006). It has also been argued that the premise-based procedure could be preferable for moral and political reasons as well. Thus it is said that only if the group votes on each of the premises will all the reasons for taking a given decision be publicly accessible and contestable (Pettit 2001).

The premise-based procedure is often thought to be preferable if time is also a relevant consideration. The claim here is that the premise-based procedure enables the collective to preserve a stable identity and pursue common goals over time as earlier interconnected decisions of a group are in this procedure regarded as premises of the proposition to be decided upon at a later time. By contrast, the conclusion-based procedure could generate inconsistencies at the collective level because each decision is voted upon according to members' views on the given issue, irrespective of the fact that this decision may potentially conflict with the conclusion that earlier judgments of the same group would logically entail (Pettit 2001, 2007).

At the same time, there are other considerations favoring the conclusion-based procedure. First, in some cases groups may want to put a premium on unanimity over simple majority. Thus notice that the conclusion-based procedure in the Tenure Committee case yields a unanimously supported decision, whereas in the premise-based procedure the aggregation of each judgment (whether p, whether q, etc.) is supported only by a majority. *Ceteris paribus*, some may regard this difference as a reason for preferring the conclusion-based procedure. Second, the conclusion-based procedure may better safeguard against unwanted strategic voting. Third, although the premise-based procedure is under most circumstances a better "truth-tracker" as mentioned above, this is not always the case (for details, see Bovens and Rabinowicz 2006). Fourth, in some cases we may want to or have to take a stand on a logically complex proposition as a whole without having a firm view on one or more of the simple propositions constituting it. The conclusion-based procedure can better accommodate such situations.

Whatever the respective merits of the premise-based and conclusion-based procedures may be in terms of these epistemic, moral, and political *desiderata*, however, the point to emphasize here is that these relative advantages are irrelevant

---

[12]I am indebted to Wlodek Rabinowicz for calling my attention to such alternative criteria for assessing the relative merits of the premise-based and conclusion-based decision procedures.

to the case at hand. The collectivist argument discussed here is based on the paradox of judgment aggregation, i.e., the inevitable conflict between the outcomes of the premise-based and conclusion-based procedures.[13]

I believe that the right individualist response should focus precisely on the unavoidability of the conflict. There is no procedure that can guarantee outcomes against which nobody can raise a legitimate complaint (List and Pettit 2002; List 2006, p. 376). If that is true, what basis is there to judge the collective culpable? What exactly is the collective collectively responsible for?

For the sake of argument, let us assume that members of the Tenure Committee were aware of the possibility of ending up straddled with the kind of paradoxical results discussed above. Still, when deliberating about the issue, there will not be an option available to the members against which no complaint could be raised. Therefore, it would follow that all options open to the Tenure Committee were culpable. But we are reluctant to hold agents responsible if every course of action available to them is equally culpable.[14]

The right individualist response therefore is to say that *in such cases there is simply nobody to be held responsible, nobody culpable, and nobody to be blamed for these paradoxical results: neither one or more individuals nor some collective as a whole*.[15] In other words, it is a mistake to take the paradoxical outcome as evidence for the occurrence of culpable wrongdoing in Tenure Committee type cases

---

[13]Collectivist authors are not always as clear on this point as one would wish them to be. Sometimes they do not really explain why they think one would have a reason to challenge the decision resulting from the aggregation of judgments. For example, discussing an example of the same structure as Tenure Committee, Pettit (2007, p. 198) only says this: "But suppose now that some external parties have a complaint against the group ... because [they] think [the collective's decision] is unfair." But he does not specify what the reason for the complaint here would be. Is it some substantial unfairness of the kind I have discussed above? That cannot be the case because the playing field was level. Is the decision challenged as unfair because a decision procedure was used which is inferior in terms of the epistemic, moral, or political criteria mentioned above? No. In fact, in this particular case Pettit allows that the collective decision be legitimately challenged, even though this group opts for the premise-based procedure which Pettit tends to describe in various places as by and large preferable in terms of the epistemic, moral, or political *desiderata* just discussed. To be fair, elsewhere (e.g., Pettit 2001), Pettit is much clearer about what he holds to be the truly relevant reason for the "challengeability" of the collective decision emphasizing that Tenure Committee type cases present a *dilemma*. These cases are dilemmatic because none of the available decision procedures is immune to challenges given the paradox of judgment aggregation.

[14]From the *metaphysical* point of view, there is an additional problem. The retort implies that the collective adopted the procedure at some point and so it implies that the collective acted. But the procedure was adopted by one or more individuals, not the collective.

[15]The collectivist can object that by accepting this claim the individualist will increase the responsibility-deficit—now in a different way than before. If it were true that nobody was to be held responsible for paradoxical outcomes of judgment-aggregation, then this would create a "perverse incentive." This is because people could now form collectives "to achieve a certain bad and self-serving effect, while arranging things so that none of them can be held fully responsible for what is done" (Pettit 2007, p. 196). But this objection is confused. If people *deliberately* arranged things in order that the aggregation of their judgments yielded such paradoxical results and hoped thereby to evade responsibility, then they would of course be individually culpable for doing so.

by any individual or collective. On second thoughts, this is not all that surprising: it is nobody's fault, not any individual's nor that of any given collective, that judgment aggregation is fraught with paradox. That is just the way the world is.

5   Harm without Responsibility

If this is correct so far, should we then not say also that nobody has been wronged in this case? I think this does not follow. In my view, there is indeed something wrong with the fact that Ms Borderline's tenure can depend solely on whether the Tenure Committee members' views are aggregated via the premises or via the conclusion.

Not all individualists agree. Some would question whether there is any valid claim for redress in Tenure Committee type situations. Why should the fact that the outcome depends on the decision procedure in the way described above constitute a legitimate reason for complaint by anyone as long as the playing field was level?—they ask. After all, the result also depended on the fact that the Committee happened to consist of three and not two or four members. By the same logic, would that dependence not be a legitimate reason for challenging the decision too? If all such procedural factors could constitute a reason for complaint, then no decision could ever be taken. What is crucial, according to these individualists, is that both the premise-based and the conclusion-based procedures are reasonable, impartial and procedurally fair—the playing field is level. If so, then there is no room for challenges on the basis that some alternative decision procedure would have produced a different result.[16]

Let me point out first of all that this argument of course would only strengthen the anti-collectivist position I have been defending. But I think it goes too far. We can see where it goes too far if we focus on the question what the content of the complaint in the Tenure Committee type case could be. If, say, the conclusion-based procedure is used and Ms Borderline is denied tenure as a result, her complaint should not be that the result of the conclusion-based procedure was unjustified. That complaint would not be legitimate since, as noted, the playing field was level and the procedure used reasonable, impartial, etc. Rather, her complaint should be that the reason why she was ultimately denied tenure was *extraneous* to her qualifications for the position. It was extraneous in the same way as flipping a coin to break a tie may be in other situations. Of course, in many cases the dependence of the decision on such extraneous factors does not make a decision unjustified. Sometimes we do need to flip a coin if the matter at hand is to be decided one way or another. By the same token, sometimes *either* the premise-based *or* the conclusion-based procedure will have to be used and we cannot use both. We cannot have our cake and eat it.

---

[16]I owe this point to Kirk Ludwig.

And yet, that the outcome can be traced back to such an extraneous factor can sometimes be, to borrow Feinberg's idea, unjust even if justified.[17] Furthermore, I believe that in some cases that sort of injustice does constitute a legitimate basis for a redress claim. What form the compensatory action should take, if any, will depend on the circumstances of the case. In Tenure Committee, it could be argued that the inconsistency between the outcome of the premise-based and conclusion-based procedures can constitute a reason for some compensatory action. The range of options include repeating the procedure by adding further criteria, or including more people in the Committee, or (if the conclusion-based procedure was used) giving Ms Borderline another chance a year later, or (if the premise-based procedure was used) creating a tenure position for Ms Secondbest as well, and so on.[18]

Given the exigencies of situations in which similar decisions have to be taken, such compensatory action is not always possible. Nor would I want to claim here that paradoxical outcomes of judgment aggregation constitute a *sufficient* reason for compensatory actions of this sort. The point is simply that such paradoxical outcomes do sometimes constitute a legitimate basis for a redress claim and may constitute *a* reason for satisfying such a claim.

I believe that this individualist analysis of the Tenure Committee example generalizes for all cases in which some harm or disadvantage is suffered due to paradoxical results of judgment aggregation. Individualism denies that such cases warrant ascriptions of responsibility to collectives. But this does not entail that individualism is morally inferior to collectivism. In fact, individualists accept that paradoxes of judgment aggregation can give rise to legitimate complaints and so can require compensatory action. What individualists deny is that the normative basis for these complaints is the ascription of collective responsibility.

---

[17] "[O]ne and the same act can be both unjust (to someone or other) and justified" (Feinberg 1970, p. 45).

[18] An anonymous referee pointed out that by insisting that members of the Tenure Committee *qua* committee members should care about redressing the unjust consequences of the decision taken, I acknowledge in effect that members of the Tenure Committee can regard themselves as individually responsible (even if not culpable) for how they voted and participated in the collective decision. In fact, it may be said to follow from what I am saying above that members can even *feel* collectively responsible, if only in an attenuated sense, since I urge that they as members of the Tenure Committee should address the complaint and do something about it if at all possible. I have no problem with these implications provided we remain clear about what is meant by "feeling collectively responsible". First, the fact that individual members are not culpable for the outcome does not mean that they cannot be required to alleviate the harmful effects of that outcome. We can often be required to redress harms for which we are not morally responsible (sometimes not even causally responsible). Such a requirement often has to do with our roles as members of organized groups or institutions. Furthermore, in some cases, redressing harms (whether or not one is morally responsible for that harm in the first place) requires cooperation with others as when I need you so that we can lift that stretcher together. Second and relatedly, it is also true that members should be individually concerned about how their individual contributions combine with those of others (and may be held individually responsible if they fail to do so) especially if those contributions, although severally harmless, have harmful effects in the aggregate. But of course all these considerations pertain to individual responsibility and do not imply collective responsibility of the kind the collectivist would want to establish.

6   The Moral High Ground

Tenure Committee type cases have also been used to make ambitious collectivist claims about the *personhood* of collectives. After all, in one version of Tenure Committee nobody except the collective as a whole judges Ms Borderline to be deserving of tenure. If groups can abstract from the views of their members in this way, collectivists claim, they can have their own irreducibly collective values, intentions, beliefs, and judgments. It follows that we may have to regard them as fully enfranchised members of the moral community together with natural persons. As noted, the collectivist thinks that this is a good thing from the ethical point of view because this allows us to call to task collective persons in the same way as natural persons (French 1979, p. 207; Pettit 2003, p. 184). Corporations, governments, international organizations can no longer claim to be merely a piece of legal fiction when facing moral criticism, blame, or sanctions.

I have put forward some arguments against this line of thought above. In closing, I want to offer an example to illustrate that enfranchising collectives with a status resembling that of natural persons can raise as many ethical problems as it may solve. In a recent landmark decision, *Citizens United v. Federal Election Commission*, the US Supreme Court lifted the ban on corporate funding of political advertising. The Supreme Court's main argument for this extremely controversial ruling was precisely that the interests of corporations are to be treated on a par with those of natural persons (Dworkin 2010).

This shows that "collectivist" talk concerning the personhood of collectives can also serve to increase the power of collectives rather than limit it. Most would agree that, even if it were legally defensible, increasing the power of collectives in the way the Supreme Court has done in this case is hardly desirable morally speaking. It is objectionable because given the infinitely richer resources which corporations have access to they acquire an enormous advantage in the competition to influence the opinions of the electorate. This advantage is not only unfair in itself, it also restricts the freedom of speech of others.

Of course, collectivists need not agree with the Supreme Court's decision in this case. They may continue to distinguish between the rights of natural as opposed to organizational persons despite their readiness to attribute responsibility to collectives *qua* collectives. So in this specific case, they may draw a line between natural and organizational persons in terms of the right to free speech.[19] But if this is the position the collectivist wishes to defend, then the individualist can rightly demand additional arguments from the collectivist why we should not distinguish between natural and organizational persons in terms of responsibility (and other attributes of personhood) even though we treat them differently in terms of the rights they enjoy, or at least differently in terms of some of the specific basic rights they enjoy.

---

[19] I thank Christian List for alerting me to this possible collectivist rejoinder.

In the bulk of this essay, I have sought to defend individualism against a specific collectivist charge. This last section constitutes an attempt to turn the tables and go on the offensive as it were. A single example is of course insufficient to support such an attack on collectivism. It does give us reason, however, to recognize the possibility that in some cases the collectivist rhetoric may actually create moral deficits which individualism can easily steer clear of.

References

Bovens, L., and W. Rabinowicz. 2006. Democratic answers to complex questions—An epistemic perspective. *Synthese* 150(1): 131–153.

Copp, D. 2006. On the agency of certain collective entities: An argument from normative autonomy. *Midwest Studies in Philosophy* 30: 194–221.

Copp, D. 2007. The collective moral autonomy thesis. *Journal of Social Philosophy* 38(3): 369–388.

Dworkin, R. 2010. The devastating decision. *New York Review of Books* 57(8): 63–67.

Feinberg, J. 1970. *Doing and deserving*. Princeton: Princeton University Press.

French, P. 1979. The corporation as a moral person. *American Philosophical Quarterly* 16(3): 207–215.

Haji, I. 2006. On the ultimate responsibility of collectives. *Midwest Studies in Philosophy* 30: 292–308.

Kutz, C. 2000. *Complicity*. Cambridge: Cambridge University Press.

List, C. 2006. The discursive dilemma and public reason. *Ethics* 116(2): 362–402.

List, C., and P. Pettit. 2002. The aggregation of sets of judgments: An impossibility result. *Economics and Philosophy* 18(1): 89–110.

McKenna, M. 2006. Collective responsibility and an agent meaning theory. *Midwest Studies in Philosophy* 30: 16–34.

Miller, S. 2007. Against the collective moral autonomy thesis. *Journal of Social Philosophy* 38(3): 389–409.

Miller, S., and P. Mäkelä. 2005. The collectivist approach to collective moral responsibility. *Metaphilosophy* 36(5): 634–651.

Parfit, D. 1984. *Reasons and persons*. Oxford: Oxford University Press.

Petersson, B. 2008. Collective omissions and responsibility. *Philosophical Papers* 37(2): 243–261.

Pettit, P. 2001. Deliberative democracy and the discursive dilemma. *Philosophical Issues* 11(1): 268–295.

Pettit, P. 2003. Groups with minds of their own. In *Socializing metaphysics*, ed. F. Schmitt, 167–194. New York: Rowman & Littlefield.

Pettit, P. 2007. Responsibility incorporated. *Ethics* 117(2): 171–201.

Pettit, P., and W. Rabinowicz. 2001. The jury theorem and the discursive dilemma. *Philosophical Issues* 11(1): 295–299.

Pettit, P., and D. Schweikard. 2006. Joint action and group agency. *Philosophy of the Social Sciences* 36(1): 18–39.

Chapter 21
Can Groups Be Autonomous Rational Agents? A Challenge to the List-Pettit Theory

Vuko Andric

Abstract Christian List and Philip Pettit argue that some groups qualify as rational agents over and above their members. Examples include churches, commercial corporations, and political parties. According to the theory developed by List and Pettit, these groups qualify as agents because they have beliefs and desires and the capacity to process them and to act on their basis. Moreover, the alleged group agents are said to be rational to a high degree and even to be fit to be held morally responsible. And the group agents under consideration are autonomous, according to the List-Pettit Theory, because their beliefs and desires cannot easily be reduced to the beliefs and desires of the groups' members. I want to show that we should not accept the List-Pettit Theory, because it implies the absurd claim that instrument-user-units, like car-driver-units, are rational agents over and above their user-parts, say drivers. The focus of my argument is on whether instrument-user-units are autonomous in relation to their user-parts on the List-Pettit Theory.

In everyday life, we often perceive groups as performing actions. Examples include football teams competing in a match, governments executing law, and commercial corporations buying real estate. These phenomena give rise to the question of whether groups are agents. According to Christian List and Philip Pettit, some of them are. List and Pettit have put forward a prominent view of the conditions under which groups are rational agents over and above their individual members.[1] In this essay, I will explain why I do not find their view convincing. I try to show that the

---

[1] Other prominent arguments for the view that groups can be rational agents have been put forward in French (1984) and May (1987).

V. Andric (✉)
Department of Philosophy, University of Konstanz, Constance, Germany
e-mail: vuko_andric@yahoo.de

A. Konzelmann Ziv and H.B. Schmid (eds.), *Institutions, Emotions, and Group Agents*,   343
Studies in the Philosophy of Sociality 2, DOI 10.1007/978-94-007-6934-2_21,

view of List and Pettit has a very absurd implication. The implication is so absurd, I think, that you will not be prepared to accept it.

The view of List and Pettit will be presented in Sect. 1. Then, in Sect. 2, I will explain why I do not find it convincing. The chapter concludes with a brief summary of the results in Sect. 3.

1   The List-Pettit Theory

Let "List-Pettit Theory"—henceforth "LP Theory"—cover all claims held by List and Pettit concerning the conditions under which a system is an autonomous rational agent. It follows from the LP Theory that some groups are rational agents over and above their members. My presentation of the LP Theory will be structured around the following questions:

1. Why do some groups qualify as *agents*?
2. In what sense and to what extent do they qualify as *rational*?
3. Why do some groups qualify as *autonomous* in relation to their members?

As to the first question, the LP Theory says that some groups qualify as *agents* because they have representational and motivational states—henceforth "beliefs" and "desires"—and the capacity to process them and to act on their basis.[2] The LP Theory contains a broadly functionalist account of agency.[3] According to *functionalism*, the states of a system are desires and beliefs if they play certain causal roles, that is, if there are characteristic causal relations between these states and other states of the system, its behavior, and its environment. Beliefs depict how things are in the environment. Desires specify how the system requires things to be in the environment. One important aspect of the functional roles of beliefs and desires is that an agent processes its beliefs and desires such that it intervenes suitably, according to its beliefs, whenever the environment fails to match its desires, at least under favorable conditions and within feasible limits (List and Pettit 2011, pp. 19–20).

It should be clear that many groups indeed have beliefs and desires in the functionalist sense. Commercial corporations endorse strategies to maximize their profit, governments pursue political goals, and religious groups share (more or less) religious aims and opinions—to name but a few. If a church, say, forms the desire to spread what it thinks is the word of God, then it will tend to send its missionaries to the heathens' strongholds.

---

[2]The conditions of agency in general are discussed in List and Pettit (2011, ch. 1, see esp. pp. 20 and 32).

[3]The functionalist foundation of the LP Theory is presented in Pettit (1993, ch. 1–2), Pettit (2009, sec. 1), and List and Pettit (2011, ch. 1, sec. 1–2).

Groups are not organisms with brains, of course. How then can their beliefs and desires be realized? As List and Pettit point out, some groups have *organizational structures*.[4] It is through these structures that roles in the generation of a group's desires and beliefs as well as in the performance of corresponding actions are assigned to group members. Such roles are salient when, for example, Coca Cola's managers bring it about that Coca Cola intends to buy some real estate, or when Coca Cola's lawyers sign a contract with the effect that Coca Cola buys some real estate. As this illustrates, a group's propositional attitudes are realized in the interplay of its members' attitudes and its organizational structure.

To sum up, according to the LP Theory some groups qualify as agents because they have beliefs and desires and the capacity to process them and to act on their basis. Group agents form their beliefs and desires and process them and act on their basis in virtue of their organizational structures in combination with the beliefs, desires and actions of the members.

Let us then come to the next question: In what sense and to what extent do the groups in question qualify as being *rational*? Agents can be more or less rational in the sense that they can perform better or worse as agents. The standards of rationality apply to the way an agent's beliefs and desires connect with its environment, to the way an agent's beliefs and desires connect with the actions by which the agent intervenes in its environment, and to the way an agent's attitudes connect with one another. List and Pettit call these three kinds of standards "attitude-to-fact", "attitude-to-action", and "attitude-to-attitude" standards of rationality.[5]

The *attitude-to-fact* standards require agents to ensure that their beliefs are true and that their desires are at least in principle realizable. Groups can, according to List and Pettit, meet these standards in virtue of the inputs they get from their members. The members' attitudes will be aggregated into group attitudes by a group's organizational structure.

It is also in virtue of their members and their organizational structures that groups can ensure the performance of actions that are rationally required by their attitudes. Hence, group agents can meet the *attitude-to-action* standards of rationality.

Attitude-to-attitude standards of rationality rule out beliefs that take propositions to be true that are not co-realizable, or desires that require such propositions to be true. So these standards rule out failures of consistency. As we will see below, the attitude-to-attitude standards of rationality are very important when it comes to the question of why some groups qualify as autonomous.

In sum, groups can be rational, according to the LP Theory, in the sense that they can meet attitude-to-fact, attitude-to-action, and attitude-to-attitude standards of rationality. All that is needed for a group to be able, in principle, to meet these standards are its members' attitudes and actions and a decent organizational structure.

---

[4]"Organizational structure" is the term used in List and Pettit (2011, see esp. pp. 60–64). Pettit (2007a) speaks of "corporations' constitutions".

[5]The standards are introduced in List and Pettit (2011, ch. 1, sec. 1, and applied to groups in ch. 1, sec. 3, see esp. pp. 35–37). See also, e.g., Pettit (2007b).

Let us now consider to what extent groups can be rational according to the LP Theory. List and Pettit (2011, pp. 29–31, 63–64) distinguish between agents who can reason and those who cannot. Agents who can reason are capable of having beliefs not only about objects in the environment and simple propositions, but also about sophisticated propositions that may include propositions as their objects. And they possess a meta-language. Thus, reasoning agents can think about the properties of propositions such as their truth, their consistency, or their desirability.

How, according to the LP Theory, is it possible for some groups to reason? The idea is that since a group's individual members can reason, the group is also capable of having beliefs and desires about sophisticated propositions. Such propositions can come on the agenda and the group can endorse or reject them via its members in whatever way is prescribed by the group's organizational structure.

The capacity to reason is crucial when it comes to moral responsibility.[6] For bearing moral responsibility requires that one has the understanding required to make normative judgments about the options one faces. Since the alleged group agents can reason, they show this understanding. They thus meet a crucial condition for their being fit to be held morally responsible for their actions. For example, Coca Cola can weigh the pros and cons of buying some piece of real estate. This activity can be brought about, let us suppose, by its managers discussing the issue in accordance with the organizational structure.

To sum up, some groups, according to the LP Theory, are rational to an extent that makes them capable of reasoning. Hence, a very important condition for their moral responsibility is met. Since the other conditions, which for brevity's sake I do not consider in this essay, are also met by some group agents, the LP Theory implies that there are group agents that are fit to be held morally responsible.

Let us now turn to the third question: why do some group agents qualify as autonomous in relation to their members? Before I answer this question—which I will do in some detail because the answer is very important for my critique in the next section—it is important to mention that not all group agents are autonomous according to the LP Theory. A degenerate case of a group agent that is constructed around a dictator, for example, should not be seen as autonomous in relation to the dictator, the LP Theory says, but as an extension of the dictator's agency.[7] As for those groups that are autonomous in relation to their members according to the LP Theory, the autonomy is epistemological rather than ontological in character. As List and Pettit put it:

> A group agent is autonomous in the relevant sense to the extent that the features that make it an agent – particularly its attitudes – are not readily reducible to features of the individual members: again, crucially, their attitudes. Under our account, there are a number of reasons why the required reduction or translation is difficult. (List and Pettit 2011, pp. 76–77)

List and Pettit (2011, p. 77) list three difficulties that stand in the way of an easy reduction of the group's attitudes to its members' attitudes:

---

[6]On a group's fitness to be held responsible, see Pettit (2007a) and List and Pettit (2011, ch. 7).
[7]For details see List and Pettit (2011, ch. 3).

Table 21.1 A discursive dilemma: How majority voting can lead to inconsistent attitudes

	Pursue P?	Pursue Q?	Pursue R?	Pursue P&Q&R?
Member 1	No	Yes	Yes	No
Member 2	Yes	No	Yes	No
Member 3	Yes	Yes	No	No
Group	Yes	Yes	Yes	No

This is a slightly modified version of a table that List and Pettit use in many articles, see, for example, Pettit (2007a, p. 182)

(i) It may be hard to precisely determine what the individual attitudes are. In this context, it is important that there can be many different combinations of individual attitudes that give rise to the same group attitude so that you cannot infer which attitudes the individuals have on the basis of the group attitude.

(ii) In the case of an autonomous group agent, the group agent's attitudes towards propositions are not derivable solely from its members' attitudes towards these propositions but are realized by the interplay of its members' attitudes towards these propositions and the group's organizational structure.[8] As List and Pettit show in detail, a non-degenerative group agent must ensure that its attitudes towards propositions are not derivable solely from its members' attitudes towards these propositions. For otherwise, the group would, in the long run, form inconsistent sets of attitudes. Thus, it would not be capable of rational agency. This is shown by discursive dilemmas and associated impossibility theorems.

It is beyond the scope of this chapter to present all discursive dilemmas and the associated impossibility theorems. Let me confine myself to one discursive dilemma in order to illustrate the argument for a case where the group's attitudes are determined simply by the majority of its members. Suppose there is a group with three members. Assume that the group's members first have to decide whether the group pursues P as a goal, then whether it pursues Q, and then whether it pursues R. On each issue two of the members will say "Yes". So the group will try to bring it about that P, that Q, and that R. But then, the members have to decide whether they want to bring it about that P&Q&R. Now each member, consistently with her or his prior votes, says "No". So the group will, inconsistently with its other views, not adopt P&Q&R as a goal. The decisions are illustrated in Table 21.1.

If the group adopted P as a goal, Q as a goal, and R as a goal and if it dismissed as a goal P&Q&R, then it would have inconsistent sets of attitudes and thus would not be capable of rational agency. Therefore the group's organizational structure will ensure that the group's attitudes towards P, Q, R, and P&Q&R are not derivable solely from its members' attitudes towards these propositions. This, according to the LP Theory, guarantees the group's autonomy.

---

[8]For details see List and Pettit (2011, ch. 3, sec. 2). The aggregation of intentional attitudes is the topic of List and Pettit (2011, ch. 2).

(iii) There are cases of group agents that involve feedback (or related phenomena) between individual and group-level attitudes. Feedback leads individuals to revise their attitudes in light of the resulting group attitudes or to adjust their votes over what the group attitudes should be. Thus, the individual attitudes may be evolving so that it becomes even more difficult to reduce the group attitudes to them.

Here is a brief summary of the LP Theory: Some groups qualify as agents because they have beliefs and desires and the capacity to process them and to act on their basis. Group agents are capable of improving their performance by reasoning and the capacity to reason also ensures (together with some other features) that group agents are fit to be held morally responsible. Some group agents are autonomous in relation to their members because their attitudes cannot easily be reduced to the attitudes of their members.

2   The List-Pettit Theory and Instrument-User-Units

Let us now come to my criticism of the LP Theory:

(1) If the LP Theory is true, then instrument-user-units are autonomous rational agents.
(2) Instrument-user-units are not autonomous rational agents.
(3) Therefore, the LP Theory is false.

I will only briefly comment on premise (2). Then I will argue at some length for premise (1). I take it that nobody who understands (2) would seriously question it. Instead of arguing for (2), I will tell three short stories that are extremely absurd. Their absurdity can best be explained by the fact that, as (2) says, instrument-user-units are not autonomous rational agents.

Story One: Michael owns a Ferrari. When Michael uses his Ferrari, both become the Michael-Ferrari-Unit, MFU. The MFU is quite dangerous. It moves through towns with the highest speed. As the police succeed in stopping it, Michael leaves his Ferrari and the chief officer says: "Mike! The MFU is guilty of moving too fast, as you know. Since you play a crucial role in it, you bear some responsibility, too ..."

Story Two: Linda takes her toothbrush. The Linda-Toothbrush-Unit, LTU, cleans its teeth. Having put aside the toothbrush, Linda smiles and considers her teeth in the mirror. She is thankful to the LTU and thinks that she does a good job as a part of it.

Story Three: After a long history of dubious doctrine, the Pope eventually comes to recognize what is really wrong with using condoms. It is not that sperm is wasted, or the like. Rather, using condoms means committing adultery. For women are not married to the man-condom-units they are having sex with.

I take these stories to illustrate that instrument-user-units are not autonomous agents, distinct from their agent-parts. In particular, nobody thinks that instrument-user-units can bear responsibility.

Table 21.2 The analogy
between group agents and
car-driver-units

Group agent	Car-driver-unit
Members	Driver
Organizational structure	Car's constitution

Let me now come to premise (1): If the LP Theory is true, then instrument-user-units are autonomous rational agents. For simplicity, I will concentrate on a special kind of instrument-user-unit, namely car-driver-units. Are car-driver-units autonomous rational agents according to the LP Theory? The first thing to notice is that car-driver-units qualify as agents on the LP Theory. Car-driver-units have beliefs and desires and the capacity to process them and to act on their basis: Car-driver-units clearly exhibit states that due to their causal relations to the car-driver-unit's behavior, to its environment, and to its other states qualify as beliefs and desires. Moreover, they can form and reform these states and act in accordance with their beliefs so as to make the environment match their desires. So given the LP Theorist's account of agency, we are justified in saying things like "the Paul-and-his-car-unit intends to stop at the next petrol station if it's not BP" or "The Paul-and-his-car-unit stops at the next petrol station".

How are the beliefs and desires of a car-driver-unit realized? Cars have technical properties that are relevant for their users. Examples include a car's size, how fast it can move, and how much fuel it needs. Let us call these properties a car's *constitution*. A car's constitution corresponds, in the analogy we are considering, to a group agent's organizational structure, see Table 21.2. LP Theorists have to say, I submit, that a car-driver-unit's propositional attitudes are realized by the interplay of its driver's attitudes and the car's constitution. Thus, car-driver-units can be agents via their drivers who behave in accordance with the cars' constitutions. For example, in virtue of Paul's intention to stop at the next petrol station the Paul-and-his-car-unit intends to stop at the next petrol station. And it is in virtue of Paul's applying the brakes that the Paul-and-his-car-unit stops at BP.

Just like the group agents considered in the last section, car-driver-units are capable of reasoning. It is in virtue of their driver-parts' ability to have beliefs about sophisticated propositions that car-driver-units are capable of having beliefs about sophisticated propositions. For example, the Paul-and-his-car-unit can weigh the pros and cons of stopping at BP stations.

Let us now come to the question of whether car-driver-units are *autonomous* in relation to their drivers. I take it that the LP Theorist will admit that car-driver-units qualify as rational agents on the LP Theory but deny that car-driver-units qualify as autonomous in relation to their driver-parts. I will, hence, argue at some length for the claim that car-driver-units are autonomous in relation to their driver-parts according to the LP Theory.

A car-driver-unit is autonomous, according to the LP Theory, if its attitudes are not easily reducible to the driver's attitudes. We have seen three reasons why the attitudes of autonomous group agents are not easily reducible to their members' attitudes. Similar reasons apply to the case of car-driver-units:

(i) In the case of group agents, the LP Theory holds, it may be hard to precisely determine the individual attitudes, especially given the fact that many different combinations of individual attitudes can give rise to the same group attitude.

Notice that this is the first of three points and List and Pettit (2011, p. 77) present the three points "in ascending order of seriousness". I am inclined not to take this point very seriously; for while it *may* be hard to precisely determine the individual attitudes, it *need not* be. Imagine someone who knows the organizational structure and the individual members of a group agent pretty well. Think, for example, of a political scientist who is concerned with political group agents such as political parties, the government, or the state. The LP Theory, as I understand it, holds that even relative to such an expert the group agents in question are autonomous, even if the expert can track most or all of a group agent's decisions and actions in a particular period of time back to the individual members. But how can the LP Theory say this if the expert sees the individuals and the organizational structure behind the group agent's decisions and actions?

In response, I think, List and Pettit should stress the "ascending order of seriousness" and say that the point indeed only concerns those people who are not experts. Ordinary people are not experts; they often do not know the attitudes of the members of the group agents in question or they do not know the organizational structures. Moreover, List and Pettit could argue, no *actual* expert may be able to look *exclusively* at the individual level of any actual autonomous group agent. Important social facts obtain on the group level and you cannot completely ignore them if you want to understand society and to live in it.

I think, however, that parallel claims can be put forward when it comes to car-driver-units. First of all, we often do not know the individual attitudes of the driver-parts of the car-driver-units prior to observing the behavior of the car-driver-units. Rather, we have to look at the level of a car-driver-unit in order to infer the respective driver's attitudes. True, there *may* be an "expert" who knows the driver's attitudes in advance. But as we have seen, there may also be experts who will know the individualistic base of what the LP Theory claims to be autonomous group agents.

Secondly, we need to keep our eyes fixed on the level of the car-driver-units because important social facts can obtain at that level, facts such as the stopping at a petrol station or a passing manoeuver. So even in cases where we know the driver's attitudes, we cannot ignore the level of the car-driver-unit.

In sum, the LP Theorist's point in favor of some group agents' autonomy does not have much force in the first place. And a parallel point with hardly less force can be defended when it comes to the autonomy of car-driver-units.

(ii) I think that the second reason for considering (non-degenerative) group agents autonomous is far more important than the first one: a group agent's organizational structure will ensure that the group agent's attitudes towards propositions are not derivable solely from the members' attitudes towards these propositions.

The same is true, however, in the case of car-driver-units. A car-driver-unit's attitudes towards propositions are not derivable solely from its driver's attitudes towards these propositions but are realized by the interplay of its driver's attitudes and the car's constitution. Here is an example that illustrates the point: Assume that you want to drive as fast as possible from Berlin to Rome without stopping. But, due to your car's constitution, you have to stop in Munich in order to refuel your car. While you have the desire not to stop in Munich, the you-and-your-car-unit has the desire to stop in Munich. This shows that the you-and-your-car-unit is autonomous in relation to you.

You could object: "While I *would* have the desire to drive as fast as possible from Berlin to Rome if I failed to take into account my car's constitution, I *do* have the desire to stop the car in Munich in order to refuel it because I do, of course, take into account the car's constitution. So the me-and-my-car-unit's desire to stop in Munich *is* derivable from my desire that the car stop in Munich. The me-and-my-car-unit, therefore, is not autonomous." Let us call such an argument against autonomy an *objection from actual attitudes*.

Objections from actual attitudes derive their force from a doctrine that we can call the actuality-principle. This principle says that:

(AP) An overall system is autonomous in relation to its subsystems only if the overall system's attitudes (at some moment) are not derivable from the attitudes the subsystems actually have (at that same moment).

The above objection from actual attitudes appeals to this principle when it states that the you-and-your-car-unit's desire to stop in Munich is derivable from your desire to stop in Munich. You do actually have this desire by the time the you-and-your-car-unit has it. Thus, the latter is derivable from the former. But then, the you-and-your-car-unit fails to be autonomous.

My reply to objections from actual attitudes against the autonomy of instrument-user-units is that proponents of the LP Theory cannot raise them on pain of incoherence. For if the rationale of these objections—that is, (AP)—is correct, then this also undermines the autonomy of some paradigmatic group agents. (AP) rules out the autonomy of some group agents because some organized groups' attitudes are derivable solely from their members' actual attitudes. Thus, (AP) allows for objections from actual attitudes against the autonomy of group agents that are claimed to be autonomous by the LP Theory. Here is such an objection with respect to the example we considered in Sect. 1: Each of three members of a group *would* have desired that the group pursues, say, that non-P&Q&R if the member had not taken into account the organizational structure. But if we suppose that the organizational structure prescribes a *deliberative* process at the end of which all members must *agree* on the group attitudes, then the desires of the members will evolve in the deliberative process. Each member will eventually desire that P&Q&R. So the group's desire that P&Q&R *is* derivable, according to (AP), from its members' desires and, therefore, the group is not autonomous.

The analogous relations between an overall system and its subsystems in the case of group agents, on the one hand, and in the case of instrument-user-units, on the other, reflect on the attitudes of the agential subsystems in both cases. Each group member will say: "We pursue P&Q&R—this decision has been made in accordance with our organizational structure. However, I, personally, would have preferred that we not pursue P&Q&R". Analogously, you will say: "Due to my car's fuel consumption, I intend to stop in Munich. But I would have preferred not to."

How, exactly, does the objection from actual attitudes relate to (AP)? As I said at the beginning of Sect. 1, by "the LP Theory" I mean all claims held by List and Pettit concerning the conditions under which a system is an autonomous rational agent. Since the LP Theory focuses on the attitudes the group members *would* have if they failed to take into account the group's organizational structure (otherwise the theory could not say that groups with deliberative formation procedures for group attitudes are autonomous), the LP Theory is incompatible with (AP). The LP Theorist therefore cannot deny the autonomy of the you-and-your-car-unit on grounds of (AP). But if we change our understanding of the LP Theory to the effect that it focuses on the *actual* attitudes of the group members, then it does not follow anymore from the LP Theory that group agents with deliberative formation procedures for group attitudes will be autonomous in relation to their members. Statements about what a group agent believes, desires, or does would be reducible to statements about what the group members believe, desire, or do. The LP Theory, then, would not show what it is supposed to show. The LP Theorist, hence, faces a *dilemma* with respect to (AP).

In sum, my reply to objections from actual attitudes is that, if such objections show that the attitudes of instrument-user-units are not derivable, in the relevant sense, from the users' attitudes, then it follows from the objections' rationale that some allegedly autonomous group agents' attitudes are not derivable, in the relevant sense, from the members' attitudes. So the LP Theorist faces a dilemma. Either the LP Theory implies that instrument-user-units are autonomous in relation to the users as far as the derivability of instrument-user-unit attitudes is concerned. Or we modify the LP Theory so that it does not provide the desired result that some group agents are autonomous in relation to the members as far as the derivability of group attitudes is concerned.

(iii) Finally, recall that the members' attitudes in the case of some group agents are evolving in accordance with the organizational structure. As we have just seen, however, something similar is going on in the example involving your trip from Berlin to Rome. You first have the desire not to stop in Munich. Then you recognize that you have to stop in Munich in order to refuel your car. After this recognition you form the desire to stop in Munich. Hence, your attitudes have evolved, due to the car's constitution. An observer, however, will not be able to say whether your desires have evolved due to the car's constitution, in particular the car's need for fuel. As far as the observer is concerned, it could as well be that you would have desired to stop in Munich even if you did not have to refuel your car there.

The upshot is that since the LP Theory says that non-degenerate group agents are autonomous in relation to their members, LP Theorists seem to be committed to saying that instrument-user-units are autonomous in relation to their user-parts, too. Instrument-user-units, hence, seem to be autonomous rational agents according to the LP Theory in a very strong sense—so strong that they are even fit to be held morally responsible. But this is absurd. Therefore, we should dismiss the LP Theory.

3 Conclusion

According to the LP Theory, organized groups such as churches, commercial corporations, and political parties qualify as rational agents over and above their members. This is a fascinating result. But we should not accept the LP Theory. For it implies that instrument-user-units, e.g. car-driver-units, are rational agents over and above their users. This implication is absurd. In order to avoid this result, the LP Theorist has to find a relevant difference between organized groups and instrument-user-units. It has to be a difference that allows the LP Theorist to say that some group agents are autonomous in relation to their members and to insist, at the same time, that instrument-user-units are not autonomous in relation to their user-parts. As long as no such difference is found, the LP Theory is not acceptable.[9]

References

French, P.A. 1984. *Collective and corporate responsibility*. New York: Columbia University Press.
List, C., and P. Pettit. 2011. *Group agency: The possibility, design, and status of corporate agents*. Oxford: Oxford University Press.
May, L. 1987. *The morality of groups: Collective responsibility, group-based harm, and corporate rights*. Notre Dame: University of Notre Dame Press.
Pettit, P. 1993. *The common mind: An essay on psychology, society and politics*. Oxford: Oxford University Press.
Pettit, P. 2007a. Responsibility incorporated. *Ethics* 117: 171–201.
Pettit, P. 2007b. Rationality, reasoning and group agency. *Dialectica* 61: 495–519.
Pettit, P. 2009. The reality of group agents. In *Philosophy of the social sciences: Philosophical theory and scientific practice*, ed. C. Mantzavinos. Cambridge: Cambridge University Press.

---

[9]For comments on earlier versions of this chapter, I want to thank participants at the *Conference on Collective Intentionality VII* (University of Basel, 2010) and at the spring school *Realität und Bedeutung kollektiver Absichtlichkeit—philosophische und rechtliche Aspekte* (University of Konstanz, 2011). I am also grateful to Fabian Hundertmark, Jeff Kochan, Peter Schulte, Marc Staudacher, and Joachim Wündisch.

Chapter 22
Direct and Indirect Common Belief

Emiliano Lorini and Andreas Herzig

Abstract We give informal definitions of the concepts of direct and indirect common belief, illustrating them by an example. We then provide an analysis of these concepts within public announcement logic (PAL). The conceptual distinction between direct common belief and indirect common belief is important because it identifies two social phenomena which rely on different forms of agents' cognitive capabilities. It is moreover relevant for speech act theory.

1 Introduction

Consider the following scenario. Giovanni and Maria meet each other for the first time at a party. They both have Italian citizenship but they do not know whether the other is Italian or French. A third person arrives who (publicly) tells them: "You both have Italian citizenship!" After the speaker's assertion Giovanni and Maria mutually believe that they are both Italian: Giovanni believes that both are Italian, Maria believes that both are Italian, Giovanni believes that Maria believes that both are Italian, and so on. Now consider a variant of our scenario in which the speaker just tells Giovanni and Maria: "You have the same citizenship!" In this case Giovanni and Maria also start to mutually believe that they are both Italian. There is however an important difference between these two common beliefs.[1] In the first version of the scenario. Giovanni and Maria's common belief is *direct*: it is a

---

[1] In this chapter we consider the sentences "Giovanni and Maria mutually believe that φ", "there is mutual belief between Giovanni and Maria that φ" and "there is common belief between Giovanni and Maria that φ" to be synonymous.

E. Lorini (✉) • A. Herzig
Institut de Recherche en Informatique de Toulouse-CNRS, Toulouse, France
e-mail: Emiliano.Lorini@irit.fr; herzig@irit.fr

A. Konzelmann Ziv and H.B. Schmid (eds.), *Institutions, Emotions, and Group Agents*,
Studies in the Philosophy of Sociality 2, DOI 10.1007/978-94-007-6934-2_22,
© Springer Science+Business Media Dordrecht 2014

direct consequence of the speaker's manifest assertion, and it was already mutually believed before the assertion that such a common belief would obtain. This is not the case in the second variant. We call the second kind of mutual belief *indirect*. In the example, Giovanni and Maria's indirect common belief is determined by what may be called a *shared inference* of the form "I (Giovanni) am Italian and, as Maria and I have the same citizenship, I will infer that Maria and I are both Italian. Moreover, as Maria believes that she is Italian and that we have the same citizenship, Maria too will infer that we are both Italian, and so on... I (Maria) am Italian and, as Giovanni and I have the same citizenship, I will infer that Giovanni and I are both Italian. Moreover, as Giovanni believes that he is Italian and that we have the same citizenship, Giovanni too will infer that we are both Italian, and so on... " In the rest of the chapter, we are going to work out the details of this distinction.

The notion of common belief has been extensively studied in the last four decades. It plays a central role in several areas of research ranging from linguistics and social philosophy to game theory, theoretical computer science, and distributed artificial intelligence. The first precise account of common belief was David Lewis's (1969). Robert Aumann was the first to provide a mathematical characterization of a similar concept using set theory (see Aumann 1976).[2] More recently, formal accounts of common belief were proposed using the tools of epistemic and doxastic logic.[3] The concept of common belief was employed to explain group activity, coordination, communication, and important social concepts like agreement and social commitment. For instance, the concept of convention, as a solution to coordination problems, is classically defined in terms of common belief (see e.g. Lewis 1969; Castelfranchi et al. 2003). It was also proved that common belief justifies the plausibility of equilibrium notions in game theory such as Nash equilibrium, iterated strict dominance, and rationalizability (see e.g. Battigalli and Bonanno 1999). Moreover, common belief has been used to define the concept of common ground in a conversation (Stalnaker 2002), which is fundamental for discourse understanding and definite reference (Schiffer 1972; Clark and Marshall 1981). Beyond that, common belief has been considered a fundamental constituent of joint activity, of shared and group intentions, and of joint agreements.[4] In computer science, common knowledge and common belief are central concepts in the analysis of properties of distributed systems. One of the results in that field is that common knowledge can only be attained if communication is reliable, as exemplified by the

---

[2]Aumann formalizes common knowledge which contrarily to belief, has the property of being truthful.

[3]See e.g. Bicchieri (1989), Bacharach (1992), Bonanno and Nehring (2000), and Fagin et al. (1995).

[4]See Tuomela (1995), Bratman (1992), Gilbert (1989), and Grosz and Kraus (1996), and Tummolini et al. "A convention or (tacit) agreement betwixt us: on reliance and its normative consequences," forthcoming in *Synthese* (published online 29 September 2012).

famous Byzantine generals' problem (alias coordinated attack problem).[5] Recently the logic of common knowledge and public announcements was studied intensely in the domain of multiagent systems[6] and public announcement logic (PAL) was applied to analyze several protocols and puzzles.[7]

Formal definitions of common belief derive from definitions of *shared belief* in the following way. We say that the agents in a group of agents G share a belief that a certain fact[8] φ is true if and only if each of the agents in G individually believes that φ is true.[9] We then say that the agents in G have a common belief that φ is true if and only if the agents in G share a belief that φ is true for every order $k \geq 1$. That is, every agent in G believes that φ, every agent in G believes that every agent in G believes that φ, and so on *ad infinitum*. This is also called the iterative definition of common belief and has been distinguished from the fixed point definition which can be stated as follows[10]: the agents in G have a common belief that φ if and only if every agent in G believes that φ and every agent in G believes that the agents in G have a common belief that φ. In the rest of this chapter we mainly deal with the iterative definition of common belief.

The rest of the chapter is organized as follows. In the first part (Sect. 2), we provide definitions of direct common belief and indirect common belief. In the second part (Sect. 3), we provide a formal analysis of direct and indirect common belief in PAL.

2   Direct vs. Indirect Common Belief

We first present the concepts of direct and indirect common belief from a general and informal perspective. While direct common belief is a mutual belief about an event or a fact that is manifest for the group, an indirect common belief is a mutual belief about something which is not openly accessible to the agents in the group and which often results from a *shared inference* by the agents in the group.

---

[5]See Lehmann (1984), Fagin et al. (1995), and Meyer and van der Hoek (1995).

[6]See van Ditmarsch et al. (2007), Kooi (2007), Kooi and van Benthem (2004), Baltag et al. (2008), and Balbiani et al. (2010).

[7]See van Ditmarsch (2003), Dechesne and Wang (2010), and van Ditmarsch et al. [un-published manuscript].

[8]We use the terms "fact" and "proposition" indistinguishably.

[9]In the present analysis, the term 'group' just denotes a set of individuals (alias agents). We use the symbols i,j,k,... to refer to individuals and G,H,J,... to refer to groups.

[10]Tuomela (2002) and Heifetz (1999).

2.1   Direct Common Belief

With the term "direct common belief" we refer to the kind of common belief of a group of agents G which is directly caused by an event that is manifest (or openly accessible) to all agents in the group. We define the latter in a way close to Robert Stalnaker (2002, p. 708).

Definition 1 (Manifest fact). We say that a certain fact ψ is manifest (or openly accessible) to all agents in a group G thanks to φ if and only if:

1. every agent in G has just learnt that φ is true, and the agents in G mutually believe that every agent in G has just learnt that φ is true, and
2. before the occurrence of φ, the agents in G mutually believed that if φ is learnt, then ψ is true.

Let us have a closer look at the particular case when $\varphi = \psi$: according to our definition the fact ψ is manifest to all agents in G thanks to ψ if and only if every agent in G has just learnt that ψ is true, the agents in G mutually believe that every agent in G has just learnt that ψ is true, and before the occurrence of ψ, the agents in G mutually believed that if ψ is learnt, then ψ is true afterwards. The last condition is nontrivial. To see this, consider the case where φ is a so-called Moore sentence, such as $p \wedge \neg B_i p$ for some agent i of G, where $B_i p$ stands for "agent i believes that p". When every agent in G learns that $p \wedge \neg B_i p$ then that fact itself can never be manifest.[11] Instead, it is only p that is manifest for G thanks to $p \wedge \neg B_i p$.

We say that a group of agents G has acquired a *direct common belief* that ψ thanks to φ if and only if, in the previous state the agents in G did not mutually believe that ψ is true, and they just started to mutually believe that ψ because φ has become manifest to them. More precisely:

Definition 2 (Direct common belief). A group of agents G has acquired a direct common belief that ψ thanks to φ if and only if:

1. the agents in G mutually believe that ψ;
2. every agent in G has just learnt that φ is true, and the agents in G mutually believe that every agent in G has just learnt that φ is true;
3. before the occurrence of φ, the agents in G did not mutually believe that ψ;
4. before the occurrence of φ, the agents in G mutually believed that if φ is learnt, then ψ is true.

Thus, if a group of agents G has acquired a direct common belief that ψ thanks to φ then ψ is manifest to all agents in the group G. Indeed, the second condition and the fourth condition in Definition 2 are together equivalent to the fact that ψ is manifest to all agents in a group G thanks to φ (Definition 1). We are going to

---

[11]Otherwise, agent i would believe both that p is true and that he does not believe that p, which makes i's beliefs contradictory as soon as we accept the principle of positive introspection, in formulas: $B_i \varphi \rightarrow B_i B_i \varphi$.

show formally that the second condition is redundant when the occurrence of φ is identified with the public announcement of φ, cf. Sect. 3.3.

The following example can help to clarify the abstract definition of direct common belief. Consider two persons called Alice and Bob who are watching TV together in the evening, and suddenly there is an unexpected strong tremor. Supposing that Alice and Bob are mutually aware of each other, after the occurrence of the earthquake, Alice and Bob have a direct common belief that an earthquake has occurred. In fact, before the tremor both Alice and Bob did not mutually believe that an earthquake was going to occur. Moreover, they perceive the earthquake and they mutually believe that each of them has perceived the earthquake. According to Definition 2, all direct consequences of the perceived fact that can be inferred from a prior mutual belief of Alice and Bob are also manifest to Alice and Bob and are the content of a direct common belief of Alice and Bob. For instance, suppose that, before the occurrence of the quake, Alice and Bob mutually believe that if they perceive a strong quake, the house might crash down. Thus, the fact that the house might crash down is manifest to Alice and Bob and consequently, after the earthquake, Alice and Bob will also have a direct common belief that the house might crash down.

2.2 Indirect Common Belief

In contrast with direct common belief, indirect common belief is the common belief that appears "out of the blue": it was not foreseen by the group and just "popped up" after the occurrence of a given event. An indirect common belief that a certain fact ψ is true has its origins in the perception of an event φ by the entire group, even though there was no prior mutual belief that "if φ is learnt, then ψ is true". More precisely, we say that:

Definition 3 (Indirect common belief). A group of agents G has acquired an indirect common belief that ψ thanks to φ if and only if:

1. the agents in G mutually believe that ψ;
2. every agent in G has just learnt that φ is true, and the agents in G mutually believe that every agent in G has just learnt that φ is true;
3. before the occurrence of φ, the agents in G did not mutually believe that ψ;
4. before the occurrence of φ, the agents in G **did not** mutually believe that if φ is learnt then ψ is true.

According to our definition, when a group of agents G acquires an indirect common belief that ψ thanks to φ then ψ is not manifest to the agents in the group. The latter is the case because prior to the occurrence of φ the agents in the group did not mutually believe that if φ occurs then ψ must be true. Indirect common belief and direct common belief are therefore disjoint: it cannot be the case that thanks to the same event φ, G simultaneously acquires an indirect common belief that ψ and a direct common belief that ψ thanks to φ.

Let us take up our running example where Giovanni and Maria meet each other for the first time, not knowing that both of them are Italian citizens. By the third person's assertion "You have the same citizenship!" Giovanni and Maria acquire an indirect common belief that they are both Italian. To see this, let us show how the four conditions in the definition of indirect common belief are satisfied in this scenario.

1. First, the fact that prior to the third person's assertion both Giovanni and Maria do not know whether the other is also Italian implies that, before the third person's assertion, Giovanni and Maria did not mutually believe that they are both Italian (condition 3).
2. Second, after the speaker's assertion, Giovanni believes that Maria and he both have Italian citizenship. Therefore Giovanni infers that the speaker's assertion also indicates to Maria that they both have Italian citizenship. Consequently Giovanni can conclude that Maria believes that they both have Italian citizenship. As Giovanni believes that Maria believes that they both have Italian citizenship, Giovanni infers that Maria infers that the speaker's assertion indicates to Giovanni that they both have Italian citizenship. Thus, after the speaker's assertion, Giovanni believes that Maria believes that Giovanni believes that they both have Italian citizenship. And so on *ad infinitum*. The same kind of reasoning applies to Maria. This means that, after the speaker's assertion, Giovanni and Maria mutually believe that they are both Italian (condition 1).
3. Third, the speaker's assertion is public for Giovanni and Maria: both Giovanni and Maria have just heard the speaker's assertion, and they mutually believe that they have just heard the speaker's assertion (condition 2).
4. Fourth, before the speaker's assertion, there was no mutual belief between Giovanni and Maria that if they learn that they have the same citizenship, then this means that they are both Italian (condition 4). Indeed, before the speaker's assertion, Giovanni considers possible a situation in which Giovanni is Italian and Maria is French and in which Maria considers possible a situation in which both Giovanni and Maria are French. That is, before the speaker's assertion, Giovanni considers possible a situation in which Maria considers possible a situation in which Giovanni and Maria have the same citizenship but they are not Italian; and the same kind of reasoning applies to Maria.

Our running example highlights that indirect common belief is often determined by what may be called a 'shared inference' by the agents in the group. The precise conditions for such a shared inference are given in the following definition.

Definition 4 (Basis of shared inference). A group of agents G is in the condition to make a shared inference that ψ thanks to the public fact φ if and only if:

1. every agent in G has just learnt that φ is true, and the agents in G mutually believe that every agent in G has just learnt that φ is true;
2. φ indicates to every agent in G that ψ is true;
3. before the occurrence of φ, the agents in G mutually believed that if ψ is learnt then 2. is true.

Following (Lewis 1969, p. 56), we say that an event φ indicates to some agent i that ψ is true if and only if, if i had reason to believe that φ occurred, i would thereby have reason to believe that ψ is true. Later we will identify this with the public announcement of φ having the effect that the agent believes ψ.

Let us consider in more detail how the 'shared inference' that ψ is true thanks to the public fact φ works on the basis of the previous three conditions. Suppose every agent in the group G has just learnt that φ is true, and the agents in G mutually believe that every agent in G has just learnt that φ is true (condition 1). Thanks to condition 2, every agent in the group G infers that ψ is true. Thus, every agent in G can conclude that ψ is true. As every agent in G believes that ψ is true, thanks to condition 3, every agent in G infers that condition 2 is true. As every agent in G believes that condition 2 is true, thanks to condition 1, every agent in G infers that every agent in G infers that ψ is true.[12] Thus, every agent in G can conclude that every agent in G believes that ψ is true. As every agent in G believes that every agent in G believes that ψ is true, thanks to condition 3, every agent in G infers that every agent in G infers that condition 2 is true. Thus, every agent in G can conclude that every agent in G believes that condition 2 is true. As every agent in G believes that every agent in G believes that condition 2 is true, thanks to condition 1, every agent in G infers that every agent in G infers that every agent in G infers that ψ is true. Thus, every agent in G can conclude that every agent in G believes that every agent in G believes that ψ is true. And so on *ad infinitum*. These chains of inferences by all agents in the group (which together constitute a 'shared inference') determine higher-order beliefs of any length for all agents in the group.

In order to better grasp the distinction between indirect and direct common belief, let us consider the first version of the previous example in which the speaker tells Giovanni and Maria "You both have Italian citizenship!". In this situation Giovanni and Maria will also acquire the common belief that they are both Italian. But, differently from the second version, in this case Giovanni and Maria's common belief is direct, as it is a direct consequence of the speaker's manifest assertion, and it is not constructed by means of a shared inference of Giovanni and Maria. Indeed, before the speaker's assertion, Giovanni and Maria mutually believed that if they learn that they are both Italian, then this means that they are both Italian.

We think that the conceptual distinction between direct common belief and indirect common belief is important because it identifies two social phenomena which rely on different forms of agents' cognitive capabilities. Differently from a direct common belief about φ, an indirect common belief about φ has an intrinsic 'constructive' nature, in the sense that it is formed starting from a mutual belief of order 1 that φ is true, and moving up progressively to mutual beliefs of higher orders by means of a *shared inference*. This is not the case for direct common belief. When forming a direct common belief about φ, φ can already be inferred from a prior common belief of the agents and, consequently, there is no need for the agents

---

[12] We are here assuming that every agent in G trusts his perception (so that he automatically believes what he perceives) and that this is mutual belief among the agents in G.

to 'construct' the new common belief by means of the shared inference. For this reason, we can argue that the formation of indirect common belief is cognitively more demanding than the formation of direct common belief.

We also think that the distinction between direct common belief and indirect common belief is relevant for the theory of language in which, following Searle (1979), direct speech acts (or direct communication) are distinguished from indirect speech acts (or indirect communication). Examples are direct vs. indirect request (such as the famous "Pass me the salt!" vs. "Can you pass me the salt?"), direct vs. indirect assertion, direct vs. indirect commitment, and direct vs. indirect agreement. For instance, in the case of an indirect commitment, the speaker becomes socially committed to do a certain action, without having performed a direct speech act with commissive force. In the case of an indirect request, the speaker communicates to the hearer his desire that the hearer will do a certain action, without performing a direct speech act with directive force. In both cases the speaker communicates something to the hearer by way of relying on their mutually shared background information, together with the general powers of rationality and inference on the part of the hearer. In the case of indirect communication, the common belief between the speaker and the hearer about the speech act's illocutionary force is often formed by means of a shared inference of the kind we have illustrated above.

3   A Logical Analysis of Indirect and Direct Common Belief

In this second part of the chapter, we provide a formal analysis of the distinction between indirect common belief and direct common belief in terms of a modal logic of belief, alias a doxastic logic.

The language of modal logics of belief has modal operators $\mathbf{B}_i$, one per agent i. The proposition $\mathbf{B}_i\varphi$ is read "agent i believes that φ". The language allows to talk about higher-order beliefs: $\mathbf{B}_i\mathbf{B}_j\varphi$ expresses that i believes that j believes that φ, $\mathbf{B}_i\mathbf{B}_j\mathbf{B}_i\varphi$ expresses that i believes that j believes that i believes that φ, and $\mathbf{B}_i(\neg\mathbf{B}_j\varphi \wedge \neg\mathbf{B}_j\neg\varphi)$ expresses that i believes that j has no opinion about φ.

The semantics of modal logics of belief is in terms of doxastic models, alias Kripke models. Such models have a set of possible worlds together with binary relations of accessibility R_i on that set, one per agent i. The idea is that when two possible worlds w and w' are related by R_i then at w, agent i considers w' possible; one also says that i cannot distinguish w from w'. The sentence "at w, agent i believes that φ", formally written $\mathbf{B}_i\varphi$, is then identified with the truth of φ at all possible worlds that are accessible from w via R_i.

We start from the standard formalization of common belief in the semantic framework of doxastic logic (Sect. 3.1).[13] In that formalization, common belief is

---

[13]Fagin et al. (1995) and Meyer and van der Hoek (1995).

reduced to individual beliefs. Syntactically this corresponds to a fixpoint definition of common belief: there is common belief between i and j that φ if and only if each of the following is the case:

- i believes φ;
- j believes φ;
- i believes that j believes φ;
- i believes that j believes that i believes φ;
- ...

So syntactically, common belief is an infinite conjunction. While such conjunctions are not in our logical language, common knowledge can however be axiomatized by means of an induction axiom.

In order to formally distinguish indirect common belief from direct common belief, we add particular events to the standard logic of common belief: informative events called public announcements (Sect. 3.2). Public announcements have been extensively studied in the recent literature on epistemic and doxastic logic as logics of information dynamics.[14] The semantics of a public announcement is in terms of an update of the doxastic model by the elimination of all those doxastic alternatives which do not satisfy the content of the announced fact. Therefore, public announcements capture the notion of manifest event as defined in Sect. 2.

In this extended logical framework integrating the concept of common belief and the concept of public announcement, we provide a formal analysis of our running example. The semantics of the logic of public announcements will help us to clarify the difference between the first assertion of the speaker ("You both have Italian citizenship!") and the second assertion ("You have the same citizenship!"). Our formal analysis will in particular make clear that in the latter situation, Giovanni and Maria will acquire an indirect common belief that they are both Italian, whereas in the former situation they will acquire a direct common belief that they are both Italian.

In the next section, we recall the logic of common belief according to the least fixpoint definition, and in Sect. 3.2, we extend it by public announcements, resulting in public announcement logic (PAL). Finally in Sect. 3.3, we take up our running example.

3.1   The Logic of Common Belief

Let $AGT = \{1, \ldots, n\}$ be a finite set of agents (or individuals), $ATM = \{p, q, \ldots\}$ a countable set of atomic formulas. Let $2^{AGT^*} = 2^{AGT} \setminus \varnothing$ be the set of non-empty sets of agents; we call them groups for simplicity.

---

[14]See e.g. Plaza (1989), van Ditmarsch et al. (2007), Kooi and van Benthem (2004), and Baltag and Moss (2004).

The set of formulas of the logic of common belief is defined as the smallest set satisfying the following conditions:

- every p ∈ ATM is a formula;
- if φ is a formula then $\neg\varphi$ is a formula;
- if φ and ψ are formulas then $\varphi\vee\psi$ is a formula;
- if φ is a formula and i ∈ AGT then $\mathbf{B}_i\varphi$ is a formula;
- if φ is a formula and G ∈ 2^{AGT^*} then $\mathbf{CB}_G\varphi$ is a formula.

The modal operators $\mathbf{B}_i$ are standard doxastic operators à la Hintikka (1962): $\mathbf{B}_i\varphi$ stands for "agent i believes that φ". The $\mathbf{CB}_G$ are modal operators for common belief: $\mathbf{CB}_G\varphi$ stands for "there is a common belief that φ in group G".

The notion of shared belief ("Everybody in group G believes that φ") is defined in the standard way as follows:

$$\mathbf{EB}_G\varphi =_{def} \wedge_{i \in AGT} \mathbf{B}_i\varphi$$

Logical formulas are interpreted in doxastic models that are defined as follows.

Definition 5 (Doxastic model). A doxastic model is a triple M = $\langle W,B,V \rangle$ where:

- W is a non-empty set of worlds or states;
- B associates to every agent i∈AGT a transitive and Euclidean accessibility relation $B_i \subseteq W \times W$[15];
- V : ATM → 2^W.

For every w ∈ W, $B_i(w) = \{v| (w, v) \in B_i\}$ is i's information state at world w: the set of worlds that are possible for agent i at world w. Note that we do not require the relations B_i to be serial.[16] The reason is that public announcements (which update a given model) might produce models that are no longer serial: public announcement logic does not allow ensuring seriality. For every G ∈ 2^{AGT^*}, we define a world v to be G-reachable from world w, and note this (w,v) ∈ B_G^+, if and only if there exist worlds $w_0,\ldots,w_n$ such that $w_0 = w$, $w_n = v$ and for all $0 \leq k \leq n-1$, there exists i ∈ G such that $(w_k,w_{k+1}) \in B_i$. Moreover, we define $B_G^+(w) = \{v \mid (w, v) \in B_G^+\}$. In other words, for every G ∈ 2^{AGT^*}, B_G^+ is the *transitive closure* of B_G with $B_G = \cup_{i \in AGT} B_i$.

Truth conditions of formulas are as follows:

- M,w ⊨ p iff w ∈ V(p)
- M,w ⊨ $\neg\varphi$ iff not M,w ⊨ φ
- M,w ⊨ $\varphi \vee\psi$ iff M,w ⊨ φ or M,w ⊨ ψ
- M,w ⊨ $\mathbf{B}_i\varphi$ iff M,v ⊨ φ for all v ∈ $B_i(w)$
- M,w ⊨ $\mathbf{CB}_G \varphi$ iff M,v ⊨ φ for all v ∈ $B_G^+(w)$

---

[15]A relation B_i is transitive if (w,v) ∈ B_i and (v,u) ∈ B_i implies (v,u) ∈ B_i. B_i is Euclidean if (w,v) ∈ B_i and (w,u) ∈ B_i implies (v,u) ∈ B_i.

[16]A relation B_i is serial if for every w ∈ W, there exists v such that (w,v) ∈ B_i.

Fig. 22.1 Example
of a doxastic model

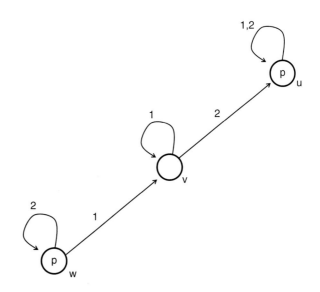

Informally speaking, at the world w of the model M, the agent i believes that φ is true if and only if, φ is true in all worlds that are *possible* for agent i at world w. Moreover, at the world w of the model M, the group G has a common belief that φ is true if and only if, φ is true in all worlds that are G-reachable from w (i.e. there exists a path of B_G-links between world w and world v). For example, in the doxastic model in Fig. 22.1 we have $(w,u) \in B_{\{1,2\}}{}^+$, as there is a path of $B_{\{1,2\}}$-links between world w and world u.

Transitivity and Euclideanity of the accessibility relations B_i correspond to the properties of positive and negative introspection over beliefs. Indeed, the following two formulas are valid in doxastic logic due to transitivity and Euclideanity of the relations:

$$\mathbf{B_i}\varphi \rightarrow \mathbf{B_i B_i}\varphi$$

$$\neg\mathbf{B_i}\varphi \rightarrow \mathbf{B_i}\neg\mathbf{B_i}\varphi$$

That is, if the agent i believes that φ is true, then i believes that i believes that φ is true; if the agent i does not believe that φ is true, then i believes that i does not believe that φ is true. We note in passing that our doxastic logic has the infamous omniscience problem: agents believe all tautologies, all the logical consequences of their beliefs, and their beliefs are closed under conjunction and material implication. In order to avoid that problem one has to restrict the inferences the agents are allowed to draw. This would make our account more complex; for example in the definition of direct and indirect common belief and of shared inference, we would have to take into account that the agents' reasoning capabilities are limited.

3.2   The Logic of Common Belief and Public Announcements PAL

We now extend the logic of common belief presented above with a notion of public announcement which has been extensively studied in the field of public announcement logic (PAL) and more generally dynamic epistemic logics.[17] Public announcements are events which are responsible for the dynamics of individual beliefs and of common beliefs. Approximately, we can say that a given fact φ is publicly announced if and only if every agent learns that φ is true and all agents have a common belief that every agent learns that φ is true.

The set of formulas of PAL is defined as the smallest set satisfying the following conditions:

- every $p \in ATM$ is a formula;
- if φ is a formula then $\neg\varphi$ is a formula;
- if φ and ψ are formulas then $\varphi\vee\psi$ is a formula;
- if φ is a formula and $i \in AGT$ then $\mathbf{B}_i\varphi$ is a formula;
- if φ is a formula and $G \in 2^{AGT^*}$ then $\mathbf{CB}_G\varphi$ is a formula;
- if φ and ψ are formulas then $[\varphi!]\psi$ is a formula.

That is, we have the language presented in Sect. 3.1 extended by the public announcement operators $[\varphi!]$. The new formula $[\varphi!]\psi$ stands for "ψ holds after the public announcement of φ". The semantics of public announcement operators is defined by means of an operation of model update which consists in restricting the agents' information states to the worlds in which the announced formula is true. That is, for every doxastic model $M = \langle W,B,V \rangle$, we define:

$$M, w \vDash [\varphi!]\psi \text{ iff } M^{\varphi!}, w \vDash \psi$$

where the updated doxastic model $M^{\varphi!}$ is the tuple $\langle W,B^{\varphi!},V \rangle$ with:

$$B_i{}^{\varphi!} = \{(w, v) \in B_i \,|\, M, v \vDash \varphi\}, \text{ for every } i \in AGT.$$

This means that at the world w of the model M it is the case that ψ holds after the public announcement of φ if and only if ψ is true at the world w of the model $M^{\varphi!}$ which results from the public announcement of φ in the model M. Figure 22.2 shows graphically how the semantics of public announcements works.

---

[17]See e.g. van Ditmarsch et al. (2007), Plaza (1989), Kooi and van Benthem (2004), and Baltag and Moss (2004).

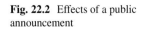

Fig. 22.2 Effects of a public announcement

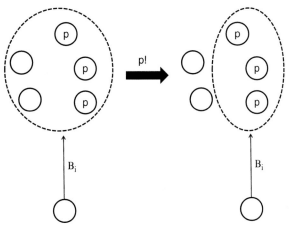

3.3   Formalization of the Running Example

Let us analyze our running example with the aid of our formal apparatus. In what follows, we identify the announcement $(i_G \wedge i_M)!$ with the speaker's assertion "You (Maria and Giovanni) both have italian citizenship!", and we identify the announcement $(i_G \wedge i_M) \vee (f_G \wedge f_M)!$ with the speaker's assertion "You (Maria and Giovanni) have the same citizenship!".[18] We are aware that this is an approximation because PAL is not a logic of speech acts. Let us first consider the situation where Giovanni and Maria learn that they both have Italian citizenship (Fig. 22.3). The left model represents the situation before the announcement $(i_G \wedge i_M)!$, whereas the right model represents the situation after the announcement.

The grey world represents the actual world. We have that:

- $\mathbf{CB}_{\{G,M\}}(i_G \wedge i_M)$ is true at the actual world of the *updated* model,
- $\mathbf{CB}_{\{G,M\}}(i_G \wedge i_M)$ is false at the actual world of the *initial* model,
- $\mathbf{CB}_{\{G,M\}}[(i_G \wedge i_M)!](i_G \wedge i_M)$ is **true** at the actual world of the *initial* model.

Therefore, in this situation Giovanni and Maria acquire a direct common belief that they are both Italian. Indeed, all four conditions of the definition of direct common belief given in Sect. 2.1 are satisfied. First, before the speaker's assertion, Giovanni and Maria did not mutually believe that they are both Italian. Second, after the speaker's assertion, Giovanni and Maria have a common belief that they are both Italian. Third, the speaker's assertion is public. Fourth, before the speaker's assertion, Giovanni and Maria mutually believed that if they learn that they are both Italian, then this means that they are both Italian.

---

[18]For simplicity, we assume that Maria and Giovanni only consider Italian citizenship and French citizenship.

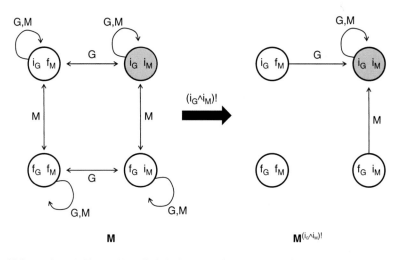

Fig. 22.3 Maria and Giovanni's beliefs before and after the speaker's assertion "You both have Italian citizenship!"

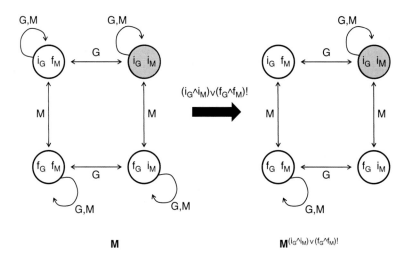

Fig. 22.4 Maria and Giovanni's beliefs before and after the announcement "You have the same citizenship!"

Let us now turn to the other variant of the scenario in which the speaker tells Giovanni and Maria that they have the same citizenship without telling them they are both Italian (Fig. 22.4). The left model represents the initial situation, whereas the right model represents the situation after the announcement $(i_M \wedge i_G) \vee (f_M \wedge f_G)!$.

This means that, thanks to the speaker's assertion, Giovanni and Maria acquire an indirect common belief that they are both Italian. Indeed, all four conditions of the definition of indirect common belief of Definition 3 in Sect. 2.1 are satisfied. First, before the speaker's assertion, Giovanni and Maria did not mutually believe that they are both Italian. Second, after the speaker's assertion, Giovanni and Maria have a common belief that they are both Italian. Third, the speaker's assertion is public. Fourth, before the speaker's assertion, Giovanni and Maria did not mutually believe that if they learn that they have the same citizenship then they are both Italian.

Notice that the three conditions for Giovanni and Maria's shared inference of $i_G \wedge i_M$ thanks to $(i_G \wedge i_M) \vee (f_G \wedge f_M)!$ that we gave in Sect. 2.1 (Definition 4) are all satisfied in this scenario:

- the public announcement of $(i_G \wedge i_M) \vee (f_G \wedge f_M)$ has just taken place,
- $[(i_G \wedge i_M) \vee (f_G \wedge f_M)!]\mathbf{EB}_{\{G,M\}}(i_G \wedge i_M)$ is true at the actual world of the *initial* model,
- $\mathbf{CB}_{\{G,M\}}((i_G \wedge i_M) \rightarrow [(i_G \wedge i_M) \vee (f_G \wedge f_M)!]\mathbf{EB}_{\{G,M\}}(i_G \wedge i_M))$ is true at the actual world of the *initial* model.

Thus, Maria and Giovanni infer that they are both Italian, because the speaker's assertion indicates to both Maria and Giovanni that they are both Italian, and because, before the speaker's assertion, Maria and Giovanni mutually believed that if they are both Italian, then the speaker's assertion indicates to them that they are both Italian.

3.4 A Remark on Lewis's Notion of Indication

Lewis's notion of indication ("φ indicates to agent i that ψ") has been expressed in the preceding section by the fact that, after learning that φ is true, agent i believes that ψ (i.e. $[\varphi!]\mathbf{B}_i\psi$). We think that our solution is interesting, because it captures the dynamic aspect of this notion. We here follow the idea of the Ramsey test in the domain of belief revision (Ramsey 1965) by claiming that— like the notion of conditional belief—the notion of indication should be seen as dynamic. That is, φ indicates to the agent i that ψ if and only if agent i will conclude that ψ is true, when adding φ to his stock of beliefs. Alternative logical treatments of Lewis's notion of indication have been proposed. For instance, Cubitt and Sugden (2003) propose a purely syntactic analysis. The analysis of Sillari (2005) is the closest to ours. In contrast with Cubitt and Sugden, Sillari also defends the idea that a semantic analysis of the notion of indication can be offered by using the tools of epistemic logic. Sillari uses a doxastic logic interpreted in a standard Kripke possible-worlds semantics in order to model the notion of reason to believe (i.e. epistemic reason) and the indication relation between epistemic reasons. Furthermore, he extends his logic with a concept of awareness in order to account for the bounded rationality aspect of Lewis's notion of common belief (i.e. the fact that agents do not necessarily have the cognitive capability of reaching mutual beliefs of any length in the common belief hierarchy). Differently from our analysis in PAL in which the formation of common belief is modeled, Sillari's analysis of common belief and of the notion of indication is purely static.

It is worth noting that in this work, we have only characterized the basis of the shared inference, without modeling the reasoning process endorsed by the agents when forming an indirect common belief. This remains an open research issue, which is not satisfactorily addressed in the present work or in the above-mentioned works. As pointed out above, Sillari's approach is static and does not allow us to model the process of forming a common belief. Cubitt and Sugden's approach is purely syntactic, thereby not being completely satisfactory from a logical point of view. We think that an approach based on PAL, as the one proposed in this work, remains the best candidate to solve such a fundamental problem in the logical theory of common belief. This research issue will be further investigated in future work.

4 Conclusion

We have identified two distinct origins of common belief: direct common belief, whose future occurrence is already mutually believed by the agents before the triggering event, and indirect common belief, of which the group only becomes aware after the triggering event by means of a shared inference. We have shown that public announcement logic allows to formally analyze the differences. In our account we have only provided a semantic analysis of the distinction between indirect and direct common belief in the PAL framework. We did not provide a logic which allows defining these two notions in the object language. Indeed, this cannot be done in PAL: it requires adding past operators. This was studied recently in the literature by Sack, Yap, and others.[19]

References

Aumann, R.J. 1976. Agreeing to disagree. *The Annals of Statistics* 4(6): 1236–1239.
Bacharach, M. 1992. The acquisition of common knowledge. In *Knowledge, belief and strategic interaction*, ed. C. Bicchieri and M.L. Dalla Chiara, 285–316. Cambridge: Cambridge University Press.
Balbiani, P., H. van Ditmarsch, A. Herzig, and T. de Lima. 2010. Tableaux for public announcement logics. *Journal of Logic and Computation* 20(1): 55–76.
Baltag, A., and L.S. Moss. 2004. Logics for epistemic programs. *Synthese* 139(2): 165–224.
Baltag, A., H. van Ditmarsch, and L. Moss. 2008. Epistemic logic and information update. In *Handbook on the philosophy of information*, ed. P. Adriaans and J. van Benthem, 369–463. Amsterdam: Elsevier Science.
Battigalli, P., and G. Bonanno. 1999. Recent results on belief, knowledge and the epistemic foundations of game theory. *Research in Economics* 53: 149–225.
Bicchieri, C. 1989. Self-refuting theories of strategic interaction: A paradox of common knowledge. *Erkenntnis* 30: 69–85.

---

[19]Hoshi and Yap (2009), Sack (2008), and Baltag et al. (2008).

Bonanno, G., and K. Nehring. 2000. Common belief with the logic of individual belief. *Mathematical Logic Quarterly* 46(1): 49–52.

Bratman, M. 1992. Shared cooperative activity. *Philosophical Review* 101(2): 327–341.

Castelfranchi, C., F. Giardini, E. Lorini, and L. Tummolini. 2003. The prescriptive destiny of predictive attitudes: From expectations to norms via conventions. In *Proceedings of the 25th annual conference of the Cognitive Science Society*, ed. R. Alterman and D. Kirsh, 222–227. Mahwah: Lawrence Erlbaum Associates.

Clark, H.H., and C. Marshall. 1981. Definite reference and mutual knowledge. In *Elements of discourse understanding*, ed. A. Joshi, B. Webber, and I. Sag, 10–63. Cambridge: Cambridge University Press.

Cubitt, R.P., and R. Sugden. 2003. Common knowledge, salience and convention: A reconstruction of David Lewis' game theory. *Economics and Philosophy* 19: 175–210.

Dechesne, F., and Y. Wang. 2010. To know or not to know—Epistemic approaches to security protocol analysis. *Synthese* 177: 51–76.

Fagin, R., J. Halpern, Y. Moses, and M. Vardi. 1995. *Reasoning about knowledge*. Cambridge, MA: MIT Press.

Gilbert, M. 1989. *On social facts*. London/New York: Routledge.

Grosz, B., and S. Kraus. 1996. Collaborative plans for complex group action. *Artificial Intelligence* 86(2): 269–357.

Heifetz, A. 1999. Iterative and fixed point common belief. *Journal of Philosophical Logic* 28(1): 61–79.

Hintikka, J. 1962. *Knowledge and belief*. New York: Cornell University Press.

Hoshi, T., and A. Yap. 2009. Dynamic epistemic logic with branching temporal structures. *Synthese* 169: 259–281.

Kooi, B. 2007. Expressivity and completeness for public update logic via reduction axioms. *Journal of Applied Non-Classical Logics* 17(2): 231–253.

Kooi, B., and J. van Benthem. 2004. Reduction axioms for epistemic actions. In Preliminary *Proceedings of the fifth advances in modal logic conference (AiML'04)*, ed. R. Schmidt, I. Pratt-Hartmann, M. Reynolds, and H. Wansing, 197–211. Manchester: Department of Computer Science, University of Manchester.

Lehmann, D.J. 1984. Knowledge, common knowledge and related puzzles (Extended summary). In *PODC'84 proceedings of the third annual ACM symposium on principles of distributed computing*, 62–67. New York, USA: ACM Press.

Lewis, D.K. 1969. *Convention: A philosophical study*. Cambridge, MA: Harvard University Press.

Meyer, J.-J.Ch, and W. van der Hoek. 1995. *Epistemic logic for AI and computer science*. Cambridge: Cambridge University Press.

Plaza, J.A. 1989. Logics of public communications. In *Proceedings of the fourth international symposium on methodologies for intelligent systems (ISMIS'89)*, ed. M.L. Emrich, M.S. Pfeifer, M. Hadzikadic, and Z.W. Ras. Oak Ridge National Laboratory, ORNL/DSRD-24, 201–216. Reprinted in *Synthese* 158(2):165–179. 2007.

Ramsey, F.P. 1965 [1931]. General propositions and causality. In *The foundations of mathematics and other logical essays*, ed. by J.B. Braithwaite, 237–255. London: Kegan Paul. 4th imprint.

Sack, J. 2008. Temporal languages for epistemic programs. *Journal of Logic, Language and Information* 17(2): 183–216.

Schiffer, S. 1972. *Meaning*. Oxford: Oxford University Press.

Searle, J.R. 1979. *Expression and meaning: Studies in the theory of speech acts*. Cambridge: Cambridge University Press.

Sillari, G. 2005. A logical framework for convention. *Synthese* 147(2): 379–400.

Stalnaker, R. 2002. Common ground. *Linguistics and Philosophy* 25: 701–721.

Tuomela, R. 1995. *The importance of us: A philosophical study of basic social notions*. Stanford: Stanford University Press.

Tuomela, R. 2002. Collective goals and communicative action. *Journal of Philosophical Research* 27: 29–64.

van Ditmarsch, H. 2003. The Russian cards problem. *Studia Logica* 75:31–62. [Special issue on dynamics of knowledge, ed. M. Wooldridge and W. van der Hoek.]

van Ditmarsch, H., W. van der Hoek, and B. Kooi. 2007. *Dynamic epistemic logic*. Berlin/Heidelberg: Springer.

Printed by Publishers' Graphics LLC